A DECADAL SURVEY OF THE SOCIAL AND BEHAVIORAL SCIENCES

A Research Agenda for
Advancing Intelligence Analysis

Committee on a Decadal Survey of Social and Behavioral Sciences
for Applications to National Security

Board on Behavioral, Cognitive, and Sensory Sciences

Division of Behavioral and Social Sciences and Education

A Consensus Study Report of

The National Academies of
SCIENCES · ENGINEERING · MEDICINE

THE NATIONAL ACADEMIES PRESS
Washington, DC
www.nap.edu

THE NATIONAL ACADEMIES PRESS   500 Fifth Street, NW   Washington, DC 20001

This activity was supported by contracts between the National Academy of Sciences and the Office of the Director of National Intelligence, Contract No. 2014-14041100003-009. Support for the work of the Board on Behavioral, Cognitive, and Sensory Sciences is provided primarily by a grant from the National Science Foundation (Award No. BCS-1729167). Any opinions, findings, conclusions, or recommendations expressed in this publication do not necessarily reflect the views of any organization or agency that provided support for the project.

International Standard Book Number-13: 978-0-309-48761-0
International Standard Book Number-10: 0-309-48761-7
Library of Congress Control Number: 2019936260
Digital Object Identifier: https://doi.org/10.17226/25335

Additional copies of this publication are available for sale from the National Academies Press, 500 Fifth Street, NW, Keck 360, Washington, DC 20001; (800) 624-6242 or (202) 334-3313; http://www.nap.edu.

Copyright 2019 by the National Academy of Sciences. All rights reserved.

Printed in the United States of America

Suggested citation: National Academies of Sciences, Engineering, and Medicine. (2019). *A Decadal Survey of the Social and Behavioral Sciences: A Research Agenda for Advancing Intelligence Analysis.* Washington, DC: The National Academies Press. doi: https://doi.org/10.17226/25335.

The National Academies of
SCIENCES · ENGINEERING · MEDICINE

The **National Academy of Sciences** was established in 1863 by an Act of Congress, signed by President Lincoln, as a private, nongovernmental institution to advise the nation on issues related to science and technology. Members are elected by their peers for outstanding contributions to research. Dr. Marcia McNutt is president.

The **National Academy of Engineering** was established in 1964 under the charter of the National Academy of Sciences to bring the practices of engineering to advising the nation. Members are elected by their peers for extraordinary contributions to engineering. Dr. C. D. Mote, Jr., is president.

The **National Academy of Medicine** (formerly the Institute of Medicine) was established in 1970 under the charter of the National Academy of Sciences to advise the nation on medical and health issues. Members are elected by their peers for distinguished contributions to medicine and health. Dr. Victor J. Dzau is president.

The three Academies work together as the **National Academies of Sciences, Engineering, and Medicine** to provide independent, objective analysis and advice to the nation and conduct other activities to solve complex problems and inform public policy decisions. The National Academies also encourage education and research, recognize outstanding contributions to knowledge, and increase public understanding in matters of science, engineering, and medicine.

Learn more about the National Academies of Sciences, Engineering, and Medicine at **www.nationalacademies.org**.

The National Academies of
SCIENCES • ENGINEERING • MEDICINE

Consensus Study Reports published by the National Academies of Sciences, Engineering, and Medicine document the evidence-based consensus on the study's statement of task by an authoring committee of experts. Reports typically include findings, conclusions, and recommendations based on information gathered by the committee and the committee's deliberations. Each report has been subjected to a rigorous and independent peer-review process and it represents the position of the National Academies on the statement of task.

Proceedings published by the National Academies of Sciences, Engineering, and Medicine chronicle the presentations and discussions at a workshop, symposium, or other event convened by the National Academies. The statements and opinions contained in proceedings are those of the participants and are not endorsed by other participants, the planning committee, or the National Academies.

For information about other products and activities of the National Academies, please visit www.nationalacademies.org/about/whatwedo.

COMMITTEE ON A DECADAL SURVEY OF SOCIAL AND BEHAVIORAL SCIENCES FOR APPLICATIONS TO NATIONAL SECURITY

PAUL R. SACKETT (*Chair*), Department of Psychology, University of Minnesota
GARY G. BERNTSON, Department of Psychology, The Ohio State University
KATHLEEN M. CARLEY, School of Computer Science, Institute for Software Research International, Carnegie Mellon University
NOSHIR S. CONTRACTOR, McCormick School of Engineering and Applied Science, School of Communications, and the Kellogg School of Management, Northwestern University
NANCY J. COOKE, The Polytechnic School, Ira A. Fulton Schools of Engineering, Arizona State University
BARBARA ANNE DOSHER (NAS), Department of Cognitive Science, University of California, Irvine
JEFFREY C. JOHNSON, Department of Anthropology, University of Florida
SALLIE KELLER, Social and Decision Analytics Division, Biocomplexity Institute, University of Virginia
DAVID MATSUMOTO, Department of Psychology, College of Science and Engineering, San Francisco State University
CARMEN MEDINA, MedinAnalytics, LLC
FRAN P. MOORE, The Financial Systemic Analysis and Resilience Center
JONATHAN D. MORENO (NAM), Department of Medical Ethics and Health Policy, Perelman School of Medicine, University of Pennsylvania
JOY ROHDE, Gerald R. Ford School of Public Policy, University of Michigan
JEFFREY W. TALIAFERRO, Department of Political Science, Tufts University
GREGORY F. TREVERTON, Dornsife College of Letters, Arts, and Sciences, School of International Relations, University of Southern California
JEREMY M. WOLFE, Departments of Ophthalmology and Radiology, Brigham and Women's Hospital, Harvard Medical School

SUJEETA BHATT, *Study Director*
ALEXANDRA BEATTY *(from March 2017)*, *Senior Program Officer*
JULIE ANNE SCHUCK, *Program Officer*
ELIZABETH TOWNSEND *(until March 2018)*, *Research Associate*
RENÉE L. WILSON GAINES *(until June 2018)*, *Senior Program Assistant*
THELMA COX, *Program Coordinator*

BOARD ON BEHAVIORAL, COGNITIVE, AND SENSORY SCIENCES

SUSAN T. FISKE (*Chair*), Department of Psychology and Woodrow Wilson School of Public and International Affairs, Princeton University
JOHN BAUGH, Department of Arts & Sciences, Washington University in St. Louis
LAURA L. CARSTENSEN, Department of Psychology, Stanford University
JUDY DUBNO, Department of Otolaryngology-Head and Neck Surgery, Medical University of South Carolina
JENNIFER EBERHARDT, Department of Psychology, Stanford University
ROBERT L. GOLDSTONE, Department of Psychological and Brain Sciences, Indiana University
DANIEL R. ILGEN, Department of Psychology, Michigan State University
NANCY G. KANWISHER, Department of Brain and Cognitive Sciences, Massachusetts Institute of Technology
JANICE KIECOLT-GLASER, Department of Psychology, The Ohio State University College of Medicine
BILL C. MAURER, School of Social Sciences, University of California, Irvine
STEVEN E. PETERSEN, Department of Neurology and Neurological Surgery, Washington University School of Medicine
DANA M. SMALL, Department of Psychiatry, Yale Medical School
TIMOTHY J. STRAUMAN, Department of Psychology and Neuroscience, Duke University
JEREMY M. WOLFE, Departments of Ophthalmology and Radiology, Brigham and Women's Hospital, Harvard Medical School

BARBARA A. WANCHISEN, *Director*

Preface

The Intelligence Community (IC) is no stranger to the valuable contributions made by research in the social and behavioral sciences (SBS) to the work of intelligence analysis. Likewise, researchers in many SBS disciplines have benefited from opportunities to work with the IC and conduct research on countless topics related to intelligence. But in an age when both technologies and national security concerns are evolving at lightning speed, the IC has recognized the critical need to more systematically take advantage of cutting-edge research from diverse SBS fields.

In this context, the Office of the Director of National Intelligence (ODNI) turned to the National Academies of Science, Engineering, and Medicine to explore opportunities for research from SBS disciplines to support the work of intelligence analysts and enhance national security. ODNI requested that the National Academies conduct a decadal survey that would support the IC in developing a 10-year agenda for SBS research with applications to intelligence analysis.

The National Academies had developed the decadal survey model to serve other federal agencies—including the National Aeronautics and Space Administration, the National Science Foundation (NSF), the U.S. Department of Energy, the National Oceanic and Atmospheric Administration, and the U.S. Geological Survey—by identifying research relevant to key policy objectives. This model had not previously been used to survey SBS fields or to serve an objective as broad as strengthening national security, so the process was an experiment for ODNI and the National Academies, as well as for the Committee on a Decadal Survey of Social and Behavioral

Sciences for Applications to National Security. This report describes the results of the work of the intrepid committee—made up of experts with decades of experience in intelligence, scholars in diverse SBS fields, and several individuals with extensive experience in both worlds—that took on this challenge.

This decadal survey was made possible by the generous sponsorship of ODNI and the invaluable insight and support of Dr. David Honey, former director of science and technology and former assistant deputy director of national intelligence for science and technology. We also appreciate the tireless support of members of the ODNI staff, including Dr. Steven D. Thompson, Mr. Melvin L. Eulau, Dr. Kent Myers, and Mr. William "Bruno" Millonig. We are particularly thankful to Ms. Debra Stanislawski for her assistance with this report. We are grateful as well for the substantive core support for the Board on Behavioral, Cognitive, and Sensory Sciences received from NSF's Social, Behavioral and Economic Sciences Directorate, which ensured necessary oversight on the project.

Many individuals contributed their time and effort to this project. They are too numerous to list here, but we are extremely grateful for the contributions of those who served on the steering committees for the summit meeting and six workshops held during the course of the study, which provided us with vital insights about the work of the IC and many lines of SBS research; those who participated in our fact-finding meetings and public workshops; and those who took the time to prepare white papers in response to our requests and participate in other ways in our extensive information-gathering efforts (see Appendix B for a full listing of contributors).

Thanks are also due to the project staff, including Alexandra Beatty, whose expertise in report organization and writing is unmatched; Julie Schuck, who was instrumental in all phases of the project; and Elizabeth Townsend who provided support through its early phases. Thelma Cox managed logistical and administrative matters. Rebecca Morgan and Jorge Mendoza-Torres of the National Academies Research Center conducted literature and data reviews and assisted with report references.

This Consensus Study Report was reviewed in draft form by individuals chosen for their diverse perspectives and technical expertise. The purpose of this independent review is to provide candid and critical comments that will assist the National Academies in making each published report as sound as possible and to ensure that it meets the institutional standards for quality, objectivity, evidence, and responsiveness to the study charge. The review comments and draft manuscript remain confidential to protect the integrity of the deliberative process.

We thank the following individuals for their review of this report: Matthew W. Brashears, Department of Sociology, University of South

Carolina; Roger Z. George, Department of Politics, Occidental College; Loch K. Johnson, Department of International Affairs, University of Georgia; Sara B. Kiesler, Human-Computer Interaction Institute, Carnegie Mellon University; Stephen Marrin, Integrated Science and Technology/Intelligence Analysis, James Madison University; John E. McLaughlin, Paul H. Nitze School of Advanced International Studies, Johns Hopkins University; John Monahan, School of Law, University of Virginia; Frederick L. Oswald, Department of Psychology, Rice University; Peter Pirolli, senior research scientist, Institute for Human and Machine Cognition; Andrew L. Ross, National Security Affairs Program, Texas A&M University; and Paul Slovic, president, Decision Research, and Department of Psychology, University of Oregon.

Although the reviewers listed above provided many constructive comments and suggestions, they were not asked to endorse the conclusions or recommendations of this report nor did they see the final draft before its release. The review of this report was overseen by Cynthia Beall, Department of Anthropology, Case Western Reserve University, and Susan J. Curry, College of Public Health, University of Iowa. They were responsible for making certain that an independent examination of this report was carried out in accordance with the standards of the National Academies and that all review comments were carefully considered. Responsibility for the final content rests entirely with the authoring committee and the National Academies.

> Paul R. Sackett, *Chair*
> Sujeeta Bhatt, *Study Director*
> Committee on a Decadal Survey of
> Social and Behavioral Sciences for
> Applications to National Security

Contents

Summary   1

1 Introduction   15
Purpose of This Study, 16
Applying the Decadal Process in a New Context, 18
Study Approach, 20
   Information Gathering, 20
   Assessment of Information Collected, 24
   Identification of Opportunities for Strengthening
      National Security, 25
Guide to This Report, 27
References, 28

PART I: CONTEXT FOR THIS DECADAL STUDY

2 Two Communities   31
The Universe of Intelligence and National Security, 31
   The Security Infrastructure, 33
   Types of Intelligence, 35
The Social and Behavioral Sciences, 36
Shared Challenges and Diverse Demands, 40
   More Data and More Ways to Analyze Them, 40
   Interdisciplinary Collaborations, 42
   Diverse Cultures, Audiences, and Demands, 44
References, 45

3 Global Context for the Decadal Study   49
   U.S. Government Documents, 49
      Assessment of the National Intelligence Council, 50
      President's National Security Policy, 53
      U.S. Department of Defense Military Strategy, 54
      National Intelligence Strategy, 55
   Statements of International Organizations, 56
      Organisation for Economic Co-operation and Development, 56
      World Economic Forum, 57
   Persistent Themes and Emerging Threats, 58
   References, 62

4 The Work of the Intelligence Analyst   65
   Sensemaking, 65
   What Analysts Do, 67
      The Analyst's Daily Activities, 69
      Sustaining Activities, 72
      Communicating Intelligence and Analysis to Others, 73
   Illustrating Analytic Work, 76
      Analytic Lens: Monitoring Terrorist Group Z, 78
      Analytic Lens: Monitoring Weapons Proliferation, 78
      Analytic Lens: Monitoring a Country, 79
   Looking Forward, 79
   References, 81

PART II: OPPORTUNITIES FOR THE IC

5 Sensemaking: Emerging Ways to Answer Intelligence Questions   85
   Approaches to Understanding Human and Social Processes, 86
      The Study of Narrative, 86
      The Study of Social Networks, 88
      The Study of Complex Systems, 90
      The Affective Sciences, 92
   Applying Social and Behavioral Science Research to Sensemaking
         for Core Analytic Problems, 94
      Understanding Power and Influence, 95
      Understanding Threats and Opportunities, 108
      Understanding Complexity, 117
   Conclusions, 122
   References, 124

CONTENTS

6 Integrating Social and Behavioral Sciences (SBS) Research
   to Enhance Security in Cyberspace   141
   What Is Social Cybersecurity Science?, 142
     Drawing on Other Disciplines, 146
     A Social Cybersecurity Approach to Studying a False
       Information Campaign, 149
   Opportunities for the IC, 152
   Example Application: Social Influence on Twitter, 154
   Research Needed in the Coming Decade, 157
     Social Cyberforensics: Identifying Who Is Conducting Social
       Cybersecurity Attacks, 158
     Information Maneuvers: Identifying the Strategies Used to
       Conduct an Attack, 160
   Intent Identification: Identifying the Perpetrator's Motive, 164
   Cross-Media Movement and Information Diffusion: Tracing the
     Attackers and the Impact of the Attack across Multiple
     Social Media Platforms, 167
     Real-Time Measurement of the Effectiveness of Information
       Campaigns: Quantifying the Effectiveness of the Attack, 168
     At-Risk Groups: Identifying Who Is Most Susceptible to
       Attacks, 169
     The Most Effective Responses: Mitigating These Attacks, 172
   Conclusions, 174
   References, 176

7 Integrating the Social and Behavioral Sciences (SBS)
   into the Design of a Human–Machine Ecosystem   189
   A New Form of Analytic Work, 191
   Research Domains, 194
     Human Capacities, 199
     Human–Machine Interaction, 205
     Human–Technology Teaming, 225
     Human–System Integration, 230
   Conclusions, 232
     A Research Program to Support Design and Development, 233
     Ethical Considerations, 234
   References, 238

8 Strengthening the Analytic Workforce for Future Challenges — 253
Selecting Individuals to Succeed in Intelligence Analyst Roles, 256
    Advances in Measurement, 256
    Outcomes of Interest, 258
    The Effectiveness and Utility of a Selection System, 260
    Workforce Selection: Implications for the Intelligence Community, 261
Retaining Effective Analysts, 262
    Dissatisfaction and the Desirability of Movement, 262
    An Unfolding Model of Turnover Decisions, 264
    Shifting the Focus from Who Leaves to Who Stays, 264
    Social Influences in the Turnover Process, 265
    Unmet Expectations and the Value of Realistic Job Previews, 266
    Collective Turnover, 267
    Retaining Effective Analysts: Implications for the Intelligence Community, 267
Developing Skills Through Formal Training and Informal Learning, 268
Supporting the Analytic Workforce, 271
Conclusions, 277
References, 280

PART III: LOOKING FORWARD

9 Strengthening Ties Between the Two Communities — 289
Lessons from Conducting the Decadal Survey, 289
    Challenges and Benefits of a Broad Charge, 290
    Challenges in Integrating Social and Behavioral Sciences (SBS) and Other Research, 291
Obstacles to Collaboration Between Researchers and the Intelligence Community (IC), 292
Building on Past Collaborations, 293
    Working Together: A Brief History, 294
    Lessons for Productive Collaboration, 296
Conclusions, 306
References, 306

10 **Capitalizing on Opportunities in Social and Behavioral
   Science (SBS) Research: A 10-Year Vision**   311
   Intelligence Analysis in 10 Years, 311
   Opportunities to Shape the Future of Intelligence Analysis, 313
      Stronger Intelligence Assessments, 314
      Tools and Technologies Optimally Designed for Human Use
         and Human–Machine Interaction, 315
      Strengthened Readiness to Confront Evolving Security
         Threats, 316
   Capitalizing on These Opportunities, 317
      Research Opportunities, 317
      Strengthening Ties Between the IC and the Research
         Community, 318
   Closing Thoughts, 325
   References, 326

Appendixes

A	Summary of National Security–Related Research Programs	329
B	Summary of the Committee's Information Gathering	337
C	Reproducibility and Validity	357
D	New Data, New Research Tools, New Ethical Questions	365
E	Biographical Sketches of Committee Members and Staff	375

Summary

Ten years from now, the job of the intelligence analyst will be transformed. Analysts responding to continuously evolving security risks will likely be tracking new combinations of nonstate and state-sponsored actors who threaten to disrupt governance and civil society. These potential adversaries will likely be motivated by both familiar and unforeseeable drivers, including the effects of global climate change, which will be manifest through such issues as scarcities of water, food, and other resources; extreme weather events; and dislocation of communities. Shifting strategic alliances, military conflicts, the presence of hostile terrorist factions and street gangs, and deteriorating local economies will further challenge stability. At the same time, adversaries and other actors of concern to the Intelligence Community (IC) will have access to new resources, including computing technologies and cyberspace operations, as well as chemical and biological weapons—perhaps even stolen nuclear weaponry—that will dramatically amplify their power to inflict harm and disrupt daily life and commerce.

Intelligence analysts themselves will have new resources based on advances in data processing and other technologies. Technologies including artificial intelligence (AI), large dataset analytics, dynamic search tools, and interactive technologies are already allowing analysts to process and integrate multiple sources of data and intelligence far more quickly and efficiently than ever before. They are also dramatically expanding opportunities for collaboration involving personnel and technology, and integration of new types of data. New knowledge, tools, and technologies with applications for understanding, forecasting, and mitigating security risks are continually emerging.

The IC will need research from the social and behavioral sciences (SBS) if it is to take maximum advantage of these developing resources and be optimally prepared for the security challenges on the horizon. But what is needed is not simply more research. Intelligence analysts already rely on SBS research, just as they already synthesize large volumes of data and information about fast-breaking developments to produce reliable and accurate assessments that can support urgent and consequential decisions.

To date, however, the influence of SBS research on intelligence analysis has been ad hoc: despite the value of many ongoing efforts, the IC has not found ways to systematically integrate research and perspectives from the academic SBS community into its work. Recognizing this gap and the crucial role of SBS research in supporting intelligence analysis, the Office of the Director of National Intelligence (ODNI), which oversees and directs the work of the agencies and organizations responsible for foreign, military, and domestic intelligence for the United States, requested that the National Academies of Sciences, Engineering, and Medicine conduct a decadal survey of SBS research with applications to national security.

The charge to the Committee on a Decadal Survey of Social and Behavioral Sciences for Applications to National Security was to (1) develop understanding and direction regarding resources from SBS disciplines with the greatest potential to augment and support the intelligence analysis process and enhance national security, which the IC can use in determining its research priorities for the coming decade; and (2) identify lessons to be learned from the application of the decadal survey process in the national security context.

STUDY PROCESS

A decadal survey is a method for engaging members of a scholarly community to identify lines of research with the greatest potential to be of use over a 10-year period in pursuit of a particular goal. The National Academies developed this type of survey to support the planning of future research for other government entities, including the National Aeronautics and Space Administration, the National Science Foundation (NSF), the U.S. Department of Energy, the National Oceanic and Atmospheric Administration, and the U.S. Geological Survey. The process has not previously been used to survey SBS research or to support the IC's research planning. In conducting the present survey, the committee adapted the methods used in previous decadal surveys; we developed a process to seek understanding of the needs of the IC and current challenges in the work of the IC analyst and to cull SBS research of potential relevance to those challenges.

We identified two broad categories of need for the IC: support in leveraging developing research and technology to improve the skills and tools used by analysts, and support in strengthening the IC workforce. Thus, our focus was on the insights provided by the SBS disciplines into human behavior, capacities, and limitations, and ways in which those insights could be integrated into both the content of intelligence analysis (understanding what people and adversaries do) and the technical means of analysis (improving and supplementing the human capacities of the analyst).

We used four criteria to identify the areas of research with the most promise for direct impact on these two categories of need:

1. the potential for impact on urgent national security priorities;
2. the strength of the supporting evidence base;
3. technical readiness, or the state of development on the continuum from basic research, to field testing and evaluation, to applied research; and
4. the potential to use or develop emerging data sources, methods, or other technical advances with potential to yield significant advances.

We also considered the ethical implications of the research itself and its applications throughout the study process.

OPPORTUNITIES TO SHAPE THE FUTURE OF INTELLIGENCE ANALYSIS: RESEARCH DIRECTIONS

Opportunities in the research we examined can contribute to the most fundamental aspects of the IC's work. To adapt to anticipated changes in both the security landscape and the way intelligence analysis is conducted, the IC will need the insights that come from deep understanding of cultural and political history and context, the way humans and social and political entities behave, and current trends and forces shaping the actions and decisions of individuals and groups. Integrating the understanding of human beings and social processes that comes from SBS research into the analyst's work as it evolves in the coming decade will be critical.

It is this knowledge base that will enable the IC to develop tools and methods that are both proactive and interactive and can effectively augment the capacities of human analysts, and, more broadly, to respond effectively to the security threats of the coming decades. We have identified research directions, summarized in our conclusions, for pursuing the opportunities in the bodies of work we examined. While there are clear, critical potential benefits to the IC in each of these areas, they are by no means the only promising ones. Nevertheless, a 10-year research agenda based on these areas would contribute significantly to the IC's analytic responsibilities, and build a strong foundation for significantly strengthening interchange between the security community and the external SBS research community.

Targeted SBS research offers the potential for stronger intelligence assessments, tools and technologies optimally designed for human use and human–machine interaction, and optimal readiness to confront evolving security threats.

Stronger Intelligence Assessments

SBS research can support the development of intelligence assessments that are **richer** 10 years from now because analysts will have the capacity to use new types of information and analyze existing types of information in new ways. SBS research involves gathering reliable and interpretable data on human behavior that does not fall within the expertise of other disciplines. It provides the essential theoretical and empirical bases for designing and using sophisticated methodologies to make complex data meaningful and enrich the analyst's understanding of the social and political worlds. Assessments may also be more **nuanced** because analysts will have tools that allow them to identify intersections and see connections in large-scale datasets that humans alone could not detect.

Assessments may be **more accurate and efficient.** Methodologies and tools described in this report may allow for faster processing of large volumes of data, integration of multiple kinds of data and other analyses, and tracking of developments—capabilities beyond those of human analysts—but only if conceptual frameworks derived from SBS work provide the basis for their design. The result will be improved forecasting and the possibility of efficiently tracking regions, populations, groups, and sources of information. New kinds of indicators based in research on, for example, manifestations of emotion or how extremist narratives exert influence, could help the analyst gauge changes in a political leader's behavior, the developing strength of a minority group's influence, or the cohesiveness of networks within which toxic narratives are spreading, and direct the analyst's attention more swiftly to those developments requiring attention.

> **CONCLUSION 5-1:**[1] Developing research on narratives, social networks, complex systems, and affect and emotion can enhance understanding of primary targets of intelligence analysis, the potential impact of actions taken by the Intelligence Community, and individual and social processes relevant to security threats. This research offers possibilities for new tools, including but not limited to

---

[1] Conclusions are numbered according to the chapters in which they are introduced.

- indicators for use in monitoring and detection of key security-related developments;
- algorithms for extracting meaning from large quantities of open-source information; and
- models for reasoning about the potential implications of various interventions or activities.

CONCLUSION 5-2: Interdisciplinary, multimethod approaches to integrating insights from social and behavioral sciences fields with sophisticated technological developments will be essential to support the development of new tools for the analysis and interpretation of data and intelligence. The Intelligence Community would benefit from pursuing a portfolio of such research focused on the development of operational methods and tools.

Tools and Technologies Optimally Designed for Human Use and Human–Machine Interaction

Tools and technologies that become operational in the coming decade and beyond—including advances in data processing and AI that support large dataset analytics, dynamic search tools, statistical modeling, and interactivity—will augment the capacities of the human analyst in vital ways, which will necessarily change the nature of human–machine interaction. Insights from SBS fields are essential to the design and development of tools and technologies that

- take advantage of the strengths of both humans and machines;
- allow humans to collaborate productively with machine partners;
- support more accurate assessment and forecasting of human activity; and
- avoid serious unintended practical and ethical consequences.

SBS research offers insights that will be needed to design tools that use AI and machine learning. It could also support the development of an ecosystem for intelligence analysis composed of human analysts and autonomous AI agents, supported by other technologies, with the capacity to derive meaning efficiently from multiple sources of information.

Existing and emerging SBS research can also provide essential support for the procurement of products from the private sector, such as commercially available software programs and other technologies. While these externally produced resources bring important efficiencies and other benefits, careful attention is needed to ensure that they reflect SBS-based insights so they provide the benefits for which they were sought. Technology used for analysis is only as strong as the understanding of the human behavior it is being used to model or explain.

> CONCLUSION 7-1: To develop a human–machine ecosystem that functions effectively for intelligence analysis, it will be necessary to integrate findings from social and behavioral sciences research into the design and development of artificial intelligence and other technologies involved. A research program for this purpose would extend theory and findings from current research on human–machine interactions to new types of interactions involving multiple agents in a complex teaming environment.

> CONCLUSION 7-2: A social and behavioral sciences research agenda to support the development of technologies and systems for effective human–machine teams for intelligence analysis should include, but not be limited to, the following goals:

- Apply methodologies from the vision sciences, the behavioral sciences, and human factors to advances in data visualization to improve understanding of how people extract meaning from visualizations and the functionality of tools designed to present information from large datasets.
- Use techniques from social network analysis to better understand how information can be transmitted effectively, as well as filtered among distributed teams of humans and machines, and how the need to use artificial intelligence (AI) to search and filter information can be balanced with the need to restrict access to certain information.
- Develop new modes of forecasting that incorporate human judgment with automated analyses by AI agents.
- Apply neuroscience-inspired strategies and tools to research on workload effects in a complex environment of networked human and AI agents.
- Examine the implications of ongoing system monitoring of work behaviors in terms of privacy issues, as well as potential interruptions to the intrinsic work habits of human analysts.
- Extend insights from the science of human teamwork to determine how to assemble and divide tasks among teams of humans and AI agents and measure performance in such teams.
- Identify guidelines for communication protocols for use in coordinating the sharing of information among multiple human and AI agents in ways that accommodate the needs and capabilities of human analysts and minimize disadvantages associated with interruption and multitasking in humans.

CONCLUSION 7-3: The design, development, and implementation of a system of human–technology teams, which would include autonomous agents, for use in intelligence analysis raise important ethical questions regarding access to certain types of data; authority to modify, store, or transmit data; and accountability and protections when systems fail. The Intelligence Community (IC) could best ensure that such systems function in an ethical manner and prepare to address unforeseeable new ethical issues by

- from the start, incorporating into the design and development process collaborative research, involving both members of the IC and the social and behavioral sciences community, on the application of ethical principles developed in other human–technology contexts to the IC context;
- ensuring that all research supported by the IC adheres to the standards for ethical conduct of research; and
- establishing a structure for ongoing review of ethical issues that may arise as the technology develops and new circumstances arise.

Optimal Readiness to Confront Evolving Security Threats

The contributions of SBS research will be vital to the capacity of the United States to react effectively to future risks. Ongoing SBS work is illuminating, for example, the nature of social networks and complex systems, protections against social cybersecurity threats, evolving ways adversaries influence hearts and minds, and the ways individuals are drawn into radicalization and extremism. Developments in numerous SBS fields are building understanding of both familiar and emerging threats. The emergence of new threats in cyberspace is already a profound challenge for the IC, one that can be expected to grow in scale and urgency in the coming decade. The developing field of social cybersecurity has the potential to offer tools, tactics, procedures, and policies for assessing, predicting, and mitigating the impact of adversarial social cyberattacks.

CONCLUSION 6-1: A comprehensive multidisciplinary research strategy for identifying, monitoring, and countering social cyberattacks, predicated on computational social science, would provide significant support for the Intelligence Community's (IC's) efforts to address the social cybersecurity threat in the coming decade. The emerging field of social cybersecurity research can yield insights that would supplement the IC's training and technology acquisition in the area of social cybersecurity threats and foster an effective social cybersafety culture. These insights could support development of the capacity to, for example, detect bots and malicious online actors and track the impact of social cyberattacks.

CONCLUSION 6-2: The Intelligence Community could strengthen its capacity to safeguard the nation against social cyber-mediated threats by supporting research with the objectives of developing

- generally applicable scientific methods for assessing bias in online data, drawing conclusions based on missing data, and triangulating to interpolate missing or incorrect data using multiple data sources; and
- new computational social science methods that would simultaneously consider change in social networks and narratives within social media–based groups from a geotemporal social-cyber perspective; and operational computational social science theories of influence and manipulation in a cyber-mediated environment that simultaneously take into account the network structure of online communities, the types of actors in those communities, social cognition, emotion, cognitive biases, narratives and counternarratives, and exploitable features of the social media technology.

Finally, SBS research can aid in strengthening the overall effectiveness of the IC workforce, an important aspect of preparedness for the security challenges of the coming decade. To the extent that foundational and current insights from industrial-organizational psychology and related fields have not already been integrated into the IC's personnel management approaches, translational research to identify the applications of a well-developed body of research and practice in this area is likely to be beneficial. Four salient areas for which robust research is available are the selection of applicants likely to be effective in analytic roles, skill development on the job through both formal training and informal learning, means of retaining and engaging effective analysts, and ways of providing support for a potentially stressed and fatigued workforce.

CONCLUSION 8-1: A range of personal attributes—including skills in critical evaluation, writing and presentation, and teamwork; openness to feedback; and a continuous learning orientation—contribute to successful job performance as an intelligence analyst. To strengthen its capacity to select individuals well suited to work as an intelligence analyst, the Intelligence Community (IC) would benefit from

- regularly updating its assessment of the facets of the analyst's job performance that are of greatest value to the IC and the attributes most useful for selection of personnel for intelligence analysis roles;
- having the capacity to measure a broad range of attributes for use in selecting individuals who possess those attributes; and

- evaluating the predictive power and potential ethical implications of such assessment devices as digital games, gleaning information about candidates from social media, and using machine learning approaches to extract information from interviews and resumés and develop scoring algorithms.

CONCLUSION 8-2: A large body of social and behavioral sciences research identifies individual and organizational factors linked to employee retention, including employees' attitudes and engagement, unit cohesiveness, and leader quality, but these factors have not been examined in the Intelligence Community (IC) context. Translational work examining the role of these potential influencing factors could aid in managing retention in the IC.

CONCLUSION 8-3: A systematic review of the degree to which the organizational culture within the agencies of the Intelligence Community supports both organizationally directed training and autonomous learning could provide valuable information that could be used to promote these means of enhancing the skills of the analytic workforce. This review could focus on practices that promote such a culture, including

- opportunities for workers to receive feedback,
- tolerance for error as employees attempt to use new skills,
- support and encouragement from supervisors and peers, and
- allocation of time for autonomous learning.

CONCLUSION 8-4: Emerging research indicates that developing tools and methods could be used to assess and mitigate issues related to the effects of work in the high-stress environment of intelligence analysis, including cognitive fatigue, reduced attention, impaired performance, and decreased efficiency. Possibilities include the application of neuroergonomics (e.g., cueing, visual or auditory warning signals, automation); neuroscience (e.g., noninvasive brain stimulation); and neuropharmacology. The development of effective and safe tools and methods ready for implementation would require (1) research on the utility and applicability of these methods in the Intelligence Community environment, and (2) careful consideration of safety and ethical issues related to their use.

CONCLUSION 8-5: To fully benefit from research findings relevant to the development of an optimal analytic workforce, the Intelligence Community (IC) would need to invest in research and evaluation to guide their application in the context of intelligence analysis. Translating key insights about selection, training, retention of, and support for the IC analytic workforce will in itself require a team approach in which members of the IC, social and behavioral sciences researchers, applied scientists, and others collaborate to help translate the approaches discussed here for the IC context and assess their effectiveness.

CAPITALIZING ON THESE OPPORTUNITIES

The ideas discussed in this report highlight the reality that technological and other developments in intelligence analysis that proceed without the benefit of SBS research are likely to be limited in their effectiveness, or worse, to result in misleading or distorted analysis.

CONCLUSION 10-1: Social and behavioral sciences (SBS) research offers a fundamental—indeed essential—contribution to the mission of the Intelligence Community (IC), a mission that requires understanding of what human beings do, how, and why. The research described in this report amply demonstrates the critical importance of

- interdisciplinary research—both foundational and applied and domestic and international—designed to take advantage of and integrate theory, methodology, and data from across SBS fields to yield new insights into human behavioral and social processes with relevance to national security;
- the integration of basic science and developing research on human behavior and social processes, as well as advances in computational methods for large-scale data analysis, with the expertise of the IC on analytic methods and challenges;
- the incorporation of a deep understanding of the IC's challenges into the identification of research questions and hypotheses to be tested, as well as the design and execution of research;
- the integration of SBS insights into the design and engineering of technologically based analytic tools; and
- translational and applied work to establish the direct utility of SBS research findings for the IC.

The range of opportunities explored in this report demonstrates both the power of the benefits SBS research offers for the IC and the extent of the challenge of fully taking advantage of these opportunities. Strengthening the relationship between the SBS community and the IC will be critical if these opportunities are to bear fruit. This report offers insights for sustaining this effort in the long term that come both from the experience of conducting this decadal survey and from a review of the history of collaboration between these two very different communities.

Overall, what initially appeared to be the greatest challenge in conducting this study—a broad charge that required looking across a very wide research landscape—turned out to be the most valuable aspect of the task. The challenge of casting such a wide net in searching for intersections between the needs of the IC and the available SBS research meant that the committee's efforts were not driven by the perspectives of a single discipline and that we had no preconceptions about where to look for relevant work. Further, despite the obvious difficulty of looking across multiple, diverse disciplines, the study process did reveal certain basic elements that would likely have emerged regardless of the methods used in the process. Without a doubt, for example, any attempt to meet our charge would have highlighted the importance of learning more about human–machine interactions, ways to make use of emerging analytics for big data, and the integration of insights about human behavior and group functioning in the pursuit of cybersecurity.

The survey process also allowed us to see firsthand some of the obstacles to integration and collaboration between the IC and the SBS community, and to observe that coordination between the two is less prevalent than would be optimal. Moreover, awareness of the potential applications of SBS research to IC needs is highly uneven across relevant SBS fields, and there is a long way to go in building awareness of these potential applications of their work among the research community.

Most of the opportunities identified in this report will depend on the integration of research from SBS fields with work from technical fields including engineering, computer science, and neuroscience. Technological developments occur in a social and economic context: SBS research is therefore essential to understanding of the potential applications and benefits, risks, and long-term effects of sophisticated technology and to its sound application, despite significant differences in theory and method between these two cultures. Therefore, we make one recommendation to the IC:

> **RECOMMENDATION 10-1:** The leadership of the Intelligence Community should make sustained collaboration with researchers in the social and behavioral sciences (SBS) community a key priority as it develops research objectives for the coming decade. A multipronged effort to integrate the knowledge and perspectives of researchers from the SBS fields into the planning and design of efforts to support intelligence analysis is most likely to reap the potential benefits described in this report.

Although the objectives and perspectives of the SBS research community and the IC are not always aligned, the two communities have always had much to learn from one another. Researchers and members of the IC have differing objectives, face differing challenges and constraints, and operate in contexts that have very different norms and expectations. Nevertheless, collaborations between the two have for decades yielded important scientific and analytic insights.

> CONCLUSION 9-1: Explicit attention to the respective intellectual goals, values, and perspectives of members of the Intelligence Community and academic researchers is a prerequisite for productive collaboration. Collaborations between the two have yielded important scientific and analytic insights, and have functioned well when funding sources and agency goals have been transparent, when social and behavioral sciences research questions and agency missions and goals have been harmonized and clear, and when ethical and value-based concerns have been treated with sufficient care. Conversely, the relationship has fractured in the past when funding sources have been kept secret or misrepresented, researchers and government agencies have struggled to balance research and agency needs, and research has touched on broader ethical or value-based disagreements.

> CONCLUSION 9-2: Ethical issues may arise at all steps of the research process, from planning, to dissemination of findings, to the operationalization of digital tools in analytic contexts. Because standards with respect to some ethical issues—particularly those concerning the use of large-scale digital datasets—are developing, and because these issues are context-sensitive, ethical assessments require careful attention throughout the research process.

> CONCLUSION 9-3: Meticulous clarity and openness about the approaches taken to ensure the reproducibility and validity of the evidence generated in the course of research conducted by or with the support of the Intelligence Community (IC) are critical to the utility of the research results. The IC can promote this standard by requiring researchers to identify project components that incorporate assessments of reproducibility, replication, and validity.

The findings presented in this report provide the foundation for what the committee hopes will become a stable and continuing process by which SBS research can be culled for its relevance to national security challenges, and promising relevant work can be supported and integrated into IC planning and operations. Effective interchange in the future is likely to involve four key ingredients:

1. building on effective examples of collaboration, such as communities of practice;
2. strengthening cultural bridges between the two communities and addressing institutional obstacles to collaboration;
3. providing opportunities for analytic staff to build their knowledge of SBS research and for researchers to improve their understanding of the IC; and
4. relying on the principles of human–systems integration to facilitate the development of collaborative systems that function effectively.

This report comes at a critical time in the nation's history: new forms of threats, as well as complex new methods and tools for understanding trends and developments, identifying immediate threats, and forecasting future problems, are making the IC analyst's work both more challenging and more critical. Without understanding of the human component of these developments, the IC analyst would be perilously hampered. Capitalizing on the research opportunities discussed in this report will require the IC to abandon procedures and ways of doing business that have been in place for a long time. The continued strengthening of the IC workforce will depend on interdisciplinary approaches in which the insights and ideas of SBS researchers are fully integrated with the needs and objectives of the IC.

Introduction

The agencies and individuals responsible for protecting the United States from international and domestic threats need to understand complex and rapidly evolving security challenges. Historically, their primary focus may have been on potential threats posed by nation-states, but the landscape has evolved. Intelligence experts anticipating risks to U.S. security in the coming decade must not only monitor nation-states but also track shifting combinations of both nonstate and state-sponsored actors, and even individuals who may have the capacity to cause large-scale harm to human life and to disrupt governance and civil society. These potential adversaries may be motivated by factors different from those that have been understood to drive nation-states, and they have access to new kinds of weapons, including computing technologies and cyberspace operations, as well as chemical and biological agents. These new weapons can dramatically amplify the power of potential adversaries to inflict harm and to "disrupt commercial activities, daily life, and military operations; cause economic damage; compromise sensitive and/or technical information; and interrupt critical infrastructure such as power grids and information networks" (U.S. Department of Defense, 2017, p. I-1). Communication in the cyber world has the potential to undermine political stability and democracy. Looking beyond the intentional actions of people and entities, moreover, intelligence analysts must seek to understand such developments as global climate change and the growth of autonomous technology.

In concert with these developments, the tools available to intelligence analysts for understanding, forecasting, and mitigating security risks are also evolving. Advances in data processing and other technologies, including artificial intelligence (AI),[1] large dataset analytics, dynamic search tools, and interactive technologies, along with access to new kinds of data, such as digital video footage, are allowing intelligence analysts to process multiple sources of data and intelligence far more quickly and efficiently than ever before. These advances are also dramatically expanding possibilities for collaboration among personnel and integration of data sources.

Even as they assimilate both evolving global threats and complex new tools, intelligence analysts continue to rely on research produced within many academic disciplines. Analysts have always synthesized large volumes of data and information on fast-breaking developments to produce reliable and accurate assessments that support urgent and consequential decisions. Those assessments must reflect lessons and insights derived from a deep understanding of cultural and political history and context, the way humans and political entities behave, and current trends and forces shaping the actions and decisions of individuals and groups. These factors remain critical even as the Intelligence Community (IC) must respond to the need both to understand human interaction with increasingly powerful technologies and to use those technologies effectively in its own work.

PURPOSE OF THIS STUDY

The deep understanding and expertise that are crucial to the work of intelligence analysts rest in large part on findings generated by research in the social and behavioral sciences (SBS)—the set of disciplines that "focus on the behavior, attitudes, beliefs, and practices of people and their organizations, communities, and institutions" (National Research Council, 2012, p. 10). This report summarizes vital opportunities to leverage this research in support of the work of intelligence analysts and thereby enhance national security.

Academic disciplines including international relations and political science, statistics, public policy, anthropology, public health and epidemiology, environmental science, sociology, demography, economics, psychology, neuroscience, and many more contribute in essential ways to the work of the intelligence analyst. A National Academy of Sciences committee recently summarized the value of SBS research for national priorities: "Nearly every major challenge the United States faces—from alleviating unemployment

---

[1] AI is commonly understood to refer to a machine performing functions that previously could be performed only by human intelligence. Computer technology makes it possible for machines to complete such tasks as recognizing patterns, speech, or images far more quickly than humans can. However, human input is essential for the programming of an AI agent: the machine can draw on and process essentially infinite amounts of data, but humans must develop the models and algorithms that direct the AI agent's actions (National Academies of Sciences, Engineering and Medicine, 2018; see also Stanford University, 2016).

to protecting itself from terrorism—requires understanding the causes and consequences of people's behavior. . . . Having a fundamental understanding of how people and societies behave, why they respond the way they do, what they find important, what they believe or value, and what and how they think about others is critical for the country's well-being in today's shrinking global world" (NASEM, 2017b, p. 1). The study of cybersecurity offers a compelling illustration of the fundamental contribution of SBS knowledge to national security. Human behavior is a critical factor in both adversaries' capacity to discover and exploit design flaws and the development and operation of cybersecurity systems to protect against such threats. Understanding human behavior is therefore vital for reducing vulnerability to cybersecurity threats (NASEM, 2017a).

Analysts, who bring backgrounds in many fields to their work, often draw on research from SBS fields. Since the 1950s, the Defense Advanced Research Projects Agency (DARPA) has supported work that integrates findings from SBS research, as does the Intelligence Advanced Research Projects Activity (IARPA), established in 2006. Likewise, the Minerva Research Initiative of the U.S. Department of Defense (DoD) was established in 2008 to draw on academic research to "improve DoD's basic understanding of the social, cultural, behavioral, and political forces that shape regions of the world of strategic importance to the U.S." (Minerva Research Initiative, 2018). The IC invests in SBS research through grants to external researchers and spending on a variety of projects carried out within its walls. (See Appendix A for a summary of SBS research efforts within the IC.)

The Office of the Director of National Intelligence (ODNI), which oversees and directs the work of the agencies and organizations responsible for foreign, military, and domestic intelligence for the United States, thus has a strong interest in research from the SBS disciplines that may be beneficial to the IC. ODNI has also noted interest in SBS research among experts such as those involved in the Intelligence Science and Technology Experts Group (ISTEG).[2] To develop a systematic understanding of the potential benefits of these disciplines for national security, ODNI requested that the National Academies of Sciences, Engineering, and Medicine conduct a decadal survey of SBS research with applications to national security. The objective was to develop understanding and direction regarding resources from these disciplines with the greatest potential to augment and support the intelligence process and national security, as well as to identify lessons that could be learned from the application of the decadal survey process in this context.

---

[2]ISTEG is an online forum in which experts from various disciplines assist ODNI in addressing key questions related to national security. It was organized by ODNI in partnership with the National Academies.

To carry out this work, the National Academies convened the Committee on the Decadal Survey of Social and Behavioral Sciences for Applications to National Security; the charge to the committee is shown in Box 1-1. This report describes the product of the decadal survey.

APPLYING THE DECADAL PROCESS IN A NEW CONTEXT

A decadal survey is a method for engaging members of a research community to identify lines of research with the greatest potential to be of use over a 10-year period in the pursuit of a particular goal. The National Academies pioneered this type of survey with a study of ground-based astronomy in 1964 (see National Academy of Sciences, 1964), and committees appointed by the National Academies have conducted more than 15 decadal surveys to date. The decadal process has become an integral resource in planning future research for the National Aeronautics and Space Administration (NASA), the National Science Foundation, the Department of Energy, the National Oceanic and Atmospheric Administration, and the U.S. Geological Survey; the two branches of the United States Congress and officials on the staff of the White House have also relied on decadal surveys (NASEM, 2015). Many research communities look to the decadal survey process as both an opportunity to share the potential benefits of their work and a source of guidance on the needs of government agencies. Agency leaders, in turn, rely on the process to provide "a science community consensus on key questions" (NASA Science, 2018).

Decadal studies have targeted many sorts of missions and have involved research disciplines within the space and earth sciences that use a range of methodologies. Many have been designed to assess research in comparatively confined sets of disciplines to address charges related to specific missions. The first such survey, for example, *Ground-Based Astronomy: A Ten-Year Program*, resulted in recommendations regarding telescopes needed for radio and optical astronomical programs (National Academy of Sciences, 1964). Subsequent decadal studies have addressed broader and more complex missions, but few if any are as broad as improving the analytic capability of agencies responsible for national security, or that draw on a range of disciplines as wide as that encompassed by the SBS.

The Decadal Survey of Social and Behavioral Sciences for Applications to National Security is the first application of this approach to SBS fields. It was planned as an opportunity for the IC to benefit more systematically from relevant research produced across these numerous fields, as well as for researchers in these fields to consider critical applications for their work of which they may not previously have been aware. However, there is no established decadal tradition in the IC: although this community relies on a wealth of research, it has not had such a mechanism for seeking input

BOX 1-1
Charge to the Committee

The National Academies will carry out a decadal survey on the social and behavioral sciences (SBS) in areas relevant to national security in two integrated phases. The first phase, a national summit (workshop) was completed in fall 2016. The statement of task for the second phase, a consensus process, is below.

An ad hoc consensus committee, drawing on membership from the summit steering committee, will be appointed to conduct the decadal survey aimed at identifying opportunities that are poised to contribute significantly to the IC's analytic responsibilities. The study will identify opportunities throughout the social sciences (e.g., sociology, demography, political science, economics, and anthropology) and from behavioral sciences (e.g., psychology, cognition, and neuroscience) and will draw on discussions at the summit to frame its inquiry. Attention will also be paid to work in allied professional disciplines such as engineering, business, and law, and a full variety of cross-disciplinary, historical, case study, participant, and phronetic approaches.

The committee will work with Office of the Director of National Intelligence (ODNI) and security community members to understand government needs and expectations. The final report will be based on the committee's consideration of broad national security priorities; relevant capabilities of elements within the security community to support and apply SBS research findings; cost and technical readiness; likely growth of research programs; emerging SBS data, procedures, personnel, and other resources; and opportunities to leverage related research activities not directly supported by government. The committee will specify a range of relevant work that could be useful to the IC for their consideration in developing future research priorities.

The committee's primary tasks will be to:

1. Assess progress in addressing selected major social and behavioral scientific challenges that might prove useful to national security. Include discussion of approaches that are gaining strength and those that are losing strength.
2. Identify SBS opportunities that can be used to guide security community investment decisions and application efforts over the next 10 years.
3. Specify approaches to facilitate productive interchange between the security community and the external social science research community.
4. Reflect on the application of the decadal model to the SBS and identify lessons learned (insights into how to approach and perform the decadal survey process) and promising practices (activities that could facilitate future decadal surveys in the SBS and similar disciplines and maximize their ultimate utilities to sponsors and the scientific community).

to its program development, planning, and allocation of funds. Similarly, the SBS community has had no systematic way of focusing on its potential contributions to national security.

STUDY APPROACH

The committee formed to conduct this study was made up of experts with decades of experience in intelligence, scholars in diverse SBS fields, and several individuals with extensive experience in both worlds. No committee could begin to reflect all the expertise that would be relevant, but we were committed to applying the well-established decadal survey process in a way that would benefit both the IC and the SBS community. We looked closely at the examples set by other decadal committees, as well as lessons documented in a 2015 National Academies consensus study of the process (NASEM, 2015). The National Academies also has released more than 500 reports on issues related to national security and conflict, and all six of the institution's divisions have contributed to this body of work. This work provided background and context for the committee's efforts, and some of it was collected in preparation for a summit held as a precursor to the present study (discussed below) (NASEM, 2017a). The committee took note as well of relevant ongoing work of the National Academies, including the projects listed in Box 1-2.

The decadal survey process has two essential elements: assessing the needs associated with the mission it is to serve and assessing the landscape of research with the potential to contribute to that mission. The committee used an iterative process to assess the needs of the IC and the strength of potential ideas from SBS research to help meet those needs.

Information Gathering

The committee used numerous methods to solicit input from the IC and the research community and to collect information about potentially relevant research; our charge was to look forward, not to synthesize the vast existing body of work from which the IC can benefit. The first phase of the study was a summit, held in October 2016, and planned by a separate steering committee. The Summit on Social and Behavioral Sciences for National Security brought together researchers, members of the IC, and government officials to explore a sampling of research relevant to national security and consider its possible benefits and limitations, and to engage in structured discussions of strategic challenges faced by the IC. The summit, which was summarized in a published document, was intended in part to broadcast the goals for this decadal study within both communities (NASEM, 2017a).

> **BOX 1-2**
> **IC-Related Work at the National Academies**
>
> The Intelligence Community Studies Board of the National Academies oversees projects on science and technology issues of importance to the IC. These include the Intelligence Science and Technology Experts Group, a standing group of experts in a range of fields who are available to provide technical advice to the Office of the Director of National Intelligence, as well as colloquia and other projects targeted at specific issues. While most of these projects have focused on technological issues, a current pilot program, Exploring the Development of Analytic Frameworks, is focused on creating innovative products that draw on research in the social and behavioral sciences to produce, for example, educational tools for junior analysts, guidance for intelligence assessments of real-world situations, and briefings for policy makers. For more information, see the following:
>
> - Intelligence Community Studies Board: http://sites.nationalacademies.org/DEPS/icsb/index.htm
> - Assessing the Minerva Research Initiative and the Contribution of Social Science to Addressing Security Concerns: http://sites.nationalacademies.org/DBASSE/BBCSS/Assessing-the-Minerva-Research-Initiative/index.htm
> - Exploring the Development of Analytic Frameworks: A Pilot Project for the Office of the Director of National Intelligence: http://sites.nationalacademies.org/DBASSE/BBCSS/Exploring-Development-of-Analytic-Frameworks/index.htm
> - Integrating Social and Behavioral Sciences within the Weather Enterprise: http://sites.nationalacademies.org/dbasse/bohsi/integrating_sbs_weather_enterprise
> - The Value of Social, Behavioral, and Economic Sciences to National Priorities: A Report for the National Science Foundation: http://sites.nationalacademies.org/dbasse/the_value_of_social_behavioral_and_economic_sciences_to_national_priorities

Once the decadal committee had been appointed, we initiated a multi-pronged effort to investigate the research literature in many salient areas and to assess IC needs. Appendix B provides a detailed description of this information-gathering process; the discussion here summarizes the primary activities with which we supplemented our own investigations. In addition to issuing announcements of our work and invitations to contribute—disseminated through e-mail blasts to networks associated with the work of the Division of Behavioral and Social Sciences and Education (DBASSE), professional organizations representing SBS disciplines, and other groups and individuals with potential interest in this study—we used four primary means of soliciting input. These sources were supplemented by the collective expertise we brought to the project and our own reviews of the relevant literature, which became increasingly refined as we identified key topics to pursue.

White Papers

An established component of the decadal survey process is the use of calls for white papers from relevant communities to solicit ideas and comments on specific topics. The committee issued two such calls: the first for input on the key questions, needs, and challenges for intelligence analysis that members of the IC regard as having the highest priority; the second focused on research solutions—concepts, methods, tools, techniques, and new ideas that could advance knowledge—in SBS fields relevant to a variety of analytic challenges and needs. This input was solicited from all SBS disciplines, not just those normally associated with national security and international relations, and notice of each call was widely distributed (see Appendix B). We received 36 responses to the first call and 62 to the second. The papers thus obtained clearly did not reflect the full range of disciplines and ideas that would be relevant, but they did provide us with a diverse set of ideas to explore, as well as an intriguing cross-section of perspectives.[3]

As noted, the solicitation of such papers has become a widely recognized procedure within communities that have adopted the decadal survey process; submission of a compelling white paper in this context is also an established step in the pursuit of significant research funding. Some decadal survey committees have received as many as several hundred submissions; our yield of white paper submissions was considerably less. However, there is currently no tradition within SBS disciplines of submitting white papers for this sort of purpose, and no reason for scholars to be looking for such opportunities. Indeed, many SBS scholars whose research may be relevant to the classified work of the IC may never have considered it in that light. Moreover, the term "social and behavioral sciences" encompasses a wide range of disciplines, methodologies, and research subjects. It would be impossible to carry out a systematic survey of such a broad terrain in the same way that one might survey the research relevant to, for example, ground telescopes. Thus, we made a concerted effort to solicit ideas with application to national security through other channels.

---

[3]We have cited specific white papers as we used them throughout this report. We did not systematically review them or provide feedback to their authors; see Appendix B for more about these papers.

INTRODUCTION 23

Structured Discussions with Researchers, Representatives of the IC, and Other Government Officials Representing Diverse Agencies and Perspectives

In the course of the study, the committee used time at its meetings to hear from 17 individuals, including researchers in the SBS disciplines, members of the IC, and other government representatives. These discussions provided an opportunity for the committee to ask questions and hear a range of perspectives.

Public Workshops

Building on the insights gained through the white papers and discussions at our meetings, the committee identified issues and questions about which we wished to learn more. Separate steering committees, each of which included members of the parent committee and outside experts, were appointed to plan six 1-day workshops aimed at exploring some of these issues. Various experts were invited to make presentations, answer questions, and engage in discussion with members of the committee and external participants, who included primarily researchers and current or former members of the IC. Thus, the committee was able to take advantage of a much broader range of expertise than could be reflected in any single 16-member committee, with the workshops serving a function similar to that of the expert panels used in many decadal studies.[4] The workshops, each summarized in a published document,[5] addressed the following:

1. Changing sociocultural dynamics and implications for national security
2. Emerging trends and methods in international security
3. Leveraging advances in social network thinking for national security
4. Learning from the science of cognition and perception for decision making
5. Workforce development and intelligence analysis
6. Understanding narratives for national security purposes

---

[4]The work of many decadal committees has been supplemented by expert panels, also appointed by the National Academies, to represent particular scientific or technical communities; they examine aspects of the parent committee's charge in detail. In this case, it was not possible to specify disciplines in advance, as the development of topics to examine and relevant disciplines was an important part of the committee's deliberations.

[5]The workshop proceedings are available at http://sites.nationalacademies.org/DBASSE/BBCSS/SBS_for_National_Security-Decadal_Survey/index.htm [December 2018].

Other Forums

The committee used several venues to spread word of its interest in hearing from members of both the IC and the research community. A virtual platform called IdeaBuzz allowed any interested user to post ideas and to comment or engage in dialogue about ideas already posted. Notice of this opportunity was widely disseminated through channels similar to those used for the white paper calls. Participation in a town hall at a meeting of the Society for Risk Analysis in 2017 was another opportunity to interact with potential contributors to the discussion and spread the word about the study. We also used announcements distributed through email to experts and academic departments throughout the country, inviting input and participation via workshops, IdeaBuzz, or simply submission of comments through the web portal for the study.

Assessment of Information Collected

The committee used multiple strategies to sort and assess the input received. A first step was to synthesize the input on the needs of the IC provided in written comments and white papers and remarks made at our meetings and workshops. The IC needs thus identified fell largely into two general categories.

One area of need was for support in taking advantage of developing research and technology to improve the skills and tools of intelligence analysts. The areas in which members of the IC cited a desire to improve included (1) ways to determine the usefulness of and analyze information and data; (2) ways to communicate findings effectively to decision makers; (3) means of monitoring and measuring current and evolving events; (4) methods for modeling and understanding complex, multiple-actor phenomena; and (5) ways to avoid errors and biases in decision making.

The second area of need was the desire for support in strengthening the IC workforce itself, taking advantage of developing research and technology to improve recruitment, selection, training, and the building of teams. Among the specific needs expressed were improved coordination and communication among researchers, analysts, policy and decision makers, and teams; the sharing of information and the organizational culture and supports available for managing workload in a high-stress environment; and strategies for identifying and mitigating incidences of insider threat.

In the process of refining our understanding of the primary needs of the IC, we also explored a large number of intriguing research topics and assessed their potential links to the needs we had identified. We deliberated at length about criteria for identifying those topics with the greatest promise for supporting the work of the intelligence analyst. Building on

INTRODUCTION 25

the guidance provided in our charge (refer to Box 1-1), we identified four primary criteria:

1. Potential for impact on urgent national security priorities
2. Strength of the supporting evidence base
3. Technical readiness, encompassing the state of development along the research continuum from basic research, to field testing and evaluation, to applied research
4. Use or development of emerging data sources, methods, or other technical advances with potential to yield significant progress

Our charge makes reference to two elements we were unable to consider fully. One was the "relevant capabilities of elements within the security community to support and apply SBS research findings." The breadth and scale of the U.S. intelligence apparatus, together with the classified nature of much of its work, prevented us from developing a detailed picture of how the IC is currently making use of research from SBS disciplines. Indeed, even a count of the analytic personnel currently employed in the agencies that make up the IC was not available to us. Given that DARPA, IARPA, and Minerva integrate work from SBS fields, it is likely that some elements of the ideas discussed in this report will be familiar among some segments of the IC. Others may not, and may be difficult for the agencies to apply immediately. Our objective was to clearly identify ways specific research could be of use for national security purposes and to be as explicit as possible about how that research might be exploited, not to address precisely how it might be implemented within the walls of the IC. The second element of our charge we were unable to address in detail was cost. Because we covered such a broad range of topics, it was simply not feasible to address any one in sufficient detail to support realistic estimates of even relative cost.

Identification of Opportunities for Strengthening National Security

Through this multistep filtering process, we identified a set of key opportunities SBS research offers for strengthening national security—specifically by supporting the work of the intelligence analyst. The intelligence analyst's key function is to make sense of information about the world that can be used to protect the United States. SBS research offers the opportunity to provide new insights about individuals, groups, and societies—using new types of data, including such artifacts as video data—that can transform intelligence analysis to improve and expand understanding of change, dynamics, and disruptions in the world.

The four broad, high-priority areas of opportunity we identified demonstrate how multiple research areas must be integrated so they can be fully exploited by the analytic community. Our focus is on a key contribution of SBS knowledge domains: the insights they provide into human behavior, capacities, and limitations, and how that understanding can be integrated into both the *content of intelligence analysis* (understanding what people and adversaries do) and the *technical means of analysis* (improving and supplementing the analyst's human capacities). We do not claim that these are the only areas of opportunity, but we are confident that they are "ripe" in the sense that they offer innovations in theory and/or application likely to bear fruit in concrete ways in the coming decade and are responsive to significant goals and needs related to the analyst's work. This report describes each of these broad opportunities and identifies objectives for research that could bring them closer to readiness for implementation by the IC.

The first two opportunities address the need for ways to improve the content of analysis, while the second two address ways to strengthen the capacity of the analytic workforce.

Opportunity 1: Emerging Ways to Answer Intelligence Questions

Advances in SBS research offer promising ways to glean answers to intelligence questions from the vast streams of information to which analysts potentially have access. New developments in such fields as cognitive and behavioral science, linguistics, psychology, and communication are providing the basis for knowledge and skills that can significantly enhance existing means of understanding many of the social phenomena important to national security. Research is expanding opportunities to apply new and familiar tools and methods, including those for analyzing new sorts of data on a very large scale and for harvesting meaning from data with respect to the behaviors and interactions of individuals, groups, and systems.

Opportunity 2: Enhancing Security in Cyberspace

Cyber-related developments have dramatically expanded the landscape of security threats, as well as the potential tools for countering those threats. Cyber experts from multiple technical disciplines have a laser focus on cybersecurity, but there is a pressing need to integrate understanding of human beings and social processes into the analyst's approach to understanding this critical set of problems. The emerging field of social cybersecurity has developed to meet this need. Researchers have been taking advantage of foundational work in SBS fields to characterize cyber-mediated changes in individual, group, societal, and political behaviors and outcomes, and also to build the cyber infrastructure needed to guard against cyber-mediated threats.

Opportunity 3: Optimal Design of a Human–Machine Ecosystem

A key emerging asset for the analyst—as well as an emerging challenge—lies in the rapidly accelerating sophistication of computer technology and AI. Collaborative computing ecosystems, in which autonomous computer agents augment the work of the human analyst, offer the potential to develop a collaborative intelligence analysis team with far greater capacity than would be possible with either humans or machines alone.

Opportunity 4: Preparing the Analytic Workforce for Future Challenges

The opportunities described in this report will pose considerable new challenges for the analytic workforce even as they provide powerful new capabilities. A significant body of existing research offers insights into how the workforce can be prepared to absorb and exploit the range of information made possible through new tools for sensemaking and the capabilities brought by collaborative computing.

GUIDE TO THIS REPORT

This report is structured in three parts. Part I provides essential context on the SBS community and the work of intelligence analysis, intended to aid readers who may not be well acquainted with one or the other of these communities. Chapter 2 provides an orientation to the two communities and identifies a few similarities and differences between them. Chapter 3 is a summary of global trends and the urgent security risks associated with those trends that are at the heart of the analyst's challenges. This chapter relies on the work of the National Intelligence Council and other entities who track such developments. Chapter 4 provides an overview of the work analysts do.

Part II (Chapters 5–8) describes opportunities offered by SBS research for enhancing national security. For each of the four areas of opportunity outlined above, these chapters describe benefits for the IC that can be reaped over the coming decade and specific areas of research that require support and development if those benefits are to be fully realized.

Part III (Chapters 9 and 10) considers how the IC can capitalize on the opportunities highlighted in Part II. Chapter 9 summarizes lessons learned in conducting this decadal study, examines the ties between the national security and SBS communities, and suggests the elements needed for productive collaboration between the two communities. Chapter 10 offers a look at intelligence analysis a decade from now. It synthesizes the primary benefits for the IC of the opportunities discussed in earlier chapters, highlights the importance of integrating research-based understanding of human and social processes into the IC's analytic capabilities, and describes what is needed to capitalize on these opportunities.

REFERENCES

Minerva Research Initiative. (2018). *Minerva Research Initiative*. Available: https://minerva.defense.gov [November 2018].

NASA Science. (2018). *Decadal Survey*. Available: https://science.nasa.gov/earth-science/decadal-surveys [November 2018].

National Academies of Sciences, Engineering, and Medicine (NASEM). (2015). *The Space Science Decadal Surveys: Lessons Learned and Best Practices*. Washington, DC: The National Academies Press.

NASEM. (2017a). *Social and Behavioral Sciences for National Security: Proceedings of a Summit*. Washington, DC: The National Academies Press.

NASEM. (2017b). *The Value of Social, Behavioral, and Economic Sciences to National Priorities: A Report for the National Science Foundation*. Washington, DC: The National Academies Press.

National Academy of Sciences. (1964). *Ground-Based Astronomy: A Ten-Year Program*. Washington, DC: National Academy Press.

National Research Council. (2012). *Using Science as Evidence in Public Policy*. Washington, DC: The National Academies Press.

Stanford University. (2016). *Artificial Intelligence and Life in 2030*. Available: https://ai100.stanford.edu/sites/default/files/ai_100_report_0831fnl.pdf [February 2019].

U.S. Department of Defense. (2017). *Joint and National Intelligence Support to Military Operations*. Joint Publication 2-01. Available: https://fas.org/irp/doddir/dod/jp2_01.pdf [November 2018].

PART I

CONTEXT FOR THIS DECADAL STUDY

Part I of this report is intended primarily for readers who may be more familiar with one of the two communities addressed in this report—that of social and behavioral science research and the Intelligence Community (IC)—than the other. An understanding of the contexts in which these professionals work and interact is an important backdrop for understanding the potential applications of the work we discuss. In Part I, we introduce the two communities and potential mismatches in the cultures of work characteristic of each, summarize the complex challenges from which it is the IC's principal mission to protect the United States, and examine the nature of the analyst's work.

2

Two Communities

The Intelligence Community (IC) and the social and behavioral sciences (SBS) research community have had many opportunities to work jointly since the early 20th century, and several structures are currently in place to facilitate that collaboration (see Chapter 9 and Appendix A). Nonetheless, each of these communities has a distinct culture and has developed specialized ways of working. For readers not already deeply familiar with the way both academic researchers and IC analysts work, it may be useful to learn more about the contexts in which their work is carried out. This chapter provides a brief introduction to the two communities and offers some observations about similarities and differences in the challenges of research and analysis they face.

THE UNIVERSE OF INTELLIGENCE AND NATIONAL SECURITY

The United States devotes considerable resources to intelligence and national security (see Box 2-1). In 2017, the total spent on intelligence was $70.3 billion, of which $53.5 billion was for national intelligence (the remainder was for military intelligence) (Miles, 2016). This work is carried out by what is loosely known as the IC, defined by the Office of the Director of National Intelligence (ODNI) as "a federation of executive branch agencies and organizations that work separately and together to conduct

> **BOX 2-1**
> **Definition of Intelligence**
>
> Intelligence is information gathered within or outside the U.S. that involves threats to our nation, its people, property, or interests; development, proliferation, or use of weapons of mass destruction; and any other matter bearing on the U.S. national or homeland security. Intelligence can provide insights not available elsewhere that warn of potential threats and opportunities, assess probable outcomes of proposed policy options, provide leadership profiles on foreign officials, and inform official travelers of counterintelligence and security threats.
>
> SOURCE: Excerpted from https://www.dni.gov/index.php/what-we-do/what-is-intelligence [January 2019].

intelligence activities necessary for the conduct of foreign relations and the protection of the national security of the United States."[1]

The work of the 17 agencies that make up the IC[2] (see Box 2-2) is not readily understood by outside observers. Much of that work is classified, and those who perform it rely on complex procedures and traditions that have developed over decades. During the past few decades, the public and the academic community have sought greater understanding of how the national security infrastructure—which carries out a function widely recognized as critical—functions. Aspects of the agencies' work have become better understood, in part because of journalists' and scholars' pressure for access to both historical and current information, and in part as a result of the work of a growing number of academic researchers drawn from such fields as history, international studies, and political science who have focused on the study of intelligence gathering and assessment (Monaghan, 2009), contributing interdisciplinary understanding of the role and functioning of spy agencies, intelligence abuses, and other issues.[3]

---

[1] Available: https://www.dni.gov/files/documents/ICD/ICD%20203%20Analytic%20Standards.pdf [January 2019].

[2] The terms "national security," "defense," "intelligence," and "Intelligence Community" are used somewhat informally to refer to related and sometimes overlapping functions associated with protecting the United States from domestic and external threats. In this report we focus on the work of intelligence analysts—those employed by the 17 IC agencies to analyze intelligence; when we refer to the IC, we mean that workforce and the agency leadership that oversees it.

[3] See, for example, the *Journal of Intelligence and National Security*, *Journal of National Security*, and *Journal of Global Security Issues*.

> **BOX 2-2**
> **The 17 Entities That Make Up the Intelligence Community**
>
> **Department of Defense Entities:**
> 1. Defense Intelligence Agency
> 2. National Geospatial-Intelligence Agency
> 3. National Reconnaissance Office
> 4. National Security Agency
> 5. U.S. Air Force Intelligence
> 6. U.S. Army Intelligence
> 7. U.S. Marine Corps Intelligence
> 8. U.S. Navy Intelligence
>
> **Non–Defense Department Entities:**
> 9. Office of the Director of National Intelligence
> 10. Central Intelligence Agency
>
> Department of Energy
> 11. *Office of Intelligence and Counter-Intelligence*
>
> Department of Justice
> 12. *Federal Bureau of Investigation's National Security Branch*
> 13. *Drug Enforcement Agency's Office of National Security Intelligence*
>
> Department of Homeland Security
> 14. *Office of Intelligence and Analysis*
> 15. *U.S. Coast Guard Intelligence*
>
> Department of State
> 16. *Bureau of Intelligence and Research*
>
> Department of the Treasury
> 17. *Office of Intelligence and Analysis*
>
> ---
>
> NOTE: Italics indicate the specific offices of the listed parent agencies that are part of the Intelligence Community.
> SOURCE: Adapted from Miles (2016).

The focus of this report is on the work of the intelligence analyst, carried out in the IC context. In this section, we provide an overview of the primary functions of the agencies dedicated to protecting the nation's security, based on information made publicly available through official documents and websites produced by the IC agencies.

The Security Infrastructure

The government officials responsible for the nation's security rely on information collected by the IC. Each of the 17 IC agencies has a particular focus and mission, but together they provide support to decision makers (often referred to as "customers" or "clients" because it is they who act on the intelligence provided) in the executive and legislative branches of government, law enforcement, and the military.

The National Security Act of 1947[4] launched the U.S. national security establishment. The changing nature of both foreign and domestic threats, as well as differing views about such issues as the purposes for which intelligence may be collected and used, the proper leadership and oversight for agencies involved in collecting it, and protections for U.S. citizens' privacy, has influenced numerous reorganizations of the IC in the course of the nation's history (Federation of American Scientists, 1996; Rosenwasser and Warner, 2017). As new agencies involved in collecting and analyzing intelligence have emerged, coordinating their work has become an increasing challenge. The Intelligence Reform and Terrorism Prevention Act of 2004 (IRTPA)[5] established ODNI to lead the IC, and charged it with synchronizing the collection, analysis, and counterintelligence carried out across the IC agencies (Office of the Director of National Intelligence, 2013).[6]

While the structure of the IC has evolved in response to the nation's changing needs, its overall responsibility has not changed: it is collectively responsible for identifying issues that need to be investigated, collecting and analyzing relevant information of many kinds, and conveying the information and analysis in a timely manner to those who need them while also keeping the information secure and complying with laws regarding its collection and handling.

Of the 17 IC agencies, all but 9 reside within the U.S. Department of Defense (DoD). While ODNI has a coordination function, it is also an agency itself, as is the Central Intelligence Agency (CIA).[7] Five departments of the executive branch have their own intelligence agencies as well: the Federal Bureau of Investigation (FBI) and the Drug Enforcement Administration (DEA) under the Department of Justice and agencies under the Departments of Energy, Homeland Security, State, and Treasury (refer to Box 2-1).

The IC agencies are guided by "a multitude of laws, executive orders, policies, and directives," and their missions overlap to some extent (Federation of American Scientists, 1996). The entire IC is guided by Executive Order 12333 (as amended),[8] but each of the IC agencies also contains many offices, directorates, and other units, each with its own areas of authority, methods, and responsibilities. For example, the CIA integrates intelligence

---

[4]*National Security Act of 1947*, Public Law No. 80-253, 61 Stat. 495 (1947).
[5]*Intelligence Reform and Terrorism Prevention Act of 2004*, Public Law No. 108-458, 118 Stat. 3638 (2004).
[6]For a detailed look at the history and culture of the agencies that make up the national security community, see George and Rishikof (2017).
[7]Available: https://www.dni.gov/index.php/what-we-do [January 2019].
[8]Exec. Order No. 12,333, 3 C.F.R. 200 (1981), reprinted in 50 U.S.C. § 401 app. at 44-51 (1982).

from all sources into a body of "national intelligence" that supports the development of foreign and domestic policy; it is also the principal collector of certain types of intelligence and has responsibility for covert action. The FBI's mission is to "protect the America people and uphold the Constitution of the United States," but it also has agents in other nations and collects intelligence of many sorts (Federal Bureau of Investigation, 2018). The Department of Homeland Security has an almost identical mission—to "safeguard the American people, our homeland, and our values"—although it focuses on threats to aviation and border security, the integrity of cyber networks, and violent extremism (U.S. Department of Homeland Security, 2018). The Defense Intelligence Agency (DIA) has a different focus: integration of intelligence collected by the various service branches into "defense intelligence" used to support the missions of U.S. military forces (Defense Intelligence Agency, 2018).

Types of Intelligence

There are many different types of intelligence that reflect the purposes for which they are collected. While no canonical definitions exist for these various types of intelligence, ODNI defines as the foundational intelligence mission of the IC the collection of the following:

- strategic intelligence—"to inform and enrich understanding of enduring national security issues";
- anticipatory intelligence—"to detect, identify, and warn of emerging issues and discontinuities"; and
- current operations—"to support ongoing actions and sensitive intelligence operations."[9]

Observers of intelligence work also commonly distinguish among strategic intelligence, used by "policymakers to make policy and military decisions at the national and international level" (Rosenbach and Peritz, 2009, p. 10); operational intelligence, used by "leaders to plan and accomplish strategic objectives within the operational area" (Rosenbach and Peritz, 2009, p. 10); and tactical intelligence, best known as the information provided to military leaders in the field to support them in planning and executing battles and engagements, helping them "accomplish immediate tactical objectives" (Rosenbach and Peritz, 2009, p. 10). As the ODNI definition indicates, strategic intelligence deals with long-range issues and needs related to the development of national strategy and policy. It is a primary source of insights into international situations, and supports the

---

[9] Available: https://www.dni.gov/index.php/what-we-do/what-is-intelligence [January 2019].

development of military plans and strategic operations (Clark, 2013; Miles, 2016). Operational intelligence concerns the capabilities and intentions of adversaries, and is used both in military contexts (e.g., to monitor events or support military campaigns) and in diplomatic contexts (e.g., to support negotiation of an arms reduction treaty). Law enforcement also may use operational intelligence to plan an operation, such as mass arrest of members of an organized crime syndicate (Clark, 2013; Miles, 2016). Tactical intelligence provides commanders with information regarding imminent threats to their forces and changes in the operational environment (Miles, 2016). Law enforcement uses tactical intelligence in a similar manner.

These categories of intelligence encompass a wide range of information needs and possible sources of information. It is important to note as well that intelligence includes more than information that is gathered through clandestine means or needs to be classified; it also includes many types of readily available information, and a key function of the analyst is to identify which information will be useful to the client. In developing strategic plans, for example, policy makers may need analyses of developments in a geographic area that are based on historical and political science research, as well as continuous monitoring of groups and trends, but that also reflect up-to-the-minute intelligence about fast-moving events. Decision makers may need support in anticipating immediate or longer-range threats or opportunities, in making sense of unexpected developments, or in responding to crises. The six basic types of raw information that make up most intelligence are described in Box 2-3. They are distinguished primarily by the methods used to collect the information, and multiple agencies may contribute to the collection of each type (Krizan, 1999; Office of the Director of National Intelligence, 2019; Rosenbach and Peritz, 2009).

The IC agency tasked with providing the intelligence and the client (i.e., user of the intelligence) must work together: the analyst must understand the client's intelligence need to identify and efficiently synthesize the information that will meet that need. As discussed in greater detail in Chapter 4, the analyst's responsibility is to provide information that is as complete and accurate as possible, but often in an extremely tight timeframe. Frequently, the client's need is both complex and urgent: the questions requiring answers may require both deep understanding of social, cultural, and historical trends and the integration of complex technologically generated information, all in the context of fast-moving developments in which lives may hang on a policy maker's decision.

THE SOCIAL AND BEHAVIORAL SCIENCES

The set of academic disciplines generally referred to as the social and behavioral sciences (SBS) is large and diverse. Researchers in these fields use

BOX 2-3
Types of Intelligence Information[a]

1. **SIGINT**—Signals intelligence is derived from signal intercepts comprising—however transmitted, and either individually or in combination—all communications intelligence (COMINT), electronic intelligence (ELINT), and foreign instrumentation signals intelligence (FISINT). The National Security Agency (NSA) is responsible for collecting, processing, and reporting SIGINT. The National SIGINT Committee within NSA advises the director, NSA, and the director of national intelligence (DNI) on SIGINT policy issues and manages the SIGINT requirements system.

2. **IMINT**—Imagery intelligence includes representations of objects reproduced electronically or by optical means on film, electronic display devices, or other media. Imagery can be derived from visual photography, radar sensors, and electro-optics. The National Geospatial-Intelligence Agency (NGA) is the manager for all IMINT activities, both classified and unclassified, within the government, including requirements, collection, processing, exploitation, dissemination, archiving, and retrieval.

3. **MASINT**—Measurement and signature intelligence is technically derived intelligence data other than SIGINT and IMINT. The data results in intelligence that locates, identifies, or describes distinctive characteristics of targets. Its collection employs a broad group of disciplines, including nuclear, optical, radio frequency, acoustics, seismic, and materials sciences. Examples might be the distinctive radar signatures of specific aircraft systems or the chemical composition of air and water samples. The Directorate for MASINT and Technical Collection (DT), a component of the Defense Intelligence Agency, is the focal point for all national and Department of Defense MASINT matters.

4. **HUMINT**—Human intelligence is derived from human sources. To the public, HUMINT remains synonymous with espionage and clandestine activities; however, most HUMINT collection is performed by overt collectors such as strategic debriefers and military attaches. HUMINT represents the oldest method for collecting information, and until the technical revolution of the mid- to late 20th century, it was the primary source of intelligence.

5. **OSINT**—Open-source intelligence is publicly available information appearing in print or electronic form, including radio; television; newspapers; journals; the Internet; commercial databases; and videos, graphics, and drawings. While OSINT collection responsibilities are broadly distributed throughout the IC, the major collectors are the DNI's Open Source Center (OSC) and the National Air and Space Intelligence Center (NASIC).

6. **GEOINT**—Geospatial intelligence is the product of the analysis and visual representation of security-related activities on the earth. It is produced through an integration of imagery, imagery intelligence, and geospatial information.

---

[a]For more information on the contributions on these types of intelligence and how they are collected, see, e.g., Krizan (1999), Office of the Director of National Intelligence (2019), and Rosenbach and Peritz (2009).
SOURCE: Adapted from Krizan (1999), Office of the Director of National Intelligence (2019), and Rosenbach and Peritz (2009).

a wide range of scientific methods, research strategies, and tools and rely on diverse theoretical approaches,[10] but what they share is "their analytic focus on the behavior, attitudes, beliefs, and practices of people and their organizations, communities, and institutions" (National Research Council, 2012, p. 10). SBS researchers inquire into people and what they do from many different stances and ask a wide variety of questions about individuals, groups, communities, societies, and nations. They may examine, for example, individual mental processes that guide behavior, ways in which cultural practices and attitudes are shared and evolve across generations, or how water shortages are influencing political developments in a particular region. Within each SBS discipline, moreover, there are multiple subspecialties that have developed their own research approaches and methodologies. This is a large research community: by one estimate it encompasses 35,490 social scientists in the United States alone, and that number does not include researchers employed outside of academic institutions (U.S. Bureau of Labor Statistics, 2018). Research collaboration and sharing of knowledge across international borders are commonplace in SBS disciplines as well; U.S. researchers expand their knowledge through international journals and academic conferences.

While it is not simple to develop a comprehensive list of SBS fields, they include areas as diverse as demography and social statistics, sociology, economics, linguistics, social anthropology, international relations, and psychology. Most—though not all—of these fields have applications important for national security. The challenges and risks discussed in this report reflect the importance of analyses that, for example, reveal implications of the aging of populations in certain countries, support forecasts of political crises, or indicate shifts in the narratives of extremist groups that provide indicators of objectives or targets.

Researchers across SBS fields use many different research approaches, including varieties of experimental and observational studies, evaluation, meta-analysis, and qualitative and mixed-methods research.[11] As discussed below, significant advances have recently been made possible by expanded computing power, increased capacity for work with large-scale datasets, and improved methods of analysis (National Research Council, 2012). A comprehensive grounding in the methods and approaches used across the

---

[10]This report addresses many aspects of SBS research. The term "research tools" is used to refer to specific means of collecting data, including both traditional means, such as questionnaires or survey instruments, and such technology-supported tools as software for use with large-scale datasets. The terms "research approach" and "theoretical approach" are used to refer to the researcher's theoretically based ideas about how to apply tools and methodology to answer a defined question.

[11]See National Research Council (2012) for an overview of research methods used in the SBS and their assets and limitations.

SBS is beyond the scope of this report, but before turning to key technological developments, we note three general trends that apply across SBS fields.

One important trend is an increase in work that cuts across disciplines, in some cases yielding new hybrid disciplines (transdisciplinary research) (Scott et al., 2015). Integrating research methods and types of data from different disciplines, including many of the physical and life sciences, has proven critical for satisfactorily investigating complex problems. For example, researchers interested in environmental sustainability have recognized that to develop a complete picture, it is necessary to combine understanding of such areas as human cognition, risk perception, economic behavior, and problem solving and decision making with understanding of climate change and its impacts on weather and infrastructure (see, e.g., Tainter et al., 2015). Interdisciplinary work is particularly important in the context of the technological advances discussed below.

Also of note—and an important intellectual backdrop for much of the research discussed in this report—is a significant evolution in thinking that has grown out of work involving not only such SBS fields as neuro- and cognitive psychology, social psychology, and sociology but also physical and life science disciplines, including neuroscience and genetics. Building on work by Bronfenbrenner and others (e.g., Bronfenbrenner, 1977, 1994) that elaborated on how the individual is influenced by family, community, and the broader social context, researchers have developed a much more sophisticated picture of these interactions.[12] Emerging work has demonstrated the dynamic interplay between human development and the environment—from the genetic and epigenetic levels to the broadest sociocultural level. Insights about the importance of culture and environment have profoundly influenced the study of many aspects of the human experience, including learning and development (see NASEM, 2018) and the factors that influence mental and behavioral disorders in young people (see NASEM, forthcoming). This rapidly developing area of study has clear implications for security-related topics, from the growth of extremist ideology in an individual to the influences that shape the beliefs and norms of a particular group or society. Application of these emerging ideas in the context of national security concerns is a promising frontier for further research.

A third trend that cuts across SBS fields is growing understanding that a significant majority of SBS research has relied on information collected within cultures that are Western, educated, industrial, rich, and democratic (WEIRD). Conclusions drawn from research conducted with samples that are limited in this way cannot readily be applied beyond the context in which the data were collected; this is known as the WEIRD problem (see, e.g., Henrich et al., 2010; Nielsen et al., 2017; see also the

---

[12]See NASEM (2018, Chapter 2) for a detailed discussion of these developments.

discussion of study populations in NASEM, 2018). Researchers across numerous fields have become increasingly circumspect about considering these characteristics in the design of studies and the analysis and reporting of results. This issue has particular relevance for the IC, not least because the IC is concerned with understanding the behavior and motivations of people and societies around the globe.

SHARED CHALLENGES AND DIVERSE DEMANDS

The accuracy and validity of research are of paramount importance for both the SBS researchers whose calling is to produce it and the intelligence analysts who rely on this and other research while also engaging in many forms of research in their own work. Moreover, understanding human behavior is, in a sense, the primary objective for each of these professional communities, and they draw on many of the same resources in their quests for that understanding. At the same time, however, very different pressures, constraints, and cultures have shaped these two professions. A brief look at an emerging phenomenon—big data—that has had a significant impact on both SBS research and intelligence analysis highlights the overlap between these two endeavors; we also look briefly at interdisciplinary collaborations and at key differences between the two communities.

More Data and More Ways to Analyze Them

The digitization of society has resulted in an exponential increase in the amount of data available to analyze, and has made access to new sorts of data easy and widespread—a phenomenon loosely referred to as "big data."[13] While there is no one best definition of the term "big data," it is generally used to refer to extremely large sets of digital data that cannot be digested without advanced analytic techniques. This development has had a profound influence on the kinds of work that can be done by both SBS researchers and the IC. It has led to increased interdisciplinary collaboration (see below), increased use of mixed methods, increased reliance on computational techniques and models, and increased reliance on online environments and publicly available data for research (Scott et al., 2015).

Digital data fall into two categories. Most broadly, virtually all existing forms of data are now routinely archived digitally. Historical information that would be of interest to the IC and was originally stored in analog form is being converted to digital form through scanning and optical character recognition. These data are stored in digital repositories accessible through

---

[13]For discussion of the analysis of large-scale data and mathematical analysis in an intelligence and defense context, see NASEM (2017a).

websites. A second, more rapidly growing category of digital data is information being generated continuously on digital platforms supported by Internet and web protocols. These data include the content—text, graphics, audio, and video—resulting from actions, interactions, and transactions that occur in digital space. In addition to this content, digital trace data provide "metadata" about, for instance, who interacts with whom, about what, and at what time.

All of these data offer unprecedented opportunities for both scholarly researchers and IC analysts. Beginning approximately a decade ago, both groups began to encounter exponentially increased volumes of data potentially relevant to their work, although much of the newer data is what statisticians term "noisy" (data whose significance is difficult or impossible to discern). This relatively new data glut has precipitated considerable progress in descriptive, predictive, and prescriptive analytic techniques as researchers have pursued ways to use newly available types of data:

- **Descriptive** analytic techniques are means of summarizing large tracts of data to discern patterns, often using exploratory data analyses. These techniques can be used, for instance, to detect a significant and abrupt growth in messaging within an adversarial social network.
- **Predictive** analytic techniques are means of discerning associations among variables, with the goal of predicting certain variables (e.g., civil unrest) based on their association with others (e.g., use of certain terms in social media chatter). Machine learning techniques are valuable for this sort of analysis: computers are "trained" with known data (e.g., available historical data about the variable of interest) to recognize the sorts of patterns in which the analyst is interested, and the resulting algorithms are used to make predictions about the variable of interest (NASEM, 2018).
- **Prescriptive** analytic techniques are particularly useful for identifying which variables can be manipulated to result in a desired change in the variable of interest. Here, recent advances in what are called optimization techniques can leverage insights from machine learning models to go beyond predicting what might happen to offering insights on what to manipulate to bring about a desired outcome. A helpful, although not entirely accurate, analogy can be found in climate science. In that field, descriptive analytics indicate the current weather conditions, while predictive analytics indicate the forecast. Prescriptive analytics might result in recommending the use of cloud seeding to trigger precipitation.

Interdisciplinary Collaborations

Advances in large-scale data collection and computational analytic techniques, as well as the continuing growth of computer power, have opened up promising new frontiers in SBS research (National Research Council, 2012). Large-scale datasets—including social media, events data, and geographic information system (GIS) data—are sources of information that analysts and policy makers can use to better monitor and understand global events in real time and at a finer granularity than was previously possible. Advances in machine learning, robust optimization, computer-assisted content analysis, social network analysis, agent-based modeling, and other emerging computational approaches are facilitating the generation of reliable and robust SBS insights using big data.

Machine learning tools such as Random Forest—an algorithm used for decision making and classification (see Breiman and Cutler, n.d.)—for example, have the potential to provide more accurate predictions of rare events, such as the outbreak of civil war, relative to traditional statistical methods (Muchlinski et al., 2016). Combining automated textual analysis and social network analysis, researchers have shown that it is possible to "analyze hacker chats and other data faster and more efficiently than had previously been possible," enabling them to identify hackers' intentions (NASEM, 2017b, p. 17). This work may improve forecasts of hacker threats (NASEM, 2017b). And recent research at the intersection of cognitive and computer science is generating new visualization tools that facilitate human exploration and understanding of the complex, multiscalar phenomena that are the subjects of computational social science (National Science Foundation, 2011).

Research at these new frontiers is often interdisciplinary, drawing on multiple methodological, theoretical, and empirical approaches. This is the case because the intellectual advances in these areas are most likely to occur at the nexus of advances in data science, computer science, and SBS research. Traditionally, SBS researchers have relied most heavily on theory-driven approaches that are either deductive (hypotheses derived from a priori theories) or inductive (theories inferred from data, sometimes referred to as "grounded theory"). In contrast, data science and computer scientists rely on data-driven approaches often focused primarily on prediction, even at the cost of theoretical explanation or understanding (Anderson, 2008). This artificial and unhelpful methodological divide can be transcended by interdisciplinary approaches that generate insights by iterating between theory-driven and data-driven approaches. The result has been renewed interest in what social scientists characterize as the abductive approach, to distinguish it from the deductive or inductive approach (Haig, 2005).

Indeed, recent assessments of the state and future of SBS research have focused on the advantages of interdisciplinary work in this area. The National Institutes of Health's Office of Behavioral and Social Research has highlighted the promise that interdisciplinary research exploiting new technologies and advances in data analytics holds for SBS knowledge (National Institutes of Health, 2017). And as emphasized by the National Science Foundation's *Rebuilding the Mosaic* report, which is based on a synthesis of more than 200 white papers from the SBS research community, the future of SBS research is "interdisciplinary, data-intensive, and collaborative" (National Science Foundation, 2011).

Another development is a recent move to thinking in terms of "broad" data, which offers researchers the unprecedented ability to fuse diverse sources of data, yielding information that is much more valuable than an undifferentiated stream of unstructured data. An example is the juxtaposition of neuroimaging and behavioral data on humans. This juxtaposition has demonstrated the potential for new theoretical advances in predicting, for instance, the efficacy of strategies designed to influence individuals' attitudes and behaviors based on activation of specific areas in the brain (Estrada et al., 2017). Another promising avenue has been the use of physical activity data on team members collected from wearable devices to offer new insights into team performance through real-time assessment of cognitive functioning (Kim et al., 2012; Pentland, 2012).

Cognitive neuroscience and related technologies are expected to continue to converge with and in some respects transform SBS research, drawing on advances in psychopharmacology, functional neuroimaging, and computational biology, among other fields. Models of psychological states and intentions are being drawn from increasingly sophisticated neurophysiological assessment technology. Noninvasive functional brain imaging technologies have been progressing rapidly (National Research Council, 2008), and may be applied to measurements of neural degeneration related to cognitive function and assessments of readiness for complex tasks.

These examples illustrate the significant potential of big data and related developments for both SBS researchers and intelligence analysts, but also highlight challenges. The scale of the available information continues to grow exponentially, and the pace of cyber-based developments also demands much faster responses. The Internet has often been described as the "wild west" because it is largely unregulated, although recent efforts to undermine democratic processes and other security threats are leading to an examination of possibilities for policing aspects of this realm. In any case, the openness and rapid pace of change characteristic of the Internet pose challenges for the IC and for researchers who hope to study the data it yields.

Diverse Cultures, Audiences, and Demands

Although challenges and opportunities presented by big data highlight possibilities that can benefit both the SBS research community and the IC, they also point to significant differences that have implications for the work the two communities do together. Many of these differences stem from the fundamentally different purposes of the researcher and the analyst. The researcher's basic purpose is to add to the sum of human knowledge using the methods of scholarship, including forming a hypothesis based on data collected, testing that hypothesis, analyzing the results, and drawing inferences based on the evidence obtained. Researchers are trained to use the methods honed within their specialty, and to apply and contribute to theoretical models designed to explain observable phenomena. They are encouraged to pursue questions because those questions are interesting and unanswered, even if the practical application of the answers is not immediately apparent. Although resource limitations—and the imperative to produce regular publications—are natural constraints, researchers generally feel relatively little pressure to produce results within a given timeframe.

Analysts, by contrast, are focused on objectives related to national security and foreign policy. As discussed in Chapter 4, they may have a range of specific assignments, which may require them to seek deep understanding of a region, historical trends, and other more general knowledge quite similar to that sought by academic researchers. But their attention does not waver from the potential application of that knowledge to security concerns: answering policy makers' questions about the world and alerting them to possible risks and opportunities. Typically, this means providing analysis that is a best guess based on the information available at the time. Researchers have the luxury of time to complete a systematic process of collecting and analyzing information and testing their conclusions, whereas analysts must often provide rapid-fire, definitive answers in urgent circumstances.

The academic researcher also generally has greater latitude than the analyst to plan a systematic approach to the collection of evidence. Few research projects afford the opportunity to collect all the data that could be of value, but means of addressing limitations can be part of the research design. Analysts, by contrast, must generally rely on data that are acquired opportunistically and are therefore not representative, unbiased samples. Bias and questions about representativeness also affect SBS research—and researchers, too, may take advantage of available data—but the data available to analysts may also be compromised by the efforts of adversaries to disguise the data or otherwise deceive, which adds a layer of questions about validity that do not affect most academic research.

Curiosity and educated guesswork likely play an important role in both academic research and intelligence analysis,[14] but a researcher is ultimately judged by his or her peers on the basis of the documented methods used in the research and the extent to which the work is substantiated by that of others. The analyst, on the other hand, is judged in practice primarily by the extent to which he or she has provided valuable information and answers to the decision makers who rely on that information.[15] The researcher's conclusions may be described in an article or book dozens or hundreds of pages long, and filled with contextual information and detailed discussion of how conclusions are supported. The analyst's results, by contrast, may be presented in a very brief text or PowerPoint presentation, or some other format, as needed by a client who must digest the results quickly and has very limited time for subtleties related to multiple alternatives or other complexities.

It is perhaps natural, then, that tensions have sometimes arisen when these two communities have collaborated, as discussed in Chapter 9. But it is also clear that the two share important interests and methods.

REFERENCES

Anderson, C. (2008). The end of theory: The data deluge makes the scientific method obsolete. *WIRED*, June 23. Available: https://www.wired.com/2008/06/pb-theory [November 2018].

Breiman, L., and Cutler, A. (n.d.). *Random Forests*. Available: https://www.stat.berkeley.edu/~breiman/RandomForests/cc_home.htm#workings theory [November 2018].

Bronfenbrenner, U. (1977). Toward an experimental ecology of human development. *American Psychologist, 32*(7), 513–531.

Bronfenbrenner, U. (1994). Ecological models of human development. In *International Encyclopedia of Education* (2nd ed., Vol. 3). Oxford, UK: Elsevier.

Clark, R. (2013). *Intelligence Collection*. Washington, DC: CQ Press.

Defense Intelligence Agency. (2018). *Office of Intelligence and Analysis Mission*. Available: https://www.dhs.gov/office-intelligence-and-analysis-mission [November 2018].

Estrada, M., Schultz, P.W., Silva-Send, N., and Boudrias, M.A. (2017). The role of social influences on pro-environment behaviors in the San Diego region. *Journal of Urban Health, 94*(2), 170–179.

Federal Bureau of Investigation. (2018). *Mission & Priorities*. Available: https://www.fbi.gov/about/mission [November 2018].

Federation of American Scientists. (1996). *An Overview of the Intelligence Community*. Available: https://fas.org/irp/offdocs/int023.html [November 2018].

George, R., and Rishikof, H. (2017). *The National Security Enterprise: Navigating the Labyrinth*. Washington, DC: Georgetown University Press.

---

[14] For discussion of the development of expertise and how it shapes an individual's capacity to integrate new information and recognize significant patterns and anomalies, see NASEM (2018); National Research Council (2000).

[15] There are analytic standards for the IC; see https://www.dni.gov/files/documents/ICD/ICD%20203%20Analytic%20Standards.pdf [January 2019].

Haig, B.D. (2005). An abductive theory of scientific method. *Psychological Methods, 10*(4), 371–388.

Henrich, J., Heine, S.J., and Norenzayan, A. (2010). The weirdest people in the world? *Behavioral and Brain Sciences, 33*(2-3), 61–135. doi:10.1017/S0140525X0999152X.

Kim, T., McFee, E., Olguin, D.O., Waber, B., and Pentland, A. (2012). Sociometric badges: Using sensor technology to capture new forms of collaboration. *Journal of Organizational Behavior, 33*(3), 412–427.

Krizan, L. (1999). *Intelligence Essentials for Everyone*. Washington, DC: Joint Military Intelligence College. Available: http://www.dtic.mil/dtic/tr/fulltext/u2/a476726.pdf [November 2018].

Miles, A.D. (2016). *Intelligence Community Programs, Management, and Enduring Issues*. Washington, DC: Congressional Research Service. Available: https://fas.org/sgp/crs/intel/R44681.pdf [November 2018].

Monaghan P. (2009). Intelligence studies. *The Chronical of Higher Education*, March 20. Available: https://www.chronicle.com/article/Intelligence-Studies/33353 [February 2019].

Muchlinski, D., Siroky, D., He, J., and Kocher, M. (2016). Comparing random forest with logistic regression for predicting class-imbalanced civil war onset data. *Political Analysis, 24*(1), 87–103.

National Academies of Sciences, Engineering, and Medicine (NASEM). (2017a). *Strengthening Data Science Methods for Department of Defense Personnel and Readiness Missions*. Washington, DC: The National Academies Press. doi:10.17226/23670.

NASEM. (2017b). *The Value of Social, Behavioral, and Economic Sciences to National Priorities: A Report for the National Science Foundation*. Washington, DC: The National Academies Press. doi:10.17226/24790.

NASEM. (2018). *How People Learn II: Learners, Contexts, and Cultures*. Washington, DC: The National Academies Press. doi:10.17226/24783.

NASEM. (forthcoming). Report of the Committee on Fostering Healthy Mental, Emotional, and Behavioral Development Among Children and Youth; see http://sites.nationalacademies.org/dbasse/bcyf/meb-health-promotion/index.htm.

National Academy of Sciences. (2018). *The Frontiers of Machine Learning: 2017 Raymond and Beverly Sackler U.S.–U.K. Scientific Forum*. Washington, DC: The National Academies Press. doi:10.17226/25021.

National Institutes of Health. (2017). *The Office of Behavioral and Social Sciences Research Strategic Plan 2017–2021*. Available: https://obssr.od.nih.gov/wp-content/uploads/2016/12/OBSSRSP-2017-2021.pdf [May 2017].

National Research Council. (2000). *How People Learn: Brain, Mind, Experience, and School: Expanded Edition*. Washington, DC: National Academy Press.

National Research Council. (2008). *Emerging Cognitive Neuroscience and Related Technologies*. Washington, DC: National Academy Press.

National Research Council. (2012). *Using Science as Evidence in Public Policy*. Committee on the Use of Social Science Knowledge in Public Policy. K. Prewitt, T.A. Schwandt, and M.L. Straf (Eds.). Division of Behavioral and Social Sciences and Education. Washington, DC: The National Academies Press.

National Science Foundation. (2011). *Rebuilding the Mosaic: Fostering Research in the Social, Behavioral, and Economic Sciences at the National Science Foundation in the Next Decade*. Arlington, VA: National Science Foundation. Available: https://www.nsf.gov/pubs/2011/nsf11086/nsf11086.pdf [November 2018].

Nielsen, M., Haun, D., Kärtner, J., and Legare, C.H. (2017). The persistent sampling bias in developmental psychology: A call to action. *Journal of Experimental Child Psychology, 162*, 31–38. doi:10.1016/j.jecp.2017.04.017.

Office of the Director of National Intelligence. (2013). *U.S. National Intelligence: An Overview*. Available: https://www.dni.gov/files/documents/USNI%202013%20Overview_web.pdf [November 2018].

Office of the Director of National Intelligence. (2019). *What Is Intelligence?* Available: https://www.dni.gov/index.php/what-we-do/what-is-intelligence [May 2019].

Pentland, A. (2012). The new science of building great teams. *Harvard Business Review*, April. Available: https://hbr.org/2012/04/the-new-science-of-building-great-teams [November 2018].

Rosenbach, E., and Peritz, A. (2009). *Confrontation or Collaboration? Congress and the Intelligence Community*. Cambridge, MA: Harvard University, Belfer Center for Science and International Affairs. Available: https://www.belfercenter.org/sites/default/files/legacy/files/energy-security.pdf [November 2018].

Rosenwasser, J., and Warner, M. (2017). History of the interagency process for foreign relations in the United States: Murphy's Law? In R. George and H. Rishikof (Eds.), *The National Security Enterprise: Navigating the Labyrinth* (2nd ed.) (pp. 13–31). Washington, DC: Georgetown University Press.

Scott, R.A., Buchmann, M.C., and Kosslyn, S.M. (2015). *Emerging Trends in the Social and Behavioral Sciences*. Hoboken, NJ: John Wiley & Sons. doi:10.1002/9781118900772.

Tainter, J.A., Taylor, T.G., Brain, R.G., and Lobo, J. (2015). *Sustainability*. Available: https://onlinelibrary.wiley.com/doi/pdf/10.1002/9781118900772.etrds0326 [November 2018].

U.S. Bureau of Labor Statistics. (2018). *Occupational Employment and Wages, May 2017: 193099 Social Scientists and Related Workers, All Other*. Available: https://www.bls.gov/oes/current/oes193099.htm [November 2018].

U.S. Department of Homeland Security. (2018). *Office of Intelligence and Analysis Mission*. Available: https://www.dhs.gov/office-intelligence-and-analysis-mission [November 2018].

3

Global Context for the Decadal Study

To identify ways in which social and behavioral sciences (SBS) research can be useful to the Intelligence Community (IC), the committee needed to have a clear, current picture of the potential sources of risk to the security of the United States. Security risks grow out of complex, interacting trends and developments around the world, including political, economic, and social developments; threats to infrastructure and stability posed by rogue, nonstate actors (see Box 3-1) or the effects of global climate change; and technological developments, such as social media, big data, and artificial intelligence (AI), that are changing the ways people work and communicate. Given the extreme complexity of the subject, we sought a range of perspectives on the highest-priority challenges and risks. We looked at several documents produced by entities of the U.S. government that include assessments of global risks and challenges. To counter the U.S. perspective reflected in these documents, we also reviewed summaries of global trends and risks produced by two international organizations—the Organisation for Economic Co-operation and Development (OECD) and the World Economic Forum. This chapter summarizes the persistent themes and emerging threats identified in these expert assessments and offers our thoughts about the role of SBS research in understanding them.

U.S. GOVERNMENT DOCUMENTS

U.S. government entities have reasons, because of their responsibilities, to develop regular assessments of risks and challenges around the world.

> **BOX 3-1**
> **Nonstate Actors**
>
> The term "nonstate actor" excludes entities and organizations established by states, such as government-organized nongovernmental organizations, intergovernmental organizations, or organizations and individuals representing political parties. Nonstate actors can be differentiated along two dimensions: (1) whether they are typically violent or nonviolent, and (2) whether they are for-profit or not-for-profit. A drug cartel is an example of a violent, for-profit nonstate actor, whereas a nongovernmental organization is an example of a nonviolent, not-for-profit nonstate actor. However, the distinctions can blur when organizations change tactics to effect change, such as when an actor that is nonviolent and not-for-profit in one situation adopts violent means and seeks profit in another (Murdie and Urpelainen, 2015; Murdie and Webeck, 2015; Peterson et al., 2018).

This section reviews several of these assessments to provide perspective on the breadth of concerns identified and themes that run across them.

Assessment of the National Intelligence Council

The National Intelligence Council (NIC) is an interagency intelligence analysis unit working for the director of national intelligence. Its primary function is to provide to the president and senior officials strategic thinking, based on interagency assessments, which is virtually always classified. An important product of the NIC is the *Global Trends* report prepared for incoming presidents, which is a widely known and respected source on primary trends in security. To develop this report, the NIC brings together experts from government, academia, and the private sector to produce unclassified strategic analyses of the forces and choices likely to shape the world over the next two decades (National Intelligence Council, 2017, p. vi). The most recent report, published in 2017, identifies seven global trends and presents an assessment of both how these trends are affecting power dynamics and how those changes, in turn, may contribute to specific rising tensions.[1] The report summarizes the seven global trends and their implications as follows (p. 6):

> **The rich are aging, the poor are not.** Working-age populations are shrinking in wealthy countries, China, and Russia but growing in developing,

---

[1] For a detailed discussion of the methodology used to develop the assessment, see pp. 7–71 of the report.

poorer countries, particularly in Africa and South Asia, increasing economic, employment, urbanization, and welfare pressures and spurring migration. Training and continuing education will be crucial in developed and developing countries alike.

The global economy is shifting. Weak economic growth will persist in the near term. Major economies will confront shrinking workforces and diminishing productivity gains while recovering from the 2008–2009 financial crisis with high debt, weak demand, and doubts about globalization. China will attempt to shift to a consumer-driven economy from its longstanding export and investment focus. Lower growth will threaten poverty reduction in developing countries. [Figure 3-1 from the report illustrates the predicted trends.]

Technology is accelerating progress but causing discontinuities. Rapid technological advancements will increase the pace of change and create new opportunities but will aggravate divisions between winners and losers. Automation and artificial intelligence threaten to change industries faster than economies can adjust, potentially displacing workers and limiting the usual route for poor countries to develop. Biotechnologies such as genome editing will revolutionize medicine and other fields, while sharpening moral differences.

Ideas and identities are driving a wave of exclusion. Growing global connectivity amid weak growth will increase tensions within and between

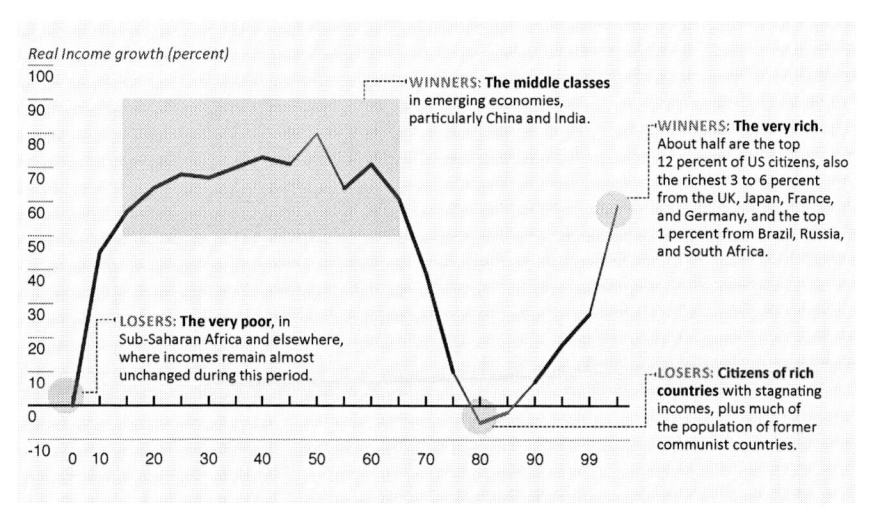

FIGURE 3-1 Changes in real income by world income percentiles.
SOURCE: National Intelligence Council (2017, p. 13).

societies. Populism will increase on the right and the left, threatening liberalism. Some leaders will use nationalism to shore up control. Religious influence will be increasingly consequential and more authoritative than many governments. Nearly all countries will see economic forces boost women's status and leadership roles, but backlash also will occur.

Governing is getting harder. Publics will demand governments deliver security and prosperity, but flat revenues, distrust, polarization, and a growing list of emerging issues will hamper government performance. Technology will expand the range of players who can block or circumvent political action. Managing global issues will become harder as actors multiply—to include nongovernmental agencies, corporations, and empowered individuals—resulting in more ad hoc, fewer encompassing efforts.

The nature of conflict is changing. The risk of conflict will increase due to diverging interests among major powers, an expanding terror threat, continued instability in weak states, and the spread of lethal, disruptive technologies. Disrupting societies will become more common, with long-range precision weapons, cyber, and robotic systems to target infrastructure from afar, and more accessible technology to create weapons of mass destruction.

Climate change, environment, and health issues will demand attention. A range of global hazards pose imminent and longer-term threats that will require collective action to address—even as cooperation becomes harder. More extreme weather, water and soil stress, and food insecurity will disrupt societies. Sea-level rise, ocean acidification, glacial melt, and pollution will change living patterns. Tensions over climate change will grow. Increased travel and poor health infrastructure will make infectious diseases harder to manage.

The report makes clear that these trends are interrelated and that their convergence may amplify tensions that are rising in both the near and longer terms (5 years into the future and beyond). It notes, for example, a number of reasons why terrorism is likely to be a growing threat, including technological advances that increase the capacity of states and other actors to recruit and inflict harm; a context of deterioration in state governance structures, particularly in the Middle East; economic dislocation for many groups; and the spread of extremist ideology. The report also describes the geopolitical outlook for world regions and highlights profound changes occurring in the international order established following World War II. The report closes with a discussion of ways leaders and nations might be able to increase their resilience and respond to recognized risks—for example, by taking advantage of advancing technologies and other developments to improve cooperation and flexibility in response to shifts such as those in power dynamics.

President's National Security Policy

Presidential administrations, by statute, regularly produce summaries of their strategies for national security that identify broad goals and specific approaches for achieving those goals (The White House, 2017).[2] The frequency of release of these documents varies among administrations, from once during an administration to annually.[3] The intended audience is the American people, U.S. allies and partners, and federal agencies. The Office of President Donald Trump published its most recent national security policy document in December 2017 (President of the United States, 2017). It identifies four broad pillars of the current national security strategy: protecting the homeland, promoting U.S. prosperity, preserving international peace, and advancing U.S. influence around the world. The document focuses on specifying those actions that will have the highest priority for pursuing goals encompassed by each of these four pillars; discussion under the first and fourth pillars identifies specific risks to be mitigated.

Under the first pillar—protecting the homeland—the document points to five primary areas of risk (President of the United States, 2017).

1. **Weapons of mass destruction.** The report notes that the "danger from hostile state and non-state actors who are trying to acquire nuclear, chemical, radiological, and biological weapons is increasing" (p. 8).
2. **Biothreats and pandemics.** The report cites both outbreaks of viruses and deliberate biological attacks.
3. **Insufficient border control and immigration policy.** The report cites risks from "terrorists, drug traffickers, and criminal cartels [that] exploit porous borders and threaten U.S. security and public safety" (p. 9).
4. **Jihadist terrorists and criminal organizations.** The report notes that "the primary transnational threats Americans face are from jihadist terrorists and transnational criminal organizations," which "rely on encrypted communication and the dark web," "thrive under conditions of state weakness," and in many cases are "sheltered and supported by states" (p. 10).
5. **Cyberattacks.** The report notes that "cyberspace offers state and non-state actors the ability to wage campaigns against American political, economic, and security interests without ever physically crossing our borders" (p. 12).

---

[2] An archive of presidential security strategies is available at http://nssarchive.us [March 2018].
[3] See http://nssarchive.us [July 2018].

The document also addresses more specific challenges facing the United States in each of six regions: Africa, Europe, the Indo-Pacific, the Middle East, South and Central Asia, and the Western Hemisphere. It identifies as consistent priorities across all regions strengthening partnerships, taking actions to encourage economic growth in the regions, and maintaining global security.

U.S. Department of Defense Military Strategy

A similar document is produced regularly by the U.S. Department of Defense to articulate the U.S. military's "strategy to compete, deter, and win" in current circumstances (U.S. Department of Defense, 2018, p. 1). This unclassified synopsis of the classified National Defense Strategy describes the strategic environment in which the U.S. military must develop its plans for protecting national security (U.S. Department of Defense, 2018). This report, referred to historically as the National Military Strategy, has been issued periodically since 1991, and was last produced in 2018.

The description in this document of the strategic environment in which the military is operating highlights areas of risk regarded by military leaders as paramount. The unclassified version of the 2018 strategy identifies the "central challenge to U.S. prosperity and security [as] the reemergence of *long-term, strategic competition* by what the National Security Strategy classifies as revisionist powers" (U.S. Department of Defense, 2018, p. 2 [italics in original]). It argues that China and Russia "want to shape a world consistent with their authoritarian model—gaining veto authority over other nations' economic, diplomatic, and security decisions" (p. 2). The document also identifies other significant risks in the strategic environment (pp. 2–3):

- a "resilient, but weakening, post-WWII international order," the guiding principles of which are being undermined by China and Russia;
- "rogue regimes such as North Korea and Iran," which are seeking new types of weaponry, sponsoring terrorism, and seeking "coercive influence";
- challenges to the U.S. military's advantage;
- "rapid technological advancements and the changing character of war";
- "terrorists, trans-national criminal organizations, cyberhackers, and other malicious non-state actors," which have increasingly sophisticated "capabilities of mass disruption";

- direct targeting of the U.S. homeland via cyber activity and political and information subversion, as well as the possibility of direct attacks on critical defenses or infrastructure; and
- weapons of mass destruction in the possession of rogue regimes.

National Intelligence Strategy

In addition, the director of national intelligence provides a regular update on the National Intelligence Strategy, also assembled by the NIC. The most recent version was presented by Director of National Intelligence Daniel Coats in January 2019 (Office of the Director of National Intelligence, 2019). It identifies priorities for the IC and describes the strategic environment in which the IC will be pursuing its objectives. The document notes that "while the IC remains focused on confronting a number of conventional challenges . . . posed by our adversaries, advances in technology are driving evolutionary and revolutionary changes across multiple fronts" (p. 4). It highlights several key threats (pp. 4–5):

- Traditional adversaries will continue attempts to gain and assert influence, taking advantage of changing conditions in the international environment—including the weakening of the post-WWII international order and dominance of Western democratic ideals, increasingly isolationist tendencies in the West, and shifts in the global economy.
- Adversaries are increasing their presence in [space] with plans to reach or exceed parity in some areas. . . . Many aspects of modern society—to include our ability to conduct military operations—rely on our access to and equipment in space.
- As the cyber capabilities of our adversaries grow, they will pose increasing threats to U.S. security, including critical infrastructure, public health and safety, economic prosperity, and stability.
- Emerging technologies, such as artificial intelligence, automation, and high performance computing . . . enable new and improved military and intelligence capabilities for our adversaries . . . the development and spread of such technologies remain uneven, increasing the potential to drastically widen the divide between the so-called "haves" and "have-nots."
- Exponentially growing amounts of information . . . [are challenging] the IC's ability to collect, process, evaluate, and analyze such enormous volumes of data quickly enough to provide relevant and useful insight to its clients.
- The ability of individuals and groups to have a larger impact than ever before—politically, militarily, economically, and ideologically—

is undermining traditional institutions. This empowerment of groups and individuals is increasing the influence of ethnic, religious, and other sources of identity, changing the nature of conflict, and challenging the ability of traditional governments to satisfy the increasing demands of their populations. . . . Some violent extremist groups will continue to take advantage of these sources and drivers of instability.

- Increasing migration and urbanization of populations are . . . further straining the capacities of governments around the world and are likely to result in further fracturing of societies, potentially creating breeding grounds for radicalization. Pressure points include growing influxes of migrants, refugees, and internally displaced persons fleeing conflict zones; areas of intense economic or resources scarcity; and areas threatened by climate changes, infectious disease outbreaks, or transnational criminal organizations.

STATEMENTS OF INTERNATIONAL ORGANIZATIONS

Organisation for Economic Co-operation and Development

The United States is not the only country concerned with social, economic, and technological trends. The OECD and the World Economic Forum both provide assessments of global trends and risks that are intended to reflect the concerns of many countries.

OECD, an independent, nonprofit organization, regularly assesses issues likely to directly affect its 34 member countries, as well as the rest of the world. Its assessments are intended to be useful for government policy makers, industry, and analysts. In 2003, OECD's International Futures Programme issued a summary of major risks for the 21st century. The report notes that a spate of large-scale disasters—including severely damaging weather patterns, emerging diseases, terrorism, and cyber-based disruption of critical infrastructure—indicate not only that "the nature of major risks . . . seems to be changing . . . but also [that] the context within which they appear and society's capacity to manage them" seem to be changing as well (Organisation for Economic Co-operation and Development, 2003, p. 4). The report identifies four primary forces that are driving these developments:

1. demographic changes, including population growth and migration;
2. environmental change, including global climate change, loss of biodiversity, and water shortages;
3. technological changes, which may "reduce some risks while aggravating others or even creating new ones" (p. 12); and

4. socioeconomic changes, including those in governments' role in managing economies, globalization, poverty, and income gaps.

The report includes recommendations with respect to forecasting and managing risks associated with these forces.

Every other year, OECD issues a similar report describing the implications of these trends for national- and international-scale policies related to science, technology, and innovation. The most recent of these reports (Organisation for Economic Co-operation and Development, 2016) reinforces the messages of the 2003 summary of major risks, noting that the above four "megatrends raise urgent issues," but that "the capacities of governments to intervene will likely face major constraints, including high public debt, increasing international security threats, a possible erosion of social cohesion, and the rise of influential non-state actors that challenge their authority and ability to act" (p. 17).

World Economic Forum

The World Economic Forum, an independent, nonprofit organization, also produces regular assessments of global challenges, which are based on surveys of experts from around the world in sectors that include economics, technology, geopolitics, and the environment (OECD contributes to the development of the report). The assessments are also intended to be useful to leaders in politics, business, and other sectors focused on global, regional, and industrial agendas, and it serves as a basis for debates at the Forum's annual meeting. The 2019 report (World Economic Forum, 2019) identifies broad themes that align with many of the concerns addressed in the U.S. government assessments discussed above. Like the report prepared by the NIC for the director of national intelligence, it synthesizes five areas of concern (paraphrased from pp. 10–17):

1. **Economic vulnerabilities,** including market volatility, slowing economic growth, the global debt burden, rising income and wealth disparities, and other strains on the global economy increase the risk of economic confrontations between major powers and erosion of multilateral rules and agreements.
2. **Geopolitical tensions** and deepening fissures in the international system, as well as polarization and weak governance, bring risk as inter-country relations are reconfigured and progress on other global challenges, particularly protecting the environment, is hampered. This environment is inauspicious for the resolution of emerging crises.

3. **Societal and political strains** within countries, including increased polarization, political fragmentation, and identity politics, undermine stable and effective governance. Diminishing social cohesion places strain on political institutions and undermines their capacity to anticipate challenges and work multilaterally with international partners.
4. **Environmental fragilities,** including rising sea levels, extreme weather, and threats to biodiversity and the food chain, pose grave risks to health, well-being, and socioeconomic development and environmental policy failure. The failure of environmental policies threatened international capacity to mitigate and adapt to the effects of climate change.
5. **Technological instabilities,** including data fraud, cyber attacks, fake news, identity theft, threats to privacy, and data breaches all contribute to the overall vulnerability of critical infrastructure and have the potential to significantly disrupt business and government.

The report emphasizes the interconnected nature of these challenges, highlighting the potential for "threshold effects," where change in one area triggers "dramatic deteriorations and cause cascading risks to crystallize" (p. 7). Figure 3-2 illustrates the complex connections among risks and trends identified in the report.

PERSISTENT THEMES AND EMERGING THREATS

These assessments are developed for different purposes and audiences and cover different time spans, and each provides a somewhat different framing of the issues that influence national security. Nevertheless, they highlight some consistent themes.

One shared concern is that the distribution of power among and across state and nonstate actors has been changing and is likely to continue to do so. Individuals and small groups continue to be empowered, opening up new opportunities but also posing new challenges, from the threat of terrorism to the increased intricacy of building international coalitions. These assessments also reflect a shared concern that international structures that have served as a force for stability and democracy are being challenged. Global environmental changes and demographic shifts are interacting to amplify the pace and effects of other changes. Such trends as economic dislocation and migration are producing an increasing disconnect between governments and the governed. Rising expectations go unmet, resulting in yet another cycle of disaffection.

GLOBAL CONTEXT FOR THE DECADAL STUDY 59

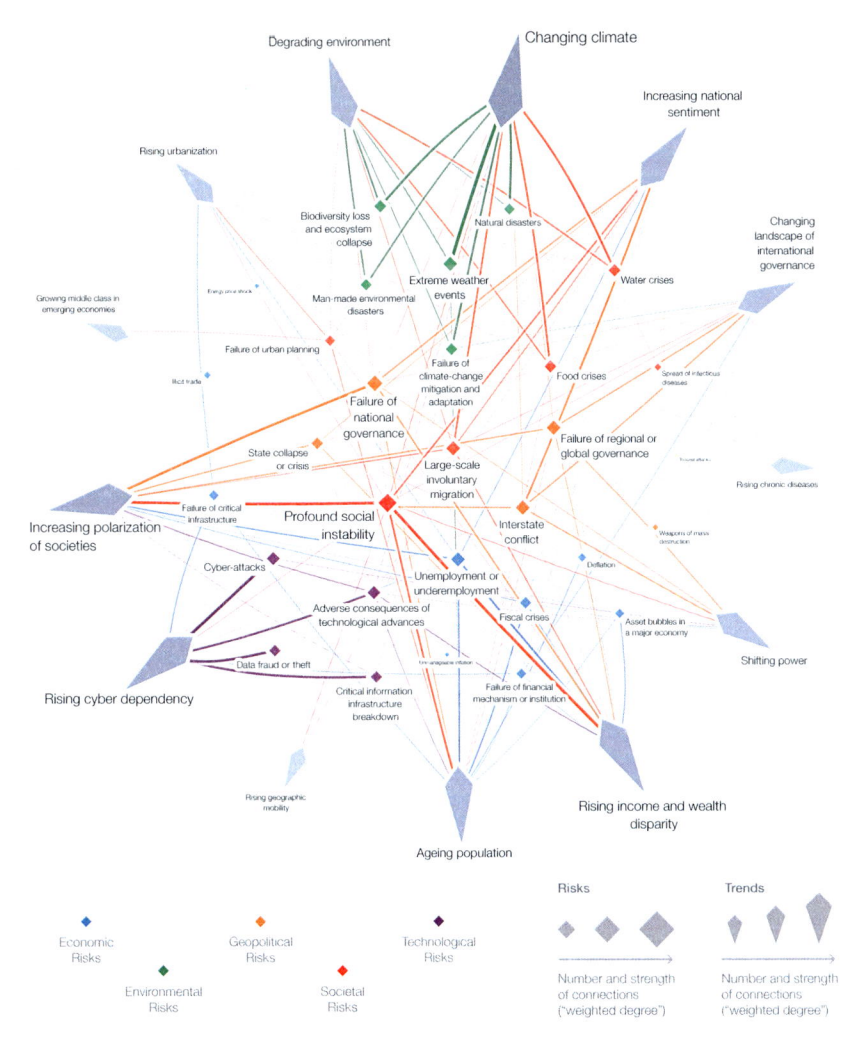

FIGURE 3-2 Connections among risks and trends.
SOURCE: World Economic Forum (2019, p. 6).

Developments in technology—particularly information technology—are also influencing the risks and challenges highlighted in the assessments discussed here. Access to massive amounts of data and computational technology, such as automation and AI, has provided both state and nonstate actors capabilities that once existed only in the realm of science fiction. Cyber-mediated communication is bringing threats to democracy and political stability. New technologies are affecting jobs, infrastructure, health, and scientific discovery in both positive and counterproductive ways. They are also affecting the nature of conflict, intelligence gathering, communication, and the spread of influence.

The new toolkit for information operations drives these trends home. To be sure, those operations are as old as conflict itself: the point of all warfare has always been to influence two inches of gray matter in the heads of leaders and their peoples. Yet the new tools available and emerging today, especially cyber but also social media–aided propaganda, have changed the calculus of risk. These tools are relatively cheap, and their nature makes it easy for the attackers who use them to hide their roles. The targets of such attacks are societies, not combatants on the battlefield; these tools can be and are used simultaneously to pursue aggressive objectives without using physical warfare.

Russia's intervention in the 2016 U.S. elections demonstrates the risk. According to a partially declassified U.S. Intelligence Community Assessment (ICA) issued in early 2017,[4] the Kremlin, in addition to its long-standing desire to undermine the U.S.-led world order, had three specific goals when it launched its influence campaign: "to undermine public faith in the U.S. democratic process, denigrate Secretary Clinton, and harm her electability and potential presidency." The Kremlin also displayed a clear preference for candidate Trump and so helped to increase his election chances.

Russia's influence campaign encompassed leaks of information Russia had stolen through cyber espionage, overt Russian propaganda, and hacks into election infrastructure—all of which were distinct but carried out simultaneously and complementarily starting at least as early as summer 2015. The first two of these lines of attack amounted to *weaponizing* information. First, emails obtained from hacks into the accounts of both the Democratic National Committee and candidate Clinton's campaign manager were released through surrogates at strategic times, such as after the Democratic convention. The second line of attack used trolls and bots on social media to cause lies—such as that Clinton was in poor health—to trend on social media so they would be picked up by the mainstream media. These operations were carried out by Russian intelligence and enjoyed the full support of the Russian government, although Russian President

---

[4]Available: https://www.dni.gov/files/documents/ICA_2017_01.pdf [December 2018].

Vladimir Putin insisted that they did not.[5] The third line of attack consisted of hacks into election infrastructure in 21 states. While U.S. intelligence found no evidence that votes were affected by those hacks, they served at the least as practice for the next time around, whether in the United States or other countries. This set of circumstances aligns closely with definitions of information warfare, as distinct from cyberwar (see Box 3-2).

Americans often think of their country as a constant pole in a world in flux. Yet the IC—not to mention the world—must take into account that the United States is a source of uncertainty. The U.S. invasion of Iraq in 2003 destroyed a tenuous, if brutal, order in the Middle East. The toppling of Libya's Muammar Gaddafi in 2011 with no "plan B" for what might come next only added to that region's chaos. Changes in world structures are being driven not just by the actions of China and Russia but also by a United States whose current approaches to international interactions, including trade, reflect a view that they are a zero-sum game to win or lose. The backdrop for these developments is the effect of global climate change, which has been described as an "accelerant of instability" and which will be manifest through such issues as scarcity of water, food, and other resources; extreme weather; and dislocation of communities and populations (American Security Project, n.d.; Goldstein, 2016; National Research Council, 2013; United Nations Climate Change, 2016).

BOX 3-2
Cyberwar vs. Information Warfare

Cyberattacks have three general purposes: espionage or exfiltration of information (such as Russia's hack of the Democratic National Committee); damage to servers and other infrastructure; and manipulation of information. Many such attacks are cybercrimes carried out for financial gain, but cyberattacks that cause massive harm—crippling society as a whole, attacking critical infrastructure, or destroying weapon systems, for example—would be termed cyberwar. Information warfare and influence operations may not cause such immediately dire consequences but can undermine an adversary by influencing the thinking, trust, and ideas of its people. Such operations may take the form of propaganda; chaos-producing operations involving high volumes of false messages; or leaks of secret, often embarrassing information to the public.

SOURCE: Committee and Herb Lin presentation, Workshop on Emerging Trends and Methods in International Security.

---

[5]During a press conference on June 1, 2017, Putin said that independent Russian hackers might have launched cyberattacks on foreign nations, but that the Russian state was uninvolved and that the hackers were motivated by their own patriotism (see Higgins, 2017).

No single committee or decadal study could address the full breadth of developing challenges and threats discussed here, and it is worth noting that there are significant trends and risks not emphasized in these assessments—for example, the rise of megacities, the broader global rate of scientific advances, and the myriad uses to which drones (unmanned aerial vehicles) may be put for purposes both good and nefarious. As the committee explored possible connections between emerging SBS research and sources of security risk, however, one thing became clear: understanding the human dimension is critical to addressing virtually any security challenge.

REFERENCES

American Security Project. (n.d.). *Climate Security*. Available: https://www.americansecurityproject.org/issues/climate-security [August 2018].

Goldstein, J.S. (2016). Climate change as a global security issue. *Journal of Global Security Studies*, 1(1), 95–98. Available: https://academic.oup.com/jogss/article-abstract/1/1/95/1841791?redirectedFrom=fulltext [November 2018].

Higgins, A. (2017). Maybe private Russian hackers meddled in election, Putin says. *New York Times*, June 1. Available: https://www.nytimes.com/2017/06/01/world/europe/vladimir-putin-donald-trump-hacking.html?mcubz=3 [November 2018].

Murdie, A., and Urpelainen, J. (2015). Why pick on us? Environmental INGOs and state shaming as a strategic substitute. *Political Studies*, 63(2), 353–372. doi:10.1111/1467-9248.12101.

Murdie, A., and Webeck, S. (2015). Responding to the call: Human security INGOs and countries with a history of civil war. *International Political Science Review*, 36(1), 3–19. doi:10.1177/0192512114547372.

National Intelligence Council. (2017). *Global Trends: Paradox of Progress*. Available: https://www.dni.gov/files/documents/nic/GT-Full-Report.pdf [July 2018].

National Research Council. (2013). *Climate and Social Stress: Implications for Security Analysis*. Washington, DC: The National Academies Press.

Office of the Director of National Intelligence. (2019). *National Intelligence Strategy of the United States of America, 2019*. Available: https://www.dni.gov/index.php/newsroom/reports-publications/item/1943-2019-national-intelligence-strategy [February 2019].

Organisation for Economic Co-operation and Development. (2003). *Emerging Risks in the 21st Century: An Agenda for Action*. Available: https://www.oecd.org/futures/globalprospects/37944611.pdf [November 2018].

Organisation for Economic Co-operation and Development. (2016). *OECD Science, Technology, and Innovation Outlook 2016*. Paris, France: OECD. Available: http://dx.doi.org/10.1787/sti_in_outlook-2016-en [July 2018].

Peterson, T., Murdie, A., and Asal, V. (2018). Human rights NGO shaming and the exports of abusive states. *British Journal of Political Science*, 48(3), 1–20. doi:10.1017/s0007123416000065.

President of the United States. (2017). *National Security Strategy of the United States of America*. Available: https://www.whitehouse.gov/wp-content/uploads/2017/12/NSS-Final-12-18-2017-0905.pdf [November 2018].

United Nations Climate Change. (2016). *Climate Change Poses Risk to Global Security*. Available: https://unfccc.int/news/climate-change-poses-risk-to-global-security [November 2018].

U.S. Department of Defense. (2018). *Summary of the 2018 National Defense Strategy of the United States of America: Sharpening the American Military's Competitive Edge*. Washington, DC: Author. Available: https://www.defense.gov/Portals/1/Documents/pubs/2018-National-Defense-Strategy-Summary.pdf [July 2018].

The White House. (2017). *A New National Security Strategy for a New Era*. Available: https://www.whitehouse.gov/articles/new-national-security-strategy-new-era [November 2018].

World Economic Forum. (2019). *The Global Risks Report 2019, 14th Edition*. Available: http://www3.weforum.org/docs/WEF_Global_Risks_Report_2019.pdf [May 2019].

4

The Work of the Intelligence Analyst

The key function of most intelligence analysts is to make sense of information about the world that can be used to protect the United States. Intelligence analysts across the nation's security agencies perform many tasks and play many roles, in line with the missions of their agencies, and they rely on diverse skills and experience as they carry out their responsibilities. Though many aspects of the agencies' work are not open to public view, the general functions and activities of the intelligence analyst can all be regarded as aspects of sensemaking—using their expertise to seek understanding within the range of material to which they have access.

This chapter sets the stage for the discussion in Part II of opportunities to use social and behavioral sciences (SBS) research in support of intelligence analysis by describing the daily work of the analyst. Before proceeding, we note both that many aspects of the analyst's work are classified and that the analyst's job varies significantly across agency and function, so we could not be certain as to exactly where new research could augment, improve, or supplant strategies and tools already in use. However, the experience of many of the committee members, supplemented by what we heard in our public meetings (see Chapter 1 and Appendix B) and what we discerned from publicly available research, was the basis for the overview that follows.

SENSEMAKING

Much of the analyst's work is primarily *tactical*; that is, analysts provide timely, high-quality insights to support immediate decision making by the president, senior policy makers, Congress, the military, and law enforcement. To develop these insights, analysts need to digest large quantities of information that comes from both sensitive intelligence sources—obtained by human and technical means—and openly available sources. A primary, ongoing challenge is to identify and assess information that is relevant, thorough, and timely enough to support the development of high-confidence, accurate insights that will allow U.S. policy makers to mitigate risks or position the United States to exploit opportunities. It is this assessment—or sensemaking process—that yields intelligence, as opposed to raw information.

In practice, the distinctions among types of intelligence are not crisp, but, as discussed in Chapter 2, intelligence work also includes *strategic* analysis, intended to help policy makers understand the broad factors or dynamics that may be shaping a geopolitical situation. The objective of this kind of analysis is to look ahead in time, to identify connections among issues, and to set particular choices that must be made within a wider context of space and time. The challenge of strategic analysis is that it often begins where the immediately relevant information ends, so the analyst relies on history, logic, and perhaps theory in looking at trends and building scenarios that can offer insight about the future.

Observers and members of the Intelligence Community (IC) have raised concern about a perceived ongoing shift away from strategic intelligence in favor of current, tactical work (see, e.g., Johnson, 2011). After nearly a generation of fighting wars—which calls for a sharp focus on the immediate—strategic analysis has not been a high priority for the U.S. IC. It is carried out primarily within the National Intelligence Council and in pockets within other agencies, especially the Central Intelligence Agency (CIA), and as a consequence, the capacity to perform strategic analysis has lagged behind tactical capabilities (Treverton and Gabbard, 2008; Stimson and Habek, 2016). The pressure to balance the two is not new, and there has been a growing need for shorter, more digestible products in response to pressing problems, perhaps at the expense of in-depth research.

We use the term "sensemaking" not to constrain the description of intelligence analysis but rather to convey its intellectual breadth. The challenge of sensemaking for intelligence analysts is akin to challenges faced by analysts in other sectors, such as business, risk analysis, or urban planning.[1] The need to find meaning in complex, data-rich environments and to understand especially challenging—"wicked"—problems is not unique

---

[1] This meaning of the term "sensemaking" was introduced in the context of organizational science (Weick, 1995; see also Anacoda, 2012).

to the IC.[2] The activities and responsibilities associated with intelligence analysis are similar to those needed for any planning or analytical task that requires expertise, the consideration of multiple variables across time and space, and the assessment of human behaviors and actions. Analysts seek to recognize patterns in behaviors, trends, and relationships among actors. Several experts have compared the work of intelligence analysts to that of medical diagnosticians because of the uncertainties involved, the complex interplay among factors, and the existential importance of the task (Marrin and Clemente, 2005; Treverton and Agrell, 2009).

Another possible comparison would be with making predictions about the performance of stocks. Stock analysts must consider diverse factors that may include trends within a single industry, as well as related industries whose fortunes may affect the one in question; the decision making of corporate leaders, consumers, and possibly policy makers in the United States and abroad; broad economic forces and trends; and even such external events as extreme weather or other consequences of global climate change, social trends, or fads. The investment analyst often must make quick decisions about the benefits of buying or selling stocks, knowing that the relevant information is limited, when potentially very large sums of money could be gained or lost.

In the context of the IC, sensemaking is a process of creating situational awareness and understanding in highly complex, emergent, or uncertain circumstances. One formulation characterizes intelligence problems as ranging from "puzzles," or challenges that have solutions; to "mysteries"; to the most difficult problems, or "complexities" (see Table 4-1) (Treverton, 2009, p. 6).

IC analysts monitor and detect events and changes in the world, anticipating likely changes and forecasting future events. They use sensemaking capabilities at the macro and micro levels and across different cultures, societies, and organizations. For IC analysts, sensemaking is used to make sense not only of the actions and motivations of humans (individuals, groups, and societies) but also of the actions and drivers of nonhumans, such as technologies, robots, organizations, and other entities.

WHAT ANALYSTS DO

Most intelligence analysts have an area of responsibility—an account—that, depending on the size and mission of the parent organization or team, may be quite broad (e.g., China's Communist Party) or more narrow (e.g.,

---

[2]The term "wicked problems," also introduced in the context of organizational management, refers to problems that are unusually challenging and difficult to define and solve, and involve complex competing factors that are difficult to reconcile.

TABLE 4-1 Puzzles, Mysteries, and Complexities

Type of Issue	Description	Intelligence Product
Puzzle	Answer exists but may not be known	*The* solution
Mystery	Answer contingent, cannot be known, but key variables can, along with sense for how they combine	Best forecast, perhaps with scenarios or excursions
Complexity	Many actors responding to changing circumstances, not repeating any established pattern	"Sensemaking"? Perhaps done orally, intense interaction of intelligence and policy

SOURCE: Treverton and Agrell (2009).

the life patterns of a particular terrorist leader). The account may lend itself more to qualitative analysis, of such questions as "How is leader X thinking about issue Y?" Or it may be more approachable through quantitative analysis, of such questions as "How much will India's economy grow over the next 10 years?" As these examples suggest, many if not most of the issues examined by intelligence analysts are also topics of study in the public domain, and analysts draw on academic research from many SBS disciplines, although mechanisms for their doing so are not as well established as they could be to serve the IC's needs, an issue discussed in Chapters 9 and 10.

Many analysts have deep expertise in their account, having studied it at the undergraduate or graduate level and worked on the issue professionally for many years. In the past two decades, many universities have begun to offer undergraduate degrees in intelligence studies, although there is ongoing discussion about the extent to which intelligence analysis should be regarded as an academic discipline (e.g., Fisher et al., 2014), and some critics have suggested that prospective analysts are better off majoring in SBS fields, languages, and other academic disciplines (Dujmovic, 2016).[3]

Not all analysts have deep expertise in specific areas relevant to their accounts, either because they are just starting their professional careers or because changing job responsibilities require changes in focus. The broad nature of national security requires expertise in a wide variety of topics, not all of which are in high demand as university majors. Thus, available

---

[3]Attention to the demands on members of the IC and how young people might best be prepared and selected for this work has also led to debates over whether intelligence analysis should be considered a profession or a craft (Gentry, 2016). This question is outside of the committee's charge, but we regard the work of the analyst as having elements of both categories.

intelligence staff may not bring all of the expertise relevant to some analytic accounts. It is possible, however, for analysts to develop expertise in particular types of intelligence problems, by, for example, working on several countries during crises.

Regardless of these differences, virtually all analysts—whatever their assigned account—engage in multiple activities. They circle back and repeat activities, and often, because of time pressures, omit certain actions entirely. Many of these activities are also performed in a team environment, with individual analysts sharing responsibility for the tasks involved, although it is not unusual for an individual analyst to perform most if not all of these activities herself (see Chapters 7 and 8 for further discussion of teaming; see also Hackman and O'Connor [2005]). Our description highlights primary functions common to most analysts' work. We look first at the recurring activities that are part of day-to-day responsibilities, then at sustaining activities through which analysts pursue the longer view of their accounts. We then look at a key element of any type of analysis, one that is both a daily and a sustaining activity: communicating it effectively so that clients can act on it.

The Analyst's Daily Activities

Maintain an Inventory of Questions That Are Important for the Analyst's Assigned Account

Analysts need to identify and track questions that reflect both their understanding of what policy makers want to know and their own appreciation of the issue at hand. They are not passive receptors of information provided by the agents who collect it and other sources; they provide parameters to help collectors focus on obtaining information that is key to narrowing intelligence gaps, and like social scientists, they help shape the design of data collection efforts. This is a foundational task: if analysts do not ask the right questions, they are likely to miss important developments on their accounts. This inventory of questions will span the range of puzzles, mysteries, and complexities, often fluctuating among them. Not infrequently, for example, a question that an analyst believed would lend itself to a linear answer—i.e., a puzzle—will reveal itself to be more complex, making it difficult to disentangle causal factors.

The analyst's inventory of key analytic questions will cover a wide range of topics. On any given day, analysts will be dealing with specific questions, such as "What is Individual X likely to do tomorrow?" But these specific questions will most often fall into more general areas of study and investigation.

Understanding power. How are decisions made in a nation, society, group, or organization? How is status allocated? Is the nature of power changing? What are the important sources of power in a particular context: economics, military might, corruption?

Understanding influence. What are the centers or networks of influence in a nation or organization? How is that influence wielded? What types of themes, narratives, and communications are influential in a society? What opportunities exist to influence a particular individual or group?

Understanding threats, opportunities, and social and organizational dynamics. What are the variables that threaten the cohesion and stability of a particular organization or society? What opportunities would the group or nation welcome and seek to take advantage of? What are its priorities, and how might they change? How stable is a particular group? What indicators should be used to track change?

Understanding complexity. Which developments are difficult to explain? What new dynamics may be emergent in a society or organization? How do seemingly disparate events combine to form new realities? What are the network effects? Which situations appear uncertain and difficult to parse—that is, wicked problems?

Understanding deception and gaps. How complete are the reporting and information available on an issue. How can the information be validated? Are certain sources of information suspect? What information is missing? What reporting appears to be "too good to be true"?

Stay Abreast of Current Information Relevant to the Account

Information of interest to the analyst includes classified intelligence collected on the account (e.g., through clandestine reporting, diplomatic reporting, or signals intelligence [SIGINT]), as well as any other information that might be relevant to the account. Indeed, defining what is relevant is itself a significant task that depends on the judgment and experience of the individual analyst. Thus, staying abreast of information involves several subactivities.

Establishing parameters and routines for information or intelligence searches. For example, the analyst may develop a search query for automated information-retrieval software or devote time each week to researching public sources and academic literature. The establishment of an information routine helps the analyst determine whether she is keeping up with the information flow or falling behind. The information routine requires monitoring and updating.

Filtering information and intelligence to determine what is deserving of more careful study. For an intelligence analyst responsible for a broad account, such as following the outlook for a particular leader, filtering what to pay attention to can be a particularly difficult, though critical, activity. How does the analyst, for example, know which popular cultural themes are important to follow? For an analyst dealing with a highly specific, narrow issue, such as the activities of a particular military unit, filtering information flow may be more straightforward, but even here, broader context may be necessary to understanding the unit's movements and actions. For example, how might the conditions of roads or timing of religious holidays affect the unit's mobility?

Filtering information with speed and accuracy is critical as no analyst wants to miss an important development because she did not spot the information. Yet for almost any account, the flow of possibly relevant information is so great that the analyst's tools and strategies for filtering are critical. Analysts often rely on filtering for the titles or subject headings assigned to discrete information items. This practice becomes problematic, however, when the originators of information describe its content or significance incorrectly. Technology can help, both in filtering and in tracking what has been filtered out in case it becomes valuable later, as discussed in subsequent chapters.

Reading selected information for understanding and meaning. Analysts take in a significant portion of their information by reading and must quickly digest large volumes of text. Reading strategies naturally vary with cognitive styles: some analysts may read important content several times, taking notes and underlining; others may read only once and move on. In many teams, analysts engage in substantive back-and-forth as they read through their information. "Did you see that report from the embassy? What do you think?" Analysts' exchanges about the information they are reviewing are a key way that they confirm assessments of credibility and other questions. Regardless, reading large volumes of material has long been a constant for most analysts.

Making judgments and evaluating the information received. Each day, sometimes every hour, an analyst will encounter new content that requires evaluation. "Is this information new? How important is this information? How should it be categorized? Is it relevant to the motivations of a leader or the interaction between two countries? Is it 'good' or 'bad' news for a particular terrorist group? Does it conflict with other information? If so, what evidence could indicate which is correct? Does this information make a bad development more or less likely? Is it unusual for this company to sell this material to country Z?" These are only examples of the hundreds if not thousands of potential questions the analyst may have to answer. Often an analyst may gain perspective on particular content only by combining it with other items of information or knowledge; for example, the fact that individual Y went to location X yesterday indicates that last week's report of an important leadership meeting may be true.

Thus, pattern recognition is a key element of the analyst's judgments about the information received, as is sensitivity to nonobvious indicators of change. Understanding of social and cultural factors is key to the analyst's capacity to search for, understand, and combine information intelligently, as are such skills as managing, coordinating, and combining information from multiple sources.

Cataloging the information. New content may need to be parsed into discrete information items to maximize its utility. A reporting cable, for instance, may have to be broken down into who, what, where, and when before its import can be entered into a database, or an analyst may maintain a descriptive list of a terrorist's daily habits that requires updating. In some units, information may be catalogued in a formal manner, perhaps being entered into a database shared by a team or an entire organization. In other cases, however, an analyst may catalog information only in his own mind, relying on memory to bring it forward when needed, or in simple records, such as chronologies of events.

Sustaining Activities

Apart from sorting through information and preparing intelligence reports, analysts, like any professionals, must engage in other activities just to maintain their expertise and advance their craft.

When—or perhaps if, given the tyranny of the present—intelligence analysts are not addressing time-sensitive issues, they will likely turn their attention to medium- or longer-term projects, such as researching a report on the emergence of a new leader in Cuba or working with an analytic methodologist on a new application of link technology that can elucidate the leadership structure of a terrorist organization. Analysts always need more time to gather information and explore new sources. An analyst may want to visit several policy makers or other clients to remain current on their intelligence needs, or meet with a collector of human intelligence (HUMINT) or SIGINT (see Chapter 2) to update intelligence requirements on a particular issue.

There are resources on which analysts can rely to supplement their own information, perspectives, and tools, such as security contractors, experts at think tanks, and university researchers. However, it is not easy for intelligence analysts to conduct independent research, such as field work to determine attitudes toward particular issues in a country they are following, in their areas of responsibility. Public perceptions of the intelligence function, along with administrative and sometimes even legal restrictions, limit the analyst's activities.

Finally, to do their jobs effectively and efficiently, analysts need to work with a model, a theory, or a set of hypotheses concerning their account. It is in fact this set of hypotheses that helps determine the analytic questions that frame the analyst's work (i.e., the first step in the analyst's daily activities). For example, an analyst may believe that country W is relatively stable or, conversely, is about to enter a volatile period. This framework will then color how the analyst sorts and interrogates the daily flow of information. Or a technical analyst will have a sense of new scientific breakthroughs in his or her field and thus be actively looking for the first signs of adoption by a particular military. Developing such heuristics, updating them on a regular basis, and refining analytic questions are the steady baseline activities for the analyst. Individual analysts and teams of colleagues continuously review and develop the theories and models that provide fundamental support for intelligence analysis. Structured analytic techniques based in the scientific method can help analysts organize their thinking about the conceptual underpinnings of their work, achieve clarity, and document uncertainties and gaps; these formal structures are the predominant way of framing analytic methodology within the IC (Heuer, 2011). Throughout these processes, proficient analysts and analytic teams will examine their worldviews, their cognitive biases, and their sources of information to identify weaknesses and apply corrective measures.

Communicating Intelligence and Analysis to Others

Effectively communicating to policy makers the information it is critical for them to have is as fundamental as developing and assessing the information in the first place. If the analysis is to be useful, it must provide sufficient context to support clients in making sound decisions, as well as a realistic, accurate indication of risk and urgency. It is also critical that the analyst (or analytic team) have the trust of the client and establish a rapport that facilitates communication (see, e.g., Hulnick, 2007; Lowenthal, 2017; Davis, n.d.). This is accomplished through informal interaction between analysts and their managers and networks of counterparts at the Departments of Defense and State, through feedback mechanisms built into the President's Daily Brief process, and in other ways both formal and informal.

Questions about what is done by policy makers in response to assessments provided by analysts are beyond the scope of this report, but a key aspect of analysts' responsibilities is to ensure that their intended messages are heard and understood. At the same time, particularly when the analysis pertains to serious or immediate risks, analysts bear a grave responsibility in considering how to convey the level of risk in a way that is actionable—providing any available guidance about possible responses—without usurping the decision maker's role (see Johnson, 2011; Davis, 2015; Wirtz, 2019; Wolfberg, 2017).[4]

As analysts absorb information, they must decide whether some of it needs to be communicated to others and if so, when and how. Analysts may be instructed to prepare intelligence reports for managers who also review the intelligence and information flow on a daily basis, or they may receive questions from policy makers. Analysts may also encounter unexpected information they recognize as important to convey to others. Their communications may be as simple as sharing their view of a particular piece of content with their teammate—for example, "This reporting looks new, but we actually saw the same information from another source 3 weeks ago." Or the task may be as obvious as the need to communicate a report of plans for a terrorist attack against a U.S. embassy to the National Security Council.

What is important to note here is that much of the information being parsed by the analyst is also being seen by hundreds of other members of the national security community. Information about a threat to a U.S. embassy, for example, would be sent to the embassy, to the White House Situation Room, to the responsible military command, and possibly to others as well. More sensitive reporting may be seen only by a few colleagues, and perhaps shared only through the President's Daily Brief. In any case, it is rare for an analyst to be the only individual to see a report, although he may be the first or only person to understand its significance. Others may not regard the threat of an attack as credible, for example, but the analyst may realize that the details of the attack are identical to those in a report from weeks ago about a terrorist group's plans to change tactics. As with the task of keeping up with the flow of information, many subactivities are involved in communicating intelligence to others.

Preparing an intelligence report. The nature of this report will vary with the organization, the urgency of the report, and the audience to whom the information is to be reported. The report may be a slide in a PowerPoint briefing, an updated coordinate on a map, a cable sent to the field, or a

---

[4]Research on the communication of risk, much of it developed in the contexts of public health and climate change, provides insights on how to communicate about the likelihood and potential impact of negative events (see, e.g., the *Journal of International Crisis and Risk Communication* [https://stars.library.ucf.edu/jicrcr] and *Journal of Risk Research* [https://www.tandfonline.com/toc/rjrr20/11/1-2]).

formal piece of intelligence analysis for the President's Daily Brief. It may be transmitted in a phone call or a classified email. If a formal, written report is necessary, a premium is placed on the quality and conciseness of the writing. Reports also need to be tailored to suit the preferences of the client: one policy maker may prefer to receive intelligence summarized, with the main points on a single page, for example, while another may prefer graphics.

Coordinating and collaborating with peers. If an analyst has a discrete account—perhaps being the only individual following events in a small country—there may be little need to discuss her findings with others. More typically, however, analysts will need to coordinate their intelligence reports with other analysts who cover the same or related issues. An intelligence report on North Korea's use of a new port in Oceania to evade military sanctions, for example, will have to be coordinated with the analysts covering North Korea and those covering Oceania, as well as with imagery experts, military analysts, experts on sanctions, and experts on port operations, just to name the most obvious. The earlier such coordination occurs, the more profitable it is likely to be. Often, however, the press of business leads to a compressed, hurried process. It is not unusual for coordination steps to be missed for a rushed item; this may in fact be a good outcome if a military commander in the field just needs a quick update. Analysts may also be unaware of individuals who could have added useful information or perspective on an issue, as is particularly the case when the coordination is occurring across agencies within the IC.

Sourcing the intelligence report. The analyst needs to assemble the most important intelligence and information that is the basis of the findings to be conveyed to others, particularly policy makers, in a formal report. This task can be time consuming for an analyst, particularly if the findings are based on multiple reports that must be interpreted in a particular way or sequence if they are to be understood accurately. Clear sourcing is important both for coordinating intelligence within the analytic community and for conveying accurate information to policy makers, who may not on their own make connections in the same way the analyst will. Another complication arises if intelligence reports are particularly sensitive and require specific approval to be shared with a broader audience.

Shepherding the intelligence report through an editorial process. Depending on the nature of the intelligence report, the analyst may need to engage with a complex editorial process designed to ensure the quality of what is essentially an organizational product. The editorial process for the President's Daily Brief is particularly complex because of the importance of its clients (the president and a very small number of aides and cabinet members). The layers of the process typically include, but are not limited to, the analyst's immediate supervisor; the leader of the analytic office; a chief editor with duties not unlike those of a newspaper or journal editor; and in the case of the President's Daily Brief, a senior reviewer representing the leadership of the IC. The analyst's job is to defend the analysis itself from editorial "fixes" that would alter the message while at the same time welcoming changes that improve clarity and readability. The analyst must also be sensitive to editorial changes that would require further coordination with colleagues. It is important to note that this editorial process is not merely or even primarily stylistic; it often identifies errors in thinking or perspective that need to be fixed. For example, it is not unusual for a reviewer to identify new experts who must be consulted to complete an intelligence report. More senior editors will be more sensitive to how a particular judgment can best be communicated to a skeptical policy maker.

Finalizing secondary details. In most IC organizations, analysts are also responsible for many auxiliary details in the communication of an intelligence report. The analyst may need to coordinate with the graphic designer to develop visuals that accurately convey the information, or create derivative versions of the report to share with a broader audience not cleared to receive the original. The analyst may need to identify the proper list of recipients for particular reports.

ILLUSTRATING ANALYTIC WORK

In discussing the opportunities SBS research offers, in Part II, we point to many aspects of the analyst's work that may not be entirely familiar to readers not directly involved in the work. To help make the applications of the research described in Part II come alive, we developed a hypothetical illustration of one aspect of intelligence analysis. As noted above, analysts must naturally focus on particular aspects of the world, and of necessity can apprehend only fragments of the entire picture at a time. Figure 4-1 illustrates several of the many possible lenses through which teams of analysts might view the world, depending on their areas of subject matter expertise and the accounts to which they have been assigned. The figure depicts a set of circumstances that teams of analysts might be following. We developed a stand-in map to avoid association with any actual geographic region, but note that the hypothetical circumstances illustrated are simpler than any real-world example would be.

In the region depicted, a number of circumstances and current developments can be observed:

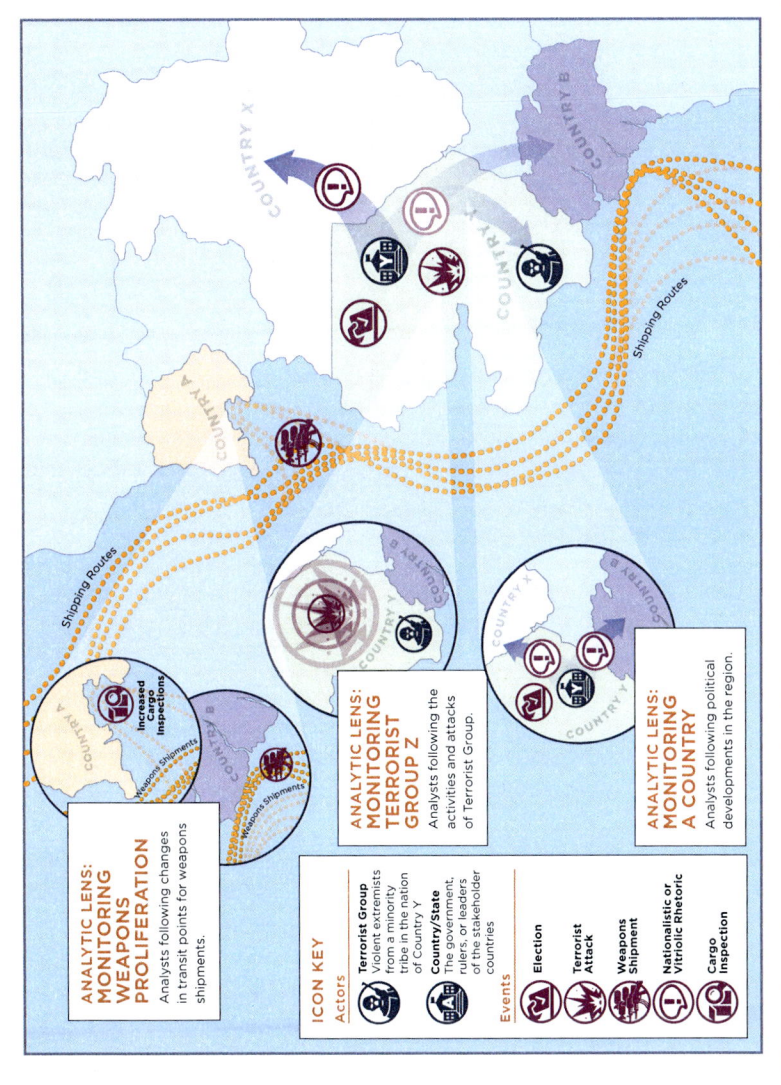

FIGURE 4-1 Illustration of how analysts with different accounts associated with a particular region will regard the same set of circumstances through different lenses. The figure depicts several events that would be monitored by groups of analysts; each group would focus their information collection and analyses on some events and not others, according to their assigned responsibilities.

- Terrorist group Z is conducting more frequent complex attacks against government installations in country Y.
- Country A has increased the rigor of customs enforcement, including cargo inspections.
- Weapons proliferators have changed transit points for weapons shipments to country B.
- Country Y's leader has increased negative rhetoric aimed at country X to shore up nationalist support in advance of national elections.

Different teams of analysts regard this region and these developments through different lenses, based on the accounts for which they are responsible.

Analytic Lens: Monitoring Terrorist Group Z

Analysts who focus on terrorist groups work to detect patterns in information they collect about the movements such groups make and their communications. In Figure 4-1, a group of analysts closely follows terrorist group Z, which is conducting attacks against government installations in country Y. While terrorist group Z acts independently, it is known to have a close relationship with country X, with which it shares cultural and religious beliefs. The analysts have observed over time that both terrorist group Z and country X see country Y as an existential threat because of its differing cultural and religious beliefs, capable military, and history of aggression. The analysts have been using an all-source data aggregator to capture all possible information on terrorist group Z's attacks, past and present, to identify patterns in the attacks. The results show that terrorist group Z's attacks against country Y are growing more complex, using powerful explosives and sophisticated detonation techniques. The analysts following terrorist group Z might decide to collaborate with those responsible for country X to determine whether the explosives' components are consistent with materials in that country's military arsenal, and, if this is confirmed, make the judgment that country X is providing material support and training for terrorist group Z.

Analytic Lens: Monitoring Weapons Proliferation

In Figure 4-1, weapons proliferation analysts, using algorithms to detect changes in transit points for weapons shipments, detect a change in shipping routes for weapons, weapons components, and other weapons-related materials. Shipments that had been transiting through country A are now transiting through country B. The analysts have assembled information on which countries and groups possess the technology to sell weapons, which have a need to buy them, and how supply chains for such weapons work. They note that country A has stepped up cargo inspections under international pressure and assess that weapons suppliers have likely identified country B as an attractive alternative transit site in the region because it requires less stringent inspections.

Analytic Lens: Monitoring a Country

Analysts who follow political developments in the region depicted in Figure 4-1 notice that the leader of country Y, who has been in power for 20 years, is facing National Assembly elections later in the year. They know from experience that he has traditionally used carrots, sticks, and low-level fraud to ensure a credible majority win for his party. The analysts discern in both intelligence reporting and open-source information that dissatisfaction with his rule is growing, and that he is increasingly preoccupied with tactics that will ensure a favorable election outcome that will be viewed as legitimate by the electorate. The analysts also know that the leader of country Y has historically used nationalist rhetoric directed at country X and terrorist group Z to shore up his base of support and justify cracking down on his domestic opposition; for example, he has publicly accused opposition leaders of colluding with terrorist group Z. The analysts are using algorithms to track the content of this leader's rhetoric over the past 6 months; their results show a major spike in negative themes involving country X, with a lesser uptick in vitriol against both terrorist group Z and a small neighboring country, country B. Since the vitriol against country B is an anomaly, the analysts may continue to focus their efforts on what experience has shown: that the leader of country Y is stirring up nationalist sentiment against country X to deflect criticism of his government's handling of the attacks by terrorist group Z and shore up his party's chances in the elections.

LOOKING FORWARD

The roles and tasks of intelligence analysts described above are classic ones, and they still apply. Analysts continuously develop new technical skills to support their analysis, but the fundamental nature and demands of the job have not changed significantly in the past few decades. Yet the world of the analyst is changing as the world itself changes. Of the changes that affect the analyst's world, the most obvious is perhaps the combination of transparency and overabundance brought by big data. A proliferation of sensors continues to dramatically increase the volumes of information that, in principle, make so much more information visible to the analyst. Advances in information technology have made it possible to harvest meaningful information from those enormous volumes. As researchers in SBS fields continue to generate new findings, the challenge of staying abreast even with, say, the literature relevant to terrorism or weapons proliferation increases weekly. Analysts struggle to make sense of a high—and constantly increasing—volume of both clandestine and openly available information. Some still worry that vital information that governments and nonstate actors take great pains to conceal is still being missed. Principal Deputy Director for National Intelligence Sue Gordon recently characterized the challenge this way (Gordon and Long, 2017, p. 4):

> We've moved from a world of data scarcity to data abundance. Where we used to go looking for single pieces of information that no one else had . . . now what we have is a world that is so much information that we have to make sense of it. How do you take advantage of the data that is now available and do something special with it so we know something a little more, a little sooner? We have to help the community build more capacity, whether that's in artificial intelligence, or in cyber, capacity and capability . . . to make use of all the data that exists.

A second set of big changes is likely in the nature of what analysts produce and how it is conveyed to their policy clients. The IC will continue to produce exquisite analyses, but rapid growth has occurred in commercial products and services that could be adapted to support intelligence analysts. For example, many of the kinds of products being produced by the National Geospatial-Intelligence Agency a generation ago are now available commercially, or even for free on the Internet (National Geospatial-Intelligence Agency, n.d.). Intelligence analysts will continue to search for new ways to add value that will intersect with policy makers' need for 24-7 access to intelligence.

As a result, the "product" of intelligence will increasingly be the analytic teams themselves, connected by new technologies to their policy counterparts and finding innovative ways to answer questions. This change will drive corresponding changes in how analysts are selected and how they are trained and evaluated. Analysts will surely need more quantitative skills so they can be sophisticated consumers of big data analytics;[5] they will also need to be adept not only at providing briefings but also at interacting with policy officers ad hoc.

---

[5]Data analytics allows for the identification of relationships and patterns across large and distributed datasets (Floridi, 2012) such that fine-grained behaviors and preferences (e.g., political opinions) can be tracked, and predictions about future behavior can be made (e.g., predictive policing or screening for insurance or employment) (Mahajan et al., 2012).

REFERENCES

Anacoda, D. (2012). Sensemaking: Framing and acting in the unknown. In S. Snook, N. Nohria, and R. Khurana (Eds.), *The Handbook for Teaching Leadership: Knowing, Doing and Being* (pp. 3–20). Thousand Oaks, CA: SAGE.

Davis, J. (n.d.). *A Policymaker's Perspective on Intelligence Analysis.* Available: https://www.cia.gov/library/center-for-the-study-of-intelligence/kent-csi/vol38no5/pdf/v38i5a02p.pdf [February 2019].

Davis, J. (2015). Intelligence analysts and policymakers: Benefits and dangers of tension in the relationship. In L.K. Johnson (Ed.), *Essentials of Strategic Intelligence* (pp. 115–138). Santa Monica, CA: Praeger.

Dujmovic, N. (2016). Colleges must be intelligent about intelligence studies. *The Washington Post*, December 30. Available: https://www.washingtonpost.com/news/grade-point/wp/2016/12/30/colleges-must-be-intelligent-about-intelligence-studies/?noredirect=on&utm_term=.9bfb3a41274b [November 2018].

Fisher, R., Johnston, R., and Clement, P. (2014). Is intelligence analysis a discipline? In R. George and J. Bruce (Eds.), *Analyzing Intelligence: National Security Practitioners' Perspectives* (2nd ed., pp. 57–80). Washington, DC: Georgetown University Press.

Floridi, L. (2012). Bid data and their epistemological challenge. *Philosophy & Technology*, 25(4), 435–437.

Gentry, J.A. (2016). The "professionalization" of intelligence analysis: A skeptical perspective. *Journal of Intelligence and Counterintelligence*, 29(4), 643–676. doi:10.1080/08850607.2016.1177393.

Gordon, S., and Long, L. (2017). *Plenary Session #6: A Conversation with Sue Gordon.* Presented at the Intelligence and National Security Summit 2017. Available: https://www.insaonline.org/wp-content/uploads/2017/09/Summit-2017-Transcript-Sue-Gordon-7Sept2017.pdf [November 2018].

Hackman, J.R., and O'Connor, M. (2005). *What Makes for a Great Analytic Team? Individual versus Team Approaches to Intelligence Analysis.* Washington, DC: Intelligence Science Board, Office of the Director of Central Intelligence. Available: https://fas.org/irp/dni/isb/analytic.pdf [February 2019].

Heuer, R.J., Jr. (2011). *Structured Analytic Techniques for Intelligence Analysis.* Washington, DC: CQ Press.

Hulnick, A.S. (2007). What's wrong with the intelligence cycle. In L.K. Johnson (Ed.), *Strategic Intelligence, Volume 2: The Intelligence Cycle* (pp. 1–22). Westport, CT: Praeger.

Johnson, L. (2011). *The Threat on the Horizon: An Inside Account of America's Search for Security after the Cold War.* New York: Oxford University Press.

Lowenthal, M.M. (2017). *Intelligence: From Secrets to Policy,* 7th ed. Los Angeles, CA: SAGE.

Mahajan, R.L., Mueller, R., Williams, C.B., Reed, J., Campbell, T.A., and Ramakrishnan, N. (2012). Cultivating emerging and black swan technologies. *ASME International Mechanical Engineering Congress and Exposition*, 6(Pts. A and B), 549–557.

Marrin, S., and Clemente, J.D. (2005). Improving intelligence analysis by looking to the medical profession. *International Journal of Intelligence and CounterIntelligence*, 18(4), 707–729.

National Geospatial-Intelligence Agency. (n.d.). *2015 NGA Strategy.* Available: https://www.nga.mil/About/NGAStrategy/Pages/default.aspx [November 2018].

Stimson, C., and Habeck, M. (2016). Reforming intelligence: A proposal for reorganizing the intelligence community and improving analysis. *The Heritage Foundation*, August 29. Available: https://www.heritage.org/defense/report/reforming-intelligence-proposal-reorganizing-the-intelligence-community-and [November 2018].

Treverton, G. (2009). *Addressing "Complexities" in Homeland Security*. Stockholm, Sweden: Center for Asymmetric Threat Studies (CATS). Available: https://medarbetarwebben. fhs.se/Documents/Externwebben/forskning/centrumbildningar/CATS/2009/publikationer/ addressing-complexities-in-homeland-security.pdf [November 2018].

Treverton, G., and Agrell, W. (2009). *National Intelligence Systems: Current Research and Future Prospects*. Cambridge, UK: Cambridge University Press.

Treverton, G., and Gabbard, C.B. (2008). *Assessing the Tradecraft of Intelligence Analysis*. Santa Monica, CA: RAND Corporation. Available: https://www.rand.org/content/dam/ rand/pubs/technical_reports/2008/RAND_TR293.pdf [November 2018].

Weick, K. (1995). *Sensemaking in Organizations*. Thousand Oaks, CA: SAGE.

Wirtz, J.J. (2019). The intelligence-policy nexus. In L.K. Johnson (Ed.), *Strategic Intelligence: Understanding the Hidden Side of Government* (vol. 1, pp. 139–150). Westport, CT: Praeger.

Wolfberg, A. (2017). The President's Daily Brief: Managing the relationship between intelligence and the policymaker. *Political Science Quarterly,* 132(2), 225–258.

PART II

OPPORTUNITIES FOR THE IC

We turn next to opportunities in the diverse landscape of social and behavioral science (SBS) research for strengthening the analytic capability of the Intelligence Community (IC) workforce. In Chapter 5, we begin with a sweep across the disciplines in this landscape, exploring examples that demonstrate both the range of potential opportunities and the importance to intelligence analysis of a sophisticated understanding of human and group behavior. Chapter 6 focuses on a specific, critical, example of the power of SBS research to enhance analysis: the emerging transdisciplinary[1] field of social cybersecurity. This field has developed for the express purpose of integrating SBS research from several disciplines to address the highly technical challenge of understanding cyber-based threats and strengthening the cybersecurity of the United States.

We then turn from ways of strengthening the substance of analysis to ways of strengthening the ways in which the analyst's work is carried out. Chapter 7 examines the rapidly expanding possibilities for sophisticated human–machine collaboration within the IC, and the vital role of research on how human beings function within teams that also rely on autonomous machine agents and supporting technologies in effective utilization of future developments in artificial intelligence and other technologies. Finally, Chapter 8 focuses on the importance of marshaling a robust body of research from industrial-organizational psychology and human resource development to strengthen the IC's capacity to attract, select, train, retain, and support a workforce that is fully ready to take advantage of these opportunities.

---

[1] A transdisciplinary field is a new academic discipline that merges the intellectual approaches of two or more existing fields.

5

Sensemaking: Emerging Ways to Answer Intelligence Questions

Understanding of social processes—insights about the functioning of individuals, groups, and societies—is essential to analysts' ability to answer enduring intelligence questions. As discussed in Chapter 4, intelligence analysts' primary function is sensemaking, drawing meaningful conclusions from the vast stream of information to which they have access, and they already make use of decades of social and behavioral sciences (SBS) research in doing this. Our charge required us to look across the current landscape of SBS research to highlight new and emerging insights with potential to improve sensemaking, including from areas that have not been consistently applied in a national security or intelligence context. Recognizing that it would not be possible to develop a comprehensive picture of all opportunities relevant to the Intelligence Community's (IC's) needs—or to be certain of the degree to which any particular opportunity is already being exploited within the IC—we focused instead on demonstrating how and why the insights from SBS research are essential to supporting the knowledge, skills, and methods analysts use to tackle core analytic challenges (see Chapter 4): the need to understand power and influence; threats, opportunities, and social and organizational dynamics; complexity; and deception and gaps in information.

Our review of a wide range of ideas and trends in SBS research revealed four areas with the potential to be particularly fruitful in supporting analysts' sensemaking efforts—the study of narrative, the study of social networks, the study of complex systems, and the affective sciences. We see in these four areas a combination of emerging developments and relevance to core analytic challenges that highlights the power of SBS research to strengthen intelligence analysis. There are undoubtedly many other developments that have not yet been fully exploited by the IC, and we hope future collaborations between the IC and the academic community will continue to identify new opportunities (see Chapter 10).

The opportunities described in this chapter can best be understood in the context of their place in the overall SBS research landscape, and the chapter therefore begins with an overview of the origins, methods, and primary contributions of research in these four areas. We then describe the specific ways in which research in each area can be applied to core analytic problems, drawing on both emerging research from contexts not typically associated with intelligence analysis and work on phenomena well recognized as key to analytic work. We suggest potential direct applications for the analyst, with the caveat that some are much readier for practical application than others.

APPROACHES TO UNDERSTANDING HUMAN AND SOCIAL PROCESSES

While each of the four areas highlighted in this chapter offers ways of understanding human behavior and social processes, they have different histories and are characterized by different theoretical models and methods. We briefly outline the unique contribution of each and recent trends that are ripe for application to core analytic challenges.

The Study of Narrative

Understanding narratives—from the meaning of cultural traditions, to political themes in press coverage, to trends in social media communications—is fundamental for the intelligence analyst, who must understand the content of communications and how and why they are conveyed. Narratives have existed since long before there was written language, and their impact and influence are evident. The study of narratives and stories has long been important in the humanities and in such social sciences as anthropology and psychology. Scholars of narrative have contributed to the broader study of culture and have developed ways of understanding the content and structure of narratives, as well as other features. This work has produced numerous definitions of what constitutes a narrative, but in essence it refers to some sort of story, conveyed verbally or nonverbally, in words, pictures, or even through gestures. New technologies have brought new kinds of narratives that analysts must understand, along with new methods for studying them.

In the past, narratives were slower (books, letters), and sources were more identifiable (authors, groups). The influence of narratives has been closely linked to the technologies available for creating and spreading them, and powerful new technologies that serve this purpose have emerged over the past two decades. The Gutenberg printing press made written stories readily available to large populations. More recently, train systems, the telegraph, and radio accelerated the speed at which stories could spread, while photography, film, and other video technologies intensified their emotional impact (Kaufer and Carley, 1993). Today, the Internet and associated digital technologies are again revolutionizing the nature and impact of narratives. Social media and other technologies allow for narratives to be generated and shared publicly at a much faster rate; narratives can quickly inspire group actions specific to time and location; and they can be shorter (e.g., presidential tweets) and more conversational.

At the same time, developments in the study of narratives have been fueled by the exponential growth in data created by social media such as Facebook and Twitter and by the fact that vast amounts of content are now stored digitally, which has made the study of narratives at a large scale much more practical. These capabilities offer new frontiers for applying the study of narratives to intelligence analysis.

Early narrative research focused on such widely shared narratives as folk tales. This research suggested that narratives have underlying patterns and structures; as early as the 1960s, computer technology was allowing researchers to identify such patterns and structures by searching large volumes of text (Colby et al., 1966). Interest in narratives has since spread beyond the traditional humanities to social science departments, and today's academic programs in this area are often multidisciplinary, drawing on psychology, sociology, anthropology, and other fields while also utilizing cutting-edge developments in the analysis of big data (see Chapter 2). New for-profit businesses have also contributed to the study and tracking of public sentiment and social media memes.

The expansion of narrative studies to additional social science domains has led to the emergence of more research questions with direct relevance to national security. Even such age-old fields of study as rhetoric have been brought to bear on security-related challenges, such as decoding of the master narratives of Islamist extremism (Halverson et al., 2011) or the deployment of traditional rhetorical charms (such as humor and ridicule) to counter extremist narratives (Goodall et al., 2012). Methods used in narrative study have obvious applications to the study of political narratives and how they both shape and are shaped by events, trends, leaders, and more. The nature of narratives is changing as social media tools proliferate. These new technologies make it possible to construct, assess, share, alter, and counter the spread of those narratives at ever faster rates. SBS research provides a basis for understanding, analyzing, and responding to these changes in narratives.

Developments in the quantitative and qualitative analysis of texts, narratives, imagery, and videos have contributed to advances in researchers' ability to characterize and anticipate human action, the contexts for issues of importance, the flow of ideas in societies or groups, and the emotional states and motivations of relevant individual populations. Advances in the use of natural language processing, machine learning, and computational approaches in the social sciences (see Chapter 2) are contributing means of analyzing big data in pursuit of questions about how narratives function and exert influence on individuals, groups, and societies. Study of multimodal communications (examining all aspects of a communication and its context) and transmedia storytelling (simultaneous transmission of a narrative across many media platforms) is helping to identify how and why some stories spread while others fizzle.

Researchers have long used several basic features that can be measured in analyzing narratives: the topics being addressed and concepts expressed, the sentiments or stances with respect to the topic that are implied or articulated, and the overall gist of the messages being conveyed. Today, new technologies are providing more sophisticated ways of using these and other measures. Machine learning tools, for example, now available for many languages, can be used to identify and track concepts. Sentiment, which formerly was assessed by coding text as positive or negative can now be assessed using such additional factors as social context, evidence of the author's ideological position, and data on the way people read (e.g., eye movements).

The use of machine learning approaches alone for the analysis of narrative has not, however, been entirely successful. Machines may identify characteristics of an author or situation inaccurately; misread socially nuanced language or cultural differences; or be tripped up by typographical errors, intentional spelling errors, emoticons, emojis, images, humor, or satire and sarcasm. Thus, effective use of machine learning, like other developing tools for narrative analysis, requires human judgment (Huang et al., 2011; Menabney, 2016).

The Study of Social Networks

Understanding the complex and dynamic relationships among and within social and institutional networks is an essential facet of intelligence analysis. One tool long used by the IC is social network analysis—a structural approach to understanding the world based on the interdependencies among actors and their influences on behavior; the flow of information, disease, resources, and other phenomena; and both the opportunities available to individuals and groups and the actions they take. Social network analysis has also played an important role in social science fields that include anthropology, communication, sociology, and political science (Borgatti et al., 2009; Johnson, 1994). The social network analysis entails representing a network in terms of nodes and relations that form an interdependent, holistic system and identifying key actors, their group identifications, and other network features.

Social network analysis predates the development of current social media, and even the field of computer science. The effort to understand society in terms of social relationships goes back as far as descriptions of lines of descent in the bible or clan histories found in other historical contexts (Freeman, 2004). However, the advent of modern social network analysis is generally attributed to Jacob L. Moreno, a sociologist who became interested in social psychology in the 1930s (Moreno, 1934). Moreno attempted to explain and understand social behavior using "socio-grams"—graphical representations of the links between an individual and others.

Computational and statistical advances in the study of social and other types of networks have increasingly involved computer scientists, physicists, statisticians, and mathematicians. For example, work by Harary (1969) provided a mathematical basis for reasoning about networks. Since the attacks of September 11, 2001, the field of social network analysis has exploded as researchers and national security experts have come to recognize its utility for understanding, identifying, and breaking terrorist groups.

Today, researchers use statistical methods, mathematical modeling, and simulation to understand social networks. They also use such tools as machine learning, big data analytics, and neural imaging to investigate network behaviors involving individuals, groups, organizations, and countries. The methods of social network analysis have been fruitfully applied as well to networks involving language, neural systems, animals, and food and supply chains; computer networks; and networks involving nonhuman agents, such as machines powered by artificial intelligence (AI) that have agency and can serve as nodes in a network alongside humans (Contractor et al., 2011; Lanham et al., 2014; Ofem et al., 2012). The analytic methods used have expanded to support the study of high-dimensional, dynamic, and spatial networks (Carley, 2003).

Cutting-edge methods for social network analysis are developing rapidly. They rest on technological advances[1]—particularly improved capacity for application at very large scales. Indeed, some of these advances have

---

[1] For example, such methods as homophily and diversity analysis, diffusion and epidemiological analysis, path analysis, and network visual analytics are being used to develop detailed profiles of networks and their functioning (National Academies of Sciences, Engineering, and Medicine, 2018b).

resulted from collaboration between researchers and the IC,[2] and all of these advances have utility for the IC in such applications as counterinsurgency analysis, tracking of terrorists, and exploitation of open-source data.

At the same time, however, the utility of this research for intelligence analysis rests on interdisciplinary work with other SBS disciplines. It has been demonstrated that social networks have profound influences on many human sentiments (an aspect of affective sciences, which are discussed below), behaviors, and actions that are of interest to the IC. These include, for example, the distribution and exchange of resources, the development of trust within a group or society, ideological contagion,[3] diffusion of beliefs, attitude formation, the establishment of normative constraints, the development of group and individual social capital,[4] group and organizational effectiveness, the evolution of organizational leadership, group and organizational resilience and robustness, and political stability, among many others. Researchers analyzing social networks examine such issues as how homogeneous the members of a network are (e.g., whether they share beliefs and how they came to do so); how ideas are transferred within the network; how some network members are uniquely positioned to influence other members; how members of a network adapt to its influences; and what ties link network members and how these ties function to create network identities (Grosser and Borgatti, 2013). Methods of social network analysis can also be applied to texts and used to understand features of narratives, how narratives have changed (Diesner and Carley, 2011; Sudhahar et al., 2015), and the rhetorical strategies (strategic framing) they use (Schultz et al., 2012). Recent work combines these approaches with the study of emotion to examine identity and influence (e.g., Joseph et al., 2016; see the discussion of affective sciences below).

The Study of Complex Systems

Intelligence analysis is challenging in part because almost all the issues of interest are complex and interact in ways that are difficult to trace and monitor. Work in a number of fields, including both mathematics and philosophy, has contributed to the development of a scientific approach

---

[2]Such advances include the development of scalable algorithms for many network measures and clustering algorithms and greater attention to cascades in networks. Currently, advances in this area involve a movement to more metrics for high-dimensional or metanetwork data, as well as new abilities to analyze changes in networks over time and assess the network dynamics, as well as to assess geospatially embedded networks.

[3]The notion that when a relatively small percentage of a population holds a new belief, that belief spreads to a majority of the population.

[4]Social relationships and networks that are the source of economic and other benefits.

to studying complex systems in which the phenomena being examined are viewed from a holistic, or integrated, perspective.

A complex system comprises many interacting parts, each acting on its own and with no singular central control. These interacting parts structure themselves into a system but behave in a nonlinear way, such that outcomes cannot be predicted based on their behavior (Bar-Yam, 2002). In addition, complex systems typically have adaptive components (including actors that learn); they operate on multiple levels, often involving dynamic social networks and processes; and they occupy "wicked" problem spaces.[5] For all these reasons, it is difficult to understand complex systems and to predict events and developments that may occur within the system or their potential consequences. As a result, people attempting to study or monitor complex systems are often caught off guard by so-called "black swan" events—consequential developments that were not expected—or by the unintended consequences of an event.

Many of the issues for which intelligence analysts are responsible exhibit the features of complex systems.[6] For example, China, whose role in the world is a key issue for the IC, is a massively complex system. Numerous factors—including economic performance, the degree of social cohesion, rural–urban migration, leadership dynamics in the Communist Party, and environmental degradation, to name but a few—are likely to interact and shape future developments in that country. Yet in the face of this complexity, intelligence analysts are expected to provide policy makers with reliable insights about how developments in China will evolve in the future. Analysis of nonstate actors in international affairs, such as terrorist organizations or subnational groups, can be even more difficult because of their informal and often hidden nature.

It is difficult not only to forecast the future state of a complex system but also to understand its current dynamics. Analysts cannot be certain that they adequately comprehend the causes of past events, and they lack proven methods for projecting how events may unfold in the future. As a result, they are often surprised by developments, even those that in hindsight appear to have been predictable. According to one veteran intelligence officer and scholar, "complexity is the phenomenon that is fueling and/or complicating the management of the government's—and indeed the nation's—most vexing strategic challenges" (Kerbel, 2015). Equally difficult

---

[5]As defined in Chapter 4, "wicked problems" are unusually challenging and difficult to define and solve and involve complex competing factors that are difficult to reconcile.

[6]We note also that the IC itself is a complex sociotechnical system, and research from this field is relevant to the management of the multiple entities and large workforce involved, a point we touch on in Chapters 6, 7, and 8.

for analysts is to help policy makers evaluate how their policy choices may interact with the complex dynamics of the issues at hand.

Subject matter experts in the IC face constant pressure, often within extremely compressed timeframes, to develop simulations and models for scenarios that are constantly changing. The need to communicate the results of modeling and simulation to policy and decision makers in relevant and timely ways is another persistent challenge.

Researchers have developed an interdisciplinary approach to studying complexity, sometimes termed complexity science, strategy, or theory. Based in systems theory that emerged in the mid–20th century, as well as developments in the natural sciences, this approach is used to study phenomena that are unpredictable and nonlinear, providing ways to identify and mitigate unintended consequences, as well as methods useful for considering a wide range of alternatives and thus supporting strategic analysis. Scholars of complexity theory use computational and mathematical methods to assess such phenomena,[7] and many SBS researchers rely on complexity theory in studying social, cultural, and technological systems. This applied approach, which relies heavily on modeling and simulation, has proven relevant for national security–related applications (Anderson, 1999; Brown and Eisenhardt, 1997); the possibilities are discussed in detail below. Researchers in the field of international relations have also used simulations and other methods of complexity theory to examine dynamics relevant to international security (see, e.g., Elder et al., 2015; Frankenstein et al., 2015).

The Affective Sciences

Emotion and affect play a fundamental role in human and social behavior. Societies and cultures would not function effectively, and humans would not survive as a species, if emotions were not regulated in culturally defined ways for the common, social good. Emotions can have extraordinary power to influence behavior and can be manipulated as a way of controlling others' attitudes and actions. Understanding how emotion and affect function and influence people's thoughts, beliefs, and actions therefore has clear utility for intelligence analysis; drawing on foundational and emerging work in this area to provide direct applications for intelligence analysis is a key frontier for SBS researchers and the IC.

The past few decades have witnessed a blossoming of research on a variety of topics under the rubric of "affective sciences," which address

---

[7]These methods include general algorithmic assessments (Flum and Crohe, 2006), computational algorithms that promote scalability, fractals, and techniques for identifying tipping points (Flake, 1998).

emotions, feelings, affect, moods, sentiments, and affectively based personality traits and psychopathologies. The study of all these components of the affective sciences, including the verbal and nonverbal signals of affective states, can provide insights into the mindsets, personalities, motivations, and intentions of the actors intelligence analysts seek to understand; help explain people's actions, judgments, and decisions; and support more nuanced and sophisticated understanding of communication.

Emotion and affect are complex phenomena, and many fields—particularly branches of psychology, psychiatry, neuroscience, and biology, but also others, including sociology and anthropology—have contributed to a growing understanding of these human phenomena. Indeed, many topics within the affective sciences are studied across disciplines. Scholars in these fields use diverse approaches—including laboratory and field-based studies and experimental and observational methods—to study how people experience and express emotion and affect, what physiological processes accompany them, and how they affect other people, among other questions. Foundational work has significantly expanded understanding of many psychological processes, such as personality, development, pathology, and social behavior, that are critical to an understanding of people's actions and behavior (Davidson et al., 2002; Gross, 2007; Matsumoto et al., 2008, 2013).

Broadly speaking, emotion refers to transient, biopsychosocial reactions to events that have consequences for an individual's welfare and potentially require immediate action. Emotion is a metaphor for a host of physiological and psychological state changes that are produced by a cognitive appraisal process, and it can have profound influences on what people do. The experience of emotion involves multiple components, including affect, physiological response, mental changes, and expressive behavior. Emotions serve intrapersonal, interpersonal, and sociocultural functions that all have implications for intelligence analysis (Hwang and Matsumoto, 2016; Keltner and Haidt, 1999; Levenson, 1999) (see Box 5-1).

Affective states—including not only emotion but also mood (state of mind) and sentiment (a view or attitude with respect to a circumstance or event)—are signaled both verbally and nonverbally. The study of nonverbal communication, defined as "the transfer and exchange of messages in any and all modalities that do not involve words," offers significant potential benefits for the IC (Matsumoto et al., 2013, p. 4). People communicate nonverbally through both conscious and unconscious actions of the face, voice, and body, such as vocal cues (e.g., tones), gestures, body postures, interpersonal distance, touching, and gaze. These communication modes serve multiple functions: they may define a communication by providing a backdrop for it, regulate a verbal communication, or constitute the message itself (see Box 5-2). Such nonverbal behaviors are observable, and thus can

> **BOX 5-1**
> **Intrapersonal, Interpersonal, and
> Sociocultural Functions of Emotion**
>
> **Intrapersonally**, emotions help people act quickly with minimal conscious awareness (Tooby and Cosmides, 2008); prepare the body for immediate action; and orchestrate such systems and functions as perception, attention, inference, learning, memory, goal choice, motivational priorities, physiological reactions, motor behaviors, and behavioral decision making (Cosmides and Tooby, 2000; Tooby and Cosmides, 2008). Emotions also influence thoughts because they are connected to cognition and memories (Wang and Ross, 2007), and they motivate future behaviors, as well as judgment and decision making (Lerner et al., 2015).
>
> **Interpersonally**, emotions expressed both verbally and nonverbally (through facial expressions, voices, gestures, body postures, and movements) influence other people and social interactions (Elfenbein and Ambady, 2002; Matsumoto, 2001).
>
> **Socioculturally**, emotions and emotional expressions help regulate behavior, allowing people to engage in socially appropriate behaviors as defined by their culture. Emotions, expressions, and behaviors are regulated by cultural rules, norms, values, beliefs, attitudes, and opinions, as reinforced by social structures, organizations, and sanctioning systems.

provide signals of potential utility to analysts. Research over the past few decades has provided strong evidence of the validity and reliability of nonverbal expressions of specific emotional states and evidence for nonverbal signals of many other cognitive and emotional states (see, e.g., Cartmill and Goldin-Meadow, 2016; Hwang and Matsumoto, 2016; Re and Rule, 2016; Scott and McGettigan, 2016).

Recent research in affective sciences has provided new insights into specific areas of interest to the IC. These include the content and power of narratives, processes of judgment and decision making, and the spread of attitudes and beliefs associated with terrorism and other security threats.

APPLYING SOCIAL AND BEHAVIORAL SCIENCE RESEARCH TO SENSEMAKING FOR CORE ANALYTIC PROBLEMS

Research in these four areas can be applied to support the analyst in tackling core sensemaking challenges, though further research is needed to bring these ideas closer to practical application. Many of the methods and ideas discussed here can be applied to more than one set of analytic problems; accordingly, this discussion of opportunities and how they may be applied is organized, somewhat arbitrarily, around the core challenges

> **BOX 5-2**
> **How Nonverbal Communications Function**
>
> Nonverbal communications may interact with a verbal message by
>
> - substituting for it, providing messages in the absence of words;
> - repeating messages so they are conveyed both verbally and nonverbally;
> - contradicting verbal messages by sending a message different from one that is spoken—for example, to convey sarcasm;
> - complementing verbal communication by amplifying it;
> - accenting a particular part of a spoken communication—for example, by using a gesture to emphasize a particular word, thus telling the listener that this concept is important; or
> - regulating verbal communication by conveying unspoken rules that keep the communication organized and efficient.

of understanding power and influence, understanding threats and opportunities, and understanding complexity (see Chapter 4). Note that, because many of the most current developments in understanding deception address cyber-based deception, those challenges are addressed in Chapter 6.

Understanding Power and Influence

The nature and sources of the power wielded by individuals, groups, and states and how these entities exert influence are fundamental topics for analysts. Examples of the specific challenges analysts confront include making sense of the power structure in a group or region, assessing lines of influence, identifying influencers (individuals who exert influence on key or emergent leaders), and tracking changes that could signal a developing shift in power. This section reviews opportunities for enhancing understanding of status and power, judgment and decision making, influences on individuals' attitudes and behaviors, the vulnerability and adaptability of social networks, and network influences on political and economic environments.

Status and Power

Research in several fields has contributed to understanding of the nature of status and power, and of how leaders, groups, and states wield power and are influenced by the status and power of other actors. The fields of political science and international relations have provided foundational understanding of the fundamental importance of status and power. International stability depends on two factors: aspiring (or rising) powers must believe in the stability of the current status hierarchy (generally maintained through the strength of leading powers, such as the United States), but they must also perceive that this hierarchy is legitimate and that the boundaries of the elite group are permeable, making admittance into that group possible (Larson and Shevchenko, 2014a; Wohlforth, 2009).

Status refers to an actor's position within a social hierarchy and is defined by acknowledgment from other actors; actors cannot achieve higher status unilaterally (NASEM, 2018a).[8] Status is important to state actors; they value their relative status and may seek to elevate it—independent of other foreign policy goals—through both violent and peaceful means (Renshon, 2016, 2017; Ward, 2013, 2017). Rising powers, such as Turkey, India, and Brazil, are especially sensitive to status concerns (Mares, 2016; Paul and Shankar, 2014), but less is known about how those concerns affect small states and middle powers. Nonstate actors play a growing role in counterinsurgencies and complex humanitarian emergencies, and it is not uncommon for nongovernmental organizations (NGOs), terrorist or insurgent groups, and state actors to come into conflict with one another (Murdie and Peksen, 2014; Murdie and Stapley, 2014; Murdie and Urpelainen, 2015).

Status and power are also framed in terms of overlapping hierarchies. That is, a person might have different statuses at home, at work, and in other contexts. Similarly, a world leader has local and international status, and an individual terrorist has status within the terrorist group, while the group has status relative to other groups. Actors of concern to the IC may be navigating within and between related yet distinct networks of power and status (see, e.g., McIntosh, 2005).

Other insights about how status can influence the actions of state actors come from social identity theory, a basic principle of social psychology that explains people's behavior through a focus on their social identity (that part of the self-construct derived from membership in a social group). Individuals tend to experience the collective triumphs and defeats of groups with which they identify as if they were their own, and they evaluate their own group's status by comparing it with that of a reference group of a similar but slightly higher rank. Researchers applying these ideas to political actors have found that they display similar dynamics. For example, whereas Russia and China might compare themselves with the United States, India might compare itself with China, while France might compare itself with Germany (Larson and Shevchenko, 2010, 2014a; Wohlforth, 2009, 2014).

---

[8]Reputation, another attribute conferred upon a state or nonstate actor by others, refers to an inference that others draw about that nonstate actor, including expectations about future behavior based on observations of past behavior (NASEM, 2018a).

Social groups (such as states) interested in increasing their relative status may use one of three identity-management strategies—social mobility, social competition, or social creativity—to challenge international status hierarchies and improve their ranking. To pursue any of these strategies, a state must possess a minimum level of "hard power," or military capability; reliance on hard power can, of course, result in conflict. States may also use other means of exerting influence that fall into the category of "soft power" (described in Box 5-3, the first of a series of boxes in this chapter on potential applications of SBS research to the work of the intelligence analyst).

The **social mobility** strategy is to seek membership in an elite group by following recognized rules and improving one's standing with respect to the group's recognized attributes. In the decade after the Cold War ended, for example, former Warsaw Pact member states adopted democracy and capitalist economies and then sought admission to the North Atlantic Treaty Organization and the European Union, not simply to attain military security and economic prosperity but also to achieve higher status.

The use of **social competition** encompasses the efforts of a lower-ranked group to equal or exceed the dominant group. Lower-ranked groups tend to use this strategy when the boundaries of the dominant group appear impermeable and the existing status hierarchy is illegitimate or unstable—for example, when higher-ranking members are perceived as bullying others or holding double standards (see Box 5-4).

Lower-status states may also use **social creativity** as a strategy for achieving higher status. This strategy tends to be used when the dominant-status

---

BOX 5-3
Potential Application: Measuring Soft Power

Soft power—the capacity of a nation-state or other actor to influence others through persuasion rather than coercion—is a potent tool (Nye, 2004). In analyzing a situation, an intelligence analyst may need to assess the effectiveness of a soft power. Measures of soft power have tended to focus on how it is exercised rather than on how it is received, often using qualitative analysis, based in political theory, of the content of narratives. Such analysis can, for example, demonstrate how coverage of international sports teams (Grix and Houlihan, 2014) or the publications of think tanks (Paradise, 2009) can be used as instruments of soft power. Social media have provided a newer tool for exercising soft power (Warren, 2014), one whose impact can be quantified (Anguelov and Kaschel, 2017). Analyzing information in the cyber-mediated environment, such as digital traces and YouTube videos, can reveal how cultural and other output from countries or groups is influencing others (Flew, 2016; Wu, 2017). Advances in social cybersecurity (see Chapter 6) are making this type of computational social science a viable tool (Martin et al., 2013).

> **BOX 5-4**
> **Potential Application: Observing Status Competition**
>
> Demands by lower-ranking members to change the rules and norms are indicators of an unstable hierarchy. In geopolitical terms, a challenger will compete with established great powers for allies, client states, and weapons. If the challenger is not powerful enough to surpass the dominant state, it may act as a spoiler by trying to humiliate the dominant state and prevent it from attaining its goals. For example, Russia currently lacks the military and economic capabilities to surpass the United States. However, President Vladimir Putin views the international status hierarchy as illegitimate because it excludes Russia as a leading power. Putin has undertaken various strategies to humiliate the United States and its allies (Larson and Shevchenko, 2014a, 2014b). Because instability in international hierarchies is a flag for analysts monitoring for unrest, tracking early signs of challenge to a dominant power can be a valuable tool.

group is impermeable, but the existing status hierarchy is believed to be both stable (e.g., a change in the hierarchy is unlikely) and legitimate (e.g., its rules and norms are perceived to be fair). In these circumstances, a state pursuing greater status may seek to change the international perception of a trait or attribute previously viewed as negative, and thereby to excel in a new dimension. If, however, the dominant state refuses to see value in this new dimension or see the aspiring state as superior in that dimension, a social creativity strategy will prove ineffective (Larson and Shevchenko, 2014a).

Other areas of SBS research have also contributed to understanding of status and power. For example, social network analysis has built on traditional understanding of international relations (Hafner-Burton et al., 2009). Theoretical work over the past several decades has developed a portrait of power dynamics and the effectiveness of charismatic authority or control of communications, for example (see, e.g., Bonacich, 1987; Brass, 1992). More recent work has used network analysis to assess these dynamics (e.g., Golbeck and Hendler, 2004; Lawler et al., 2011).

Complexity models are also used to understand and reason about power. By taking into account sociological and biological findings on trust and reciprocity, for example, researchers can use computational models to consistently calculate scores of agents' trust and reputation (Mui et al., 2002). Other complexity models point to the role of credibility in building and maintaining reputation (Herbig et al., 1994), as well as to the roles of trust (Prietula and Carley, 2001), rumor (Prietula, 2001), and the volatility of the environment (Carley and Prietula, 1993). Such models yield understanding of the conditions under which status, power, and reputation can be disrupted.

> **Research Directions**
>
> ***Apply existing methods to pursue understanding of violent, for-profit organizations and individual nonstate actors.***
>
> The past decade has seen an increase in systematic and quantitative research on terrorist organizations, NGOs, and religious organizations, but less attention has been given to the role of violent for-profit organizations and individual nonstate actors in international security. Methods for assessing the potential influence of nonstate actors include counting the number of organizations or measuring their output (e.g., dissemination of a report or press release, the number of terrorist events or their lethality, media attention to those outputs). Other research topics might include perceptions of nonstate actors among others in their communities and other actors, such as states and international governmental organizations, and the influence of individual nonstate actors, such as celebrity activists (e.g., Leonardo de Caprio and Angelina Jolie) and religious leaders (e.g., the Dali Lama and Pope Francis). Finally, since the terrorist attacks of September 11, 2001, there has been a general decline in the influence of civil society, including NGOs and other social organizations. While some states have sought to prevent funding from reaching terrorists through networks of nonstate actors, other states have used counterterrorism as a justification to restrict the activities of even purely humanitarian organizations (Murdie and Purser, 2017). Additional research is needed to understand the conditions that have led to such crackdowns and how they affect nonstate actors.

Judgment and Decision Making

One problem set facing intelligence analysts involves understanding and trying to anticipate the judgments and decisions of political leaders and other actors who wield power. These human processes have been studied by researchers in many fields, including anthropology, psychology, economics, sociology, political science, communication, and organization science. This work was long dominated by cognitive theories based on the premise that human beings are rational agents who make decisions based primarily on logical reasoning about possible alternatives (Camerer, 2003). Subsequent work showed, however, that humans make decisions under constraints of bounded rationality and that rational choices must be understood within cognitive and situational constraints (e.g., Gigerenzer and Selten, 2002; Kahneman and Tversky, 1979; Thaler et al., 2013).

Research by Kahneman and Tversky (1979), for example, provided models of decision making incorporating a complex combination of cognitive processes that could be predicted. Since then, examinations of economic decision making (Naqvi et al., 2006) and decision making in stressful situations (Starcke and Brand, 2016) have contributed to the development of new theoretical models, and a significant body of work has focused on the role of emotions in these processes. This work indicates that emotions and cognition interact and portrays the processes of judgment and decision making as being imbued with emotion at multiple stages (Lerner et al., 2015).

Other work has explored the role of context in decision making. A number of researchers, for example, have examined the effects of context on choice behavior in the face of multiple alternatives. This research has shown that context limits what alternatives are considered (see, e.g., Bartels and Johnson, 2015; Becharaet al., 2000; Schwartz, 2000; Trueblood et al., 2013; Tversky and Simonson, 1993).

Research Directions

Explore how the interaction of cognitive, emotional, and contextual factors to affect and influence judgment and decision making can be applied to assessments of actors of interest to the IC (see Box 5-5).

The IC would benefit from both basic and applied research that could provide more detailed understanding of

- the kinds of cognitive, emotional, and contextual factors that have the greatest effect on the judgments and decisions of actors of interest to the IC;
- how uncertain, ambiguous, or risky contexts or situations affect these processes;
- how these processes are affected by specific emotions; and
- the impacts of stress, particularly on ambiguous or uncertain decisions.

Influences on Individuals' Attitudes and Behaviors

Several fields shed light on how ideas, beliefs, and attitudes form, evolve, and spread through a given population.

Analysis of human networks. Some researchers have used network analysis to explore the behavior of humans and groups. For example, study of the diffusion of innovations initially focused on the characteristics of individual potential adopters (such as their education levels). Subsequent work, however, showed that the network in which potential adopters were embedded was significantly more powerful in both explaining and predicting the dif-

> **BOX 5-5**
> **Potential Application: Indicators of Actors' Intentions**
>
> Advances in research on judgment and decision making could allow analysts to carry out more sophisticated assessments of the likely intentions of actors they are following. For example, a reliable way to determine a leader's preferred decision-making style would allow analysts to anticipate how long a particular leader would take to make a decision or the likelihood that a leader would reverse a policy move. Research has shown that emotions can affect decision making (e.g., by modulating attention and/or memory), and has identified specific behavioral and physiological markers of emotion that can be applied in assessing the role of emotion in decision making (Brosch et al., 2013; Lerner et al., 2015; Phelps et al., 2014; Stasi et al., 2018). Such research could provide the basis for using signals of mental states or situational cues as indicators of potentially consequential emotional states or changes in those states among leaders or other powerful actors, or as indicators of their thinking. These methods could be applied to help analysts assess the inclinations of leaders involved in high-stakes encounters with the United States, such as Iraqi President Saddam Hussein during the two Gulf Wars and North Korean leader Kim Jong-un.

fusion of innovations and adoption behavior (Johnson and Brown, 1986; Rogers, 2003; Rogers and Kincaid, 1981; Valente, 1996).

Research on social influence—the process through which individuals' states (such emotions as happiness, or other states, such as health or obesity) evolve over time as a result of social influence—has shown that it is one of the key dynamics involved in the diffusion of ideas (Carley, 1986; Carley et al., 2009; Christakis and James, 2011; Delre et al., 2007). Models of social influence, validated in both laboratory experiments and real-world settings (Algesheimer et al., 2005; Friedkin, 2006; Marsden and Friedkin, 1993), have been used successfully to predict political voting and reasoning about such events as the fall of the Berlin Wall (de Mesquita, 1998; Stokman and Van Oosten, 1994).

Affective sciences. Influencers are influential not only because of the persuasiveness of their logic and arguments but also because of the way they craft their messages to express specific emotions associated with their logic and arguments. Such communication packages may include the strategic use of nonverbal communication and behavior to reinforce their messages. These nonverbal signals may include contextual cues in the background as well as nonverbal behaviors of the influencer—facial expressions, tone of voice, and gesture. Indeed, these nonverbal cues are often critical to the power of an argument. The IC today depends largely on intelligence reporting to identify the key influencers in a particular group or society. Improved understanding of emotion and how verbal and nonverbal communications work, especially in contexts relevant to the IC, could yield additional methods for evaluating influencers and interpreting the behavior of actors of interest.

Research Directions

Distinguish the effects of a network on people's attitudes and behaviors from the effects of people's attitudes and behaviors on network formation (Steglich et al., 2010).

Some work suggests that these two effects evolve together (Carley et al., 2009), but longitudinal data (see, e.g., Mercken et al., 2012) are needed to examine this question empirically. Lacking longitudinal data, researchers have relied on network data collected via surveys. However, survey methodologies do not scale easily to large networks of actors, and survey data quickly grow out of date. It is, moreover, not practical to solicit network data from covert adversarial actors.

Network analysis of digital data. Other research has focused on digital data that can be collected from, for example, interactions on social media platforms; digitized texts; and online commercial transactions, including video and audio posted online. This work includes both analysis of digital trace data and interdisciplinary approaches to this rich source of information.

Analysis of digital trace data. Internet users create data, in most cases unknowingly, as they use websites and interact on social media platforms, because they leave traces (known as digital trace data) that can be analyzed. Events occurring online, such as posted messages or comments, can be represented as individual interactions (e.g., by coding the sender, receiver, and time, possibly with other attributes of the sender, receiver, or interaction) and collected as a record of all events from a particular online platform.

Before digital trace data were available, researchers studying social network dynamics would examine a network at a single point in time and compare the resulting data with data collected at other discrete times (e.g., Graham and Carley, 2006; Palinkas et al., 2000). The availability of digital trace data has now made it possible to study any digital interaction in the context of all other such interactions occurring on a single social media platform.[9] However, the nature of the data—both the volume and the rapidity of interactions—has created the need for new dynamic network methods for streaming the data and "chunking" it into time periods.

Using time-stamped data, network researchers have in the past decade been able to jump-start the development of new statistical techniques for studying network dynamics (Brandes et al., 2009; Butts, 2008; McCulloh et al., 2012), sometimes in conjunction with machine learning techniques (Huang and Carley, 2018). This approach has made it possible to conduct longitudinal research at a much higher level of temporal resolution, and has the potential to yield substantial advances in theoretical understanding of social and behavioral processes for which relational event data (datasets that capture interactions among multiple actors or actions) are available (Leenders et al., 2016; Magelinski and Carley, 2018). This work has been the basis for the development of methods for assessing the importance of network nodes, tracking the trajectory of ideas, and other advances (Merrill et al., 2015) (see Box 5-6).

Integration of social network analysis with narrative research. The integration of social network analysis with narrative research offers additional possibilities for the intelligence analyst. Most social network researchers examine social influence on individuals in terms of the network structures in which they are embedded. There is, however, a robust body of literature in communication and psychology that considers social influence on networks as explained by the content of persuasive messages (Cialdini, 1984; Cialdini and Goldstein, 2004; O'Keefe, 2016). Combining these two approaches can provide a richer picture of networks and how they exert influence.

BOX 5-6
Potential Application: Using Dynamic Network Analysis to Track Security-Related Developments

Dynamic network techniques can support understanding of, for example, how groups or regions transition from stability to instability (Merrill et al., 2015) and how factions form (Magelinski and Carley, 2018). These techniques may also provide indicators and metrics of reductions or increases in the power of key actors (Kas et al., 2013), help identify emergent groups (Campedelli et al., 2018; Xie et al., 2013), and aid in identifying anomalous network activity (Heard et al., 2010).

---

[9]Cross-platform analysis is possible in theory; however, identifying actors across platforms is challenging, and combining data across platforms can lead to privacy breaches.

For example, computational models have been used to merge these two approaches to support reasoning about the coevolution of groups and what they talk about (Carley et al., 2009). Such models can be useful for assessing how interventions can affect groups or which media are most effective in carrying messages. These developments could be used to identify indicators for monitoring the developing strength of a minority opposition group's message (Maxwell and Carley, 2009) (see Box 5-7).

Research Directions

Conduct interdisciplinary work combining social network analysis with narrative analysis.

Such an integrated approach has the potential to benefit the IC by providing improved understanding of

- how and where narratives emerge within networks and how they spread and change over time;
- the characteristics of ideological cutpoints (the points that divide topic groups) in social media networks and their role in the spread of beliefs and ideologies;
- the types of network motifs and structures that are resistant to disinformation or misinformation;
- the ways in which competing narratives, ideologies, and beliefs evolve in social networks and how these networks maintain or lose insularity (i.e., the degree to which they exist in an "information bubble");
- how online influence operations might be identified based on high-dimensional network behaviors;
- the aspects of social networks that facilitate or impede the viral spread of ideas;
- the specific emotions and sentiments underlying narratives that emerge from social network analysis that make those narratives powerful in different ways and drive changes in attitudes, values, and beliefs; and
- the way networks and individuals' network positions are reshaped by emotional messaging and online influence operations.

The Vulnerability and Adaptability of Social Networks

Since the attacks of September 11, 2001, the IC has had an intensified interest in research on social networks, particularly terrorist networks (Ressler, 2006), and researchers have responded.[10] One area of interest to

---

[10]See, for example, work on particular terrorist networks (Perliger and Pedahzur, 2011; Sageman, 2004), the network position of lone wolf terrorists (Weimann, 2012), criminal networks (Carrington, 2011), adaptation in terrorist groups (Horgan et al., 2014), destabilization of terrorist networks (Carley et al., 2001), and target prediction (Campedelli et al., 2018).

> **BOX 5-7**
> **Potential Application: Understanding How Networks and Persuasive Messages Together Influence Individuals**
>
> The integration of social network analysis with analysis of narrative content could be the basis for a robust analytic approach to assessing the influences of and on social networks. For instance, this combined approach could be used to test the cohesiveness of a network in which toxic narrative is spreading, identify how changes in power structure may affect narratives, or reveal how changes in leaders' narratives coincide with changes in their networks (Contractor and DeChurch, 2014; Edwards, 2010). Such an approach, for example, could have helped analysts track the rise of ISIS in the Middle East and the relative decline in the appeal of Al Qaeda.

analysts that has been addressed by social network research is the functioning, viability, and vulnerability of groups and organizations. This research has helped answer questions about what makes some groups or organizations effective while others are dysfunctional or fail, and what makes some more resilient than others.

Terrorists' power is heavily dependent on their connection to others who can provide material and other forms of support. However, covert networks must constantly weigh the benefits of activating a network tie against the potential of unintentionally revealing that tie to the IC. Researchers have explored ways to exploit this tension, with the aim of suggesting ways to break up terrorist networks or inhibit their ability to function effectively. Much of this research has focused on how to remove the actors or linkages whose loss will optimally disrupt the network, sometimes referred to as the "key player" problem (Borgatti, 2002).

The complexity of the dynamics of social networks complicates such efforts. Networks have properties that help them resist such disturbances as the removal of a specific entity or relationship and adapt to changing circumstances (National Research Council, 2003; Sheffi, 2001). In examining how to break up the structure of terrorist and other "dark" networks, such as criminal cartels, and inhibit their effectiveness, researchers have used mathematical algorithms (Farley, 2003), simulation (Carley et al., 2001), mixed network analysis and simulation (Tsvetovat and Carley, 2005), and optimization algorithms (Chan et al., 2014). However, dismantling terrorist groups is a complex problem. Breaking up a covert network, for example, may paradoxically make it more efficient (Levitsky, 2003), as illustrated by the fact that suspending potential terrorist groups from social media platforms can simply send them to other venues that are more difficult to monitor.

Research Directions

Develop new dynamic network analytic methods, and conduct fundamental research on how human networks, such as social, knowledge, semantic, and task networks, adapt or evolve.

This work would include research on the relationship between networks' emergent properties (those that are not properties of the network's individual elements, only of the network itself) and their functioning, dynamics, and evolution as part of a general adaptive system. It would also include research exploring multitheoretical and multilevel motivations for covert networks to create, maintain, and dissolve network ties (Monge and Contractor, 2003) and the mechanisms by which networks are rebuilt (Tsvetovat and Carley, 2005; Wright et al., 2016). Specific areas such research could help illuminate include

- the functioning, viability, and vulnerability of groups and organizations, such as terrorist groups, social movements, and leadership networks involving state actors;
- the emergent properties of social networks, particularly dark networks, that make them resilient or susceptible to disturbances and direct interventions;
- the role of redundancy in the functioning, adaptation, evolution, and resiliency of multidimensional networks (e.g., when multiple actors have access to the same resources, tasks, or other actors) or in multilevel networks (e.g., when a group at one level, such as an organization, has two alternative supporting nodes or sources of input at a different level, such as communities that can provide workers);
- how the latent or hidden properties of network actors influence network adaptation, evolution, or resilience;
- how adaptive capacities in networks might be identified and possibly circumvented;
- what makes for effective network leadership and how it might influence network resilience;
- whether particular network structural and adaptive features make terrorist or dark networks more or less effective;
- when there is competition for leadership in a network and how it might be used to influence network functioning and vulnerability; and
- dynamic network-based indicators and warnings of faction formation and dissolution, conversion of a network to become more extremist or hostile, and other events of interest to the IC.

Network Influences on Political and Economic Environments

Social networks that operate at large scales, such as the relationships that exist within and among cities and countries, also have important security implications. Social network analysis can serve as a valuable supplement to the work of such fields as political science and sociology for studying political and economic developments and international power dynamics.

Current theory and methods in social network analysis have yielded important insights into organizational, urban, and global dynamics. Research on organizational networks, for example, has revealed the importance of investigating cross-level network phenomena to making sense of complex network dynamics (Brass et al., 2004), the need for multilevel models combining characteristics of individuals with structural network models (Borgatti and Foster, 2003), and the important role of social networks in rapid globalization (Zhou et al., 2007). Research on urban and regional networks has examined global and regional patterns (Knox and Pinch, 2010); the robustness of transportation systems (Nagurney and Qiang, 2007); the spatial diffusion of illnesses and ideas (Carrington et al., 2005); and the effects of community infrastructures on sustainability (Dempsey et al., 2011), community cohesion (Gilchrist, 2009; Moody and White, 2003), segregation (Laurence, 2009), and polarization (Lee et al., 2014). Similar work has examined global organizational networks—for example, to identify cities at particular risk during global ecological and economic crises (Taylor and Derudder, 2015). And a multimethods approach blending computer simulation and network analysis has been used to gain a better understanding of ways to limit the impact of biological threats (Carley et al., 2006; Eubank et al., 2004); of information diffusion (Rahmandad and Sterman, 2008); and of how positive and negative alliances influence the use of weapons of mass destruction (Frankenstein et al., 2015).

> **Research Directions**
>
> *Apply recent developments in statistical network analysis and dynamic network modeling to global dynamics.*
>
> This approach could help improve analysts' assessment and forecasting capabilities at both the global and regional scales. Specific benefits to the IC might include improved understanding of
>
> - the influence of inter- and intrastate economic and political networks on the behaviors of strategic state and nonstate actors;
> - indicators and warnings based on changes in positive and negative network relations among nation-states that can help predict shifts in state actors' positions with respect to weapons of mass destruction;
> - the economic and political factors that affect how connected one state is to others (centrality), as well as changes in those connections;
> - factors that contribute to the declining network dominance and influence of a nation-state;
> - the development and adaptation of global criminal and terrorist networks and the associated regional constraints on these networks; and
> - how shifts in such factors as international trade alliances, pacts, crypto-currency payments from one country to another, and trade routes (because of climate change) affect the global network of cities and the network dominance of states and nonstate actors.

Understanding Threats and Opportunities

Analysts constantly monitor and assess developing situations to understand whether they are likely to bring security threats, or perhaps open up opportunities for the United States to pursue a security, policy, or diplomatic objective. They use the results of these analyses to advise policy makers as to the possible interventions that might prevent a problem from occurring, or identify when the conditions in a society have changed or new actors and influencers have emerged that make that society amenable to a peaceful solution to a long-standing problem. Recent developments in Colombia illustrate this more positive analytic work: assessment involving a multitude of factors, including notice of the disarmament of guerilla groups and an assessment that the time was ripe, guided U.S. policy makers who worked to support negotiations that led to a peace agreement between the government and the Revolutionary Armed Forces of Colombia (FARC) in 2016.

This is a very broad arena, so we highlight here just a few areas with potential to enhance the analyst's capacity to recognize threats and opportunities and understand complex situations: radicalization and extremism, parsing of the narratives used by actors and groups, insider threat, and deception.

Radicalization and Extremism

Recently, a considerable body of research in affective studies has emerged on the processes of indoctrination and radicalization and the characteristics of extremism. This work has shed light on the motivations of lead bad actors for committing acts of violence (Gill, 2016; Gill et al., 2017; Gurski, 2015; Horgan, 2014; McCauley and Moskalenko, 2008; Meloy and Gill, 2016; Meloy and Yakeley, 2014; Meloy et al., 2015; Moskalenko and McCauley, 2009; Speckhard, 2012). Horgan (2008), for example, points to three motivational factors: perceived injustice, identity (pursuing an individual purpose), and the desire for a sense of belonging.

This body of work strongly suggests that no set of demographic characteristics reliably distinguishes terrorists from nonterrorists (Gill et al., 2017; Meloy and Gill, 2016). Becoming a terrorist is a complex process, and terrorism is not understood as a disorder in the individual. Rather, becoming a terrorist can be viewed as a tool that individuals adopt in pursuit of their aims (Kruglanski and Fishman, 2006). Moghaddam (2005), for example, identifies stages an individual may go through on a path to adopting terrorism. The process often begins with a perception of injustice, a search for a solution, and anger when no solution is available. An individual may go on to engage morally with a terrorist organization and develop an alternative persona. The next stage entails irrevocably joining a terrorist organization and escalating one's commitment, ultimately developing a belief that because the terrorists are fundamentally different from their enemies, engaging in violence on the organization's behalf is acceptable.

> **Research Directions**
>
> ***Conduct follow-up research on potential indicators of individuals' movement along a path to terrorism or extremism.***
>
> Current understanding of radicalization and extremism provides a foundation for research on behavioral markers useful for flagging terrorists and other bad actors. Researchers have identified possible indicators that an individual is moving along a path toward extremism or contemplation of violence (Meloy and Gill, 2016; Meloy et al., 2012), as well as nonverbal behaviors that may be useful as indicators that an actor is on the immediate cusp of engaging in acts of violence (discussed below). Progress in these areas could allow analysts to diversify their sources of information and scan for relatively indirect indicators of potential radicalization. Recent work, for example, illustrates the connection between the high price young men in some cultures must pay for brides and a heightened likelihood of radicalization. Such research can provide pointers to other economic or social indices that correlate with radicalization.
>
> Improved understanding of the emotional elements underlying the narratives of bad actors as they motivate their members to engage in acts of violence could also be of value to analysts, although this research is currently in its infancy. Among the questions that could contribute to analysts' capacity to assess the development of violent extremism are the following:
>
> - How long do underlying emotions, including hatred and others, need to fester before an individual reaches a tipping point?
> - How do these emotions spread within a social network? Who are the leaders of networks that foster hatred, extremism, or violence, and what are the nodes of such networks?
> - Can the emotions that fuel terrorism be incited in previously neutral actors?
> - How might these emotions be deescalated, minimized, or neutralized?
> - How do such emotions as hatred and their verbal and nonverbal signals combine with other verbal and linguistic markers of threat, such as integrative complexity (the degree to which the reasoning of a writer or speaker integrates multiple perspectives and/or solutions to problems)?
> - Can these markers be used in predicting changes in group mood[11] or terrorist acts? (See Box 5-8.)

---

[11]Some research has focused specifically on the moods or emotional dispositions of groups, examining such questions as how group moods develop and are influenced and how they affect individuals' behavior.

> **BOX 5-8**
> **Potential Application: Using Automation to Flag Potential Terrorist Threats**
>
> Detailed analysis of the language used by terrorist groups offers the potential to refine tools for flagging potential attacks by such groups. An approach for assessing the integrative complexity of language used by a particular group has been suggested (Chambers, 2017). Applying this approach would require collaboration among experts in terrorism, language, semantics and rhetoric, computational linguistics, and social science methods and coding, who would identify and code text features characteristic of a particular group and use machine learning to develop a method of automated classification that could potentially be applied to other groups. A related possibility is to integrate research on integrative complexity and other social and behavioral sciences approaches (e.g., identifying affective signals of hatred) with technologies for automated flagging.
>
> SOURCE: Adapted from Chambers (2017).

Parsing of the Narratives Used by Actors and Groups

Analysts know that narrative has significant power to shape and influence attitudes, values, beliefs, and motivations. Large organizations, for example, including nation-states, exercise influence by controlling their stories and their brands, and powerful institutions have generally been dominant in the production and proliferation of public narratives. Today, the Internet and social media have reduced the costs of creating and transmitting narratives, allowing individuals, organizations, states, and loose alliances to develop storylines with the potential to influence and mobilize other populations. Disaffected individuals and groups can more easily challenge narratives with which they disagree, and narratives are a particularly important weapon for nonstate actors, who deploy them to gain supporters and allies.

It is vital for analysts to track these developments. Narrative and network analysis and the study of emotion offer pathways for supplementing existing approaches for understanding the meaning of narratives and their influence.

Research Directions: Using Narrative Analysis

Apply new methods for analyzing the content of large volumes of data to identify changing narratives and their sources.

One example of how this can be done was described at a workshop held by the committee (see Chapter 1). Red Hen Lab, a consortium that conducts communication research, has compiled a vast collection of data consisting of approximately 4 billion words and 360,000 hours of audiovisual broadcasts that can be searched using natural language processing and optical character recognition software.[12] Researchers in such fields as linguistics, social networks, and machine learning are collaborating to develop ways to search such databases—for example, using linguistic forms and grammar patterns, semantic patterns, and topic identification—to detect significant events or changes in discourse. Developments made possible by such tools include

- improved understanding of persistent structures in narratives (Zhao et al., 2013), enabled, for example, by software programs that allow researchers to document the typical arcs in storylines, and to detect deviations from such arcs that may signal changes or be useful for assessing sentiments (NASEM, 2018c; Reagan et al., 2016);[13]
- improved understanding of stories told by particular groups (e.g., ISIS [Bodine-Baron et al., 2016]) and identification of the narratives of liars or truth tellers (Hancock et al., 2007);
- analysis of visual narratives, using such techniques as image annotation (Tuffield et al., 2006), to provide a more comprehensive assessment of narratives and answer such questions as how terrorists use images to reinforce or challenge narratives (Annesley-Mair, 2016); and
- translation of models developed for one language to other languages (Poibeau et al., 2013).

Such developments have the potential to provide analysts with tools that could be used to, for example,

- monitor narratives in multiple languages used by actors of national security concern;
- provide ongoing insights about discourse associated with the politics of social groups of interest;
- support more precise detection of shifting political sentiments or increasing persuasiveness of groups' messages; or
- allow for the assessment of narratives in near real time, quickly enough to be of practical use for analysts trying to answer questions.

---

[12] Red Hen Lab was discussed at a workshop held by the committee on January 24, 2018, the proceedings of which are summarized in NASEM (2018c). Also see http://www.redhenlab.org [September 2018] for more information.

[13] See, e.g., work on autogenerating narratives (Young, 2007); theme, topic, and gist identification and modeling (Mohr and Bogdanov, 2013); entity extraction (Etzioni et al., 2005); and opinion, sentiment, and stance mining (Liu, 2012; Pang and Lee, 2008; Snajder and Boltuzic, 2014).

Research Directions: Using Affective Sciences

Apply research on emotion in analysis of security-related contexts.

It is by conveying emotions that narratives often influence those who consume them. Researchers have shown, for example, that the triad of anger, contempt, and disgust plays an important role in the development of group-level hatred toward other groups, and that group leaders' expression of such emotions toward an outgroup frequently precedes violence against the outgroup (Matsumoto et al., 2013, 2014a, 2014b, 2015b, 2016, 2017). The study of emotion has also contributed to understanding of peace negotiations (Halperin et al., 2011); the causes of conflicts and wars (Bar-tal et al., 2007; Halperin, 2008; Halperin and Gross, 2011; Halperin and Pliskin, 2015); and stereotypes about other groups (Fiske et al., 1999, 2002; Kahn et al., 2016) (see Box 5-9).

BOX 5-9
Potential Application: Taxonomy of Emotional Profiles

Research on the relationships between expressions of emotion and behavior could serve as the basis for the development of tools that would help analysts understand how narratives exert their influence. For example, existing methods for characterizing emotion profiles and scripts for narratives (e.g., such basic narrative building blocks as fear, appeasement, hostility, and agitation) and linking them to behavioral outcomes could be applied in analyzing the narratives of groups of interest to the IC. Researchers working collaboratively with members of the IC could develop a taxonomy of narratives according to a limited number of emotional profiles and scripts associated with likely decision-making and action outcomes for groups of interest.

Insider Threat

A perennial threat within the IC is the possibility that an individual may use access to classified protected information or other opportunities afforded by his position within the IC in ways that pose a threat to security. Corporations are also affected by insider threat or industrial espionage (Crane, 2005). Inadvertent leaks are another risk for the IC as well as business interests (Carley and Morgan, 2016; Johnson and Dynes, 2007). The IC regards this phenomenon as a serious risk and has a robust structure for addressing it.[14] While the committee has no information about the IC's strategies for deterring such acts and detecting them when they occur

---

[14] Available: https://www.dni.gov/index.php/ncsc-what-we-do/ncsc-insider-threat [June 2018].

beyond what is publicly available, we offer insights from recent research that may be useful to the IC, and suggest research directions.

Research has provided a general portrait of the nature of insider threat (e.g., Cappelli et al., 2012; Irvin and Charney, 2014; Warkentin and Willison, 2009), demonstrating that no single underlying psychological, economic, or political cause is consistent across all such cases (Colwill, 2009). Many cases begin with an inadvertent leak of classified or proprietary information (Carley and Morgan, 2016). Research also has shown that individuals who become insider threats share certain characteristics with individuals who engage in other types of clandestine subversive behavior (Moore et al., 2015). For example, individuals who will later become insider threats often begin to reduce or limit contact with family and work colleagues; increase contacts with those to whom they will leak documents; and keep those individuals separate from colleagues, friends, and family members (Moore et al., 2015). Over time, they change their patterns of interaction, often dropping ties with some family members and work colleagues while establishing links with outsiders or malicious actors (Moore et al., 2015).

Researchers have brought additional perspectives to bear in elaborating this general portrait. The example of Chelsea Manning, a U.S. Army intelligence analyst who released more than 750,000 classified or sensitive U.S. military and diplomatic documents to WikiLeaks in 2013, offers a useful case for exploring the possibilities from various disciplinary perspectives.

Some of the insights gained from the Manning case are psychological. Manning has been characterized as a shy individual who is idealistic, psychologically troubled by struggles with gender identification issues, and socially inept. She has a troubled family history, and prior to the leaks had a limited personal network (see Nicks, 2012). While serving a tour of duty during the war in Iraq, she was also introverted and had a few negative and violent altercations (Brevini et al., 2013). She used the Internet to establish relationships, including with individuals who sought her confidence but later turned her in. She felt understood by the individuals who sought the leaks and noted during her trial that she had believed she would be helping people by sharing the leaked information (Brevini et al., 2013).

Manning exhibited many of the characteristics of a lone wolf (Marlatt, 2016; Ranieri and Barrs, 2011). Such an individual (who may become either a terrorist or an insider threat [e.g., Spaaij, 2010]) often, though not always, suffers from social ineptitude and psychological disturbances, and acts in illicit ways to address both personal frustration and social, political, or religious aims. Some work suggests that for many lone wolves, ideas of justice and empathy are more critical than association with a radical group in determining their choices (Moskalenko and McCauley, 2011).

Insider threat is also usefully viewed as a complex sociotechnical problem for which simulation models have been developed. For example,

Sokolowski and colleagues (2016) developed a model of the likelihood that each employee in an organization would become an insider threat, focusing in particular on how individuals become disgruntled. The model includes both individual-level factors (e.g., affect, risk tolerance, reward, threat) and organization-level factors (e.g., rate of change, organizational culture).[15] Casey and colleagues (2016) modeled insider threat as a compliance game. Their findings suggest characteristics of settings that are relatively protected from insider threat: organizational responses and policies with respect to trusting employees and checking their activities are difficult to predict, and employees are continually learning in response to changing circumstances. Such simulations could be used to assess the potential effects of complex interacting influences—in Manning's case, for example, tensions between her religious upbringing and her change in gender identification, or between the disciplined culture of the army and the rebellious appeal of her Internet contacts.

In related work, the National Consortium for the Study of Terrorism and Responses to Terrorism (START) at the University of Maryland has assessed means of deterring insider threat using safety, security, and other systems.[16] Other related areas of interest include identifying attributes most associated with individuals who choose to report possible threat behavior they witness and possibilities for promoting such choices (Bradley et al., 2017).

Another related issue is trust, although the term lacks a universally agreed-upon definition. In economics, trust is understood in the context of a cost-benefit calculation of material gain (or loss), a calculation of the likelihood of defection or mutual cooperation in a bargaining situation. In psychology, by contrast, the concept of trust implies a willingness to be vulnerable to another actor—a specific trustee—whose behavior cannot be controlled or monitored (Dunning, 2018; Mayer, 2018). In general, trust connotes a presumption that the other party will adhere to certain ethical or moral guidelines, whether explicit or implicit. Perceptions of ability, benevolence, and integrity all contribute to a decision about whether to trust an individual, group, organization, or information source (Mayer et al., 1995).

A sizable body of research has examined the dynamics of interpersonal trust, as well as the dynamics of trust within small groups and large organizations (Colquitt et al., 2007). Deception can occur only to the extent that its target—whether an individual or members of a group—is receptive to

---

[15]This model was validated using comparison with measures of workforce ethics derived from a survey and observed level of misconduct. The model suggests that more than 40 percent of actors have the potential to be threats and that organizational climate can affect their decisions in this regard.

[16]See https://www.start.umd.edu [October 2018].

the false, misleading, or even partially true but selectively tailored information provided by the deceiver. That receptivity, in turn, is a function of the target's trust in the information or the information source.

Research Directions

Conduct transdisciplinary research that brings together the disparate threads involved in the study of insider threat.

No single approach has proven sufficient to explain insider threat, so a multidisciplinary research approach is most likely to yield breakthroughs in the ability to identify potential insider threats and deal with this risk. Current research provides valuable insights about the social networks that exist both online and elsewhere. Other work sheds light on the social, cognitive, and psychological processes observable in restrictive organizational cultures, and this work can be applied to settings, such as the IC, where the actors have access to secret information and online communication tools that can be exploited.

One of the limitations of research on insider threat has been that most salient datasets are sampled on the dependent variable: those individuals who have already engaged in sharing secret information. More comprehensive study that includes collecting data on individuals who both do and do not manifest currently recognized markers of risk for becoming an insider threat and analyzing those data together with data on the organizations in which these individuals are embedded could contribute to the development of improved strategies for recognizing these potential risks and deterring risk behaviors. Thus network metrics commonly used in team science research might be insufficient to identify those teams that are at risk for the emergence of an insider threat, but the utility of these metrics could be greatly enhanced if they were combined with work on the dynamics of interpersonal trust and of trust within small groups and large organizations (Colquitt et al., 2007). Doing so may require the development of a transdisciplinary approach in which the intellectual tools of the two disciplines would be formally integrated.

Deception

The potential for insider threat is one reason analysts are concerned with deception and trust, but of course external actors that analysts follow also deceive. They may manipulate intelligence by intentionally introducing information that is false, misleading, or partially true but selectively tailored; they may also introduce errors in logic into information collection channels with the objective of influencing an adversary's judgments and actions (Lowenthal, 2016).[17] The ability to recognize that deception may

---

[17] The use of misinformation as part of an information operation is sometimes referred to as the "four Ds": dismissing a current narrative, sowing distrust or dismay, or distracting the audience with a new narrative (Snegovaya, 2015).

be occurring, to evaluate truthfulness, and to assess credibility is critical for intelligence analysts (and collectors), especially when they are analyzing human-generated source data (e.g., videos, interviews, interrogations) (Heuer, 1999).

Many recent developments related to deception are occurring in the context of cyber activity, the subject of Chapter 6. Here we briefly review the traditional framework for the study of deception and the foundation it provides for intelligence analysis applications. For example, evidence supports the idea that understanding of emotion and nonverbal communication and behavior can be used in detecting deception and assessing credibility (Matsumoto and Hwang, 2018b; Matsumoto et al., 2014c; Novotny et al., 2018; Vrij et al., 2008; Warren et al., 2009). The effects of false information on such phenomena as hate crimes or violent protest have been studied, although the accuracy of predictions has been mixed (Alden and Parker, 2005; Hossain et al., 2018).

Other work points to possibilities for developing markers associated with both veracity and deception that could be used as indicators. Possibilities include verbal (Guitart-Masip et al., 2012), linguistic (Bachenko et al., 2008), and grammatical (Burgoon et al., 2012) markers, as well as eye and body movements (Zhang et al., 2013). Machine learning models are key tools for the development of such indicators: computational modeling is used to identify signals of veracity and deception in narratives, documents, images, videos, and other forms of communication (see, e.g., Bachenko et al., 2008; Burgoon et al., 2012; Hauch et al., 2012, 2015; Matsumoto and Hwang, 2018b; Zhang et al., 2013). It is important to note, however, that cultural understanding is critical to the development of effective indicators, and that pure machine learning models on their own have not been effective at identifying specific emotions that are important for motivation, judgment, and decision making (Hauch et al., 2015; Matsumoto et al., 2015a). More precise analysis of emotions, intentions, and preferences could be valuable to the IC. Similarly, SBS approaches such as the use of discourse analysis to evaluate the linguistic content of speech are needed to provide reliable indicators of tone, honesty, audience, formality, and cognitive decline.

Understanding Complexity

In this chapter, complexity is discussed both as a discipline—the study of complex systems—and as a core challenge for the analyst. Almost by definition, analysts are responsible for making sense of sometimes extraordinarily complex circumstances. Many—perhaps most—of the actors and entities monitored by intelligence analysts are functioning as elements of a system, and perhaps multiple systems; isolated individuals rarely hold significant power, and even seemingly lone actors may be subject to influences not immediately apparent. As discussed earlier in this chapter, as well as in Chapter 4, many of the problems analysts seek to understand are so-called "wicked" problems—ones that are unusually challenging and difficult to define and solve, and that involve complex competing factors that are difficult to reconcile. An example in international affairs is the collapse of the Soviet Union in the 1990s: analysts had no precedents to help them analyze what happens when a Communist superpower disintegrates. Under such volatile circumstances, reliance on previous models, even successful ones, can be particularly dangerous (see Box 5-10).

The general contributions of the study of complex systems were discussed earlier. Here we look more closely at developments in modeling and simulation and in human–systems integration that offer possibilities for intelligence analysis.

Modeling and Simulation

Work in the fields of complexity theory and network systems has clear applications to the analytic challenge of understanding complexity, offering the possibility of measuring, modeling, and interpreting complex phenomena and developments, as well as forecasting change.[18] Scalable high-level network algorithms, for example, have made possible advances in modeling of the relationships between processes and networks. This type of modeling can support analysts in understanding the dynamic nature of systems, and in monitoring the emergence of new phenomena and move-

---

BOX 5-10
Causality and Chance

Unpredictable interactions between causality and chance are a key source of complexity. Unintended developments and chance connections may have powerful consequences that individual humans cannot readily identify in real time. After the fact, for example, observers determined that the Soviet invasion of Afghanistan eventually led to the emergence of Al Qaeda and the attacks of September 11, 2001 (Burke, 2004; Gerges, 2011). In this case, a chance encounter caused members of an Al Qaeda cell to change their plans and travel to Afghanistan, where they met Osama bin Laden and subsequently began to train for the attacks (Atwan, 2008). This is a sequence of events in which both chance and a complex set of existing relationships and related circumstances played key roles.

---

[18]For a detailed discussion of modeling in SBS fields, see Davis et al. (2018).

ments in the international system. Simulations developed in the context of computational social science are supported by data (quantitative, text) from real-world contexts but are also grounded in theory.[19] Such simulations can be tested with real data and modified on the basis of their own results. Simulation has been used in the IC in a number of ways, including forecasting Soviet defense spending (Firth and Noren, 1998), predicting a subject's decision making (Sticha et al., 2005), reasoning about a leader's personality (Sticha et al., 2009), and predicting insider threat (Moore et al., 2011).

Tools for modeling and simulation can help analysts see connections among people, ideas, corporations, and other entities that are components of complex systems (see Box 5-11). These data networks are dynamic and often scale to billions if not trillions of nodes. Analyzing such networks is essential to understanding nonstate actors involved in global affairs, such as terrorist organizations, which often lack fixed organizational structures and constantly adapt to their environment; the emergence of new leaders and changes in power structure; vulnerability in nation-state alliances; and trade and hostility structures (see Box 5-12).

Tools that can be used in mining, analyzing, and visualizing high-dimensional network data (data that capture, for example, not only the substance of discussion but also where and when the discussion occurred, what changes it reflects, or how it is structured) are already available to the IC (Carley et al., 2015). These tools, which include those that can be used for

---

BOX 5-11
Methods for Modeling Complex Systems

Modeling of complex systems generally makes use of four basic methods:

1. Qualitatively assessing a system as complex, drawing on arguments about such characteristics as nonlinearity, competing factors, and multiple stakeholders (see, e.g., Byrne, 2002).
2. Modeling the system as a social network and measuring complexity using network metrics (Estrada et al., 2010).
3. Modeling the system as a high-dimensional dynamic network in which changes at one level can lead to changes at another (Frankenstein et al., 2015).
4. Conducting a simulation (Edmonds, 2005).

---

[19] A model is a representation of a complex phenomenon, such as a system, in which mathematical procedures are used to represent the phenomenon's parameters as accurately as possible; simulation is the use of a model to explore possible outcomes in the case of hypothetical changes.

> **BOX 5-12**
> **Potential Application: Studying Transnational Crime Networks**
>
> Transnational crime networks function through webs of relationships and access to needed resources. They are opportunistic, agile, and manipulative. They can create favorable conditions for their activities by bribing officials, identifying contacts for useful services, or developing dual roles in business and governance. Research involving criminology, economics, and computer science has contributed to growing understanding of these complex networks. For example, Shelley (2014) describes networks of relationships among criminals, officials, and terrorists that enable criminal and terrorist acts, including within the United States. Chayes (2015) demonstrates the dangers to security posed by organized illicit relationships when they are part of patronage networks within governance structures. These dangers can contribute to conflict when the relationships form criminalized power structures (Dziedzic, 2015). Other work has explored the digital drug market (Duxbury and Haynie, 2018), the economics of online crime (Moore et al., 2009), and issues related to Bitcoin and cryptocurrency (Vasek et al., 2014; Hamrick et al., 2018).
>
> More study of the changes, evolutions, and relationship dynamics of transnational criminal networks would yield benefits for national security interests.
>
> SOURCE: Excerpted from Mendosa (2017).

both modeling and simulation,[20] have been applied to such security-related challenges as deterrence of violent behavior (Davis, 2014), the settlement of Syrian refugees (Hattle et al., 2016), and the relationship between European Union policies on immigration and subsequent refugee crises (Melis, 2001).

Despite advances in this area and the increasing use of simulation by the Department of Defense and the IC, however, no one approach has yet proven adequate to the challenge of modeling complex real-world situations. For example, the Defense Advanced Research Project Agency's (DARPA's) Integrated Crisis Early Warning System did lead to a series of integrated, geographically based models for forecasting crises (Ward et al., 2012). But the strength of these models was that, using machine algorithms, they could assess change in the level of a critical event and the likelihood that another, similar event would occur in a region; the models could not forecast entirely unusual events, such as the Syrian refugee crisis. One of the key outcomes of this modeling effort, however, was an event database that can support future modeling efforts (Ward et al., 2013).

---

[20]These include agent-based (Bonabeau, 2002; Davidsson, 2002; Van Dam et al., 2012) and agent-based dynamic-network models (e.g., Morgan et al., 2017); event-history models (Box-Steffensmeier, 2004); and system dynamic models (Mohaghegh et al., 2009; Sterman, 2001).

Society-level modeling is not yet fully developed for several reasons. First, this type of modeling is resource-intensive: it typically requires very large datasets that require careful cleaning and archiving. Thus the development of such models is quite time-consuming. At a theoretical level, moreover, existing models cannot readily handle multilevel systems, such as systems relevant to the IC in which individuals, organizations, and states interact, each affecting the behavior, learning, and adaptation of the others. In general, the more tuned to a specific problem a model is, the more costly it is to develop but the more informative are its results. Thus, models that accurately depict circumstances at the cognitive and task levels do not scale to the community or even large-group level. The reverse is also true: models that are informative about populations are inaccurate at the cognitive level.

Dynamic network modeling helps bridge this gap, as does modeling of social cognition (Morgan et al., 2017). However, models offering true multilevel accuracy and scalability do not yet exist; most simulation models are one-off. Efforts to develop testbeds that can support reuse and model integration have failed for reasons that include overly constraining components; premature ontologies; lack of support for multiple timeframes, spatial frames, and procedural frames; forced validation using inappropriate validation theory; and difficulties in creating and maintaining a comprehensive database for all component models.

Another issue is that validation methods for simulations of social systems are still in their infancy.[21] Methods for modeling uncertainty and validating results developed in other contexts (Schefzik et al., 2013; Slotte and Smørgrav, 2008) do not readily transfer to social simulation models, which must include hundreds of variables and have many sources of nonlinearity. Many societal-level simulations, moreover, are centered on events for which there are no historical analogs, so that past data cannot readily be used for validation purposes. Thus while the science of validation is well developed for models of physical systems (Sargent, 2013), such is not the case for social simulation models.

In response to these challenges, researchers in the field are moving toward hybrid modeling and a "system of systems" approach that makes use of interoperable models (models designed to interface with one another). A key advantage of these models is that they make gaps in the underlying theories explicit; support comparison, integration, and development of theories; and allow users to create a framework with which they can rapidly reason about alternative explanations (useful forensically) or alternative

---

[21]We note that the DARPA SocialSim program has the potential to promote improved models of social behavior and new testbeds and integration platforms in which diverse models can be linked together, tested, and evaluated; see https://www.darpa.mil/program/computational-simulation-of-online-social-behavior [October 2018].

courses of action (useful for planning) (Gilbert and Troitzsch, 2005). Yet while hybrid models are increasingly being used to link micro-, meso- and macro-level processes (such as those at the individual, organization, and state levels), such models are still difficult to reuse, take a long time to develop, may require massive amounts of data that need to be cleaned and fused. Generating the data needed for realistically sized, complex sociotechnical systems also takes a long time.

Computer simulation requires extensive resources, person power, and time. The Pentagon has those prerequisites, and so has been able to make good use of computer simulations over the years to predict the military responses of adversaries and to reason about other state and nonstate actors (National Research Council, 2008). Because of the rate of change in problems faced by the IC and the resources available, however, the IC's use of computer simulation has been more limited. Before the IC can use computer simulation more extensively, the field will have to mature, the requirements will have to become less onerous, and the IC will have to invest in the needed research.

Application of Human–Systems Integration

Research in the field of human–systems integration (discussed in greater detail in Chapter 7) considers the integration of humans with technology in the context of a rich sociotechnical system (National Research Council, 2007). This research relies on methods for understanding a system at multiple levels and the interactions within and between those levels. Research in this area has led to the development of methods for understanding and modeling complex sociotechnical systems (Waterson et al., 2015). Agent-based models are another example of this approach (see, e.g., Sun, 2006). Methods developed to understand particular system levels (e.g., the team level) can be extended to the analysis of other levels (Cooke and Gorman, 2009). Nonetheless, these methods are often tedious and time-consuming, and research is therefore needed to develop human–systems integration methods that allow for real-time monitoring and automatic analysis of a system at all levels (Gorman et al., 2012). This research direction is promising not only for work on human–systems integration but also as an aid to the IC in understanding complex sociotechnical systems, subtle interactions within those systems, and possible unintended consequences.

CONCLUSIONS

The work explored in this chapter demonstrates the potential of SBS research to deepen, strengthen, and enhance the accuracy of intelligence analysis. We have examined a large and growing body of work that is interdisciplinary, draws on multiple methods, and makes use of new types of data (especially data captured from cyberspace).

The examples we have discussed illustrate how basic research provides a theoretical and empirical foundation for the development of sophisticated analysis methods. For example, accurate computer modeling of complex, sophisticated sociopolitical systems rests on foundational understanding of the nature of status and power, socioemotional processes, and linguistic structures. The potential for developing such tools and approaches rests on the marriage of technological advances and insights from SBS fields. Examples include the use of digital trace data to assess the importance of network nodes that pose potential security threats or to track the trajectory of political ideas, the use of understanding of how nonverbal cues can enhance the power and influence of political messages to assess such messages, and the application of traditional techniques of narrative analysis to machine computational analysis of discourse among social media groups.

Sophisticated methods such as computational analysis of large datasets would make little sense without theoretical frameworks to guide the development of algorithms, such as those for classification of narrative structures or analysis of the functioning of social networks. Similarly, insights from SBS research are important to guide the development of implementable indicators of, for example, potentially consequential emotional states or changes in leaders or other powerful actors, the developing strength of a minority group's message, or the cohesiveness of networks in which toxic narratives are spreading.

> CONCLUSION 5-1: Developing research on narratives, social networks, complex systems, and affect and emotion can enhance understanding of primary targets of intelligence analysis, the potential impact of actions taken by the Intelligence Community, and individual and social processes relevant to security threats. This research offers possibilities for new tools, including but not limited to
>
> - indicators for use in monitoring and detection of key security-related developments;
> - algorithms for extracting meaning from large quantities of open-source information; and
> - models for reasoning about the potential implications of various interventions or activities.

There is considerable variation in how directly SBS research has been applied to questions of interest to the IC, in how close it is to providing the basis for practical application for analysts, and in the aspects of intelligence analysis it could potentially support. Tools for social network analysis, for example, are close to being operational, and simulation groups within the IC are using models to address complex situations. Research on other tools, such as those based on understanding of unconscious behavior and nonverbal cues, is still emerging. Nonetheless, existing SBS research provides the basis for a forward-looking program of interdisciplinary research aimed directly at leveraging developments in theory, understanding, and technology to support the work of the intelligence analyst at a time when the nature of threats to security is evolving.

Further progress in the development of applications that can serve the IC's needs will depend on interdisciplinary collaboration. For example, the integration of recent advances in analysis of narratives, networks, and affect would provide a framework for supporting dramatic advances in the assessment of narratives and counternarratives, early detection of polarization, assessment of group vulnerability to disinformation, and detection and mitigation of diverse information maneuvers. Similarly, applying multidisciplinary, multimethods research to IC issues from a complexity perspective—using modeling and simulation, representation, and understanding of human factors—would yield significantly stronger methods of forecasting surprising events or developments.

Advances in the use of large-scale data are likely to be at the heart of significant developments for the IC in the coming decade, but new technologies will be only as strong as the understanding of the human behaviors they are used to model or explain. The committee anticipates progress in the development and validation of computational models, the reuse of simulation modes, and the integration of social networks with computational models, advances with the potential to enable near-real-time assessment of competing actors, messages, or groups and the interventions that influence them.

CONCLUSION 5-2: Interdisciplinary, multimethod approaches to integrating insights from social and behavior sciences fields with sophisticated technological developments will be essential to support the development of new tools for the analysis and interpretation of data and intelligence. The Intelligence Community would benefit from pursuing a portfolio of such research focused on the development of operational methods and tools.

REFERENCES

Alden, H.L., and Parker, K.F. (2005). Gender role ideology, homophobia and hate crime: Linking attitudes to macro-level, anti-gay, and lesbian hate crimes. *Deviant Behavior*, 26(4), 321–343.

Algesheimer, R., Dholakia, U.M., and Herrmann, A. (2005). The social influence of brand community: Evidence from European car clubs. *Journal of Marketing*, 69(3), 19–34.

Anderson, P. (1999). Perspective: Complexity theory and organization science. *Organization Science, 10*(3), 216–232.
Anguelov, N., and Kaschel, T. (2017). Toward quantifying soft power: The impact of the proliferation of information technology on governance in the Middle East. *Palgrave Communications, 3*, art. 17016. Available: https://www.nature.com/articles/palcomms201716 [December 2018].
Annesley-Mair, G. (2016). *How Do Images of Female Jihad Challenge and Reinforce Narratives Surrounding Women's Agency in Terrorist Violence in the Areas Occupied by the Islamic State of Iraq and Syria?* Available: http://hummedia.manchester.ac.uk/schools/soss/politics/conference/Grace%20Annesley-Mair%20-%20How%20do%20images%20of%20female%20jihad%20challenge%20and%20reinforce%20narratives%20surrounding%20women%E2%80%99s%20agency%20in.pdf [February 2019].
Atwan, A.B. (2008). *The Secret History of Al Qaeda*. Berkeley: University of California Press.
Bachenko, J., Fitzpatrick, E., and Schonwetter. M. (2008). Verification and implementation of language-based deception indicators in civil and criminal narratives. In *Proceedings of the 22nd International Conference on Computational Linguistics* (vol. 1, pp. 41–48). Stroudsburg, PA: Association for Computational Linguistics. Available: http://www.aclweb.org/anthology/C08-1006 [February 2019].
Bar-tal, D., Halperin, E., and De Rivera, J. (2007). Collective emotions in conflict situations: Societal implications. *Journal of Social Issues, 63*(2), 441–460.
Bartels, D.M., and Johnson, E.J. (2015). Connecting cognition and consumer choice. *Cognition, 135*, 47–51. doi:10.1016/j.cognition.2014.11.024.
Bar-Yam, Y. (2002). General features of complex systems. In *Encyclopedia of Life Support Systems (EOLSS)*. Oxford, UK: UNESCO.
Bechara, A., Damasio, H., and Damasio, A.R. (2000). Emotion, decision making, and the orbitofrontal cortex. *Cerebral Cortex, 10*(3), 295–307.
Bodine-Baron, E., Helmus, T.C., Magnuson, M., and Winkelman, Z. (2016). *Examining ISIS Support and Opposition Networks on Twitter*. Santa Monica, CA: RAND. Available: https://www.rand.org/pubs/research_reports/RR1328.html [February 2019].
Bonabeau, E. (2002). Agent-based modeling: Methods and techniques for simulating human systems. *Proceedings of the National Academy of Sciences of the United States of America, 99*(Suppl. 3), 7280–7287.
Bonacich, P. (1987). Power and centrality: A family of measures. *American Journal of Sociology, 92*(5), 1170–1182.
Borgatti, S.P. (2002). The key player problem. *SSRN*. doi:10.2139/ssrn.1149843.
Borgatti, S.P., and Foster, P.C. (2003). The network paradigm in organizational research: A review and typology. *Journal of Management, 29*(6), 991–1013.
Borgatti, S.P., Mehra, A., Brass, D.J., and Labianca, G. (2009). Network analysis in the social sciences. *Science, 323*(5916), 892–895.
Box-Steffensmeier, J.M. (2004). *Event History Modeling: A Guide for Social Scientists*. New York: Cambridge University Press.
Bradley, P., Chambers, W., Davenport, C., and Saner, L. (2017). *A National Research Agenda on Insider Threat*. Available: https://sites.nationalacademies.org/cs/groups/dbassesite/documents/webpage/dbasse_179892.pdf [December 2018].
Brandes, U., Lerner, J., and Snijders, T.A.B. (2009). Networks evolving step by step: Statistical analysis of dyadic event data. In *2009 International Conference on Advances in Social Network Analysis and Mining*. Institute of Electrical and Electronics Engineers. doi:10.1109/ASONAM.2009.28.
Brass, D.J. (1992). Power in organizations: A social network perspective. *Research in Politics and Society, 4*, 295–323.

Brass, D.J., Galaskiewicz, J., Greve, H.R., and Tsai, W. (2004). Taking stock of networks and organizations: A multilevel perspective. *Academy of Management Journal*, 47(6), 795–817.

Brevini, B., Hintz, A., and McCurdy, P. (2013). *Beyond WikiLeaks: Implications for the Future of Communications, Journalism and Society*. London, UK: Palgrave Macmillan.

Brosch, T., Scherer, K.R., Grandjean, D., and Sander, D. (2013). The impact of emotion on perception, attention, memory, and decision-making. *Swiss Medical Weekly*, 143, w13786. doi:10.4414/smw.2013.13786.

Brown, S.L., and Eisenhardt, K.M. (1997). The art of continuous change: Linking complexity theory and time-paced evolution in relentlessly shifting organizations. *Administrative Science Quarterly*, 42(1), 1–34.

Burgoon, J.K., Hamel, L., and Qin, T. (2012). Predicting veracity from linguistic indicators. In *2012 European Intelligence and Security Informatics Conference*. Institute of Electrical and Electronics Engineers. doi:10.1109/EISIC.2012.21.

Burke, J. (2004). *Al-Qaeda: The True Story of Radical Islam*. New York: I.B. Tauris.

Butts, C.T. (2008). A relational event framework for social action. *Sociological Methodology*, 38(1), 155–200.

Byrne, D. (2002). *Complexity Theory and the Social Sciences: An Introduction*. London, UK: Routledge.

Camerer, C. (2003). *Behavioral Game Theory Experiments in Strategic Interaction*. Princeton, NJ: Princeton University Press.

Campedelli, G.M., Cruickshank I., and Carley K.M. (2018). Complex networks for terrorist target prediction. In R. Thomson, C. Dancy, A. Hyder, and H. Bisgin (Eds.), *Social, Cultural, and Behavioral Modeling. SBP-BRiMS 2018. Lecture Notes in Computer Science* (Vol. 10899). Basel, Switzerland: Springer, Cham.

Cappelli, D.M., Moore, A.P., and Trzeciak, R.F. (2012). *The CERT Guide to Insider Threats: How to Prevent, Detect, and Respond to Information Technology Crimes (Theft, Sabotage, Fraud)*. Westford, MA: Pearson Education.

Carley, K.M. (1986). Knowledge acquisition as a social phenomenon. *Instructional Science*, 14(3–4), 381–438.

Carley, K.M. (2003). Dynamic network analysis. In National Research Council (Ed.), *Dynamic Social Network Modeling and Analysis: Workshop Summary and Papers*. Washington, DC: The National Academies Press.

Carley, K.M., and Morgan, G.P. (2016). Inadvertent leaks: Exploration via agent-based dynamic network simulation. *Journal of Computational & Mathematical Organization Theory*, 22(3), 288–317.

Carley, K.M., and Prietula, M.J. (1993). Plural-soar: Towards the development of a cognitively motivated theory of organizations. In *Proceedings of the 1993 Coordination Theory and Collaboration Technology Workshop*. Available: http://www.academia.edu/24920625/Plural-Soar_A_Prolegomenon_to_Artificial_Agents_and_Organizational_Behavior [February 2019].

Carley, K., Lee, J.-S., and Krackhardt, D. (2001). Destabilizing networks. *Connections*, 24(3), 31–32.

Carley, K.M., Fridsma, D., Casman, E., Yahja, A., Altman, N., Chen, L.-C., Kaminsky, B., and Nave, D. (2006). BioWar: Scalable agent-based model of bioattacks. *IEEE Transactions on Systems, Man and Cybernetics-Part A*, 36(2), 252–265.

Carley, K.M., Martin, M.K., and Hirshman, B.R. (2009). The etiology of social change. *Topics in Cognitive Science*, 1(4), 621–650. doi:10.1111/j.1756-8765.2009.01037.x.

Carley, K.M., Wei, W., and Joseph, K. (2015). High dimensional network analytics: Mapping topic networks in Twitter data during the Arab Spring. In S. Cui, A. Hero, Z.-Q. Luo, and J. Moura (Eds.), *Big Data Over Networks* (pp. 278–299). Cambridge, UK: Cambridge University Press.

Carrington, P.J. (2011). Crime and social network analysis. In J. Scott and P.J. Carrington (Eds.), *The SAGE Handbook of Social Network Analysis* (pp. 236-255). Thousand Oaks, CA: SAGE.

Carrington, P.J., Scott, J., and Wasserman, S. (2005). *Models and Methods in Social Network Analysis*. Cambridge, UK: Cambridge University Press.

Cartmill, E.A., and Goldin-Meadow, S. (2016). Gesture. In D. Matsumoto, H.C. Hwang, and M.G. Frank (Eds.), *APA Handbook of Nonverbal Communication* (pp. 307-333). Washington, DC: American Psychological Association.

Casey, W., Morales, J.A., Wright, E., Zhu, Q., and Mishra, B. (2016). Compliance signaling games: Toward modeling the deterrence of insider threats. *Computational and Mathematical Organization Theory*, 22(3), 318-349.

Chambers, W. (2017). *Predicting Terrorist Attacks by Automating Integrative Complexity* [White Paper]. Available: http://sites.nationalacademies.org/cs/groups/dbassesite/documents/webpage/dbasse_179901.pdf [February 2019].

Chan, H., Akoglu, L., and Tong, H. (2014). Make it or break it: Manipulating robustness in large networks. In *Proceedings of the 2014 SIAM International Conference on Data Mining* (pp. 325-333). doi:10.1137/1.9781611973440.37.

Chayes, S. (2015). *Thieves of State: Why Corruption Threatens Global Security*. New York: W.W. Norton & Co.

Christakis, N.A., and James, F.H. (2011). *Connected: The Surprising Power of Our Social Networks and How They Shape Our Lives—How Your Friends' Friends' Friends Affect Everything You Feel, Think, and Do*. Boston, MA: Back Bay Books.

Cialdini, R.B. (1984). *Influence: How and Why People Agree to Things*. New York: William Morrow & Co.

Cialdini, R.B., and Goldstein, N.J. (2004). Social influence: Compliance and conformity. *Annual Reviews of Psychology*, 55, 591-621. doi:10.1146/annurev.psych.55.090902.142015.

Colby, K.M., Watt, J.B., and Gilbert, J.P. (1966). A computer method of psychotherapy: Preliminary communication. *Journal of Nervous and Mental Disease*, 142(2), 148-152.

Colquitt, J.A., Scott, B.A., and LePine, J.A. (2007). Trust, trustworthiness, and trust propensity: A meta-analytic test of their unique relationships with risk taking and job performance. *Journal of Applied Psychology*, 92(4), 909-927.

Colwill, C. (2009). Human factors in information security: The insider threat—who can you trust these days? *Information Security Technical Report*, 14(4), 186-196.

Contractor, N.S., and DeChurch, L.A. (2014). Integrating social networks and human social motives to achieve social influence at scale. *Proceedings of the National Academy of Sciences of the United States of America*, 111(Suppl. 4), 13650-13657.

Contractor, N., Monge, P., and Leonardi, P. (2011). Multidimensional networks and the dynamics of sociomateriality: Bringing technology inside the network. *International Journal of Communication*, 5(1), 682-720.

Cooke, N.J., and Gorman, J.C. (2009). Interaction-based measures of cognitive systems. *Journal of Cognitive Engineering and Decision Making*, 3(1), 27-46.

Cosmides, L., and Tooby, J. (2000). Evolutionary psychology and the emotions. In M. Lewis and J.M. Haviland-Jones (Eds.), *Handbook of Emotions* (2nd ed., pp. 91-115). New York: Guilford Press.

Crane, A. (2005). In the company of spies: When competitive intelligence gathering becomes industrial espionage. *Business Horizons*, 48(3), 233-240.

Davidson, R.J., Scherer, K.R., and Goldsmith, H.H. (2002). *Handbook of Affective Sciences*. Oxford, UK: Oxford University Press.

Davidsson, P. (2002). Agent-based social simulation: A computer science view. *Journal of Artificial Societies and Social Simulation*, 5(1), 1-7.

Davis, P.K. (2014). *Toward Theory for Dissuasion (or Deterrence) by Denial: Using Simple Cognitive Models of the Adversary to Inform Strategy*. Santa Monica, CA: RAND.

Davis, P.K., O'Mahony, A., Gulden, T.R., Osoba, O., and Sieck, K. (2018). *Priority Challenges for Social and Behavioral Research and Its Modeling*. Santa Monica, CA: RAND.
de Mesquita, B.B. (1998). The end of the cold war: Predicting an emergent property. *The Journal of Conflict Resolution, 42*(2), 131–155.
Delre, S.A., Jager, W., and Janssen, M.A. (2007). Diffusion dynamics in small-world networks with heterogeneous consumers. *Computational and Mathematical Organization Theory, 13*(2), 185–202.
Dempsey, N., Bramley, G., Power, S., and Brown, C. (2011). The social dimension of sustainable development: Defining urban social sustainability. *Sustainable Development, 19*(5), 289–300.
Diesner, J., and Carley, K. (2011). Semantic networks. In *Encyclopedia of Social Networks* (Vol. 1) (pp. 767–769). Thousand Oaks, CA: SAGE.
Dunning, D. (2018). *Interpersonal Trust: Current Findings and Mysteries*. Presentation submitted to the Committee on a Decadal Survey of Social and Behavioral Sciences and Applications to National Security, National Academies of Sciences, Engineering, and Medicine. Available: https://vimeo.com/258003972 [February 2019].
Duxbury, S.W., and Haynie, D.L. (2018). Building them up, breaking them down: Topology, vendor selection patterns, and a digital drug market's robustness to disruption. *Social Networks, 52*, 238–250. doi:10.1016/j.socnet.2017.09.002.
Dziedzic, M. (Ed.). (2015). *Criminalized Power Structures: The Overlooked Enemies of Peace*. London, UK: Rowman & Littlefield.
Edmonds, B. (2005). Simulation and complexity—how they can relate. In V. Feldmann and K. Mühlfeld (Eds.), *Virtual Worlds of Precision—Computer-based Simulations in the Sciences and Social Sciences* (pp. 5–32). Münster, Germany: Lit Verlag.
Edwards, G. (2010). *Mixed-Method Approaches to Social Network Analysis*. Ecomonic & Social Research Council National Centre for Research Methods. Available: http://eprints.ncrm.ac.uk/842/1/Social_Network_analysis_Edwards.pdf [December 2018].
Elder, R.J., Levis, A.H., and Yousefi, B. (2015). Alternatives to cyber warfare: Deterrence and assurance. In S. Jajodia, P. Shakarian, V.S. Subrahmanian, V. Swarup, and C. Wang (Eds.), *Cyber Warfare: Building the Scientific Foundation* (ch. 2, pp. 15–35). Basel, Switzerland: Springer, Cham. Available: https://doi.org/10.1007/978-3-319-14039-1.
Elfenbein, H.A., and Ambady, N. (2002). Is there an in-group advantage in emotion recognition? *Psychology Bulletin, 128*(2), 243–249.
Estrada, E., Fox, M., Higham, D.J., and Oppo, G.L. (2010). *Network Science: Complexity in Nature and Technology*. London, UK: Springer.
Etzioni, O., Cafarella, M., Downey, D., Popescu, A.M., Shaked, T., Soderland, S., Weld, D.S., and Yates, A. (2005). Unsupervised named-entity extraction from the web: An experimental study. *Artificial Intelligence, 165*(1), 91–134.
Eubank, S., Guclu, H., Kumar, V.S.A., Marathe, M.V., Srinivasan, A., Toroczkai, Z., and Wang, N. (2004). Modelling disease outbreaks in realistic urban social networks. *Nature, 429*(6988), 180–184.
Farley, J.D. (2003). Breaking Al Qaeda cells: A mathematical analysis of counterterrorism operations (a guide for risk assessment and decision making). *Studies in Conflict and Terrorism, 26*(6), 399–411.
Firth, N.E., and Noren, J.H. (1998). *Soviet Defense Spending: A History of CIA Estimates, 1950–1990* (Vol. 58). Houston: Texas A&M University Press.
Fiske, S.T., Xu, J., and Cuddy, A.C. (1999). (Dis)respecting versus (dis)liking: Status and interdependence predict ambivalent stereotypes of competence and warmth. *Journal of Social Issues, 55*(3), 473–489.

Fiske, S.T., Cuddy, A.J., Glick, P., and Xu, J. (2002). A model of (often mixed) stereotype content: Competence and warmth respectively follow from perceived status and competition. *Journal of Personality and Social Psychology, 82*(6), 878–902.

Flake, G.W. (1998). *The Computational Beauty of Nature: Computer Explorations of Fractals, Chaos, Complex Systems, and Adaptation.* Cambridge, MA: MIT Press.

Flew, T. (2016). Entertainment media, cultural power, and post-globalization: The case of China's international media expansion and the discourse of soft power. *Global Media and China, 1*(4), 278–294.

Flum, J., and Crohe, M. (2006). *Parameterized Complexity Theory.* Berlin/Heidelberg, Germany: Springer.

Frankenstein, W., Mezzour, G., Carley, K.M., and Carley, L.R. (2015). Remote assessment of countries' nuclear, biological, and cyber capabilities: Joint motivation and latent capability approach. *Social Network Analysis and Mining, 5*(1), 1–21.

Freeman, L.C. (2004). *The Development of Social Network Analysis: A Study in the Sociology of Science.* Vancouver, BC: Empirical Press.

Friedkin, N.E. (2006). *A Structural Theory of Social Influence.* Cambridge, UK: Cambridge University Press.

Gerges, F.A. (2011). *The Rise and Fall of Al-Qaeda.* Oxford, UK: Oxford University Press.

Gigerenzer, G., and Selten, R. (2002). *Bounded Rationality: The Adaptive Toolbox.* Cambridge, MA: MIT Press.

Gilbert, N., and Troitzsch, K.G. (2005). *Simulation for the Social Scientist.* London, UK: Open University Press.

Gilchrist, A. (2009). *The Well-Connected Community (Second Edition): A Networking Approach to Community Development.* Bristol, UK: Bristol University Press.

Gill, P. (2016). *Lone Actor Terrorists: A Behavioural Analysis.* New York: Routledge.

Gill, P., Silver, J., Horgan, J., and Corner, E. (2017). Shooting alone: The pre-attack experiences and behaviors of U.S. solo mass murderers. *Journal of Forensic Sciences, 62*(3), 710–714.

Golbeck, J., and Hendler, J. (2004). Accuracy of metrics for inferring trust and reputation in semantic web-based social networks. In *EKAW 2004: Engineering Knowledge in the Age of the Semantic Web* (pp. 116–131). Berlin/Heidelberg, Germany: Springer.

Goodall, H.L., Cheong, P.H., Fleischer, K., and Corman, S.R. (2012). Rhetorical charms: The promise and pitfalls of humor and ridicule as strategies to counter extremist narrative. *Perspectives on Terrorism, 6*(1), 70–80.

Gorman, J.C., Hessler, E.E., Amazeen, P.G., Cooke, N.J., and Shope, S.M. (2012). Dynamical analysis in real time: Detecting perturbations to team communication. *Ergonomics, 55*(8), 825–839.

Graham, J.M., and Carley, K.C. (2006). Dynamic network analysis in information operations: A process for near real-time assessment of atmospherics, socio-political landscape and leverage points. In *Proceedings of National Security Methods Conference.* Santa Monica, CA: RAND.

Grix, J., and Houlihan, B. (2014). Sports mega-events as part of a nation's soft power strategy: The cases of Germany (2006) and the UK (2012). *The British Journal of Politics and International Relations, 16*(4), 572–596.

Gross, J.J. (2007). *Handbook of Emotion Regulation.* New York: Guilford Press.

Grosser, T.J., and Borgatti, S.P. (2013). Network theory/social network analysis. In R.J. McGee and R.L. Warms (Eds.), *Theory in Social and Cultural Anthropology* (pp. 595–597). Thousand Oaks, CA: SAGE.

Guitart-Masip, M., Huys, Q.J., Fuentemilla, L., Dayan, P., Duzel, E., and Dolan, R.J. (2012). Go and no-go learning in reward and punishment: Interactions between affect and effect. *Neuroimage, 62*(1), 154–166.

Gurski, P. (2015). *The Threat from Within: Recognizing Al Qaeda-Inspired Radicalization and Terrorism in the West*. London, UK: Rowman & Littlefield.
Hafner-Burton, E., Kahler, M., and Montgomery, A. (2009). Network analysis for international relations. *International Organization, 63*(3), 559–592.
Halperin, E. (2008). Group-based hatred in intractable conflict in Israel. *Journal of Conflict Resolution, 52*(5), 713–736.
Halperin, E., and Gross, J.J. (2011). Intergroup anger in intractable conflict: Long-term sentiments predict anger responses during the Gaza war. *Group Processes and Intergroup Relations, 14*(4), 477–488.
Halperin, E., and Pliskin, R. (2015). Emotions and emotion regulation in intractable conflict: Studying emotional processes within a unique context. *Political Psychology, 36*(Suppl. 1), 119–150.
Halperin, E., Russell, A.G., Trzesniewski, K.H., Gross, J.J., and Dweck, C.S. (2011). Promoting the Middle East peace process by changing beliefs about group malleability. *Science, 333*(6050), 1767–1769.
Halverson, J.R., Goodall, H.L., Jr., and Corman, S.R. (2011). *Master Narratives of Islamist Extremism*. New York: Palgrave Macmillan.
Hamrick, J.T., Rouhi, F., Mukherjee, A., Feder, A., Gandal, N., Moore, T., and Vasek, M. (2018). The *Economics of Cryptocurrency Pump and Dump Schemes*. Available: https://ssrn.com/abstract=3303365 [February 2019]. doi:10.2139/ssrn.3303365.
Hancock, J.T., Curry, L.E., Goorha, S., and Woodworth, M. (2007). On lying and being lied to: A linguistic analysis of deception in computer-mediated communication. *Discourse Processes, 45*(1), 1–23.
Harary, F. (1969). *Graph Theory*. Reading, MA: Addison-Wesley.
Hattle, A., Yang, K.S., and Zeng, S. (2016). Modeling the Syrian refugee crisis with agents and systems. *The UMAP Journal, 37*(2), 195–213.
Hauch, V., Blandón-Gitlin, I., Masip, J., and Sporer, S. (2012). Linguistic cues to deception assessed by computer programs: A meta-analysis. In E. Fitzpatrick, J. Bachenko, and T. Fornaciari (Eds.), *Proceedings of the Workshop on Computational Approaches to Deception Detection* (pp. 1–4). Stroudsburg, PA: Association for Computational Linguistics. Available: http://www.aclweb.org/anthology/W12-0401 [February 2019].
Hauch, V., Blandón-Gitlin, I., Masip, J., and Sporer, S.L. (2015). Are computers effective lie detectors? A meta-analysis of linguistic cues to deception. *Personality and Social Psychology Review, 19*(4), 307–342.
Heard, N.A., Weston, D.J., Platanioti, K., and Hand, D.J. (2010). Bayesian anomaly detection methods for social networks. *Annals of Applied Statistics, 4*(2), 645–662.
Herbig, P., Milewicz, J., and Golden, J. (1994). A model of reputation building and destruction. *Journal of Business Research, 31*(1), 23–31. doi:10.1016/0148-2963(94)90042-6.
Heuer, R.J. (1999). *Psychology of Intelligence Analysis*. Washington, DC: Center for the Study of Intelligence. Available: https://www.cia.gov/library/center-for-the-study-of-intelligence/csi-publications/books-and-monographs/psychology-of-intelligence-analysis/PsychofIntel-New.pdf [December 2018].
Horgan, J. (2008). From profiles to pathways and roots to routes: Perspectives from psychology on radicalization into terrorism. *Annals of the American Academy of Political and Social Science, 618*(1), 80–94.
Horgan, J. (2014). *The Psychology of Terrorism*. New York: Routledge.
Horgan, J., Kenney, M., Horne, C., Vining, P., Carley, K. M., Bigrigg, M., Bloom, M., and Braddock, K. (2014). Competitive adaptation in terrorist networks: Preliminary findings from an Islamist case study. In A. Stedmon and G. Lawson (Eds.), *Counter-terrorism & Hostile Intent: Human Factors Theory and Application*. London, UK: Ashgate.

Hossain, K.S.M., Gao, S., Kennedy, B., Galstyan, A., and Natarajan, P. (2018). Forecasting violent events in the Middle East and North Africa using the Hidden Markov Model and regularized autoregressive models. *The Journal of Defense Modeling and Simulation*, 1–15. doi:10.1177/1548512918814698.

Huang, B., and Carley, K.M. (2018). Location order recovery in trails with low temporal resolution. In *IEEE Transactions on Network Science and Engineering*. Institute of Electrical and Electronics Engineers. doi:10.1109/TNSE.2018.2871783.

Huang, L., Joseph, A.D., Nelson, B., Rubinstein, B.I.P., and Tygar, J.D. (2011). Adversarial machine learning. In *AISec '11 Proceedings of the 4th ACM Workshop on Security and Artificial Intelligence* (pp. 43–58). New York: Association for Computing Machinery.

Hwang, H.C., and Matsumoto, D. (2016). Facial expressions. In *APA Handbook of Nonverbal Communication* (pp. 257–287). Washington, DC: American Psychological Association.

Irvin, J.A., and Charney, D.L. (2014). Stopping the next Snowden: The problem isn't that he could. It's that he wanted to. *Politico Magazine*, March 25. Available: https://www.politico.com/magazine/story/2014/03/stopping-next-edward-snowden-105004 [February 2019].

Johnson, J.C. (1994). Anthropological contributions to the study of social networks: A review. In S. Wasserman and J. Galaskiewicz (Eds.), *Advances in Social Network Analysis* (pp. 113–151). Thousand Oaks, CA: SAGE.

Johnson, M.E., and Dynes, S. (2007). Inadvertent disclosure: Information leaks in the extended enterprise. *Proceedings of the Sixth Workshop on the Economics of Information Security*, Carnegie Mellon University, June 7–8. Available: https://www.econinfosec.org/archive/weis2007/papers/43.pdf [February 2019].

Johnson, N., and Brown, W.B. (1986). The dissemination and use of innovative knowledge. *The Journal of Product Innovation Management*, 3(2), 127–135.

Joseph, K., Wei, W., Benigni, M., and Carley, K.M. (2016). A social-event based approach to sentiment analysis of identities and behaviors in text. *The Journal of Mathematical Sociology*, 40(3), 137–166.

Kahn, D.T., Liberman, V., Halperin, E., and Ross, L. (2016). Intergroup sentiments, political identity, and their influence on responses to potentially ameliorative proposals in the context of an intractable conflict. *Journal of Conflict Resolution*, 60(1), 61–88.

Kahneman, D., and Tversky, A. (1979). Prospect theory: An analysis of decision under risk. *Econometrica*, 47(2), 263–291.

Kas, M., Carley, K.M., and Carley, L.R. (2013). Incremental closeness centrality for dynamically changing social networks. In *Proceedings of the 2013 IEEE/ACM International Conference on Advances in Social Networks Analysis and Mining (ASONAM 2013)* (pp. 33–40). Institute of Electrical and Electronics Engineers. doi:10.1109/ASONAM.2013.6785863.

Kaufer, D.S., and Carley, K.M. (1993). *Communication at a Distance: The Influence of Print on Sociocultural Organization and Change*. Hillsdale, NJ: Lawrence Erlbaum Associates.

Keltner, D., and Haidt, J. (1999). Social functions of emotions at four levels of analysis. *Cognition and Emotion*, 13(5), 505–521.

Kerbel, J. (2015). The complexity challenge: The U.S. government's struggle to keep up with the times. *The National Interest*, August 26. Available: https://nationalinterest.org/feature/the-complexity-challenge-the-us-governments-struggle-keep-13698 [December 2018].

Knox, P., and Pinch, S. (2010). *Urban Social Geography: An Introduction*. London, UK: Pearson Education Limited.

Kruglanski, A.W., and Fishman, S. (2006). Terrorism between "syndrome" and "tool." *Current Directions in Psychological Science*, 15(1), 45–48.

Lanham, M.J., Morgan, G.P., and Carley, K.M. (2014). Social network modeling and agent-based simulation in support of crisis de-escalation. *IEEE Transactions on Systems, Man, and Cybernetics: Systems*, 44(1), 103–110.

Larson, D.W., and Shevchenko, A. (2010). Status seekers: Chinese and Russian responses to U.S. primacy. *International Security*, 34(4), 63–95.

Larson, D.W., and Shevchenko, A. (2014a). Managing rising powers: The role of status concerns. In D. Welch Larson, T.V. Paul, and W.C. Wohlforth (Eds.), *Status in World Politics* (pp. 33–57). Cambridge, UK: Cambridge University Press.

Larson, D.W., and Shevchenko, A. (2014b). Russia says no: Power, status, and emotions in foreign policy. *Communist and Post-Communist Studies*, 47(3–4), 269–279.

Laurence, J. (2009). The effect of ethnic diversity and community disadvantage on social cohesion: A multi-level analysis of social capital and interethnic relations in UK communities. *European Sociological Review*, 27(1), 70–89.

Lawler, B., Loh, E., Martino, P.J., and Pincus, M. (2011). *Methods and Apparatus for Integrating Social Network Metrics and Reputation Data*. U.S. Patent 8,010,619, issued August 30, 2011.

Lee, J.K., Choi, J., Kim, C., and Kim, Y. (2014). Social media, network heterogeneity, and opinion polarization. *Journal of Communication*, 64(4), 702–722.

Leenders, R., Contractor, N.S., and DeChurch, L.A. (2016). Once upon a time: Understanding team processes as relational event networks. *Organizational Psychology Review*, 6(1), 92–115.

Lerner, J.S., Li, Y., Valdesolo, P., and Kassam, K.S. (2015). Emotion and decision making. *Annual Review of Psychology*, 66(1), 799–823.

Levenson, R.W. (1999). The intrapersonal functions of emotion. *Cognition and Emotion*, 13(5), 481–504.

Levitsky, M. (2003). Transnational criminal networks and international security. *Syracuse Journal of International Law and Commerce*, 30(2), 227–240.

Liu, B. (2012). *Sentiment Analysis and Opinion Mining*. Williston, VT: Morgan & Claypool. doi:10.2200/S00416ED1V01Y201204HLT016.

Lowenthal, M.M. (2016). *Intelligence: From Secrets to Policy*. Thousand Oaks, CA: CQ Press.

Magelinski, T., and Carley, K.M. (2018). Legislative voting dynamics in Ukraine. In R. Thomson, C. Dancy, A. Hyder, and H. Bisgin (Eds.), *Social, Cultural, and Behavioral Modeling* (pp. 82–88). Cham, Switzerland: Springer International.

Mares, D.R. (2016). Brazil: Revising the status quo with soft power? In T.V. Paul (Ed.), *Accommodating Rising Powers: Past, Present, and Future* (pp. 246–267). Cambridge, UK: Cambridge University Press.

Marlatt, G.E. (2016). *Lone Wolf Terrorism—A Brief Bibliography*. Available: https://www.hsdl.org/?view&did=727224 [February 2019].

Marsden, P.V., and Friedkin, N.E. (1993). Network studies of social influence. *Contemporary Sociology*, 22(2), 127–151.

Martin, C., Jagla, L., and Firestone, C. (2013). *Integrating Diplomacy and Social Media: A Report of the First Annual Aspen Institute Dialogue on Diplomacy and Technology*. Washington, DC: The Aspen Institute.

Matsumoto, D. (2001). Culture and emotion. In D. Matsumoto (Ed.), *The Handbook of Culture and Psychology* (pp. 171–194). New York: Oxford University Press.

Matsumoto, D., and Hwang, H.C. (2018a). Clusters of nonverbal behaviors differ according to type of question and veracity in investigative interviews in a mock crime context. *Journal of Police and Criminal Psychology*, 33(4), 302–315. doi:10.1007/s11896-017-9250-0.

Matsumoto, D., and Hwang, H.C. (2018b). Social influence in investigative interviews: The effects of reciprocity. *Applied Cognitive Psychology*, 32(2), 163–170.

Matsumoto, D., Keltner, D., Shiota, M.N., O'Sullivan, M., and Frank, M. (2008). Facial expressions of emotion. In *Handbook of Emotions* (3rd ed., pp. 211–234). New York: Guilford Press.

Matsumoto, D., Frank, M.G., and Hwang, H.C. (2013). *Nonverbal Communication: Science and Applications*. Thousand Oaks, CA: SAGE.

Matsumoto, D., Hwang, H.C., and Frank, M.G. (2014a). Emotions expressed by leaders in videos predict political aggression. *Behavioral Sciences of Terrorism and Political Aggression*, 6(3), 212–218.

Matsumoto, D., Hwang, H.C., and Frank, M.G. (2014b). Emotions expressed in speeches by leaders of ideologically motivated groups predict aggression. *Behavioral Sciences of Terrorism and Political Aggression*, 6(1), 1–18.

Matsumoto, D., Hwang, H.C., Skinner, L.G., and Frank, M.G. (2014c). Positive effects in detecting lies from training to recognize behavioral anomalies. *Journal of Police and Criminal Psychology*, 29(1), 28–35.

Matsumoto, D., Hwang, H.C., and Sandoval, V.A. (2015a). Cross-language applicability of linguistic features associated with veracity and deception. *Journal of Police and Criminal Psychology*, 30(4), 229–241.

Matsumoto, D., Frank, M.G., and Hwang, H.C. (2015b). The role of intergroup emotions in political violence. *Current Directions in Psychological Science*, 24(5), 369–373.

Matsumoto, D., Hwang, H.C., and Frank, M.G. (2016). The effects of incidental anger, contempt, and disgust on hostile language and implicit behaviors. *Journal of Applied Social Psychology*, 46(8), 437–452.

Matsumoto, D., Hwang, H.C., and Frank, M.G. (2017). Emotion and aggressive intergroup cognitions: The ANCODI hypothesis. *Aggressive Behavior*, 43(1), 93–107.

Maxwell, D.T., and Carley, K.M. (2009). Principles for effectively representing heterogeneous populations in multi-agent simulations. In A. Tolk and L.C. Jain (Eds.), *Complex Systems in Knowledge-based Environments: Theory, Models and Applications. Studies in Computational Intelligence* (pp. 199–227). Berlin/Heidelberg: Springer. doi:10.1007/978-3-540-88075-2_8.

Mayer, R. (2018). *The Importance of Interpersonal Trust: Now More Than Ever*. Presentation submitted to the Committee on a Decadal Survey of Social and Behavioral Sciences and Applications to National Security, National Academies of Sciences, Engineering, and Medicine. Available: https://vimeo.com/258004014 [February 2019].

Mayer, R.C., Davis, J.H., and Schoorman, F.D. (1995). An integrative model of organizational trust. *The Academy of Management Review*, 20(3), 709–734.

McCauley, C., and Moskalenko, S. (2008). Mechanisms of political radicalization: Pathways toward terrorism. *Terrorism and Political Violence*, 20(3), 415–433.

McCulloh, I.A., Johnson, A.N., and Carley, K.M. (2012). Spectral analysis of social networks to identify periodicity. *Journal of Mathematical Sociology*, 36(2), 80–96.

McIntosh, S.K. (Ed.). (2005). *Beyond Chiefdoms: Pathways to Complexity in Africa*. New York: Cambridge University Press.

Melis, B. (2001). *Negotiating Europe's Immigration Frontiers*. Boston, MA: Kluwer Law International.

Meloy, J.R., and Gill, P. (2016). The lone actor terrorist and the TRAP-18. *Journal of Threat Assessment and Management*, 3(1), 37–52.

Meloy, J.R., and Yakeley, J. (2014). The violent true believer as a "lone wolf"—psychoanalytic perspectives on terrorism. *Behavioral Sciences and the Law*, 32(3), 347–365.

Meloy, J.R., Hoffmann, J., Guldimann, A., and James, D. (2012). The role of warning behaviors in threat assessment: An exploration and suggested typology. *Behavioral Sciences and the Law*, 30(3), 256–279.

Meloy, J.R., Roshdi, K., Glaz-Ocik, J., and Hoffmann, J. (2015). Investigating the individual terrorist in Europe. *Journal of Threat Assessment and Management, 2*(3–4), 140–152.

Menabney, D. (2016). In 2017, narrative intelligence will be your edge over artificial intelligence. *Medium*, December 30. Available: https://medium.com/@darmenab/in-2017-narrative-intelligence-will-be-your-edge-over-artificial-intelligence-d978e9427c35 [December 2018].

Mendosa, J. (2017). *Transnational Organized Crime: An Evolving Challenge* [White Paper]. Available: https://sites.nationalacademies.org/cs/groups/dbassesite/documents/webpage/dbasse_179826.pdf [December 2018].

Mercken, L., Steglich, C., Sinclair, P., Holliday, J., and Moore, L. (2012). A longitudinal social network analysis of peer influence, peer selection, and smoking behavior among adolescents in British schools. *Health Psychology, 31*(4), 450–459.

Merrill, J.A., Sheehan, B.M., Carley, K.M., and Stetson, P.D. (2015). Transition networks in a cohort of patients with congestive heart failure: A novel application of informatics methods to inform care coordination. *Applied Clinical Informatics, 6*(3), 548–564.

Moghaddam, F.M. (2005). The staircase to terrorism a psychological exploration. *American Psychologist, 60*(2), 161–169.

Mohaghegh, Z., Kazemi, R., and Mosleh, A. (2009). Incorporating organizational factors into Probabilistic Risk Assessment (PRA) of complex socio-technical systems: A hybrid technique formalization. *Reliability Engineering and System Safety, 94*(5), 1000–1018.

Mohr, J.W., and Bogdanov, P. (2013). Introduction-topic models: What they are and why they matter. *Poetics, 41*(6), 545–569.

Monge, P.R., and Contractor, N. (2003). *Theories of Communication Networks*. Oxford, UK: Oxford University Press.

Moody, J., and White, D.R. (2003). Structural cohesion and embeddedness: A hierarchical concept of social groups. *American Sociological Review, 68*(1), 103–127.

Moore, T., Clayton, R., and Anderson, R. (2009). The economics of online crime. *Journal of Economic Perspectives, 23*(3), 3–20.

Moore, A.P., Cappelli, D.M., Caron, T.C., Shaw, E.D., Spooner, D., and Trzeciak, R.F. (2011). *A Preliminary Model of Insider Theft of Intellectual Property*. (No. MU/SEI-2011-TN-013). Pittsburgh, PA: Carnegie-Mellon University, Software Engineering Institute.

Moore, A.P., Carley, K.M., Collins, M.L., and Altman, N.W. (2015). Social network dynamics of insider threats: A preliminary model. In *Proceedings of the International Conference of the System Dynamics Society*. Albany, NY: System Dynamics Society. Available: https://resources.sei.cmu.edu/asset_files/ConferencePaper/2015_021_001_506866.pdf [December 2018].

Moreno, J.L. (1934). *Who Shall Survive? A New Approach to the Problem of Human Interrelations*. Washington, DC: Nervous and Mental Disease.

Morgan, G.P., Joseph, K., and Carley, K.M. (2017). The power of social cognition. *Journal of Social Structure, 18*(3), 1–22.

Moskalenko, S., and McCauley, C. (2009). Measuring political mobilization: The distinction between activism and radicalism. *Terrorism and Political Violence, 21*(2), 239–260.

Moskalenko, S., and McCauley, C. (2011). The psychology of lone-wolf terrorism. *Counselling Psychology Quarterly, 24*(2), 115–126.

Mui, L., Mohtashemi, M., and Halberstadt, A. (2002). A computational model of trust and reputation. In *HICSS '02 Proceedings of the 35th Annual Hawaii International Conference on System Sciences (HICSS'02)* (Vol. 7, p. 188). Washington, DC: IEEE Computer Society.

Murdie, A., and Peksen, D. (2014). The impact of human rights INGO shaming on humanitarian interventions. *The Journal of Politics, 76*(1), 215–228.

Murdie, A., and Purser, C. (2017). How protest affects opinions of peaceful demonstration and expression rights. *Journal of Human Rights, 16*(3), 351–369.

Murdie, A., and Stapley, C. (2014). Why target the "good guys"? The determinants of terrorism against NGOs. *International Interactions, 40*(1). doi:10.1080/03050629.2013.863192.

Murdie, A., and Urpelainen, J. (2015). Why pick on us? Environmental INGOs and state shaming as a strategic substitute. *Political Studies, 63*(2), 353–372.

Nagurney, A., and Qiang, Q. (2007). Robustness of transportation networks subject to degradable links. *EPL (Europhysics Letters), 80*(6), 68001. doi:10.1209/0295-5075/80/68001.

Naqvi, N., Shiv, B., and Bechara, A. (2006). The role of emotion in decision making: A cognitive neuroscience perspective. *Current Directions in Psychological Science, 15*(5), 260–264.

National Academies of Sciences, Engineering, and Medicine (NASEM). (2018a). *Emerging Trends and Methods in International Security: Proceedings of a Workshop*. Washington, DC: The National Academies Press. doi:10.17226/25058.

NASEM. (2018b). *Leveraging Advances in Social Network Thinking for National Security: Proceedings of a Workshop*. Washington, DC: The National Academies Press. doi:10.17226/25057.

NASEM. (2018c). *Understanding Narratives for National Security: Proceedings of a Workshop*. Washington, DC: The National Academies Press. doi:10.17226/25119.

National Research Council. (2003). *Dynamic Social Network Modeling and Analysis: Workshop Summary and Papers*. Washington, DC: The National Academies Press.

National Research Council. (2007). *Human-System Integration in the System Development Process: A New Look*. Committee on Human-System Design Support for Changing Technology. R.W. Pew and A.S. Mavor (Eds.). Committee on Human Factors, Division of Behavioral and Social Sciences and Education. Washington, DC: The National Academies Press.

National Research Council. (2008). *Behavioral Modeling and Simulation: From Individuals to Societies*. Committee on Organizational Modeling: From Individuals to Societies. G.L. Zacharias, J. MacMillan, and S. Van Hemel (Eds.). Board on Behavioral, Cognitive, and Sensory Sciences; Division of Behavioral and Social Sciences and Education. Washington, DC: The National Academies Press.

Nicks, D. (2012). *Private: Bradley Manning, WikiLeaks, and the Biggest Exposure of Official Secrets in American History*. Chicago, IL: Chicago Review Press.

Novotny, E., Carr, Z., Frank, M.G., Dietrich, S.B., Shaddock, T., Cardwell, M., and Decker, A. (2018). How people really suspect and discover lies. *Journal of Nonverbal Behavior, 42*(1), 41–52.

Nye, J.S. (2004). Soft power and American foreign policy. *Political Science Quarterly, 119*(2), 255–270.

O'Keefe, D.J. (2016). *Persuasion: Theory and Research*. Thousand Oaks, CA: SAGE.

Ofem, B., Floyd, T.M., and Borgatti, S.P. (2012). Social networks and organizations. In D.D. Caulkins and A.T. Jordan (Eds.), *A Companion to Organizational Anthropology* (pp. 147–166). Hoboken, NJ: Blackwell.

Palinkas, L.A., Gunderson, E.K.E., Holland, A., Miller, C., and Johnson, J.C. (2000). Predictors of behavior and performance in extreme environments: The Antarctic Space Analogue Program. *Aviation, Space, and Environmental Medicine, 71*(41), 1–7.

Pang, B., and Lee, L. (2008). Opinion mining and sentiment analysis. *Foundations and Trends in Information Retrieval, 2*(1–2), 1–135.

Paradise, J.F. (2009). China and international harmony: The role of Confucius institutes in bolstering Beijing's soft power. *Asian Survey, 49*(4), 647–669.

Paul, T.V., and Shankar, M. (2014). Status accommodation through institutional means: India's rise and the global order. In T. Paul, D. Welch Larson, and W. Wohlforth (Eds.), *Status in World Politics* (pp. 192–218). Cambridge, UK: Cambridge University Press.

Perliger, A., and Pedahzur, A. (2011). Social network analysis in the study of terrorism and political violence. *PS: Political Science & Politics, 44*(1), 45–50.

Phelps, E.A., Lempert, K.M., and Sokol-Hessner, P. (2014). Emotion and decision making: Multiple modulatory neural circuits. *Annual Review of Neuroscience, 37,* 263–287. doi:10.1146/annurev-neuro-071013-014119.

Poibeau, T., Saggion, H., Piskorski, J., and Yangarber, R. (2013). *Multi-Source, Multilingual Information Extraction and Summarization.* Berlin/Heidelberg, Germany: Springer-Verlag.

Prietula, M. (2001). Advice, trust and gossip among artificial agents. In A. Lomi and E.R. Larsen (Eds.), *Dynamics of Organizations: Computational Modeling and Organization Theories* (pp. 141–177). Menlo Park, CA: American Association for Artificial Intelligence.

Prietula, M., and Carley, K. (2001). Boundedly rational and emotional agents cooperation, trust and rumor. In C. Castelfranchi and Y.-H. Tan (Eds.), *Trust and Deception in Virtual Societies* (pp. 169–194). Norwell, MA: Kluwer Academic.

Rahmandad, H., and Sterman, J. (2008). Heterogeneity and network structure in the dynamics of diffusion: Comparing agent-based and differential equation models. *Management Science, 54*(5), 998–1014.

Ranieri, T.F., and Barrs, S. (2011). Internet and ideology: The military counterintelligence challenges of the "Net Wolf." *American Intelligence Journal, 29*(2), 80–89.

Re, D.E., and Rule, N.O. (2016). Appearance and physiognomy. In D. Matsumoto, H.C. Hwang, and M.G. Frank (Eds.), *APA Handbook of Nonverbal Communication.* (pp. 221–256). Washington, DC: American Psychological Association.

Reagan, A.J., Mitchell, L., Kiley, D., Danforth, C.M., and Dodds, P.S. (2016). The emotional arcs of stories are dominated by six basic shapes. *EPJ Data Science, 5*(1), 31. doi:10.1140/epjds/s13688-016-0093-1.

Renshon, J. (2016). Status deficits and war. *International Organization, 70*(3), 513–550.

Renshon, J. (2017). *Fighting for Status: Hierarchy and Conflict in World Politics.* Princeton, NJ: Princeton University Press.

Ressler, S. (2006). Social network analysis as an approach to combat terrorism: Past, present, and future research. *Homeland Security Affairs, 2*(2), 1–10.

Rogers, E.M. (2003). *Diffusion of Innovations* (5th ed.). New York: Free Press.

Rogers, E.M., and Kincaid, D.L. (1981). *Communication Networks: Towards a New Paradigm for Research.* New York: Free Press.

Sageman, M. (2004). *Understanding Terror Networks.* Philadelphia, PA: University of Pennsylvania Press.

Sargent, R.G. (2013). Verification and validation of simulation models. *Journal of Simulation, 7*(1), 12–24.

Schefzik, R., Thorarinsdottir, T.L., and Gneiting, T. (2013). Uncertainty quantification in complex simulation models using ensemble copula coupling. *Statistical Science, 28*(4), 616–640.

Schultz, F., Kleinnijenhuis, J., Oegema, D., Utz, S., and van Atteveldt, W. (2012). Strategic framing in the BP crisis: A semantic network analysis of associative frames. *Public Relations Review, 38*(1), 97–107.

Schwartz, B. (2000). Self-determination: The tyranny of freedom. *American Psychologist, 55*(1), 79–88.

Scott, S., and McGettigan, C. (2016). The voice: From identity to interactions. In D. Matsumoto, H.C. Hwang, and M.G. Frank (Eds.), *APA Handbook of Nonverbal Communication* (pp. 289–305). Washington, DC: American Psychological Association.

Sheffi, Y. (2001). Supply chain management under the threat of international terrorism. *The International Journal of Logistics Management*, *12*(2), 1–11.
Shelley, L.I. (2014). *Dirty Entanglements: Corruption, Crime, and Terrorism*. New York: Cambridge University Press.
Slotte, P.A., and Smørgrav, E. (2008). *Response Surface Methodology Approach for History Matching and Uncertainty Assessment of Reservoir Simulation Models*. Richardson, TX: Society of Petroleum Engineers. doi:10.2118/113390-MS.
Snajder, J., and Boltuzic, F. (2014). Back up your stance: Recognising arguments in online discussions. In *Proceedings of the First Workshop on Argumentation Mining* (pp. 49–58). Available: https://pdfs.semanticscholar.org/54dd/7247a4e900a7aae90d4028dc80e5e0e-6aeec.pdf [February 2019].
Snegovaya, M. (2015). Russia report 1: Putin's information warfare in Ukraine. *Institute for the Study of War*, September 17. Available: http://iswresearch.blogspot.com/sites/default/files/Russian%20Report%201%20Putin's%20Information%20Warfare%20in%20Ukraine-%20Soviet%20Origins%20of%20Russias%20Hybrid%20Warfare.pdf [December 2018].
Sokolowski, J.A., Banks, C.M., and Dover, T.J. (2016). An agent-based approach to modeling insider threat. *Computational and Mathematical Organization Theory*, *22*(3), 273–287.
Spaaij, R. (2010). The enigma of lone wolf terrorism: An assessment. *Studies in Conflict and Terrorism*, *33*(9), 854–870.
Speckhard, A. (2012). *Talking to Terrorists: Understanding the Psycho-Social Motivations of Militant Jihadi Terrorists, Mass Hostage Takers, Suicide Bombers, and "Martyrs."* McLean, VA: Advances Press.
Starcke, K., and Brand, M. (2016). Effects of stress on decisions under uncertainty: A meta-analysis. *Psychological Bulletin*, *142*(9), 909–933.
Stasi, A., Songa, G., Mauri, M., Ciceri, A., Diotallevi, F., Nardone, G., and Russo, V. (2018). Neuromarketing empirical approaches and food choice: A systematic review. *Food Research International*, *108*, 650–664. doi:10.1016/j.foodres.2017.11.049.
Steglich, C., Snijders, T.A.B., and Pearson, M. (2010). Dynamic networks and behavior: Separating selection from influence. *Methods for the Analysis of Social Network Data*, *40*(1), 329–393.
Sterman, J. (2001). System dynamics modeling: Tools for learning in a complex world. *California Management Review*, *43*(4), 8–25. doi:10.2307/41166098.
Sticha, P., Buede, D., and Rees, R.L. (2005). APOLLO: An analytical tool for predicting a subject's decision making. In *Proceedings of the 2005 International Conference on Intelligence Analysis*. Available: http://www.au.af.mil/bia/documents/sticha_et_al_apollo_mitre.pdf [February 2019].
Sticha, P.J., Weaver, E.A., Tatman, J.A., Mahoney, S.M., and Buede, D.M. (2009). Reading the behavior signature: Predicting leader personality from individual and group actions. In *AAAI Spring Symposium: Technosocial Predictive Analytics* (pp. 130–136). Palo Alto, CA: Association for the Advancement of Artificial Intelligence. Available: http://www.aaai.org/Library/Symposia/Spring/2009/ss09-09-024.php [February 2019].
Stokman, F., and Van Oosten, R. (1994). The exchange of voting positions: An object oriented model of policy networks. In B. Bueno de Mesquita and F.N. Stokman (Eds.), *Decision Making in the European Community: Models, Applications, and Comparisons* (pp. 105–128). New Haven, CT: Yale University Press.
Sudhahar, S., De Fazio, G., Franzosi, R., and Cristianini, N. (2015). Network analysis of narrative content in large corporations. *Natural Language Engineering*, *21*(1), 81–112.
Sun, R. (Ed.). (2006). *Cognition and Multi-Agent Interaction: From Cognitive Modeling to Social Simulation*. New York: Cambridge University Press.

Taylor, P.J., and Derudder, B. (2015). *World City Network: A Global Urban Analysis* (2nd ed.). London, UK: Routledge.

Thaler, R.H., Sunstein, C.R., and Balz, J.P. (2013). Choice architecture. In E. Shafir (Ed.), *The Behavioral Foundations of Public Policy* (pp. 428–439). Princeton, NJ: Princeton University Press.

Tooby, J., and Cosmides, L. (2008). The evolutionary psychology of the emotions and their relationship to internal regulatory variables. In M. Lewis and J.M. Haviland-Jones (Eds.), *Handbook of Emotions* (3rd ed., pp. 114–137). New York: Guilford Press.

Trueblood, J.S., Brown, S.D., Heathcote, A., and Busemeyer, J.R. (2013). Not just for consumers: Context effects are fundamental to decision making. *Psychological Science, 24*(6), 901–908.

Tsvetovat, M., and Carley, K.M. (2005). Structural knowledge and success of anti-terrorist activity: The downside of structural equivalence. *Journal of Social Structure, 6*(2), 1–38.

Tuffield, M.M., Harris, S., Dupplaw, D.P., Chakravarthy, A., Brewster, C., Gibbins, N., O'Hara, K., Ciravegna, F., Sleeman, D., Shadbolt, N.R., and Wilks, Y. (2006). Image annotation with photocopain. *Proceedings of the First International Workshop on Semantic Web Annotations for Multimedia (SWAMM)*, Edinburgh, UK, May 22–26. Available: https://research.aston.ac.uk/portal/files/189581/Tuffield_SWAMM06.pdf [February 2019].

Tversky, A., and Simonson, I. (1993). Context-dependent preferences. *Management Science, 39*(10), 1179–1189.

Valente, T.W. (1996). Social network thresholds in the diffusion of innovations. *Social Networks, 18*(1), 69–89.

Van Dam, K.H., Nikolic, I., and Lukszo, Z. (Eds.). (2012). *Agent-based Modelling of Socio-Technical Systems* (Vol. 9). Dordrecht, Germany: Springer Science & Business Media.

Vasek, M., Thornton, M., and Moore, T. (2014) Empirical analysis of denial-of-service attacks in the bitcoin ecosystem. In R. Böhme, M. Brenner, T. Moore, and M. Smith (Eds.), *Financial Cryptography and Data Security. FC 2014. Lecture Notes in Computer Science* (Vol. 8438). Berlin, Germany: Springer.

Vrij, A., Fisher, R., Mann, S., and Leal, S. (2008). A cognitive load approach to lie detection. *Journal of Investigative Psychology and Offender Profiling, 5*(1–2), 39–43.

Wang, Q., and Ross, M. (2007). Culture and memory. In *Handbook of Cultural Psychology* (pp. 645–667). New York: Guilford Press.

Ward, M.D., Metternich, N.W., Carrington, C., Dorff, C., Gallop, M., Hollenbach, F.M., Schultz, A., and Weschle, S. (2013). Geographical models of crises: Evidence from ICEWS. In D.D. Schmorrow and D.M. Nicholson (Eds.), *Advances in Design for Cross-Cultural Activities* (pp. 429–438). Boca Raton, FL: CRC Press LLC.

Ward, S. (2013). Race, status, and Japanese revisionism in the early 1930s. *Security Studies, 22*(4), 607–639.

Ward, S. (2017). *Status and the Challenge of Rising Powers*. Cambridge, UK: Cambridge University Press.

Warkentin, M., and Willison, R. (2009). Behavioral and policy issues in information systems security: The insider threat. *European Journal of Information Systems, 18*(2), 101–105.

Warren, T.C. (2014). Not by the sword alone: Soft power, mass media, and the production of state sovereignty. *International Organization, 68*(1), 111–141.

Warren, G., Schertler, E., and Bull, P. (2009). Detecting deception from emotional and unemotional cues. *Journal of Nonverbal Behavior, 33*(1), 59–69.

Waterson, P., Robertson, M.M., Cooke, N.J., Militello, L., Roth, E., and Stanton, N.A. (2015). Defining the methodological challenges and opportunities for an effective science of sociotechnical systems and safety. *Ergonomics, 58*(4), 565–599.

Weimann, G. (2012). Lone wolves in cyberspace. *Contemporary Voices: St Andrews Journal of International Relations, 3*(2). doi:10.15664/jtr.105.

Wohlforth, W.C. (2009). Unipolarity, status competition, and great power war. *World Politics, 61*(1), 28–57.

Wohlforth, W.C. (2014). Status dilemmas and interstate conflict. In T. Paul (Ed.), *Status in World Politics* (pp. 115–140). Cambridge, UK: Cambridge University Press.

Wright, S., Denney, D., Pinkerton, A., Jansen, V., and Bryden, J. (2016). Resurgent insurgents: Quantitative research into Jihadists who get suspended but return on Twitter. *Journal of Terrorism Research, 7*(2). Available: https://cvir.st-andrews.ac.uk/article/10.15664/jtr.1213 [December 2018].

Wu, I. (2017). *Measuring Soft Power with Conventional and Unconventional Data* [White Paper]. Available: http://sites.nationalacademies.org/dbasse/bbcss/dbasse_178412 [February 2019].

Xie, J., Chen, M., and Szymanski, B.K. (2013). LabelrankT: Incremental community detection in dynamic networks via label propagation. In *Proceedings of the Workshop on Dynamic Networks Management and Mining* (pp. 25–32). New York: Association for Computing Machinery. Available: https://dl.acm.org/citation.cfm?id=2489247 [May 2019].

Young, R.M. (2007). Story and discourse: A bipartite model of narrative generation in virtual worlds. *Interaction Studies, 8*(2), 177–208.

Zhang, K., Frumkin, L.A., Stedmon, A., and Lawson, G. (2013). Deception in context: Coding nonverbal cues, situational variables and risk of detection. *Journal of Police and Criminal Psychology, 28*(2), 150–161. doi:10.1007/s11896-013-9127-9.

Zhao, E.Y., Ishihara, M., and Lounsbury, M. (2013). Overcoming the illegitimacy discount: Cultural entrepreneurship in the U.S. feature film industry. *Organization Studies, 34*(12), 1747–1776.

Zhou, L., Wu, W.P., and Luo, X. (2007). Internationalization and the performance of born-global SMEs: The mediating role of social networks. *Journal of International Business Studies, 38*(4), 673–690.

6

Integrating Social and Behavioral Sciences (SBS) Research to Enhance Security in Cyberspace

Cyber-related developments have both dramatically altered the nature of security threats and expanded the landscape of potential tools for countering those threats. Experts from multiple disciplines, including electrical engineering, software engineering, computer science, and computer engineering, have a laser focus on cybersecurity, but that focus has been primarily on technical or data challenges, such as identification and prevention of malware, prevention of denial-of-service attacks, self-fixing code, unauthorized data breaches, tools for the cyber analyst, and privacy. Indeed, cybersecurity is often characterized as the set of techniques used to protect the integrity of networks, programs, and data from attack, damage, or unauthorized access.[1] These techniques have undisputed value, but they address only technological challenges, not the human behaviors and motivations that shape those challenges.

The tools of cybersecurity have obvious relevance for national security. Intelligence analysts, however, seek to understand a different but related set of critical problems—those that involve cyber-mediated communication (communication that takes place through computer networks). To understand this phenomenon, it is necessary to integrate insights about constantly evolving technology with understanding of fundamentally human phenomena. The emerging field of social cybersecurity science has developed to

---

[1] For examples, see https://searchsecurity.techtarget.com/definition/cybersecurity December 2018] and https://www.paloaltonetworks.com/cyberpedia/what-is-cyber-security [December 2018].

fill this need.[2] Researchers in this field build on foundational work in the social and behavioral sciences (SBS) to characterize cyber-mediated changes in individual, group, societal, and political behaviors and outcomes, as well as to support the building of the cyber infrastructure needed to guard against cyber-mediated threats. This chapter describes this emerging discipline, explores the opportunities it offers for the Intelligence Community (IC), illustrates its relevance to intelligence analysis with an example, and describes research needed in the coming decade to fully exploit the field's applications to the work of intelligence analysis.

WHAT IS SOCIAL CYBERSECURITY SCIENCE?

The field of social cybersecurity developed to meet a national need. It was developed by researchers with backgrounds in numerous fields to meet two primary objectives:

1. characterize, understand, and forecast cyber-mediated changes in human behavior and in social, cultural, and political outcomes; and
2. build a social cyber infrastructure that will allow the essential character of a society to persist in a cyber-mediated information environment that is characterized by changing conditions, actual or imminent social cyberthreats, and cyber-mediated threats.

Scientists in this field seek to develop the technology and theory needed to assess, predict, and mitigate instances of individual influence and community manipulation in which either humans or bots attempt to alter or control the cyber-mediated information environment (Carley et al., 2018). While researchers in the social cybersecurity area come from a large number of disciplines, many identify themselves as computational social scientists. The field is rapidly expanding to meet a growing need; the number of academic papers published in this area has risen exponentially in the past 10 years (Carley et al., 2018). The number of researchers in this area is also

---

[2] The term "social cybersecurity" is also sometimes used to refer to cyber-mediated security threats themselves, with emphasis on the human, as opposed to the technological, aspects of those threats. Examples of such threats are recruitment of members of covert groups and their training in social media, the spread of fake news and disinformation, attacks on democracy through manipulation of how citizens receive news, the fomenting of crises by creating a perception of the rampant spread of disease or state instability, phishing and spear phishing attacks (i.e., attempts to obtain sensitive or protected information online by posing as a trustworthy entity), recruitment of individuals to act as insider threats (see Chapter 5) through social media, and online brand manipulation and rumors designed to destroy corporations.

growing because of widespread concern about the global consequences of such social cybersecurity attacks as disinformation campaigns, social media manipulation, and phishing to develop insider threats. Many researchers came to this area of study independently, but they are quickly coalescing as a formal discipline through participation in emerging groups, such as the social cybersecurity working group,[3] and domestic and international conferences, such as the International Conference on Social Computing, Behavioral-Cultural Modeling, and Prediction and Behavior Representation in Modeling and Simulation.[4]

Experts in cybersecurity focus on attacks made on and through the cyber infrastructure that are intended to interfere with technology, steal or destroy information, or steal money or identities (Reveron, 2012). While cybersecurity experts do draw on social science research (see Box 6-1), social cybersecurity researchers have a different approach: they focus on activities aimed at influencing or manipulating individuals, groups, or communities, particularly activities that have large consequences for social groups, organizations, and countries. The solutions to some problems, such as denial-of-service attacks, malware distribution, and insider threats, require both types of expertise, but the emphasis in the two fields is quite different. What links researchers in social cybersecurity is that they

- take the sociopolitical context of cyber activity into account both methodologically and empirically;
- integrate theory and research on influence, persuasion, and manipulation with study of human behavior in the cyber-mediated environment; and
- focus on identifying operationally useful applications of their research.

The boundaries between cybersecurity and social cybersecurity are not altogether sharp, but Table 6-1 lists some key differences between the two. Because cybersecurity focuses primarily on technology, for example, a cyberbreach conducted to steal or compromise data would be in that realm (Carley et al., 2018). In contrast, the manipulation of groups to provide funding for covert actors or extremist groups (Benigni et al., 2017b), sway opinion to win elections (Allcott and Gentzkow, 2017), artificially boost the perceived popularity of actors (Woolley, 2016), or build groups so as

---

[3]Available: www.social-cybersecurity.org [February 2019].
[4]See http://sbp-brims.org/2019/about [January 2019].

BOX 6-1
Social and Behavioral Science (SBS) Fields in Cybersecurity

Cybersecurity involves humans who may be attackers, defenders, network administrators, computer users, organizations, and even children surfing the Internet. It is not surprising, then, that SBS research has been applied to many aspects of cybersecurity. In many cases, these applications have been focused on cybersecurity for the end user. This work has addressed questions about cyber-hygiene (practices adopted by system users to maintain the system's health and security), data privacy, passwords, user authentication, identity theft, and end-user beliefs and mindsets and appears regularly in the *Proceedings of the Symposium on Usable Privacy and Security.*[a]

Other research has applied SBS methods to understand cybersecurity operations. D'Amico and colleagues have used task analyses to understand the work of cyber defenders (D'Amico and Whitley, 2008; D'Amico et al., 2005; Gutzwiller et al., 2016, 2018; Horn and D'Amico, 2011; Vieane et al., 2016). Similarly, cognitive modeling in the form of instance-based learning theory (a type of learning algorithm in which comparison to prior examples is the basis for analysis) has been used to model the analyst and the detection of attacks (Dutt et al., 2011, 2013).

Human factors research has played a prominent role in attempts to improve cybersecurity analysis by examining the effects of distraction (Gutzwiller et al., 2018), situation awareness (Gutzwiller et al., 2016; Liu et al., 2017), and interruption (Vieane et al., 2017) on the cyber defender's task. In addition, research on teamwork among cyber analysts has shown that while it is generally minimal in practice, it enables analysts to detect a wider array of threats (Rajivan and Cooke, 2018). Armed with a better understanding of the cyber defender's task, human factors researchers have developed visualizations (Goodall, 2009), coordinated displays (Vieane et al., 2016), and other tools designed to facilitate the performance of that task.

Finally, in a recent article, Dawson and Thomson (2018) describe the competencies that will be needed in the future cybersecurity workforce. They emphasize that cyber workers will need competencies that extend beyond technical skills, such as systematic thinking, teamwork skills, communication skills, and social skills.

---

[a] Available: https://www.usenix.org/sites/default/files/soups2018_full_proceedings.pdf [February 2019].

TABLE 6-1 Key Differences between Cybersecurity and Social Cybersecurity

Characteristic	Cybersecurity	Social Cybersecurity
Core Disciplines	Electrical engineering, software engineering, computer science, computer engineering	Computational social science, societal computing, data science, policy studies
Illustrative Problems	Encryption, malware detection. denial-of-service attack protection	Spread of disinformation, spam, altering who appears influential, creating echo chambers
Core Methods	Cryptography, software engineering, computer forensics, biometrics	Network science/social networks, language technologies, social media analytics
Illustrative Level of Data	Packets	Social media posts
Focus on the Issue of Insider Threat	Encryption to prevent ease of reading, software to prevent or detect illicit data sharing, firewalls	Social engineering to seduce insiders to share information, information leakage in social media
Focus on the Issue of Spreading Malware via Kitten Images on Twitter	How malware is embedded and detected	Use of bots to promote message sharing, what groups are at risk to download
Focus on the Issue of Denial-of-Service Attacks	Technology to detect, enable, or prevent denial-of-service attacks	Social media and dark web identification of hackers who perpetrate denial-of-service attacks; analysis of how these hackers are trained
Illustrative Tools	SysInternals, Windows GodMode, Microsoft EMET, Secure@Source, Q-Radar, ArcSight	ORA-PRO, Maltego, TalkWalker, Scraawl, Pulse, TweetTracker, BlogTrackers
National Infrastructure Support	United States Computer Emergency Readiness Team (US-CERT)	Nothing comparable—emergent self-management by social media providers
Illustrative Central Conferences	RSA, Black Hat, DEFCON, InfoSec World, International Conference on Cybersecurity	World Wide Web, SBP-BRiMS, ASONAM, Social Com, Web and Social Media

to have an audience for recruitment (Benigni et al., 2019) would all best be addressed by social cybersecurity.

Drawing on Other Disciplines

SBS research plays a role in both cybersecurity and social cybersecurity; examples include research on deception and motivations for attacks at the individual and state levels (discussed below) and research on teams (see Chapter 7). Both cybersecurity and social cybersecurity are applied fields in which new technologies are developed and tested. The field of social cybersecurity does not simply supplant the important work of SBS research. Rather, researchers in the field build on some existing work and extend other work to generate new knowledge and in some cases develop new theory and methods that arise from the transdisciplinary approach for studying the cyber environment. Social cybersecurity is a computational social science, one of a growing number of social science fields that are using digital data and developing computational tools and models (Mann, 2016). Computational social science is not the application of computer science techniques to social science problems and data (Wallach, 2018); it is the use of social science theories to drive the development of new computational techniques, combined with further development of those theories using computational techniques for data collection, analysis, and simulation.

In the case of social cybersecurity science, computer scientists and engineers on the one hand and social scientists and policy analysts on the other have not always recognized the implications of each other's perspectives for their own research. For example, computer scientists' attempts to identify disinformation usually begin with fact checking. However, most disinformation campaigns rely less on blatant falsehood than on other strategies, such as illogic, satire, facts out of context, misuse of statistics, dismissal of topics, intimidation, appeals to ethnic bias, and simple distraction, all topics of SBS research (Babcock et al., 2018). Similarly, when SBS researchers seek to invent or reinvent computer science techniques, the results typically do not scale, are difficult to maintain, and lack generalizability. For example, affect control theory (a valuable computational model of human emotions based on social psychology) cannot be scaled to handle large social groups and populations. Computational social science, in contrast, requires deep engagement in and integration of knowledge, theories, and methods from both computer science and social science. Social cybersecurity science is often viewed as going beyond the interdisciplinary approach of integrating the methods and knowledge of diverse disciplines, having become a truly transdisciplinary science in the sense that it is creating new knowledge, theories, and methods. The objective of social cyber experts is to account for the peculiarities of the cyber environment and the specific opportunities for exploitation available in the communication and entertainment technology used by actors engaged, explicitly or implicitly, in information warfare or marketing.

As the field has matured, "social cybersecurity" has become the recognized term for this work, but the approach has been associated with other terms, including "social cyberforensics," "social cyberattack," "social media analytics," "cyber-physical-social based security," "social cyberdefense," "computational propaganda," and "social media information warfare," and a variety of terms are used for key concepts in the field. Table 6-2, although not comprehensive, indicates this variety.

One constant for researchers in social cybersecurity is the application of network science and social network analysis (see Chapter 5), often in combination with other methods. The field also builds on other computational social science methods, including those used in data science, visual analytics, machine learning, text mining, natural language processing, social media analytics, and spatiotemporal data mining. Key methods include detection of change in networks, assessment and forecasting of diffusion, study of belief formation, influence assessment, identification of network elites, group identification, analysis of mergers and breakups, cyberforensics, actor activity prediction, and topic analysis. As evidence mounts that social media manipulation involves manipulation of both social and knowledge networks, researchers in this area increasingly combine social network analysis and narrative methods (see Chapter 5).

Another constant is reliance on social media data. Social cybersecurity experts are particularly concerned with social influence and group manipulation, the emergence of norms within and between online groups, and the formation or destruction of groups that are either receptive to or proponents of particular ideas and willing to engage in particular actions. Thus, key areas of study include models and methods associated with dynamically evolving data, patterns of life, information and belief diffusion, social influence, narrative construction and manipulation, group inoculation, and group resilience. Increasingly, research in the field is concerned with cultural variations, which often manifest as geographically specific enablers, constraints, and variation. Researchers seek to understand differences across groups by exploring variations in how people in different parts of the world generate, consume, and are affected by social media. They also explore how geospatial constraints, such as the location of ports, the existence of water features, the characteristics of landscape, and the types of natural disasters to which an area is prone may influence how information spreads in cyberspace, and why. Research areas include methods of psychological and social manipulation, cognitive biases in information handling, social biases in accessing information, trust building, and disinformation strategies.

TABLE 6-2 Intersections between Social Cybersecurity and Other Disciplines

Discipline	Key Terms	Key Methods Other Than Network Science/ Social Networks	Key Sources of Data Other Than Social Media	Illustrative Question
Sociology	Influence in social media, online influence	Language technology	Demographics	Do online groups and group processes resemble those offline?
Forensics	Social cyberforensics	Forensics	Website scraping, dark web	Who is responsible for a particular social cybersecurity attack?
Political Science	Digital democracy, participatory democracy	Forum creation	Forums, legal and policy documents	How can social media be used to support or cripple democracy?
Anthropology	Digital anthropology, online ethnography	Rapid ethnographic assessment, area studies	Interviews, participant observation	How do people in different cultures use social media?
Information Science	Cyber-physical-social security, social media analytics	Machine learning	Phone and banking data	How and when does information diffuse in social media?
Psychology	Social engineering	Social media analytics, case studies	E-mail, laboratory experiments	When do people contribute to conversations in social media?

TABLE 6-2 Continued

Discipline	Key Terms	Key Methods Other Than Network Science/ Social Networks	Key Sources of Data Other Than Social Media	Illustrative Question
Marketing	Viral marketing, online marketing	Social media analytics, statistics	Economic indicators, brand diagnostics	How can social media be exploited to market goods and services?
International Relations	Social cyberattacks, social cyberdefense, e-government	Case studies, historical and policy assessment	News reports, court cases, dark web	How can state and nonstate actors use social media to gain influence and win battles via nonkinetic activities?
Economics	Digital economy, cybersecurity economics	Economic incentive assessment, econometrics	Money trails, price indices, cryptocurrency rates and usage	How do social media influence the economy?

A Social Cybersecurity Approach to Studying a False Information Campaign

The issue of the spread of false information on Twitter illustrates the distinction between the approaches of social cybersecurity and either pure computer science or pure social science.

Analysis of this problem using a purely computer science machine learning approach would begin with a training set containing tweets that had been marked as containing false information, such as a doctored image or a fact that had been checked and found to be inaccurate. Narrative would be assessed in terms of what words, concepts, sentiment, or gist could be extracted computationally (see Chapter 5). These extracted features would become part of the vector of information used in the machine learning model, and as a result, values for these features would become associated with the presence of false news. A desired end-result might be an automated fact checker, similar to spam checkers, which could run on multiple platforms independently of human intervention.

It is not uncommon for a reliable training set to have 2,000 to 10,000 marked items. This set might be split in half, with some tweets used to train new algorithms and others used to assess their efficacy. Algorithms would then be devised for empirically categorizing tweets according to whether, and with what certainty, they contained false information. The utility of the new algorithms would then be determined by comparing their precision and recall against those features of older algorithms. The new algorithms would have limited utility in any context other than that in which they had been developed. It is common for other researchers to reuse such training data in developing alternative models for comparison, but a mislabeled training set can yield misleading conclusions. Box 6-2 highlights other data challenges for this research, which would affect all three approaches.

In contrast, a pure social science approach to the same problem might be to begin by defining false information and its nuances in the context of

---

BOX 6-2
Challenges in Data Access

The fields of computer science, social science, and social cybersecurity all face several challenges in data access. The first is variation in the policies, laws, and regulations of the corporations that build the data platforms or collect the data, the federal government, states, and the governments of foreign countries with respect to social media and privacy and data access, storage, and sharing, which change frequently (Anderson, 2017). Communication and entertainment technologies are evolving rapidly, their potentially exploitable features are constantly changing, and new adversarial and marketing technologies for making use of the data are continually appearing (Van Dijck and Poell, 2013). These policy and technology changes alter what researchers can study, what the IC can do, and how easy it is for adversaries to manipulate the information environment (e.g., Stribley, 2018).

Other factors limit data sharing. The process of collecting, cleaning, and validating social media data is extremely time-consuming, and researchers may be reluctant to share their data out of concern that others may not take its nuances into account. It is possible to purchase some kinds of data, but the prices are well beyond the means of most researchers. Policies related to data storage and cleaning, such as the Twitter policy of removing access to tweets from users who are suspended, also inhibit research (Wei et al., 2015, 2016; Thomas et al., 2011).

As a result, there is a paucity of publicly available, sharable data (Baggili and Breitinger, 2015). These issues also make it far more challenging—sometimes impossible—to replicate the results of research (see Chapter 9 and Appendix C). Sharing of data and results is challenging even within the IC because of varying policies and regulations regarding what sorts of data agencies can collect, store, and link (Lawson, 2014; Kris, 2017; Konkel, 2014).

a set of tweets, so that false tweets relative to that context could be identified. Then a quantitative researcher might statistically assess differences between sets of tweets with false information and sets of tweets without false information, using such metrics as the number of tweets, the topic areas addressed, the number of times tweets were retweeted or liked, and so on. This analysis would test a series of hypotheses derived from theories of human behavior (not technology) about, for example, rumor diffusion, attitude formation, persuasion, and social influence. Given the same set of tweets used by the computer scientists for training, the social scientist might assess the characteristics of the tweets and tweeters that affected interrater reliability[5] in determining whether a tweet contained false information.

Social science researchers would likely use multiple qualitative and/or quantitative methods to support the utility of their theoretical model—for example, to understand whether narratives containing false information were different from those without such information, whether different actors used different narratives, what characteristics of actors or groups made them susceptible to believing false information, or what features of narratives containing false information made them persuasive.

In other words, the computer scientist might seek to develop algorithms for identifying false news and deceptive actors in order to eliminate vulnerabilities in social media technologies to prevent the spread of misinformation. In contrast, the social scientist might seek to understand the differences in types of disinformation; the social, economic, and psychological motivations behind deception; and the aspects of human cognition, social cognition, and attitude formation that affect when an individual or group is susceptible to false information.

Drawing on the potential benefits of both of these approaches, a social cybersecurity researcher would take into account the following:

- how social media technology can be manipulated to affect who receives which messages at which times;
- the way the messages are presented and accessed;
- the way humans, individually and in groups, can create, access, be influenced by, and influence others using these features of the technology;
- how the content of a message can be manipulated to affect its persuasiveness, or the tendency of the technology to suspend the sender or recommend the message;
- the features of the content that affect its longevity (e.g., the presence of images);

---

[5]Interrater reliability refers to the level of agreement between those rating or coding a particular item.

- the similarities and differences among messages and the narratives and counternarratives coming from, going to, and being accessed by different users; and
- how the messages and technology could be manipulated to build up, link, or break down groups, and manipulate both the social network and people's perception of it.

Social cybersecurity researchers engage simultaneously in developing both method and theory and determining whether SBS hypotheses hold up in real-world settings. They would use high-dimensional network analytics[6] to analyze such questions as who is interacting with whom and who shares what narratives with whom. They would use visual analytics, statistics, and text mining to extract narrative features in order to characterize the empirical profile of messages that do and do not contain false information, the dialogues in which those messages are embedded, the narratives and counternarratives under discussion, the users that do and do not send the messages, the types of users and their motivations for sending those messages, and the groups that are or are not receptive to the messages. New methods would likely be tested on a combination of new and old data. As theoretical accounts are modified, social cybersecurity researchers develop new algorithms for collecting data on specific activities or measuring key features of those activities. The utility of these new methods and theories resides in the extent to which they support explanation and prediction in the wild, are reusable, and can be extended to new domains.

OPPORTUNITIES FOR THE IC

The field of social cybersecurity offers two primary benefits for the IC. First, it provides a means of strengthening the capacity of the United States to assess, predict, and mitigate the impact of attacks in the cyber-mediated environment that are aimed at affecting the hearts, minds, and welfare of U.S. citizens, corporations, and institutions. Second, the field provides a means of increasing U.S. capacity to assess, monitor, and forecast changes in behavior in other countries using social cyberintelligence.

The United States is engaged in an ongoing war in cyberspace, which is being conducted to a significant degree in and through social media (Shallcross, 2017; Waltzman, 2015): social cybersecurity threats are pervasive and on the rise because foreign adversaries and criminals exploit features of social media; 50 percent of the 10 worst social media–based

---

[6]High-dimensional network analytics is the use of networks with multiple dimensions, such as a series of time-varying networks, networks with geocoordinates (geonetworks), or a set of networks varying in types of nodes and links (a metanetwork) (Carley, 2002).

cyberattacks occurred in 2017 (Wolfe, 2017). Spear phishing (sending a malicious file or link through an innocuous message) is also on the rise (Frenkel, 2017).

A key role of the intelligence analyst is to understand, explain, assess, and forecast the social threats in cyberspace and to counter those threats, which include the manipulation of information for nefarious purposes. Russia and China both have and use technologies that can manipulate content on social media by altering or disguising what is being said or who appears to be saying it, and influencing who will read or receive what information. Social cyber-mediated interference in elections is common. Bots, trolls, and cyborgs have supported information and disinformation campaigns aimed at influencing elections in the United States, Britain, Germany, and Sweden. Social cybersecurity attacks are prevalent: by one estimate, as many as one in five businesses have been subjected to a social media–based malware attack.[7] Such cyberattacks are conducted by individuals, groups, nonstate actors, state actors, and actors sponsored by states, often supported by the use of bots. Because these actors vary in their capabilities, so, too, does the quality of their information maneuvers (Darczewska, 2014; Snegovaya, 2015; Zheng and Wu, 2005).

Virtually anything that can be represented in digital form can be falsified. Tools for falsifying content include fake actors (personas) (Mansfield-Devine, 2008), fake antivirus software (Stone-Gross et al., 2013), and fake websites (Holz et al., 2009). The spread of such intentionally deceptive material, particularly the spread of false information, has the potential to undermine societies and is a growing concern for governments around the world (Allcott and Gentzkow, 2017; Roozenbeek and van der Linden, 2018; van der Linden et al., 2017). The accuracy of recorded sound and images can no longer be taken for granted. Software can be used to alter digital images, mimic the sounds of human voices, and create simulated videos (e.g., Piotrowski and Gajewski, 2007; Kim et al., 2018). This technology can be used to portray people saying things they did not say and doing things that never actually occurred. The growing ability to fabricate audio and digital information not only complicates the task of societies in distinguishing between reality and false narratives but also complicates the intelligence analyst's task in detecting deception (Joseph, 2017).

The IC must rely on open-source information in addressing a range of issues (Best and Cumming, 2007; Bean, 2011). Intelligence analysts collect, manage, and assess open-source data, seeking to understand the biases contained in the data, recognize when the data have been manipulated by an adversarial party, and recognize when individuals and communities in the

---

[7]See https://www.pandasecurity.com/mediacenter/social-media/uh-oh-one-out-of-five-businesses-are-infected-by-malware-through-social-media [July 2018].

United States are under attack in the open-source information environment (Omand et al., 2012). Social cybersecurity science provides many of the tools and methods that can help meet these challenges.

Finally, the analyst has a need to understand which individuals, groups, and communities are at risk of being manipulated through social media and how that risk can be mitigated. This task includes understanding when the analyst and the IC organization are at risk. Meeting this challenge requires effective means of training IC analysts to recognize indicators and warnings that social cyberattacks are occurring, to be aware of the kinds of social cyber-mediated attacks that can occur and their consequences, and to operate safely in the social cyberenvironment. The IC needs to recognize quickly when it is under social cyberattack, as well as to identify the ways in which it is susceptible to related risks, such as insider threat, information maneuvers designed to discredit an investigation, or denial-of-service events conducted through social media. The field of social cybersecurity offers important perspectives on how to recognize and respond to such attacks. Other SBS research, particularly in the application of organization theory to high-risk organizations, provides guidance on how to promote heedful interaction in the cyber-mediated realm and how to develop and sustain an effective social cybersafety culture.

EXAMPLE APPLICATION: SOCIAL INFLUENCE ON TWITTER

An example illustrates the contributions of the social cybersecurity approach to intelligence analysis. The Islamic State of Iraq and ash-Sham (ISIS) makes extensive use of social media in its operations (Blaker, 2015; Veilleux-Lepage, 2015). It uses social media for recruitment (Berger and Morgan, 2015; Gates and Podder, 2015); information warfare on local populations (Farwell, 2014); and possibly intelligence gathering and training. Similarly, Russian information operations use social media to influence social opinion and alter behavior. Social cybersecurity theories and methods have been used to identify what tactics are being used for these purposes and to explore their potential impact. Much of this work has been done using data extracted from Twitter, although cyberforensic techniques allow researchers to connect to information in other media (e.g., Facebook and YouTube) as well.

Consider an influence operation using Twitter to benefit ISIS. The high volume of tweets is such that Twitter may not have the resources to send every tweet from a particular user to all of that user's followers, so prioritization schemes are needed to determine what to send and to whom. Twitter is organized organically into a set of topic-groups—dense communities of users that frequently mention each other and share topics, as shown in

Figure 6-1 (Benigni et al., 2017a, 2017b). A topic-group is simply the way humans self-organize in many social media systems. Social media platforms often have ways of measuring the size of these topic-groups and use information about the group's size, membership, and topics of discussion to determine what messages, topics, or people to prioritize in various lists.

In our example, one of these topic-groups is focused on issues related to Syria. Initially, it also included many individuals who were, if not members of ISIS, at least sympathizers, and much of the discussion was related to ISIS recruitment and propaganda. Within Twitter topic-groups, users vary in their communicative power, so some individuals have a disproportionate ability to reach others in the topic-group when they tweet. These individuals are often identified using metrics from social network analysis such as page rank, superspreader, or superfriend. Superspreaders in particular have a large number of followers and are central figures in their topic-group. When such individuals tweet, their messages are more likely to be read and/or retweeted than are the messages of others in the topic-group, and tweets that mention such users are more likely to be retweeted, in part because of the algorithms used by Twitter to prioritize messages and users. The analytic theories and methods used in narrative studies, especially regarding what gives certain narratives and messages power (e.g., an underlying emotional message that leads to specific attitudes and beliefs), are relevant to this challenge (see Chapter 5). However, the application of these theories to social media technologies work needs further study, particularly because of the limits in how emotions can be conveyed in or understood from short text statements.

Twitter's algorithms seem to prioritize tweets from superspreaders in the set of tweets received by other users. The term "echo chamber" refers to a set of users who tend to mention one another. The closer a topic-group is to being an echo chamber, the more rapidly information will diffuse within it. In these situations, emotions can escalate rapidly, and contradictory information is less likely to be broadcast. Messages from echo chambers appear to be prioritized in the set of messages Twitter sends to the topic-groups associated with those echo chambers. Thus if an echo chamber retweets a message from a superspreader, the members of the echo chamber are more likely to appear in the list of messages received by members of the topic-group.

Within the Syrian topic-group in our example, one superspreader is an imam. At this point, it is not known whether he is associated with ISIS or Enter the Firibi Gnome bot (an automated agent that engages in Internet activity and sends tweets) as shown in Figure 6-1. This bot—actually a network of bots—functions as a pure echo chamber. It retweeted messages from the imam, which caused members of the bot network to appear in the feeds of other members of the topic-group, who were often human. Thus,

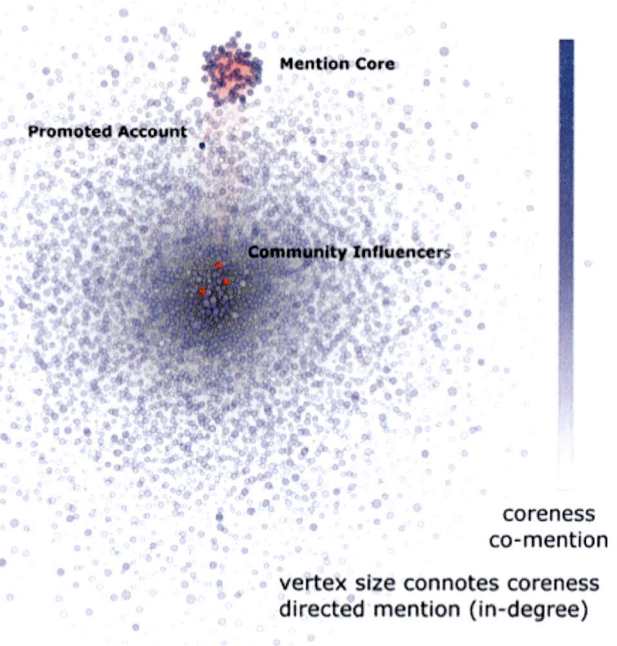

FIGURE 6-1 ISIS and Syrian online extremist community and Firibi Gnome bot on Twitter.
NOTE: Each dot (vertex) is a Twitter user who has sent a tweet about a topic of interest. Dots in red are linked to the Firibi Gnome bot. The mention core is the set of Twitter users who are densely connected by mentions. The largest, densest mention core is near the top. The Firibi Gnome bot is in that core. The promoted account is the Twitter site associated with a website that is collecting money for the children of Syria. The influencer is the imam's Twitter account.
SOURCE: Benigni et al. (2019).

members of the topic-group began to follow these bots. At some point, the bot network started tweeting messages with a link to a charity website that was ostensibly collecting money for the children of Syria, a site that some believe is linked to money laundering for ISIS. Without any active behavior from the imam, members of the topic-group were swayed by this bot to give money. Retweets by those who sympathized with messages from the bot were sufficient to manipulate the topic-group and to change the Twitter algorithm's prioritization of messages and their recipients (refer to Figure 6-1).

Social cyber researchers have developed methods that make it possible to track and understand such online developments. These methods can be used to identify topic-groups and echo chambers (Benigni et al., 2017b); identify influential users in social media, such as superspreaders and superfriends (Altman et al., 2018); identify core topics (Alvanaki et al., 2012); identify cross-media linkages (Dawson et al., 2018); and measure the potential reach of a message (Hong et al., 2011). Research is also under way on technology that could be used to support the identification or spread of false information. Examples include technology for fact checking (Rubin et al., 2015; Snopes[8]); image modification (Schneider and Chang, 1996); duplication of images (Ke et al., 2004); brandjacking attacks[9] (Youngblood, 2016); sentiment mining (Pang and Lee, 2008); stance[10] detection (Somasundaran and Wiebe, 2010); personality, gender, and age identification (Schwartz et al., 2013); location identification (Huan and Carley, 2017); and event detection (Wei et al., 2015). This work builds on ongoing computer science research that is well funded and in which advances are already being made.

Social cybersecurity research based on this work uses these computational methods in developing new sociotechnical theories and methods focused on the spread of multiple types of information maneuvers that were previously treated as a single phenomenon.

RESEARCH NEEDED IN THE COMING DECADE

Research in the field of social cybersecurity is needed on two parallel fronts: (1) research to establish new scientific methods and techniques capable of processing and analyzing the new types of data and high-dimensional networks made prevalent by social media; and (2) research to translate the resulting findings and techniques to operational tools that can be used by the IC.

---

[8]Available: https://www.snopes.com/fact-check/category/fake-news [November 2018].

[9]Brandjacking is the practice of mimicking the online identity of a business for the purpose of deceiving or defrauding users.

[10]In this context, "stance" refers to a publicly stated opinion, particularly one that is shared by an online community.

Advances in computer science, such as in the use and application of machine learning, have provided powerful tools for analyzing online activity. However, these advances are not readily transferable to the analysis of online activity in real time, nor are they sufficient to illuminate the broader context in which the activity is taking place. Multidisciplinary computational social science research building on both technological advances in computer science and SBS research has the potential to advance the research infrastructure in the field of social cybersecurity and expand the intelligence analyst's capability to address cybersecurity questions.

Having the tools necessary to predict and prevent attacks in the social cyberspace will require an aggressive research effort to identify, characterize, and understand such attacks. The committee sees opportunities to address a number of issues of concern for intelligence analysis:

- identifying who is conducting social cybersecurity attacks,
- identifying the strategies used to conduct such an attack,
- identifying the perpetrator's motive,
- tracing the attackers and the impact of the attack across multiple social media platforms,
- quantifying the effectiveness of the attack,
- identifying who is most susceptible to such attacks, and
- mitigating these attacks.

For each of these opportunities, we provide an overview of the challenge, summarize the recent work on which future developments would build, and specify the nature of further work that can pay significant dividends in the coming decade.

Social Cyberforensics: Identifying Who Is Conducting Social Cybersecurity Attacks

One of the keys to mitigating and responding to social cybersecurity attacks is being able to identify the perpetrators and impose sanctions against them. However, identification of perpetrators is a difficult problem in the cyber-mediated environment. Overcoming technical issues such as IP spoofing[11] can partly address this problem (Tanase, 2003), but the possibilities for overcoming the problem would be greatly expanded if it were possible to identify behavioral patterns at the individual and group

---

[11]IP spoofing has been defined as an attack in which "a hacker uses tools to modify the source address in the packet header to make the receiving computer system think the packet is from a trusted source, such as another computer on a legitimate network, and accept it"; see https://usa.kaspersky.com/resource-center/threats/ip-spoofing [January 2019].

levels, such as those associated with language use, location, credit taking, patterns of verbal communication, and use of images (e.g., Chen, 2015; Krombholz et al., 2015). Yet another need is the capacity to identify two actors appearing in two different media as in fact the same actor (such as when terrorist group members move from Twitter to a site on the dark web) (Maddox et al., 2016).

To illustrate, a writer's identity may be revealed through the linguistic style of a piece of text, and some work has suggested that such clues can be traced. Researchers have developed a method of encoding stylistic attributes to develop so-called "writeprints" (markers akin to fingerprints) (Abbasi and Chen, 2008). This method is based on the premise that aspects of any individual writer's usage (e.g., lexical, syntactic, structural, content-specific, and idiosyncratic features) are unconscious and persist from one document to another, so that they can be used to effectively identify an individual author (Pearl and Steyvers, 2012). Topic models have been built using these features. Thus it is now theoretically possible to develop documents that can exactly match the features of a particular author. Most of this work, however, is in early stages and is limited to English (Mbaziira and Jones, 2016).

Other detection tools are possible in the near term. Recent advances in social network/network science (Benigni et al., 2019) and social cyber-forensic techniques (Al-Khateeb et al., 2017) offer promising possibilities for identifying perpetrators. The social media reach of perpetrators is often enhanced by the use of bot, cyborg, Sybil, or troll techniques (Johansson et al., 2013; Klausen, 2015).[12] Indeed, as discussed above, many of the actors in social media may be bots; one study suggests that this may be the case for 48 million Twitter accounts (Varol et al., 2017). And according to a recent Pew Research Center report, two-thirds of all links shared on Twitter were shared by suspected bots (Wojcik, 2018). Emerging techniques are making it easier to identify whether perpetrators are humans, bots, or cyborgs, and further research is needed to increase the operational utility of these techniques for the intelligence analyst (e.g., Beskow and Carley, 2018; Morstatter et al., 2016). Bots and cyborgs that are used to influence and manipulate individuals and communities, often by exploiting features of a particular social medium, are evolving in sophistication and form as media platforms and bot-detection techniques evolve. At present, however, understanding of how bots and cyborgs evolve is limited to knowing that they are becoming more sophisticated, and no technology for predicting their evolution exists.

---

[12]A cyborg is an actor that is part human and part bot, frequently a human assisted by algorithms. Sybil is another, less widely used name for a bot. A troll is a user who posts inflammatory or off-topic messages in an online community in order to start quarrels or upset people; a troll account may be used by a single person, a group, or cyborgs.

> **Research Directions**
>
> *Continue work on developing better theories and methods for identifying perpetrators of cyberattacks.*
>
> This research could build on cyberforensic techniques, coupled with social network/network science techniques, machine learning, and deep understanding of sociopolitical contexts and the skills needed by perpetrators to manipulate social media and entertainment technologies. Some promising avenues include
>
> - research to improve the capacity to detect online behavioral patterns of perpetrators;
> - translational research to improve the utility for the IC of existing computational social science research techniques for identifying whether apparent attacks stem from humans, bots, or cyborgs;
> - interdisciplinary research led by SBS researchers (those with deep understanding of how and why people manipulate media technology) to develop tools for predicting how bots and cyborgs will evolve in the future; and
> - the development of sharable and continuously expanding data about known bots and cyborgs.

Information Maneuvers: Identifying the Strategies Used to Conduct an Attack

Used to manipulate individuals and groups, an information maneuver is any communication strategy intended to exaggerate or mitigate the spread of selected information or opinions, garner information, influence opinion, build or break connections among individuals to enable or prevent the spread of information or opinion, or exaggerate or minimize the influence of key actors (Al-Khateeb and Agarwal, 2016). A typical analytic approach to identifying information maneuvers is to look for something odd in social media posts, such as an increase in messages or the appearance of a new actor, and then collect specific data related to this anomaly. In so doing, an analyst working today would conduct detailed legwork involving tracking and reading messages. This approach is inherently costly, cannot be applied on a large scale, and is difficult to teach. A growing body of multidisciplinary research, however, has laid the foundation for new tools to augment intelligence analysis by detecting information maneuvers in a semiautomated fashion, identifying their intended audience, and classifying them by type. Much of this research has grown out of work on information warfare, marketing studies, and analyses of bot activity.

As discussed in Chapter 5, a central research challenge has been to investigate how fragilities of human social cognition and emotion can be exploited in an online context to shape information access and opinions, as well as how primary influencers exert their influence, and to better understand the nature of groups that are influenced through social media. These questions are important in seeking to understand information maneuvers and social cyberattacks, which typically operate at both the social network level (who is communicating with whom/influenced by whom) and the knowledge network level (who shares what information or opinions with whom). Such attacks typically exploit social cognition, including people's perception of the generalized other (that nebulous entity that represents one's opinion of what is common across the group), generalization strategies, and social influence procedures (Benigni et al., 2017a).

Information maneuvers can take different forms with very subtle nuances, and they require elaborate setups. Examples include maneuvers to manipulate an election (Metaxas and Mustafaraj, 2012), social engineering campaigns (Kandias et al., 2013), and satire campaigns (Babcock et al., 2018).

A social engineering campaign is the psychological manipulation of individuals to get them to perform specific actions, such as divulging confidential information or state secrets. Social engineering is one of the many tactics used in social influence campaigns on social media, such as those aimed at insiders (Kandias et al., 2013). Social engineering attacks, such as phishing and vishing (voice phishing), exploit not only factors well known to drive people's responses (see, e.g., Kumaraguru et al., 2007) but also how those responses are constrained and amplified by new technology. Traditional social science theories suggest that, whether they are conscious of it or not, people are motivated by (Cialdini, 2001):

- reciprocity, or a sense of obligation to return favors;
- commitment, or a sense of obligation to do what one says one will;
- authority, or an inclination to obey or follow authority figures;
- social influence, or a tendency to do what others do;
- sociability, or a tendency to do what those one likes suggest; and
- scarcity reduction, or a tendency to desire what is scarce.

In a cyber-mediated environment, these motivations act somewhat differently because of the influence of other factors, such as a preference for easy modes of response, readily available information, and minimization of effort. Further, the features of the communication technologies influence who is motivated by what, and when, by making it possible to alter

- the way information is prioritized;
- constraints on choices;
- the attractiveness of options (e.g., using color, font and images, or repetition); and
- how easy it is to tell whether one is interacting with people, organizations, or bots.

A satire campaign is the use of exaggeration, humor, or irony to expose the inappropriate actions or views of particular people, groups, or organizations. In social media contexts, however, satire often appears out of context and so may not be recognized as such. Satire attacks can go viral and may be mistaken for news and then recharacterized as "fake news." This latter pattern is sometimes referred to as "the Stewart/Colbert effect," referring to the unintended persuasiveness of comedians' personas (Amarasingam, 2011). Satire attacks are among the many tactics used in social influence campaigns on social media, such as those aimed at political groups Babcock et al., 2018).

The literature on information warfare also sheds some light on new forms of information maneuvers. Research on information warfare typically considers four broad strategies: distort, dissuade, distract, and dismay (Snegovaya, 2015). Classically, these strategies depend on how messages are constructed and communicated; there are well-known rhetorical strategies for persuasion (Ferris, 1994). Although forms of information maneuvers would fit into these four broad strategies, it is not yet known whether there are other strategic purposes to consider, or whether automatic characterization of an information maneuver or social media campaign as representing one of these strategies is possible. In addition, recent research has demonstrated that information maneuvers in social media may not only manipulate what is being said but also foster or undermine online communities or topic-groups associated with a message (Benigni et al., 2017b) or identities and brands (i.e., brand-jacking [e.g., Ramsey, 2010]).

Researchers are currently seeking ways to use features of social media posts and actors and the delivery/response sequence in characterizing information maneuvers. They have identified features that could work, including manipulation of emotions (Stieglitz and Dang-Xuan, 2013), presence (Naylor et al., 2012), group formation (Benigni et al., 2019), image manipulation (Tsikerdekis and Zeadally, 2014a), speed of spread (Vosoughi et al., 2018), and manipulation of the message and the group by bots (Benigni et al., 2017b). A large body of research explores the relationships among emotions, emotion manipulation, and the presentation of emotion in social media (Asur and Huberman, 2010; Gilbert and Hutto, 2014; Liu and Zhang, 2012; Pang and Lee, 2008; Steiglitz and Dang-Xuan, 2013). Additionally, particular emotions have specific triggers and functions, all of which lead to different cognitions and prime different actions/decisions. Thus, research on how specific discrete underlying emotional states lead to different consequences would be useful.

Much of the work in this area uses highly simplistic measures of emotion focused on the valence and strength of words in general, in context, or across a body of posts (stance). Meanwhile, more sophisticated approaches to emotion, such as affect control theory and discrete emotions theory (Heise, 1987; Robinson et al., 2006), provide the basis for relating emotions to behavior and identity construction empirically. However, these approaches are generally not applied to social media (an exception being Joseph and Carley [2016]). The research on social media and emotions, however, is still not well connected to the research on affect control, emotion management, and group behavior.

Another approach to characterizing information maneuvers—the use of images and videos, including doctored or fake images—has become possible with the advent of new platforms that better support images and videos, as well as increasing bandwidth, the prevalence of smartphones, and growing consumer interest in moving from text to images or videos to communicate. Recent studies in this area have explored the use of images and videos in social media by terrorist groups to recruit, spread messages, distort opinions, sow fear, and spread misleading health information (Farwell, 2014; Huey, 2015; Mangold and Faulds, 200; Syed-Abdul et al., 2013). Automated image and video analysis, however, is being carried out largely in the field of computer science and has not made its way to the field of social cybersecurity. Although hundreds of social cybersecurity studies have used computational text analysis methods, there appear to be only a few that have used any form of computational image or video processing.[13] An area of research prime for breakthroughs in the near future, then, is understanding how the presentation of emotion-laden messages and images in social media can influence groups, how such presentation varies across messages containing true and false information, and how the impact of such messages and images can be countered within and through information maneuvers.

---

[13]This observation is based on an examination of all papers identified by Carley and colleagues (2018) as being in the area of social cybersecurity.

> **Research Directions**
>
> ***Conduct interdisciplinary research to develop computational models and theories about information maneuvers in cyberspace and the respective strategies of influence and manipulation.***
>
> This research in social cybersecurity can build on foundational work on information warfare in political science, social psychology, and military science; rhetoric and communication theories relevant to marketing and manipulation; theories of social influence, social cognition, and group identification in anthropology, sociology, psychology, and political science; and studies of emotions and affect control in cognitive science and psychology. Moving beyond these theories to account for the technical, global, and temporal nature of the new cyber environment will be a valuable step forward. Promising avenues include
>
> - research to understand how operational features of specific social media and entertainment technologies are being exploited as part of these information maneuvers;
> - research expanding on new work to characterize information maneuvers and to develop a unified list of such maneuvers and associated data;
> - research to develop theories for identifying, explaining, predicting, and countering information maneuvers in cyberspace;
> - research to further develop tactics, techniques, and procedures, currently in their infancy, for detecting information manipulation as it is happening and identifying the strategies being used, and for reducing the societal and group-level risks of such manipulation; and
> - translational research on the operational technology that can allow the IC to identify and characterize information maneuvers and their intended audience rapidly, at scale, and in a semiautomated fashion.

Intent Identification: Identifying the Perpetrator's Motive

Although progress is being made in the development of methods for identifying when information maneuvers have occurred, understanding the intent behind these maneuvers presents its own challenges (e.g., Sydell, 2016). People choose to deceive others for many reasons, including to avoid something negative; to fulfill a desire for fun, economic benefit, or personal advantage; to bolster self-esteem, make others laugh, or act altruistically; or to be polite. They may also, of course, seek to deceive for malicious reasons (Bhattacharjee, 2017). Research on deception by state and nonstate actors in cyberspace has distinguished among three types of cyberattacks: they may be conducted for economic reasons (Lotrionte, 2014) or strategic cyberespionage and military reasons (Geers et al., 2013), or be opportunistic and politically motivated (Kumar et al., 2016).

An intriguing aspect of the motivation for information maneuvers is that much of the activity in social media is not malicious, but is aimed at spreading news or information on new products, sharing information on social activities, and building communities of like interest and concern. At a high level, bots and information maneuvers have been used in similar ways for both illicit and legal gain and with both malicious and nonmalicious intent. Thus information maneuvers useful for spreading false information are also useful for spreading true information. Tactics used to market real products (e.g., Safko, 2010; Scott, 2015) are also used to market illegal products (Benigni et al., 2019). And procedures used to recruit and support followers for sports teams are also used to recruit and support followers for terrorist groups (compare Henderson and Bowley [2010] and Farwell [2014]). Researchers have suggested that differences in metadata, word choice, and timing of messages may provide clues to the intent behind messages (Java et al., 2007; King, 2008), but determining the intent of a particular actor, or at least distinguishing malicious and nonmalicious activity in an automated fashion, remains a challenge.

Assessment of images and videos is frequently used to develop insight into the intent of those who spread deceptive information. In one example, a dismay maneuver used images of a bomb attack in the White House with the intent to spread terror (Weimann, 2014). In another case, a Russian information operation used fake images, some from video games (Luhn, 2017; Murphy, 2017), in tweets and Facebook posts claiming that the United States was supporting ISIS. Fake images of frightening phenomena, such as sharks in subways or airports flooded with water, are routinely circulated in the immediate aftermath of disasters to contribute to disruption (Gupta et al., 2013). Indeed, compendiums of such images have been developed, so many are reused or doctored and reused whenever disasters occur. Image analysis holds promise for understanding intent in such cases.

Researchers are also exploring other possible indicators that can be used to identify deception, including linguistic markers (Briscoe et al., 2014; Zhou and Zhang, 2008; Zhou et al., 2003); activity indicators (e.g., those used in detecting bots [Subrahamainian et al., 2016]); nonverbal behavior and the use of multiple accounts (Tsikerdekis and Zeadally, 2014a); and social structural behavior (i.e., behaviors that change who is interacting with whom and who is important in the social network) (Pak and Zhou, 2014). However, the ability to engage in deceptive behavior and the types of behaviors possible are dependent on the technology itself (Tsikerdekis and Zeadally, 2014b), language (Levine, 2014), the human social network (Chow and Chan, 2008; Tsikerdekis and Zeadally, 2014b), and human cognition (Spence et al., 2004). Other research has examined the profiles, characteristics, and motivations of hackers or cybercriminals who create fakeries or use deception or deceptive messages (Décary-Hétu et al., 2012;

Papadimitriou, 2009; Seigfried-Spellar and Treadway, 2014). Still other work seeks to identify the characteristics of individuals and groups that make them vulnerable to deceptive messaging (Pennycook and Rand, 2018).

Some of this work has led to automated fact checkers that rely on both human- and machine-labeled input (e.g., Snopes;[14] Hassan et al., 2015), software tools for identifying deception based on verbal cues in texts (Zhou et al., 2004), tools for creating and detecting fake personas (even those that create personas with disabilities) (DeMello et al., 2005; Schultz and Fuglerud, 2012), and software for modifying text and auditory and video/image data streams to engender trust in the false information (Emam, 2006; Stamm et al., 2010). While there has been a fair amount of work on detecting in-person deception based on auditory and visual cues, tools for autoidentification based on findings about auditory or visual human "tells" are less well developed (Vrij et al., 2010). Thus, ongoing research in social cybersecurity is seeking ways to uncover intent and deception computationally.

Research Directions

Conduct research to develop techniques and tools with the capabilities to determine automatically and rapidly the intent of those conducting social cybersecurity information maneuvers.

Although such techniques and tools exist, they need to be better linked to theories of motivation and tools for linking motivation to behaviors. Future research in this area would build on work in social psychology, forensics, historical analysis, anthropology, sociology, cognitive psychology, political science, and statistical comparison. Some current work ripe for expansion includes

- the development of methods for linking available metadata to actors' intents;
- the development of methods for linking image and video analysis at scale to network science analysis and language technologies;
- identification of nonverbal indicators of veracity and deception in social media encounters and the combinations of linguistic, nonverbal, and audiovisual elements that signal truthfulness versus deception on the part of persons of interest to the IC, such as the leaders of states and nonstate entities, their followers, criminals, money launderers, and other bad actors in both online and offline interactions; and
- determination of differences in early indicators and motivations for types of deception employed at the individual, state, and nonstate actor levels.

---

[14] Available: https://www.snopes.com/fact-check/fake-news-stories [October 12, 2018].

Cross-Media Movement and Information Diffusion: Tracing the Attackers and the Impact of the Attack across Multiple Social Media Platforms

Classic theories of information diffusion are largely agnostic with respect to what media are used, and those that consider the media used often focus on social presence (Cheung et al., 2011), speed and network externality effects (Lin and Lu, 2011), and media features (Lee et al., 2015). In social media, however, there is not one medium but many. Studies have shown that movement among media or links from a message in one medium to another can increase the spread and reach of messages (Agarwal and Bandeli, 2017; Suh et al., 2010). Such movement among media can be engineered by bots (Wojcik, 2018), and allows actors to "hide," moving groups and messages they take with them when they move between media (Al-Khateeb and Agarwal, 2016; Liang, 2015), which allows them to create safe havens.[15] An article on the online news site *Wired* describes the phenomenon this way:

> The Islamic State maximized its reach by exploiting a variety of platforms: social media networks such as Twitter and Facebook, peer-to-peer messaging apps like Telegram and Surespot, and content sharing systems like JustPaste.it. More important, it decentralized its media operations, keeping its feeds flush with content made by autonomous production units from West Africa to the Caucasus—a geographical range that illustrates why it is no longer accurate to refer to the group merely as the Islamic State of Iraq and al-Sham (ISIS), a moniker that undersells its current breadth.[16]

Some social media platforms are more likely to be used to receive rather than to generate messages. Most rumors on Twitter, for example, originate in other media (Liu et al., 2015), most notably in blogs. People in general use different media for different purposes (Haythornthwaite and Wellman, 1998). To be sure, diffusion models exist for social media such as Twitter (Xiong et al., 2012) and Flickr (Zhao et al., 2010). However, there are only a few theories of or models for information diffusion when multiple social media are present and in use (an exception being a model called Construct [Carley et al., 2009, 2014]), and even this model needs to be extended to account for the newer social media platforms). Although technologies are available for tracking a message or an individual across media (e.g.,

---

[15]For example, "terrorists and extremists are increasingly moving their activities online—and areas of the web have become a safe haven for Islamic State to plot its next attacks, according to a report published last week by the London-based Henry Jackson Society" (quoted from http://www.homelandsecuritynewswire.com/dr20180409-stealth-terrorists-use-encryption-the-darknet-and-cryptocurrencies [April 2018]).

[16]See https://www.wired.com/2016/03/isis-winning-social-media-war-heres-beat [April 2018].

Maltego), theories on and the ability to predict such moves do not exist (Al-Khateeb et al., 2017). Work in this area is currently limited by barriers to data collection, diffusion theories that do not account for who uses what media when, and a lack of good digital forensic skills and techniques (Bidgoli, 2006; Huber et al., 2011). Thus, most of this research considers only a single medium, such as blogs (Gruhl et al., 2004), Twitter (Romero et al., 2011), or e-mail (Mezzour and Carley, 2014). In stark contrast, most marketing guidance recommends the use of multiple media (e.g., Hovde, 2017). The technology exists to conduct cross-media assessment, but it is in its infancy and not widely available.

Research Directions

Conduct research to develop multimedia diffusion theories and a better understanding of the co-movement of people and ideas through cyberspace.

As the technology for cross-media assessment becomes more prevalent, SBS research in this area should be highly productive. This research can build on social cyberforensics technologies, social network/network science techniques, and social theories of information diffusion and group formation. New theories of information diffusion that account for multimedia use in cyberspace can then be applied to the development of techniques and tools for tracking, explaining, and predicting the movement of individuals, groups, ideas, and beliefs through and across multiple social media.

Real-Time Measurement of the Effectiveness of Information Campaigns: Quantifying the Effectiveness of the Attack

Real-time measurement of the impacts of information campaigns is a classically difficult problem, as those impacts often are slow to develop. In general, research is sparse on how to assess empirically and in real time the impact or success of an information maneuver (Carrier-Sabourin, 2011). The vast quantity of data and increased speed of communication that characterize social media create an environment in which it may be possible to make progress in this area. A number of metrics for measuring the reach and influence of messages and actors on social media have been suggested (Hoffman and Fodor, 2010; Sterne, 2010). Some of these are predicated on notions of social network influence (Benigni et al., 2019) and still others on rhetoric-based conceptions of reach (Carley and Kaufer, 1993). Nevertheless, there is little consensus among researchers on what to measure, how to use these measures strategically, and whether proposed metrics are valid (Barger and Labrecque, 2013). Furthermore, it is unknown how the data collection strategy affects these metrics and whether, as a consequence, the measurement results could be biased. Another key challenge in this area is the creation and use of measures that can capture the dynamics of the underlying social and knowledge networks. Although approaches for assessing network dynamics exist (Ahn et al., 2011; Carley, 2017; Snijders, 2001), only those that can be used for incremental assessment scale well (Kas et al., 2013). Existing methods also cannot handle high-dimensional networks and so cannot assess impact in the social and knowledge networks simultaneously.

Research Directions

Develop methods for measuring the impact of an information campaign, in both the short and long terms.

Given the benefits of such methods for intelligence analysis, progress on real-time measurement of the effects of information maneuvers in cyberspace is an important area for future research in social cybersecurity. Such research could build on research on social networks and change detection, communication theories, and studies on group formation and participation in sociology and political science. Promising avenues include research to

- identify, operationalize, and validate these metrics;
- remove bias related to data collection; and
- assess the certainty of the results for large-scale, dynamic, high-dimensional networks.

At-Risk Groups: Identifying Who Is Most Susceptible to Attacks

The risk of being susceptible to information maneuvers has traditionally been considered greatest among those who are socially or economically disadvantaged, and risk reduction has been viewed as a function of education, awareness, empowerment, and reduction of disparities. Studies focused on the 2016 elections, however, found that while education was positively associated with accurate recognition of the falsity of news stories, so, too, were age and total media consumption (Alcott and Gentzkow, 2017). Current research suggests several factors that could influence those at risk: lost trust in mainstream media (Ekovich, 2017), overly filtered information through the use of personalized news (Flaxman et al., 2016), being embedded in topic-groups that are echo chambers (Benigni et al., 2019), and the inability to recognize that the information received is from bots (Benigni et al., 2017b). Other research, however, suggests that the majority of people do not trust information on social media (Ekovich, 2017) and that the spare empirical evidence available is not definitive on the impact of filtering (Zuiderveen Borgesius et al., 2016).

Inoculation techniques to reduce the susceptibility of individuals and groups to the spread of disinformation and to being affected by information warfare activities often take the form of media education. These techniques, however, are not based on empirical evidence and a deep understanding of the features of communication and entertainment technologies that can be exploited to spread disinformation. Such features include the short length of tweets, which makes it difficult to tell whether a message is satire (Babcock et al., 2018); marketing services that use bots to send tweets from an individual's account as that person (Benigni et al., 2017b); and the removal (by Google) of image information that had made it easier to identify the falsity of information (Stribley, 2018).

SBS research shows that people will continue to persist in beliefs even when the evidence for those beliefs is discredited; facts do not change opinions (Kolbert, 2017). Thus knowing that news is manufactured does not keep people from believing it (Lilienfeld, 2014). A variety of mechanisms underlie this phenomenon (Shermer, 2002)—for example, (1) the belief that the untrue is fun, (2) the belief that true information from an untrusted source is not trustworthy, (3) social influence, (4) a reduction in cognitive dissonance, and (5) confirmation bias. Given the high volume of data in social media, it is often argued that trust in the source is used as a way of filtering information and reducing cognitive load, in which case false information from a trusted source is more trusted than true information from an untrusted source (Tang and Liu, 2015). Furthermore, a number of mechanisms have been suggested as supporting the sharing of false information, such as a preference for believing and sharing novel over more familiar information; a preference for stories that generate particular emotional reactions, such as surprise or disgust (see, e.g., Aral and Van Alstyne, 2011; Berger and Milkman, 2012; Itti and Baldi, 2009); a preference for believing what others believe (Friedkin, 2006); and appeals to the generalized other (Benigni et al., 2019).

It has become commonplace for social media providers, such as Facebook and Twitter, to use hidden algorithms to guide users to particular types of content and to other users with similar interests. This algorithmic strategy increases the likelihood that users will experience repeated exposure to particular individuals, groups, messages, and narratives. Bots and cyborgs can exploit these algorithms and create online communities in which alternative messages are suppressed, appeals to the generalized other foster group acceptance (Holdsworth and Morgan, 2007; Mead, 1934), images and humor are used to limit discussion (Meyer, 2000), and users are exposed to artificially enhanced social influence (Benigni et al., 2019). Social influence is critical in affecting one's beliefs and attitudes (Friedkin, 2006), and repeat exposure to these "contained" online communities increases the likelihood that an individual will embrace particular information and messages.[17] Spammed messages to email or social media accounts is another mechanism that has been instrumental in driving people to fake websites and the adoption of malware (Moore et al., 2009).

Research has explored the spread of false information and has begun to document its potency. In a recent large-scale study, for example, Vosoughi and colleagues (2018) found that false information diffused "significantly farther, faster, deeper and more broadly than the truth in all categories of information" (p. 1147), although other studies have found that this is the case only when an offline receptive group exists (Babcock et al., 2018).

Research Directions

Better characterize those groups at risk of social cyberattacks, and identify ways to increase awareness of malicious information maneuvers and strengthen the resistance of at-risk topic-groups to such attacks.

Such research could build on research in education and social psychology; theories of social influence, marketing, participatory democracy, and cognitive bias reduction; and social and political theories of group formation and dissolution. Promising avenues include

- empirical research on the key factors that put individuals and groups at risk of being targeted by information maneuvers in cyberspace, how these factors and the individuals and groups targeted may vary depending on the specific social media platform, and how that risk can be measured and reduced in specific media;
- research to better understand how recipients are influenced by information maneuvers, and any differences among certain populations; and
- research to develop techniques for measuring the actual and potential impacts of deceptive action or the misplacement of trust at the group or population level.

---

[17]For examples, see work by Unkelbach (2007); Unkelbach and Stahl (2009); Alter and Oppenheimer (2009); and Fazio et al. (2015).

The Most Effective Responses: Mitigating These Attacks

Direct counterattacks on those conducting information maneuvers are often unsuccessful. Terrorists suspended from Twitter, for example, will recreate new accounts and engage in this activity even more vigorously (Al-Khateeb et al., 2017). Strategies focused on the receivers of the information and countermessages tend to be more effective,[18] but the success of such strategies depends on how messages are constructed and communicated vis-à-vis the group that is to be counterinfluenced. Deep understanding of the sociopolitical context is also necessary to keep the messaging attempt from backfiring. Research has yielded numerous guidelines for the creation of effective countermessages—for example, increasing credibility through the use of visuals (Murakami et al., 2009), not engaging in direct confrontation (Goulston, 2015), including a URL (Suh et al., 2010), being unyielding in stance (Lajeunesse, 2008), creating trust in the source (Tarran, 2017), and providing for sufficient resources and planning (Southwell et al., 2017). Because information maneuvers in social media involve manipulation of both groups and messages, moreover, new approaches to countermessages that include attention to the nature of the group are needed. Examples of such approaches include the application of research on participatory democracy and deliberative democracy techniques (Mutz, 2006), as well as influence maximization (Chen et al., 2010).

Although such research provides some information to guide countermessaging, it does not address a key problem occurring in social media—that, as discussed earlier, those with similar opinions form topic-groups through which they receive constant social support for not listening to counterarguments (the echo chamber effect [Bakshy et al., 2015]). Individuals confined to a topic-group may attend selectively only to certain messages and not even be exposed to any counterarguments (what is known as the filter-bubble effect [Flaxman et al., 2016]). One potential countermessaging approach to address this problem is the use of a context-aware system that directs messages from one actor to another (Conroy et al., 2015; Fischer, 2012).

A key limitation of this research, however, is that it tends to focus either on winning the argument or on diffusing the message, and not on winning a diffusion contest against a competing message. The majority of the empirical work on the diffusion of competing ideas has used simulation (e.g., Carley, 1990; Krackhardt, 2001). However, these studies do not address how the type of communication medium affects the spread of ideas. A practical challenge in this area is that even if the perfect counter-

---

[18] In operation, policies dictate which kinds of strategies are permitted under the law.

messaging strategy were known, its use might not be possible under current rules governing the IC.

With respect to such issues as the spread of malware through social media and phishing attacks, research has expanded to look at policies, defenses, and engineering solutions that can mitigate the impact of such attacks (Fette et al., 2007; Galbally et al., 2014; Kumar et al., 2016; Lin et al., 2009; Yin et al., 2007; Zahedi et al., 2015; Zargar et al., 2013). At the organizational level, much of this work has focused on technical solutions to preventing or minimizing the impact of malware spread by social media (Timm and Perez, 2010) and on training and toolbars to avoid phishing (Wu et al., 2006). Research is increasingly showing that a mitigation strategy needs to employ a three-pronged approach, encompassing corporate policy, social cybersecurity training, and technology (Cross, 2013; Oxley, 2013). Much of this research has been based in the areas of policy and cybersecurity without drawing on the wealth of research in organizational science. The organizational literature suggests that in general, when in a high-risk situation, an organization needs to have a safety culture (Guldenmund, 2000), elements of which include heedful interaction, awareness of the risk, and support for maintaining a safe environment. Although much of the work in this area has focused on health (Pronovost and Sexton, 2005) and nuclear power plants (Pidgeon, 1991), its general claims are equally relevant to social cybersecurity risks. Engaging in heedful social cyber interaction and developing and maintaining a social cybersafety culture can potentially reduce risks associated with social cyberattacks. The IC has itself been a victim of such attacks, and therefore may wish to explore how an IC-specific social cybersecurity safety culture can be instituted.

Research Directions

Support the design of countermessaging strategies in cyberspace.

Such research could build on work on information warfare from social psychology; research on cognitive biases, marketing, and communication; theories of social cognition; and knowledge of participation and group formation gleaned from sociology and political science. Promising avenues include

- research focused specifically on identifying effective countermessaging strategies while taking into account the technical features of the social media;
- research directed at identifying effective countermessaging strategies while taking into account the authorities governing those doing the countermessaging; and
- research on how to implement, measure the prevalence of, and assess the effectiveness of a social cybersecurity safety culture.

CONCLUSIONS

Cyber-mediated threats are a growing area of concern for the IC. Because their use is increasing and their platforms change rapidly, social media serve both as a mechanism for monitoring developments and cyber-mediated threats and as a mechanism that can be manipulated to influence behaviors in ways that may pose threats to national security. We note that current work related to cyberspace issues—including data collection, cybersecurity, and social cybersecurity—is fragmented across a large number of U.S. government agencies and parts of the IC. The tools used by these entities, the authority they have to collect information, and their agreements with third-party vendors to collect data or run assessments all vary. The IC may wish to explore whether a central office to coordinate cyberintelligence efforts is needed. We caution, however, that issues associated with terrorism, social cybersecurity, and cybersecurity each demand distinct sets of skills and authorities.

Designing ways to protect against such threats requires the ability to collect data on and analyze and visualize high-dimensional dynamic networks with both social network and knowledge network components; Twitter networks, for example, generate both social data on who replies, retweets, or mentions or which individuals are quoted, and knowledge data on hashtags or topics that co-occur. However, available machine learning techniques and standard computer science methods are of limited utility for answering nuanced questions about developing situations (Lazer et al., 2014). Nor are traditional social science methods sufficient to address complex issues in today's information environment.

The promising next frontier is the combining of computer science techniques with deep understanding of how the media and entertainment technology used to collect these data operate, the sociocultural phenomena being studied, and relevant social and cognitive science theories (Carley et al., 2018; Wang et al., 2007). Social network/network science methods coupled with language technologies, geospatial crowdsourced information, or machine learning and applied to large-scale data form the methodological cornerstone on which new advances will be realized. This kind of data is "big" not only because of the quantity involved, but also because of the number of networks in which the messages are embedded over time (National Research Council, 2013).

Empirical assessment of influence and manipulation in social cyberspace is yielding methods capable of processing large volumes of data, often from multiple media, and carrying out high-dimensional network analysis. Such methods have been used for successfully addressing a number of issues, such as the likelihood of retweeting (Suh et al., 2010), information diffusion (Romero et al., 2011), disaster planning (Landwehr et al.,

2016), extremist recruiting (Benigni et al., 2019), and political polarization (Conover et al., 2011). Furthermore, geospatial assessments have shown great diversity in the ways in which social media are used by region, time, and political context (Carley et al., 2015).

This work provides a starting point for the development of tools that could be used by the IC for efficiently identifying propaganda, false information, and other social cyberthreats. In addition to building a body of research in this new field, researchers will need to address a number of methodological and data challenges if social cybersecurity research is to make the progress that is needed in the coming decade. These challenges include the development of both policy solutions for improving researchers' access to data and more sophisticated techniques for working with large but often incomplete and biased datasets (Tufekci, 2014).

> CONCLUSION 6-1: A comprehensive multidisciplinary research strategy for identifying, monitoring, and countering social cyberattacks, predicated on computational social science, would provide significant support for the Intelligence Community's (IC's) efforts to address the social cybersecurity threat in the coming decade. The emerging field of social cybersecurity research can yield insights that would supplement the IC's training and technology acquisition in the area of social cybersecurity threats and foster an effective social cybersafety culture. These insights could support development of the capacity to, for example, detect bots and malicious online actors and track the impact of social cyberattacks.
>
> CONCLUSION 6-2: The Intelligence Community could strengthen its capacity to safeguard the nation against social cyber-mediated threats by supporting research with the objectives of developing
>
> - generally applicable scientific methods for assessing bias in online data, drawing conclusions based on missing data, and triangulating to interpolate missing or incorrect data using multiple data sources; and
> - new computational social science methods that would simultaneously consider change in social networks and narratives within social media–based groups from a geotemporal social-cyber perspective; and operational computational social science theories of influence and manipulation in a cyber-mediated environment that simultaneously take into account the network structure of online communities, the types of actors in those communities, social cognition, emotion, cognitive biases, narratives and counternarratives, and exploitable features of the social media technology.

REFERENCES

Abbasi, A., and Chen, H. (2008). Cybergate: A design framework and system for text analysis of computer-mediated communication. *MIS Quarterly: Management Information Systems, 32*(4), 811–837.

Agarwal, N., and Bandeli, K.K. (2017). Blogs, fake news, and information activities. In G. Bertolin (Ed.), *Digital Hydra: Security Implications of False Information Online* (pp. 31–46). Riga, Latvia: NATO Strategic Communications Centre of Excellence.

Ahn, J., Taieb-Maimon, M., Sopan, A., Plaisant, C., and Shneiderman, B. (2011). Temporal visualization of social network dynamics: Prototypes for nation of neighbors. In *International Conference on Social Computing, Behavioral-Cultural Modeling, and Prediction* (pp. 309–316). Berlin/Heidelberg, Germany: Springer. Available: http://www.cs.umd.edu/hcil/trs/2010-28/2010-28.pdf [December 2018].

Al-Khateeb, S., and Agarwal, N. (2016). Understanding strategic information maneuvers in network media to advance cyber operations: A case study analysing pro-Russian separatists' cyber information operations in Crimean water crisis. *Journal on Baltic Security, 2*(1), 6–27.

Al-Khateeb, S., Hussain, M.N., and Agarwal, N. (2017). Analyzing deviant socio-technical behaviors using social network analysis and cyber forensics-based methodologies. In O. Savas and J. Deng (Eds.), *Big Data Analytics in Cybersecurity and IT Management* (Chapter 12). New York: CRC Press, Taylor & Francis.

Allcott, H., and Gentzkow, M. (2017). Social media and fake news in the 2016 election. *Journal of Economic Perspectives, 31*(2), 211–236.

Alter, A.L., and Oppenheimer, D.M. (2009). Uniting the tribes of fluency to form a metacognitive nation. *Personality and Social Psychology Review, 13*(3), 219–235. doi:10.1177/1088868309341564.

Altman, N., Carley, K.C., and Reminga, J. (2018). *ORA User's Guide 2018*. Technical Report CMU-ISR-18-103. Pittsburgh, PA: Carnegie Mellon University, School of Computer Science, Institute for Software Research.

Alvanaki, F., Michel, S., Ramamritham, K., and Weikum, G. (2012). See what's enBlogue: Real-time emergent topic identification in social media. In *Proceedings of the 15th International Conference on Extending Database Technology* (pp. 336–347). New York: Association for Computing Machinery.

Amarasingam, A. (Ed.). (2011). *The Stewart/Colbert Effect: Essays on the Real Impacts of Fake News*. Jefferson, NC: McFarland & Company.

Anderson, K.E. (2017). Getting acquainted with social networks and apps: Social media in 2017. *Library Hi Tech News, 34*(10), 1–6.

Aral, S., and Van Alstyne, M. (2011). The diversity-bandwidth trade-off. *American Journal of Sociology, 117*(1), 90–171.

Asur, S., and Huberman, B.A. (2010). Predicting the future with social media. In *Proceedings of the 2010 IEEE/WIC/ACM International Conference on Web Intelligence and Intelligent Agent Technology* (vol. 1, pp. 492–499). Washington, DC: IEEE Computer Society.

Babcock, M., Beskow, D., and Carley, K.M. (2018). Beaten up on Twitter? Exploring fake news and satirical responses during the Black Panther movie event. In R. Thomson, C. Dancy, A. Hyder, and H. Bisgin (Eds.), *Proceedings of the 2018 SBP-BRiMS Conference on Social Computing, Behavioral-Cultural Modeling, & Prediction and Behavior Representation in Modeling and Simulation* (pp. 97–103). Washington, DC: Springer. Available: https://link.springer.com/chapter/10.1007/978-3-319-93372-6_12 [December 2018].

Baggili, I., and Breitinger, F. (2015). Data sources for advancing cyber forensics: What the social world has to offer. In *Sociotechnical Behavior Mining: From Data to Decisions? Papers from the 2015 AAAI Spring Symposium* (pp. 6–9). Palo Alto, CA: Association for the Advancement of Artificial Intelligence.

Bakshy, E., Messing, S., and Adamic, L.A. (2015). Exposure to ideologically diverse news and opinion on Facebook. *Science, 318*(6239), 1130–1132.

Barger, V.A., and Labrecque, L. (2013). An integrated marketing communications perspective on social media metrics. *International Journal of Integrated Marketing Communications*, 64–76. Available: https://ssrn.com/abstract=2280132 [December 2018].

Bean, H. (2011). *No More Secrets: Open Source Information and the Reshaping of U.S. Intelligence.* Santa Barbara, CA: ABC-CLIO.

Benigni, M., Joseph, K., and Carley, K.M. (2017a). Mining online communities to inform strategic messaging: Practical methods to identify community-level insights. *Computational and Mathematical Organization Theory*, 1–19. doi:10.1007/s10588-017-9255-3.

Benigni, M., Joseph, K., and Carley, K.M. (2017b). Online extremism and the communities that sustain it: Detecting the ISIS supporting community on Twitter. *PLOS ONE, 12*(12), e0181405.

Benigni, M., Joseph, K., and Carley, K.M. (2019). Bot-ivistm: Assessing information manipulation in social media using network analytics. In N. Agrawal, N. Dokoohaki, and S. Tokdemir (Eds.), *Emerging Research Challenges and Opportunities in Social Network Analysis and Mining* (pp. 19–42). Cham, Switzerland: Springer.

Berger, J.M., and Milkman, K.L. (2012). What makes online content viral? *Journal of Marketing Research, 49*(2), 192–205. doi:10.1509/jmr.10.0353.

Berger, J.M., and Morgan J. (2015). Defining and describing the population of ISIS supporters on Twitter. *Brookings*, March 5. Available: http://www.brookings.edu/research/papers/2015/03/isis-twitter-census-berger-morgan [December 2018].

Beskow, D.M., and Carley, K.M. (2018). Bot conversations are different: Leveraging network metrics for bot detection in Twitter. In *2018 IEEE/ACM International Conference on Advances in Social Networks Analysis and Mining (ASONAM)* (pp. 825–832). Washington, DC: IEEE Computer Society. doi:10.1109/ASONAM.2018.8508322.

Best Jr., R.A., and Cumming, A. (2007). *Open Source Intelligence (OSINT): Issues for Congress.* Available: https://fas.org/sgp/crs/intel/RL34270.pdf [December 2018].

Bhattacharjee, Y. (2017). *Why We Lie: The Science Behind Our Deceptive Ways.* Available: https://www.nationalgeographic.com/magazine/2017/06/lying-hoax-false-fibs-science [December 2018].

Bidgoli, H. (2006). *Handbook of Information Security, Information Warfare, Social, Legal, and International Issues and Security Foundations.* Hoboken, NJ: John Wiley & Sons.

Blaker, L. (2015). The Islamic State's use of online social media. *Military Cyber Affairs, 1*(1), Article 4. doi:10.5038/2378-0789.1.1.1004.

Briscoe, E.J., Appling, D.S., and Hayes, H. (2014). Cues to deception in social media communications. In *47th Hawaii International Conference on System Sciences* (HICSS) (pp. 1435–1443). Washington, DC: IEEE Computer Society. doi:10.1109/HICSS.2014.186.

Carley, K.M. (1990). Group stability: A socio-cognitive approach. In E. Lawler, B. Markovsky, C. Ridgeway, and H. Walker (Eds.), *Advances in Group Processes: Theory and Research* (vol. VII, pp. 1–44). Greenwich, CN: JAI Press.

Carley, K.M. (2002). Smart agents and organizations of the future. In L. Lievrouw and S. Livingstone (Eds.), *The Handbook of New Media* (pp. 206–220). Thousand Oaks, CA, SAGE.

Carley, K.M. (2017). ORA: A toolkit for dynamic network analysis and visualization. In R. Alhajj and J. Rokne (Eds.), *Encyclopedia of Social Network Analysis and Mining.* Washington, DC: Springer. doi:10.1007/978-1-4614-7163-9_309-1.

Carley, K.M., and Kaufer, D. (1993). Semantic connectivity: An approach for analyzing semantic networks. *Communication Theory, 3*(3), 183–213.

Carley, K.M., Martin, M.K., and Hirshman, B. (2009). The etiology of social change. *Topics in Cognitive Science, 1*(4), 621–650.

Carley, K.M., Lanham, M.J., Joseph, K., Kowalchuck, M., and Morgan, G.P. (2014). *Construct User's Guide*. Report CMU-ISR-14-105R. Pittsburgh, PA: School of Computer Science, Institute for Software Research. Available: http://reports-archive.adm.cs.cmu.edu/anon/isr2014/CMU-ISR-14-105R.pdf [December 2018].

Carley, K.M., Wei, W., and Joseph, K. (2015). High dimensional network analytics: Mapping topic networks in Twitter data during the Arab Spring. In S. Cui, A. Hero, Z.-Q. Luo, and J. Moura (Eds.), *Big Data Over Networks* (pp. 278–300). Cambridge, MA: Cambridge University Press.

Carley, K.M., Cervone, G., Agarwal, N., and Liu, H. (2018). Social cyber-security. In R. Thomson, C. Dancy, A. Hyder, and H. Bisgin (Eds.), *Proceedings of the 2018 SBP-BRiMS Conference on Social Computing, Behavioral-Cultural Modeling, & Prediction and Behavior Representation in Modeling and Simulation* (pp. 389–394). Washington, DC: Springer. doi:10.1007/978-3-319-93372-6_42.

Carrier-Sabourin, K. (2011). *Measuring Effects and Success in Influence Operations: Challenges, Limitations and Opportunities*. Available: http://www.dtic.mil/dtic/tr/fulltext/u2/a568381.pdf [April 2018].

Chen, A. (2015). The agency. *The New York Times Magazine*, June 2. Available: https://www.nytimes.com/2015/06/07/magazine/the-agency.html [December 2018].

Chen, W., Wang, C., and Wang, Y. (2010). Scalable influence maximization for prevalent viral marketing in large-scale social networks. In *Proceedings of the 16th ACM SIGKDD International Conference on Knowledge Discovery and Data Mining* (pp. 1029–1038). New York: Association for Computing Machinery.

Cheung, C.M.K., Chiu, P.-Y., and Lee, M.K.O. (2011). Online social networks: Why do students use Facebook?. *Computers in Human Behavior, 27*(4), 1337–1343.

Chow, W.S., and Chan, L.S. (2008). Social network, social trust and shared goals in organizational knowledge sharing. *Information & Management, 45*(7), 458–465. doi:10.1016/j.im.2008.06.007.

Cialdini, R.B. (1987). *Influence* (Vol. 3). Port Harcourt, Nigeria: Albin Michel.

Cialdini, R.B. (2001). The science of persuasion. *Scientific American, 284*(2), 76–81.

Conover, M., Ratkiewicz, J., Francisco, M.R., Gonçalves, B., Menczer, F., and Flammini, A. (2011). Political polarization on Twitter. In *Proceedings of the Fifth International AAAI Conference on Weblogs and Social Media* (vol. 133, pp. 89–96). Available: https://www.aaai.org/ocs/index.php/ICWSM/ICWSM11/paper/viewFile/2847/3275 [December 2018].

Conroy, N.J., Rubin, V.L., and Chen, Y. (2015). Automatic deception detection: Methods for finding fake news. In *Proceedings of the 78th ASIS&T Annual Meeting: Information Science with Impact: Research in and for the Community* (p. 82). St. Louis, MO: American Society for Information Science. Available: https://pdfs.semanticscholar.org/939f/eec48ae1abb222cf9881932680b7ec3c68a7.pdf [December 2018].

Cross, M. (2013). Social media security: Leveraging social networking while mitigating risk. *Newnes*, November 1.

D'Amico, A.D., and Whitley, K. (2008). The real work of computer network defense analysts: The analysis roles and processes that transform network data into security situation awareness. In J. Goodall, G. Conti, and K. Ma (Eds.), *Proceedings of the Workshop on Visualization for Computer Security* (pp. 19–37). Berlin/Heidelberg, Germany: Springer. doi:10.1007/978-3-540-78243-8_2.

D'Amico, A., Whitley, K., Tesone, D., O'Brien, B., and Roth, E. (2005). Achieving cyber defense situational awareness: A cognitive task analysis of information assurance analysts. *Human Factors and Ergonomics Society Annual Meeting Proceedings, 49*(3), 229–233. doi:10.1177/154193120504900304.

Darczewska, J. (2014). *The Anatomy of Russian Information Warfare. The Crimean Operation, a Case Study*. Available: https://www.osw.waw.pl/en/publikacje/point-view/2014-05-22/anatomy-russian-information-warfare-crimean-operation-a-case-study [December 2018].

Dawson, J., and Thomson, R. (2018). The future cybersecurity workforce: Going beyond technical skills for successful cyber performance. *Frontiers in Psychology*, 9, 744. doi:10.3389/fpsyg.2018.00744.

Dawson, M., Lieble, M., and Adeboje, A. (2018). Open source intelligence: Performing data mining and link analysis to track terrorist activities. In *Information Technology-New Generations* (pp. 159–163). Cham, Switzerland: Springer.

Décary-Hétu, D., Morselli, C., and Leman-Langlois, S. (2012). Welcome to the scene: A study of social organization and recognition among Warez hackers. *Journal of Research in Crime and Delinquency*, 49(3), 359–382. doi:10.1177/0022427811420876.

DeMello, M.A., Keely, L.B., Byrum, F.D., Yaacovi, Y., and Hughes, K.E. (2005). *Method and System for Binding Enhanced Software Features to a Persona*. U.S. Patent 6,891,953, issued May 10, 2005. Available: https://patents.google.com/patent/WO2002001330A3/en [February 2019].

Dutt, V., Ahn, Y., and Gonzalez, C. (2011). Cyber situation awareness: Modeling the security analyst in a cyber-attack scenario through Instance-Based Learning. In Y. Li (Ed.), *Lecture Notes on Computer Science: Data and Applications Security and Privacy XXV* (pp. 280–292). International Federation for Information Processing. Available: https://pdfs.semanticscholar.org/f09a/9c917a376fe937ce8dc168a53cdb0c8cf040.pdf [December 2018].

Dutt, V., Ahn, Y.-S., and Gonzalez, C. (2013). Cyber situation awareness: Modeling detection of cyber attacks with instance-based learning theory. *Human Factors*, 55(3), 605–618.

Ekovich, S.R. (2017). Listening to Donald Trump. *Contemporary French and Francophone Studies*, 21(5), 498–506.

Emam, O. (2006). *System and Method for Creating Artificial TV News Programs*. U.S. Patent Application 11/236,457, filed June 22, 2006.

Farwell, J.P. (2014). The media strategy of ISIS. *Survival*, 56(6), 49–55.

Fazio, L.K., Brashier, N.M., Payne, B.K., and Marsh, E.J. (2015). Knowledge does not protect against illusory truth. *Journal of Experimental Psychology: General*, 144(5), 993–1002. doi.org/10.1037/xge0000098.

Ferris, D.R. (1994). Rhetorical strategies in student persuasive writing: Differences between native and non-native English speakers. *Research in the Teaching of English*, 28(1), 45–65. Available: https://www.jstor.org/stable/40171324 [December 2018].

Fette, I., Sadeh, N., and Tomasic. A. (2007). Learning to detect phishing emails. In *Proceedings of the 16th International Conference on World Wide Web* (pp. 649–656). New York: Association for Computing Machinery.

Fischer, G. (2012). Context-aware systems: The "right" information, at the "right" time, in the "right" place, in the "right" way, to the "right" person. In *Proceedings of the International Working Conference on Advanced Visual Interfaces* (pp. 287–294). New York: Association for Computing Machinery. doi:10.1145/2254556.2254611.

Flaxman, S., Goel, S., and Rao, J.M. (2016). Filter bubbles, echo chambers, and online news consumption. *Public Opinion Quarterly*, 80(S1), 298–320.

Frenkel, S. (2017). Hackers hide cyberattacks in social media posts. *The New York Times*, May 28. https://www.nytimes.com/2017/05/28/technology/hackers-hide-cyberattacks-in-social-media-posts.html [April 2018].

Friedkin, N.E. (2006). *A Structural Theory of Social Influence* (Vol. 13). Cambridge, MA: Cambridge University Press.

Galbally, J., Marcel, S., and Fierrez, J. (2014). Image quality assessment for fake biometric detection: Application to iris, fingerprint, and face recognition. *IEEE Transactions on Image Processing*, 23(2), 710–724.

Gates, S., and Podder, S. (2015). Social media, recruitment, allegiance and the Islamic State. *Perspectives on Terrorism*, 9(4), 107–116.

Geers, K., Kindlund, D., Moran, N., and Rachwald, R. (2013). *World War C: Understanding Nation–State Motives Behind Today's Advanced Cyber Attacks*. Available: https://www.fireeye.com/content/dam/fireeye-www/global/en/current-threats/pdfs/fireeye-wwc-report.pdf [February 2019].

Gilbert, C.J., and Hutto, E. (2014). VADER: A parsimonious rule-based model for sentiment analysis of social media text. *Eighth International Conference on Weblogs and Social Media (ICWSM-14)*. Available: http://comp.social.gatech.edu/papers/icwsm14.vader.hutto.pdf [December 2018].

Goodall, J.R. (2009). Visualization is better! A comparative evaluation. In *International Workshop on Visualization for Cyber Security* (pp. 57–68). Available: https://web.ornl.gov/~jgoodall/goodall-vizsec09.pdf [December 2018].

Goulston, M.J. (2015). *Talking to "Crazy": How to Deal with the Irrational and Impossible People in Your Life*. New York: American Management Association.

Gruhl, D., Guha, R., Liben-Nowell, D., and Tomkins, A. (2004). Information diffusion through blogspace. In *Proceedings of the 13th International Conference on World Wide Web* (pp. 491–501). New York: Association for Computing Machinery.

Guldenmund, F.W. (2000). The nature of safety culture: A review of theory and research. *Safety Science*, 34(1-3), 215–257. doi:10.1016/S0925-7535(00)00014-X.

Gupta, A., Lamba, H., Kumaraguru, P., and Joshi, A. (2013). Faking Sandy: Characterizing and identifying fake images on Twitter during Hurricane Sandy. In *Proceedings of the 22nd International Conference on World Wide Web* (pp. 729–736). New York: Association for Computing Machinery.

Gutzwiller, R.S., Hunt, S.M., and Lange, D.S. (2016). A task analysis toward characterizing cyber-cognitive situation awareness (CCSA) in cyber defense analysts. In *2016 IEEE International Multi-Disciplinary Conference on Cognitive Methods in Situation Awareness and Decision Support, CogSIMA 2016* (pp. 14–20). doi:10.1109/COGSIMA.2016.7497780.

Gutzwiller, R.S., Ferguson-Walter, K., Fugate, S., and Rogers, A. (2018). "Oh, look, a butterfly!" A framework for distracting attackers to improve cyber defense. *Proceedings of the Human Factors and Ergonomics Society*, 62(1), 272–276. doi:10.1177/1541931218621063.

Hassan, N., Adair, B., Hamilton, J.T., Li, C., Tremayne, M., Yang, J., and Yu, C. (2015). *The Quest to Automate Fact-Checking*. Available: http://cj2015.brown.columbia.edu/papers/automate-fact-checking.pdf [December 2018].

Haythornthwaite, C., and Wellman, B. (1998). Work, friendship, and media use for information exchange in a networked organization. *Journal of the American Society for Information Science*, 49(12), 1101–1114.

Heise, D.R. (1987). Affect control theory: Concepts and model. *Journal of Mathematical Sociology*, 13(1-2), 1–33.

Henderson, A., and Bowley, R. (2010). Authentic dialogue? The role of "friendship" in a social media recruitment campaign. *Journal of Communication Management*, 14(3), 237–257.

Hoffman, D.L., and Fodor, M. (2010). Can you measure the ROI of your social media marketing?. *MIT Sloan Management Review*, 52(1), 41. Available: https://sloanreview.mit.edu/article/can-you-measure-the-roi-of-your-social-media-marketing [December 2018].

Holdsworth, C., and Morgan, D. (2007). Revisiting the generalized other: An exploration. *Sociology*, 41(3), 401–417.

Holz, T., Engelberth, M., and Freiling, F. (2009). Learning more about the underground economy: A case-study of keyloggers and dropzones. In *European Symposium on Research in Computer Security* (pp. 1–18). Berlin/Heidelberg, Germany: Springer.

Hong, L.G., Dan, O., and Davison, B.D. (2011). Predicting popular messages in Twitter. *Proceedings of the 20th International Conference Companion on World Wide Web* (pp. 57–58). New York: Association for Computing Machinery. Available: http://www.cse.lehigh.edu/~brian/pubs/2011/WWW/predicting-popular-messages-twitter.pdf [February 2019].

Horn, C., and D'Amico, A. (2011). Visual analysis of goal-directed network defense decisions. In *Proceedings of the 8th International Symposium on Visualization for Cyber Security. VizSec '11* (Article No. 5). New York: Association for Computing Machinery. doi:10.1145/2016904.2016909.

Hovde, K. (2017). Why every business should be using multiple social media accounts. *Business.com*, February 22. Available: https://www.business.com/articles/why-every-business-should-be-using-multiple-social-media-accounts [April 2018].

Huan, B., and Carley, K.M. (2017). On predicting geolocation of tweets using convolutional neural network. In D. Lee, Y. Lin, R. Thompson, and N. Osgood (Eds.), *Proceedings of the International Conference on Social Computing, Behavioral-Cultural Modeling and Prediction and Behavior Representation in Modeling and Simulation (SBP-BRiMS 2017)* (pp. 281–291). Washington, DC: Springer.

Huber, M., Mulazzani, M., Leithner, M., Schrittwieser, S., Wondracek, G., and Weippl, E. (2011). Social snapshots: Digital forensics for online social networks. In *Proceedings of the 27th Annual Computer Security Applications Conference* (pp. 113–122). New York: Association for Computing Machinery. doi:10.1145/2076732.2076748.

Huey, L. (2015). This is not your mother's terrorism: Social media, online radicalization and the practice of political jamming. *Journal of Terrorism Research*, 6(2). doi:10.15664/jtr.1159.

Itti, L., and Baldi, P. (2009). Bayesian surprise attacks human attention. *Vision Research*, 49(10), 1295–1306. doi:10.1016/j.visres.2008.09.007.

Java, A., Song, X., Finin, T., and Tseng, B. (2007). Why we Twitter: Understanding microblogging usage and communities. In *Proceedings of the 9th WebKDD and 1st SNA-KDD 2007 Workshop on Web Mining and Social Network Analysis* (pp. 56–65). New York: Association for Computing Machinery.

Johansson, F., Kaati, L., and Shrestha, A. (2013). Detecting multiple aliases in social media. In *Proceedings of the 2013 IEEE/ACM International Conference on Advances in Social Networks Analysis and Mining* (pp. 1004–1011). New York: Association for Computing Machinery.

Joseph, R. (2017). *Supersynthizers: Confronting the Coming Analytical Crisis in an Age of Influence*. Presentation at the National Academies of Sciences, Engineering, and Medicine's Workshop on Leveraging Advances in Social Network Thinking for National Security. October 11, 2017.

Joseph, K., and Carley, K.M. (2016). Relating semantic similarity and semantic association to how humans label other people. In *Proceedings of 2016 EMNLP Workshop on Natural Language Processing and Computational Social Science* (pp. 1–10). Austin, TX: Association for Computational Linguistics. Available: http://www.aclweb.org/anthology/W16-5601 [December 2018].

Kandias, M., Galbogini, K., Mitrou, L., and Gritzalis, D. (2013). Insiders trapped in the mirror reveal themselves in social media. In *International Conference on Network and System Security* (pp. 220–235). Berlin/Heidelberg, Germany: Springer.

Kas, M., Wachs, M., Carley, K.M., and Carley, L.R. (2013). Incremental algorithm for updating betweenness centrality in dynamically growing networks. In *Advances in Social Networks Analysis and Mining (ASONAM), 2013 IEEE/ACM International Conference* (pp. 33–40). Piscataway, NJ: Institute of Electrical and Electronics Engineers. doi:10.1109/ASONAM.2013.6785684.

Ke, Y., Sukthankar, R., and Houston, L. (2004). Efficient near-duplicate detection and sub-image retrieval. In *ACM International Conference on Multimedia* (pp. 869–876). New York: Association for Computing Machinery. Available: http://www.cs.cmu.edu/~rahuls/pub/mm2004-pcasift-rahuls.pdf [February 2019].

Kim, H., Garrido, P., Tewari, A., Xu, W., Thies, J., Nießner, M., Pérez, P., Richardt, C., Zollhöfer, M., and Theobalt, C. (2018). *Deep Video Portraits*. Available: https://web.stanford.edu/~zollhoef/papers/SG2018_DeepVideo/paper.pdf [December 2018].

King, R. (2008). How companies use Twitter to bolster their brands. *Bloomberg*, September 6. Available: https://www.bloomberg.com/news/articles/2008-09-06/how-companies-use-twitter-to-bolster-their-brandsbusinessweek-business-news-stock-market-and-financial-advice [December 2018].

Klausen, J. (2015). Tweeting the Jihad: Social media networks of Western foreign fighters in Syria and Iraq. *Studies in Conflict & Terrorism, 38*(1), 1–22.

Kolbert, E. (2017). Why facts don't change our minds. *The New Yorker*, February 27. Available: https://www.newyorker.com/magazine/2017/02/27/why-facts-dont-change-our-minds [December 2017].

Konkel, F. (2014). The intelligence community's big-data problem. *FCW*, March 13. Available: https://fcw.com/articles/2014/03/13/ic-big-data.aspx [December 2018].

Krackhardt, D. (2001). Viscosity models and the diffusion of controversial innovation. In A. Lomi and E.R. Larsen (Eds.), *Dynamics of Organizations: Computational Modeling and Organization Theories* (pp. 243–268). Cambridge, MA: MIT Press.

Kris, D. (2017). The CIA's new guidelines governing publicly available information. *Lawfare*, March 21. Available: https://www.lawfareblog.com/cias-new-guidelines-governing-publicly-available-information [December 2018].

Krombholz, K., Hobel, H., Huber, M., and Weippl, E. (2015). Advanced social engineering attacks. *Journal of Information Security and Applications, 22*, 113–122. doi:10.1016/j.jisa.2014.09.005.

Kumar, S., Benigni, M., and Carley, K.M. (2016). The impact of U.S. cyber policies on cyber-attacks trend. In *Proceedings of the 2016 IEEE Conference on Intelligence and Security Informatics (ISI)* (pp. 181–186). doi:10.1109/ISI.2016.7745464.

Kumaraguru, P., Rhee, Y., Acquisti, A., Cranor, L.F., Hong, J., and Nunge, E. (2007). Protecting people from phishing: The design and evaluation of an embedded training email system. In *Proceedings of the SIGCHI Conference on Human Factors in Computing Systems (CHI '07)* (pp. 905–914). doi:10.1145/1240624.1240760.

Lajeunesse, G.C. (2008). Winning the war of ideas. *Small Wars Journal*. Available: http://smallwarsjournal.com/blog/journal/docs-temp/110-lajeunesse.pdf [December 2018].

Landwehr, P.M., Wei, W., Kowalchuck, M., and Carley, K.M. (2016). Using Tweets to support disaster planning, warning and response. *Safety Science, 90*, 33–47. doi:10.1016/j.ssci.2016.04.012.

Lawson, S. (2014). The U.S. military's social media civil war: Technology as antagonism in discourses of information-age conflict. *Cambridge Review of International Affairs, 27*(2), 226–245.

Lazer, D., Kennedy, R., King, G., and Vespignani, A. (2014). The parable of Google Flu: Traps in big data analysis. *Science, 343*(6176), 1203–1205.

Lee, E., Lee, J.-A., Moon, J.H., and Sung, Y. (2015). Pictures speak louder than words: Motivations for using Instagram. *Cyberpsychology, Behavior, and Social Networking, 18*(9), 552–556.

Levine, T.R. (2014). Truth-Default Theory (TDT): A theory of human deception and deception detection. *Journal of Language and Social Psychology, 33*(4), 378–392.

Liang, C.S. (2015). *Cyber Jihad: Understanding and Countering Islamic State Propaganda*. GSCP Policy Paper 2015/2. Available: https://www.gcsp.ch/News-Knowledge/Publications/Cyber-Jihad-Understanding-and-Countering-Islamic-State-Propaganda [December 2018].

Lilienfeld, S. (2014). Evidence-based practice: The misunderstandings continue. *Psychology Today*, January 27. Available: https://www.psychologytoday.com/us/blog/the-skeptical-psychologist/201401/evidence-based-practice-the-misunderstandings-continue [February 2019].

Lin, K.-Y., and Lu, H.-P. (2011). Why people use social networking sites: An empirical study integrating network externalities and motivation theory. *Computers in Human Behavior, 27*(3), 1152–1161.

Lin, Z., He, J., Tang, X., and Tang, C.-K. (2009). Fast, automatic and fine-grained tampered JPEG image detection via DCT coefficient analysis. *Pattern Recognition*, 42(11), 2492–2501.

Liu, B., and Zhang, L. (2012). A survey of opinion mining and sentiment analysis. In C. Aggarwal and C. Zhai (Eds.), *Mining Text Data* (pp. 415–463). Boston, MA: Springer. doi:10.1007/978-1-4614-3223-4_13.

Liu, X., Nourbakhsh, A., Li, Q., Fang, R., and Shah, S. (2015). Real-time rumor debunking on Twitter. In *Proceedings of the 24th ACM International Conference on Information and Knowledge Management* (pp. 1867–1870). New York: Association for Computing Machinery.

Liu, P., Jajodia, S., and Wang, C. (Eds.). (2017). *Recent Advances in Cyber Situation Awareness*. Boston, MA: Springer.

Lotrionte, C. (2014). Countering state-sponsored cyber economic espionage under international law. *NCJ Int'l L. & Com. Reg.*, 40, 443.

Luhn, A. (2017). Russia uses video game pictures to claim U.S. helped ISIL. *The Telegraph*, November 9. Available: https://www.telegraph.co.uk/news/2017/11/14/russia-use-video-game-picture-claim-us-helped-isil [February 2019].

Maddox, A., Barratt, M.J., Allen, M., and Lenton, S. (2016). Constructive activism in the dark web: Cryptomarkets and illicit drugs in the digital "demimonde." *Information, Communication & Society*, 19(1), 111–126.

Mangold, W.G., and Faulds, D.J. (2009). Social media: The new hybrid element of the promotion mix. *Business Horizons*, 52(4), 357–365.

Mann, A. (2016). Core concept: Computational social science. *Proceedings of the National Academy of Sciences of the United States of America*, 113(3), 468–470.

Mansfield-Devine, S. (2008). Anti-social networking: Exploiting the trusting environment of Web 2.0. *Network Security*, 2008(11), 4–7. doi:10.1016/S1353-4858(08)70127-2.

Mbaziira, A., and Jones, J. (2016). A text-based deception detection model for cybercrime. In *International Conference on Technology and Management*. Available: https://www.researchgate.net/publication/307594168_A_Text-based_Deception_Detection_Model_for_Cybercrime [December 2018].

Mead, G.H. (1934). *Mind, Self and Society* (Vol. 111). Chicago, IL: University of Chicago Press.

Metaxas, P.T., and Mustafaraj, E. (2012). Social media and the elections. *Science*, 338(6106), 472–473. doi:10.1126/science.1230456.

Meyer, J.C. (2000). Humor as a double-edged sword: Four functions of humor in communication. *Communication Theory*, 10(3), 310–331.

Mezzour, G., and Carley, K.M. (2014). Spam diffusion in a social network initiated by hacked e-mail accounts. *International Journal of Security and Networks*, 9(3), 144–153.

Moore, T., Clayton, R., and Stern, H. (2009). Temporal correlations between spam and phishing websites. In *Proceedings (LEET'09) of the 2nd USENIX Conference on Large-scale Exploits and Emergent Threats: Botnets, Spyware, Worms, and More* (p. 5). Berkeley, CA: USENIX Association. Available: https://www.cl.cam.ac.uk/~rnc1/leet09.pdf [February 2019].

Morstatter, F., Wu, L., Nazer, T.H., Carley, K.M., and Liu, H., (2016). A new approach to bot detection: The importance of recall. In *Proceedings of the 2016 IEEE/ACM International Conference on Advances in Social Networks Analysis and Mining* (pp. 533–540). Piscataway, NJ: IEEE Press.

Murakami, K., Nichols, E., Matsuyoshi, S., Sumida, A., Masuda, S., Inui, K., and Matumoto, Y. (2009). Statement map: Assisting information credibility analysis by visualizing arguments. In *Proceedings of the 3rd Workshop on Information Credibility on the Web* (pp. 43–50). New York: Association for Computing Machinery.

Murphy, P. (2017). Russia uses fake photos to accuse U.S. of supporting ISIS. *CNN*, November 14. Available: https://www.cnn.com/2017/11/14/us/russia-fake-photos-accusation-trnd/index.html [February 2019].

Mutz, D.C. (2006). *Hearing the Other Side: Deliberative versus Participatory Democracy*. New York: Cambridge University Press.

National Research Council. (2013). *Frontiers in Massive Data Analysis*. Committee on the Analysis of Massive Data, Committee on Applied and Theoretical Statistics, Board on Mathematical Sciences and Their Applications, Division on Engineering and Physical Sciences. Washington DC: The National Academies Press. doi:10.17226/18374.

Naylor, R.W., Lamberton, C.P., and West, P.M. (2012). Beyond the "like" button: The impact of mere virtual presence on brand evaluations and purchase intentions in social media settings. *Journal of Marketing*, 76(6), 105–120.

Omand, D., Bartlett, J., and Miller, C. (2012). Introducing social media intelligence (SOCMINT). *Intelligence and National Security*, 27(6), 801–823. doi:10.1080/02684527.2012.716965.

Oxley, A. (2013). *Security Risks in Social Media Technologies: Safe Practices in Public Service Applications*. Oxford, UK: Chandos.

Pak, J., and Zhou, L. (2014). Social structural behavior of deception in computer-mediated communication. *Decision Support Systems*, 63, 95–103. doi:10.1016/j.dss.2013.08.010.

Pang, B., and Lee, L. (2008). Opinion mining and sentiment analysis. *Foundations and Trends in Information Retrieval*, 2(1–2), 1–135.

Papadimitriou, F. (2009). A nexus of cyber-geography and cyber-psychology: Topos/"notopia" and identity in hacking. *Computers in Human Behavior*, 25(6), 1331–1334. doi:10.1016/j.chb.2009.05.009.

Pearl, L., and Steyvers, M. (2012). Detecting authorship deception: A supervised machine learning approach using author writeprints. *Literary and Linguistic Computing*, 27(2), 183–196.

Pennycook, G., and Rand, D. G. (2018). *Who Falls for Fake News? The Roles of Bullshit Receptivity, Overclaiming, Familiarity, and Analytic Thinking*. doi:10.2139/ssrn.3023545.

Pidgeon, N.F. (1991). Safety culture and risk management in organizations. *Journal of Cross-Cultural Psychology*, 22(1), 129–140. doi:10.1177/0022022191221009.

Piotrowski, Z., and Gajewski, P. (2007). Voice spoofing as an impersonation attack and the way of protection. *Journal of Information Assurance and Security*, 2(3), 223–225.

Pronovost, P., and Sexton, B. (2005). Assessing safety culture: Guidelines and recommendations. *Quality and Safety in Health Care*, 14(4), 231–233. doi:10.1136/qshc.2005.015180.

Rajivan, P., and Cooke, N.J. (2018). Information pooling bias in collaborative security incident correlation analysis. *Human Factors*, 60(5), 626–639. doi:10.1177/0018720818769249.

Ramsey, L.P. (2010). Brandjacking on social networks: Trademark infringement by impersonation of markholders. *Buffalo Law Review*, 58, 851–929. Available: http://www.buffalolawreview.org/past_issues/58_4/Ramsey.pdf [December 2018].

Reveron, D.S. (2012). An introduction to national security and cyberspace. In D.S. Reveron (Ed.), *Cyberspace and National Security: Threats, Opportunities, and Power in a Virtual World*. Washington, DC: Georgetown University Press.

Robinson, D.T., Smith-Lovin, L., and Wisecup, A.K. (2006). Affect control theory. In *Handbook of the Sociology of Emotions* (pp. 179–202). Boston, MA: Springer.

Romero, D.M., Meeder, B., and Kleinberg, J. (2011). Differences in the mechanics of information diffusion across topics: Idioms, political hashtags, and complex contagion on Twitter. In *Proceedings of the 20th International Conference on World Wide Web* (pp. 695–704). New York: Association for Computing Machinery. doi:10.1145/1963405.1963503.

Roozenbeek, J., and van der Linden, S. (2018). The fake news game: Actively inoculating against the risk of misinformation. *Journal of Risk Research*. doi:10.1080/13669877.2018.1443491.

Rubin, V.L., Chen, Y., and Conroy, N.J. (2015). Deception detection for news: Three types of fakes. *Proceedings of the Association for Information Science and Technology, 52*(1), 1–4.

Safko, L. (2010). *The Social Media Bible: Tactics, Tools, and Strategies for Business Success*. Hoboken, NJ: John Wiley & Sons.

Schneider, M., and Chang, S.-F. (1996). A robust content based digital signature for image authentication. In *Proceedings of 3rd IEEE International Conference on Image Processing* (vol. 3, pp. 227–230). doi:10.1109/ICIP.1996.560425.

Schultz, T., and Fuglerud, K.S. (2012). Creating personas with disabilities. In *International Conference on Computers for Handicapped Persons* (pp. 145–152). Berlin/Heidelberg, Germany: Springer.

Schwartz, H.A., Eichstaedt, J.C., Kern, M.L., Dziurzynski, L., Ramones, S.M., Agrawal, M., Shah, A., Kosinski, M., Stillwell, D., Seligman, M.E., and Ungar, L.H. (2013). Personality, gender, and age in the language of social media: The open-vocabulary approach. *PLoS One, 8*(9), e73791. doi:10.1371/journal.pone.0073791.

Scott, D.M. (2015). *The New Rules of Marketing and PR: How to Use Social Media, Online Video, Mobile Applications, Blogs, News Releases, and Viral Marketing to Reach Buyers Directly*. Hoboken, NJ: John Wiley & Sons.

Seigfried-Spellar, K.C., and Treadway, K.N (2014). Differentiating hackers, identity thieves, cyberbullies, and virus writers by college major and individual differences. *Deviant Behavior, 35*(10), 782–803. doi:10.1080/01639625.2014.884333.

Shallcross, N. (2017). Social media and information operations in the 21st century. *Journal of Information Warfare, 16*(1), 1–12.

Shermer, M. (2002). *Why People Believe Weird Things: Pseudoscience, Superstition, and Other Confusions of Our Time*. New York: Henry Holt and Company.

Snegovaya, M. (2015). *Putin's Information Warfare in Ukraine: Soviet Origins of Russia's Hybrid Warfare*. Washington, DC: Institute for the Study of War. Available: https://www.stratcomcoe.org/msnegovaya-putins-information-warfare-ukraine [December 2018].

Snijders, T.A.B. (2001). The statistical evaluation of social network dynamics. *Sociological Methodology, 31*(1), 361–395.

Somasundaran, S., and Wiebe, J. (2010). Recognizing stances in ideological on-line debates. In *Proceedings of the NAACL HLT 2010 Workshop on Computational Approaches to Analysis and Generation of Emotion in Text* (pp. 116–124). Los Angeles, CA: Association for Computational Linguistics. Available: http://anthology.aclweb.org/W/W10/W10-0214.pdf [December 2018].

Southwell, B.G., Thorson, E.A., and Sheble, L. (2017). The persistence and peril of misinformation. *American Scientist, 105*(6), 372–375.

Spence, S.A., Hunter, M.D., Farrow, T.F.D., Green, R.D., Leung, D.H., Hughes, C.J., and Ganesan, V. (2004). A cognitive neurobiological account of deception: Evidence from functional neuroimaging. *Philosophical Transactions of the Royal Society B: Biological Sciences, 359*(1451), 1755–1762. doi:10.1098/rstb.2004.1555.

Stamm, M.C., Tjoa, S.K., Lin, W.S., and Liu, K.J.R. (2010). Undetectable image tampering through JPEG compression anti-forensics. In *Image Processing (ICIP), 2010 17th IEEE International Conference* (pp. 2109–2112). doi:10.1109/ICIP.2010.5652553.

Sterne, J. (2010). *Social Media Metrics: How to Measure and Optimize Your Marketing Investment*. Hoboken, NJ: John Wiley & Sons.

Stieglitz, S., and Dang-Xuan, L. (2013). Emotions and information diffusion in social media—sentiment of microblogs and sharing behavior. *Journal of Management Information Systems, 29*(4), 217–248.

Stone-Gross, B., Abman, R., Kemmerer, R.A., Kruegel, C., Steigerwald, D.G., and Vigna, G. (2013). The underground economy of fake antivirus software. In *Economics of Information Security and Privacy III* (pp. 55–78). New York: Springer. doi:10.1007/978-1-4614-1981-5_4.

Stribley, R.A. (2018). Google just made it harder to spot fake news. *Medium*, February 22. Available: https://medium.com/s/story/google-just-made-it-harder-to-spot-fake-news-39a1ecff4c40 [April 20, 2018].

Subrahmanian, V.S., Azaria, A., Durst, S., Kagan, V., Galstyan, A., Lerman, K., Zhu, L., Ferrara, E., Flammini, A., and Menczer, F. (2016). The DARPA Twitter bot challenge. *Computer, 49*(6), 38–46. doi:10.1109/MC.2016.183.

Suh, B., Hong, L., Pirolli, P., and Chi, E.H. (2010). Want to be retweeted? Large scale analytics on factors impacting retweet in Twitter network. In *SOCIALCOM '10 Proceedings of the 2010 IEEE Second International Conference on Social Computing* (pp. 177–184). Washington, DC: IEEE Computer Society. doi:10.1109/SocialCom.2010.33.

Sydell, L. (2016). We tracked down a fake-news creator in the suburbs. Here's what we learned. *National Public Radio*, November 23. Available: https://www.npr.org/sections/alltechconsidered/2016/11/23/503146770/npr-finds-the-head-of-a-covert-fake-news-operation-in-the-suburbs [December 2018].

Syed-Abdul, S., Fernandez-Luque, L., Jian, W.S., Li, Y.C., Crain, S., Hsu, M.-H., Wang, Y.C., Khandregzen, D., Chuluunbaatar, E., Nguyen, P.A., and Liou, D.M. (2013). Misleading health-related information promoted through video-based social media: Anorexia on YouTube. *Journal of Medical Internet Research, 15*(2):e30. doi:10.2196/jmir.2237.

Tanase, M. (2003). IP spoofing: An introduction. *Symantec*, March 11. Available: https://www.symantec.com/connect/articles/ip-spoofing-introduction [December 2018].

Tang, J., and Liu, H. (2015). Trust in social media. *Synthesis Lectures on Information Security, Privacy, & Trust, 10*(1), 1–129.

Tarran, B. (2017). Why facts are not enough in the fight against fake news. *Significance, 14*(5), 6–7.

Thomas, K., Grier, C., Song, D., and Paxson, V. (2011). Suspended accounts in retrospect: An analysis of Twitter spam. In *Proceedings of the 2011 ACM SIGCOMM Conference on Internet Measurement Conference* (p. 243–258). New York: Association for Computing Machinery. Available: http://www.icir.org/vern/papers/twitter-susp-accounts.imc2011.pdf [February 2019].

Timm, C., and Perez, R. (2010). *Seven Deadliest Social Network Attacks (Syngress Seven Deadliest Attacks)*. Burlington, MA: Elsevier. doi:10.1016/C2009-0-61910-3.

Tsikerdekis, M., and Zeadally, S. (2014a). Multiple account identity deception detection in social media using nonverbal behavior. *IEEE Transactions on Information Forensics and Security, 9*(8), 1311–1321.

Tsikerdekis, M., and Zeadally, S. (2014b). Online deception in social media. *Communications of the ACM, 57*(9), 72–80.

Tufekci, Z. (2014). Big questions for social media big data: Representativeness, validity and other methodological pitfalls. In *ICWSM '14: Proceedings of the 8th International AAAI Conference on Weblogs and Social Media* (pp. 505–514). Available: https://arxiv.org/ftp/arxiv/papers/1403/1403.7400.pdf [December 2018].

Unkelbach, C. (2007). Reversing the truth effect: Learning the interpretation of processing fluency in judgments of truth. *Journal of Experimental Psychology: Learning, Memory, and Cognition, 33*(1), 219–230. doi:10.1037/0278-7393.33.1.219.

Unkelbach, C., and Stahl, C. (2009). A multinomial modeling approach to dissociate different components of the truth effect. *Consciousness and Cognition, 18*(1), 22–38. doi:10.1016/j.concog.2008.09.006.

van der Linden, S., Maibach, E., Cook, J., Leiserowitz, A., and Lewandowsky, S. (2017). Inoculating against misinformation. *Science, 358*(6367), 1141–1142.

Van Dijck, J., and Poell, T. (2013). Understanding social media logic. *Media and Communication, 1*(1), 2–14. doi:10.17645/mac.v1i1.70.

Varol, O., Ferrara, E., Davis, C.A., Menczer, F., and Flammini, A. (2017). Online human-bot interactions: Detection, estimation, and characterization. In *Proceedings of the Eleventh International AAAI Conference on Web and Social Media (ICWSM 2017)* (pp. 280–289). Available: https://aaai.org/ocs/index.php/ICWSM/ICWSM17/paper/view/15587/14817 [December 2018].

Veilleux-Lepage, Y. (2015). Paradigmatic shifts in Jihadism in cyberspace: The emerging role of unaffiliated sympathizers in the Islamic state's social media strategy. *Journal of Terrorism Research, 7*(1), 36–51. doi:10.15664/jtr.1183.

Vieane, A., Funke, G., Mancuso, V., Greenlee, E., Dye, G., Borghetti, B., Miller, B., Menke, L., and Brown, R. (2016). Coordinated displays to assist cyber defenders. *Proceedings of the Human Factors and Ergonomics Society Annual Meeting, 60*(1), 344–348. doi:10.1177/1541931213601078.

Vieane, A., Funke, G., Greenlee, E., Mancuso, V., Borghetti, B., Miller, B., Menke, L., Brown, R., Foroughi, C.K., and Boehm-Davis, D. (2017). Task interruptions undermine cyber defense. *Proceedings of the Human Factors and Ergonomics Society Annual Meeting, 61*(1), 375–379. doi:10.1177/1541931213601576.

Vosoughi, S., Roy, D., and Aral, S. (2018). The spread of true and false news online. *Science, 359*(6380), 1146–1151. doi:10.1126/science.aap9559.

Vrij, A., Granhag, P.A., and Porter, S. (2010). Pitfalls and opportunities in nonverbal and verbal lie detection. *Psychological Science in the Public Interest, 11*(3), 89–121.

Wallach, H. (2018). Computational social science ≠ computer science + social data. *Communications of the ACM, 61*(3), 42–44. doi:10.1145/3132698. Available: https://cacm.acm.org/magazines/2018/3/225484-computational-social-science-computer-science-social-data/fulltext [April 16, 2018].

Waltzman, R. (2015). The U.S. is losing the social media war. *TIME*, October 12. http://time.com/4064698/social-media-propaganda [March 1, 2018].

Wang, F.Y., Carley, K.M., Zeng, D., and Mao, W. (2007). Social computing: From social informatics to social intelligence. *IEEE Intelligent Systems, 22*(2), 79–83. Available: https://pdfs.semanticscholar.org/f430/9d8913cc9f0d72ec08a4bfb9829866d321d1.pdf [December 2018].

Weeks, B.E., Ardèvol-Abreu, A., and de Zúñiga, H.G. (2017). Online influence? Social media use, opinion leadership, and political persuasion. *International Journal of Public Opinion Research, 29*(2), 214–239.

Wei, W., Joseph, K., Wei, L., and Carley, K.M. (2015). A Bayesian graphical model to discover latent events from Twitter. In *Proceedings of the 9th The International AAAI Conference on Web and Social Media (ICWSM'2015)*. Available: https://www.cs.cmu.edu/~kjoseph/papers/wei_icwsm_15.pdf [December 2018].

Wei, W., Joseph, K., Liu, H., and Carley, K.M. (2016). Exploring characteristics of suspended users and network stability on Twitter. *Social Network Analysis and Mining, 6*(1), 51.

Weimann, G. (2014). *New Terrorism and New Media*. Washington, DC: Commons Lab of the Woodrow Wilson International Center for Scholars.

Wojcik, S. (2018). 5 things to know about bots on Twitter. *Pew Research Center*, April 9. Available: http://www.pewresearch.org/fact-tank/2018/04/09/5-things-to-know-about-bots-on-twitter [April 2018].

Wolfe, S. (2017). The top 10 worst social media cyber-attacks. *Infosecurity*, October 20. https://www.infosecurity-magazine.com/blogs/top-10-worst-social-media-cyber [December 2018].

Woolley, S.C. (2016). Automating power: Social bot interference in global politics. *First Monday, 21*(4). Available: https://firstmonday.org/article/view/6161/5300 [December 2018].

Wu, M., Miller, R.C., and Garfinkel, S.L. (2006). Do security toolbars actually prevent phishing attacks?. In *Proceedings of the SIGCHI conference on Human Factors in Computing Systems* (pp. 601–610). New York: Association for Computing Machinery.

Xiong, F., Liu, Y., Zhang, Z.-J., Zhu, J., and Zhang, Y. (2012). An information diffusion model based on retweeting mechanism for online social media. *Physics Letters A, 376*(30-31), 2103–2108.

Yin, H., Song, D., Egele, M., Kruegel, C., and Kirda, E. (2007). Panorama: Capturing system-wide information flow for malware detection and analysis. In *Proceedings of the 14th ACM Conference on Computer and Communications Security* (pp. 116–127). New York: Association for Computing Machinery.

Youngblood, J.R. (2016). *Business Theft and Fraud: Detection and Prevention*. Boca Raton, FL: CRC Press.

Zahedi, F.M., Abbasi, A., and Chen, Y. (2015). Fake-website detection tools: Identifying elements that promote individuals' use and enhance their performance. *Journal of the Association for Information Systems, 16*(6), Article 2. Available: https://aisel.aisnet.org/jais/vol16/iss6/2 [December 2018].

Zargar, S.T., Joshi, J., and Tipper, D. (2013). A survey of defense mechanisms against distributed denial of service (DDoS) flooding attacks. *IEEE Communications Surveys & Tutorials, 15*(4), 2046–2069.

Zhao, J., Wu, J., and Xu, K. (2010). Weak ties: Subtle role of information diffusion in online social networks. *Physical Review E, 82*(1), 016105.

Zhou, L., and Zhang, D.S. (2008). Following linguistic footprints: Automatic deception detection in online communications. *Communications of the ACM, 5*(9), 119–112. doi:10.1145/1378727.1389972.

Zhou, L., Burgoon, J., and Twitchell, D.P. (2003). A longitudinal analysis of language behavior of deception in e-mail. In H. Chen, R. Miranda, D. Zeng, T. Madhusudan, C. Demchak, and J. Schroeder (Eds.), *Proceedings of the First NSF/NIJ Symposium on Intelligence and Security Informatics (ISI 2003), Lecture Notes in Computer Science (LNCS 2665)* (pp. 102–110). Berlin/Heidelberg, Germany: Springer-Verlag.

Zheng, Y., and Wu, G. (2005). Information technology, public space, and collective action in China. *Comparative Political Studies, 38*(5), 507–536.

Zuiderveen Borgesius, F., Trilling, D., Moeller, J., Bodó, B., de Vreese, C.H., and Helberger, N. (2016). Should we worry about filter bubbles? *Internet Policy Review, 5*(1). doi:10.14763/2016.1.401.

7

Integrating the Social and Behavioral Sciences (SBS) into the Design of a Human–Machine Ecosystem

With the next generation of artificial intelligence (AI), technologies and tools used to help filter and analyze data would not only be inserted into the current work of the intelligence analyst as they are now but also would transform the very way intelligence analysis is conducted. As a recent report on AI notes, "the field of AI [research] is shifting toward building intelligent systems that can collaborate effectively with people, and that are more generally human-aware,[1] including creative ways to develop interactive and scalable ways for people to teach robots" (2015 Study Panel of the One Hundred Year Study of Artificial Intelligence, 2016, p. 9). Future technology could support the design of a human–machine ecosystem for intelligence analysis: an ecosystem composed of human analysts and autonomous AI agents, supported by other technologies that could work in true collaboration. This ecosystem could transform intelligence analysis by

- proactively addressing core analytic challenges more comprehensively than humans alone could, by, for example, systematically monitoring large volumes of data and mining large archives of potentially relevant background material;
- reaching across controlled-access networks within the Intelligence Community (IC) efficiently and securely; and
- identifying patterns and associations in data more rapidly than

---

[1] Systems that are human-aware "specifically model, and are specifically designed for, the characteristics of the people with whom they are meant to interact" (p. 17).

humans alone could do, and in real time, uncovering connections that previously would not have been detectable.

The design and implementation of a successful human–machine ecosystem will depend on research from the SBS. Given the increasing sophistication of AI applications and the many possible modes of human–technology partnering, there are many unanswered questions about how best to integrate humans with AI agents in analytic tasks. Existing SBS research will be relevant, but the complexity of a human–machine ecosystem will pose new kinds of challenges for the human analyst, challenges that will require new research if the IC is to take advantage of this fundamental technological opportunity.

This chapter explores key questions about human–machine interactions that need to be addressed if the development of new AI collaborators is to produce trusted teammates, not simply assistive devices. The committee's objective was not to propose a plan for developing a human–machine ecosystem, but to describe the SBS research the IC will need if it is to create, use, and maintain one. We begin with an overview of what would be different if such an ecosystem were developed for the IC: a look at the nature of the agents and technologies that would orchestrate the work and at how intelligence analysis would be transformed. We then turn to what is needed to exploit this opportunity. We examine primary insights from SBS fields that can guide designers, engineers, and computer scientists, at all stages from design to implementation, in creating technologies that will interact optimally with human analysts and support high-functioning systems of human and machines.

We also consider what new research will be needed to bring this opportunity to fruition. For simplicity, the discussion is divided into four domains: (1) human capacities, (2) human–machine interaction, (3) human–technology teaming, and (4) human–system integration. Although this list appears to suggest a hierarchy of work from studies of human capacity to system integration, an optimal research program will require the synergistic interplay of research in each of these domains as knowledge accumulates. Continuous research in each domain will form components of a larger research program that supports the development of an operational human–machine ecosystem to support intelligence analysis.

We note that the set of research topics that could potentially advance the development of a human–machine ecosystem is vast. We identified many other lines of inquiry that might be pursued, and this chapter offers a foundation for what would likely need to be an ongoing program of research. The chapter ends with conclusions about how the IC might move forward to pursue this opportunity, including ideas for planning and conducting the research that is needed, as well as key ethical considerations.

A NEW FORM OF ANALYTIC WORK

The development of a human–machine ecosystem for intelligence analysis would not alter the essential sensemaking challenge described in Chapter 4, but the nature of the activities an analyst might carry out in collaboration with AI agents would be very different. The primary benefits of such a system would lie in its capacity to marry capabilities that are uniquely human—those that presumably no machine could ever replace—with the computing power that outperforms human capacity for some tasks. By doing so, the human–machine ecosystem could, for example, filter and analyze vast quantities of data at an exponentially faster rate than would be possible for any team of humans; reveal questions, connections, and patterns that humans would likely or certainly miss; process a range of inputs—from text in multiple languages to geospatial data—that would require diverse expertise far beyond what a team of individual humans could offer; and tirelessly perform certain functions 24 hours a day.[2]

Many of the potential benefits relate to the availability of vast and constantly growing quantities and types of data. As discussed in Chapter 5, there are many computational approaches with potential application to issues of interest to the intelligence analyst, all of which require considerable computing power. Some types of data will need to be collected and integrated over long periods, while other streams of information will need to be monitored continuously for new data of value. Automated data collection, monitoring, and analysis supported by new AI techniques would offer means of exploiting large datasets. However, not all analytic work can be automated or turned over to AI. The human analyst will still play a critical role in information processing and decision making, exercising the complex capacity to make judgments in the face of the high levels of uncertainty and risk associated with intelligence analysis.

The key characteristic of a human–machine ecosystem would be the integration of contributions of multiple agents and technologies. There are many ways to describe such agents and technologies, but we distinguish here between those that have agency (humans and autonomous systems or AI) and those that simply provide services or information (e.g., cameras, sensing devices, algorithms for automatic data collection or interpretation). A simple depiction of a human–machine ecosystem in Figure 7-1 shows that people are an integral part of operations. The figure portrays three analytic teams that correspond to the three analytic lenses depicted in Figure 4-1 in Chapter 4. These teams, as well as individual agents, are working in collaboration with and connected to other teams through AI systems.

---

[2]Several of the white papers received by the committee (see Chapter 1) provided valuable suggestions about what improved human–machine interactions might offer (see Dien et al., 2017; Phillips et al., 2017; Sagan and McCormick, 2017).

FIGURE 7-1 A human–machine ecosystem for intelligence analysis.
NOTE: This figure is a simple illustration of a human–machine ecosystem in which analysts work in collaboration with and are connected through AI systems. It shows three teams from the hypothetical illustration of analytic work in Chapter 4. The figure also reflects the fact that analysts will be able to work individually while remaining connected to the ecosystem. A variety of sensors (shown surrounding the ecosystem) provide information to the human and AI agents for a number of different purposes, from monitoring and analyzing data pertinent to intelligence analysis to collecting and processing data from interactions between analysts and AI to improve performance.

An agent has been defined as "anything that can be viewed as perceiving its environment through sensors and acting upon that environment through effectors" (Russell and Norvig, 2010, p. 34). Human agents are capable of perceiving through their senses; thinking with their brains; and acting with their hands, mouths, and other parts of the body. Machines that are designed as intelligent agents are able to perceive their environment through sensors (e.g., cameras, infrared rangefinders) and use actuators, motors, and embedded algorithms to make decisions and perform actions. Many intelligent machines (e.g., vacuums, robots for assembly lines, game systems) have been developed to accomplish finite, rule-based tasks.

Most machines perform automated functions, which means they are designed to complete a task or set of tasks in a predictable fashion and with predictable outcomes, usually with a human operator performing any tasks necessary before or after the automated sequence. A machine has autonomy when it can use knowledge it has accumulated from experience, together with sensory input and its built-in knowledge, to perform an action; that is, it has the flexibility to identify a course of action in response to a unique circumstance (National Research Council, 2014; Russell and Norvig, 2010). In a human–machine ecosystem, some machines would need to have that capability. Autonomous systems suitable for intelligence analysis may not be available now, but they are coming. We use the term "semiautonomous agents" for such machines to stress the essential involvement of humans in critical decisions.

These semiautonomous agents would receive inputs from their environment through sensors and supporting technologies, as well as from other agents; select action(s) in pursuit of goals; and then influence their environment either by passing information along or by engaging in physical actions. For example, a useful semiautonomous agent might be a robot capable of physically moving material from one place to another, or an agent capable of alerting an analyst of an event requiring attention through vibrations on a device such as a smartphone. Ideally, these agents would learn from feedback and from their own experiences so they could adapt future actions to improve performance within the ecosystem. There is a long history of research and AI development improving the capability of machines to learn (McCorduck, 2004).

Semiautonomous machines could work with human agents, augmenting working memory, for example, or indicating potentially useful information during an analytic task. They could also work independently, performing complex monitoring functions or data analysis that were beyond human capabilities, or taking on tasks normally performed by humans when the workload became excessive. Either way, they would need to be able to interact regularly with other semiautonomous and human agents, as well as other types of machines.

194   A DECADAL SURVEY OF THE SOCIAL AND BEHAVIORAL SCIENCES

Other machines in the ecosystem would not have the capacity for adaptive operations; they would be designed to provide necessary and predictable information or services, automatically or on request, to support the work of human and semiautonomous agents. We refer to these types of machines either as sensors (devices useful for monitoring the state of the human and semiautonomous agents, as well as the environment within the ecosystem) or as tools or supporting technologies (devices that will be helpful in acquiring or processing data or executing analyses across many forms of information[3]).

The IC already uses many kinds of tools to track a broad range of security threats. This capacity will only expand as it becomes possible to implement more and improved automated analyses or data processing tools to monitor broad areas of interest. Semiautonomous AI agents could foreseeably be of particular benefit in meeting the challenge of identifying significant intersections in a vast range of data and analytic output and, as discussed in Chapter 5, their connections to sociopolitical developments and emerging threats. They would require the capacity to integrate critical information—such as data and findings culled from images, communications, environmental measurements, and other collected intelligence—into the workflow of human agents to help them uncover significant connections. (Box 7-1 illustrates the possible effect on information available to analysts.)

In a human–machine ecosystem, analysts would work collaboratively with these semiautonomous AI agents to conduct the analytic activities of sensemaking. Table 7-1 illustrates some of the specific ways in which analytic activities carried out by a human–machine ecosystem would differ from those carried out in the traditional manner.

RESEARCH DOMAINS

If AI technology becomes powerful and autonomous enough to support an ecosystem for intelligence analysis, that system will be useful only to the extent that human analysts benefit from and are able to take advantage of the assistance it offers. SBS research is essential to ensuring that developers of such an ecosystem for the IC understand the strengths and limitations of human agents. Numerous disciplines—such as cognitive science, communications, human factors, human–systems integration, neuroscience, and psychology—contribute to this understanding of human characteristics and their interactions with machines. Most of the questions of interest

---

[3]Information of relevance to intelligence analysis includes varied types of data, such as those from satellite surveillance and open-source communications and the tracking of critical supply chains, environmental measurements, and indicators of disease contagion.

BOX 7-1
Finding New Connections in a Human–Machine Ecosystem

Recall the three analytic lenses presented in Chapter 4 (refer to Figure 4-1): (1) monitoring a terrorist group, (2) tracking weapons proliferation, and (3) following the strategies of the leader of country Y. Traditionally, analyst teams working on these issues separately would assess new information within the context of their own knowledge base and keep their own records of recent developments.

The goal of a human–machine ecosystem would be to capitalize on opportunities to expand analytic resources by alerting analysts to relationships that are in the data but not visible through their specific lenses. The ecosystem helps connect analysts who may profit from discussing newly discovered information that may be useful to all.

For example, analysts working on terrorist group Z issues (who discovered the use of more powerful explosives requiring a specialized triggering device) and analysts following weapons proliferation (who detected the change in weapons shipments from country A to country B) could be alerted that the explosives and detonators are a potential common factor in the observed changes in explosives and weapons shipments. While it is often difficult to identify specific cargo, data analyses by tools within the human–machine ecosystem might discern that the supplier of the cargo in question is the leading exporter of those particular explosives and triggering devices. Semiautonomous agents would pass that information to appropriate analysts, and analysts following terrorist group Z might then suspect that those explosive and triggering devices are among the weapons shipments being tracked by the weapons proliferation analysts. The analysts could then consider conducting more research to see whether there was a true connection between the weapons shipments and the materials terrorist group Z was using in its attacks.

Analysts tracking weapons proliferation also could be alerted that country B is a common factor in the observed changes in weapons shipments and is a new target of country Y's vitriol. A group of analysts monitoring country B that is usually a marginal player on questions of terrorism, weapons proliferation, and regional political powers might either decide or be asked to bring its perspective into the collaborative analysis.

In discussion, the country B analysts could provide the context that country B and country Y share a border and that a century ago, country Y ceded territory along the border to country B to end years of conflict. In collaboration, the analysts could recognize that the political and military clout of country Y has grown, while that of country B has waned. In addition, they might discern that the leader of country Y had focused rhetorically on redressing the "mistake."

In a human–machine ecosystem, the different analyst teams working on terrorist group Z, country Y, and weapons proliferation could all be alerted to explore the factors common among their areas of focus, and a different analysis might emerge—that country B, not country X, was supplying terrorist group Z with explosives.

TABLE 7-1 Comparison of Analytic Activities Conducted Traditionally and in a Human–Machine Ecosystem

Analytic Activity of an Individual Analyst	Traditional Human Process	Process in a Human–Machine Ecosystem (HME)
Maintain Inventory of Important Questions	• Analyst maintains own record of important questions • Analyst revises own record as necessary when presented with new information from colleagues, policy makers, current events, and/or own study of the issues	• Analyst enters questions in the database of the HME and rates them according to importance • HME has access to all important questions entered and ratings by different analysts, along with ability to search efficiently for common factors, and may offer questions for analyst to consider
Stay Abreast of Current Information	• Analyst establishes own parameters and search routines for finding useful information • Analyst updates own routines when necessary • Analyst employs own strategy to filter the found information and focus attention on that of most relevance • Analyst reads and digests selected information, discussing material with available colleagues as relevant	• HME learns from analyst's parameters and search routines (as well as from those of other analysts), and using a recommender system, proactively identifies relevant information and presents it to analyst • Analyst interacts with HME to rate relevance and value of identified information, allowing HME to continuously improve its recommendations • HME finds connection between analyst's search for information and that of another analyst's investigation and sends alerts to the two analysts to talk to each other • Analyst may initiate new information searches with this new connection • HME assembles relevant information into a graphical display (or other form of sensory presentation) for analyst's review • Analyst interacts with HME to rate relevance and value of graphical display (and HME continuously improves how it displays connected information to analyst)

197

Analyze Assembled Information	• Analyst considers importance and accuracy of reviewed information • Analyst uses expertise to recognize patterns and connections between new information and previous information or knowledge • Many potential questions could be asked regarding significance of reviewed information, but analyst may be limited to considering only a few • Analyst catalogues important information in own record or a database shared by analytic team or organization	• Together, analyst and HME create hypotheses of outcomes regarding assembled information • Analyst, drawing on own expertise, interacts with HME to rate hypotheses considered • HME can interact concurrently with other relevant analysts to gather feedback on hypotheses • HME mines all available data for supporting and conflicting evidence for top-rated hypotheses
Communicate Intelligence and Analysis to Others	• Analyst may informally share an important insight with colleagues, update a shared document, or prepare a formal intelligence report • Analyst will coordinate and collaborate with relevant colleagues to prepare the formal report • Analysts will source report, assembling information used in the analysis such that it can be understood by analytic colleagues and policy makers • Analyst will revise and defend report in response to edits	• HME identifies other analysts working on related issues, proactively shares important insights, and makes connections • When a formal report is needed, analyst selects a working hypothesis, and HME automatically prepares draft report for review by analyst

continued

TABLE 7-1 Continued

Analytic Activity of an Individual Analyst	Traditional Human Process	Process in a Human–Machine Ecosystem (HME)
Sustain and Build Expertise in Analytic Area (when time permits)	• Analyst may visit policy makers or other clients to assess current intelligence needs • Analyst may work with analytic methodologist to explore new tools for discerning links between different sets of information • Analyst may explore new models and theories on issues of interest and update own framework for gathering and filtering information	• HME stays abreast of relevant models and theories • HME identifies information that does not appear to fit into any existing models—i.e., flagging analyst to consider whether information is irrelevant or a new model is needed

NOTE: Descriptions of analysts' activities are based on discussion in Chapter 4.

will require interdisciplinary work that brings researchers together both from across the SBS disciplines and with those in AI fields and computer science. The discussion here divides the needed research into four domains: (1) human capacities, (2) human–machine interaction, (3) human–technology teaming, and (4) human–system integration. Although it is not possible to discuss all the relevant research questions comprehensively within the scope of this study, we offer in each domain some of the critical areas that should be investigated. As noted above, the optimal research program will require the synergistic interplay of research in each of these domains as knowledge accumulates.

Human Capacities

While human agents bring sophisticated and contextualized reasoning to the process of analysis and inference, they are also limited in significant ways in their ability to process information. Understanding those limits, particularly in the context of intelligence analysis, is an important step in designing the technologies to augment them. The limitations to humans' capacity for perception, attention, and cognition are at the root of many errors, both in everyday life and in expert settings such as medicine (Krupinski, 1996; Nodine and Kundel, 1987; Waite et al., 2016), and there is every reason to believe that the same is true for intelligence analysis. While existing research provides insights into these limitations, the complexity of an environment of human–machine teams for intelligence analysis would require more detailed understanding, derived from many research areas, of how these limitations should be factored into a system's design. In this section, we illustrate the possibilities with a discussion of two such areas: we explore findings from vision sciences that shed light on human limits in attention and memory, and review the literature on workload to consider what is known about how individuals manage interruptions and multiple tasks.

Fundamental Capacity Limits

Humans have finite capabilities. At a perceptual level, many of these limits are fairly self-evident, and centuries of research and development have been devoted to extending human capacity. For example, human acuity is limited to resolving details of about 1 minute of arc (a unit of measure for angles), so microscopes and telescopes were invented to bring small or distant objects into view. Other devices (e.g., infrared night-vision glasses) were created to detect and render visible electromagnetic radiation outside the range of wavelengths of 400–700 nanometers, which humans cannot see. Microphones and amplifiers allow humans to detect otherwise inaudible sounds, while other devices extend their chemical senses of taste and smell. And the seismograph that detects a remote earthquake or underground nuclear blast can be thought of as an enhancement of humans' sense of touch.

Attention limits are less fully understood than perceptual limits, and accordingly, less progress has been made in developing the technologies to support them. In fact, research has shown that humans are imperfectly aware of their own attention limits. Many people can recognize that they will fail to see something if it is too small to resolve or if the lights are out, but it may be less obvious to them that they can fail to notice a fairly dramatic change between two visible instances of the same thing (e.g., missing that someone previously had a beard [Simons and Levin, 1998] or failing to perceive an object right in front of them [Cohen et al., 2016; Simons and Chabris, 1999]).

Figure 7-2 can be used to illustrate the complex relationship between attention and what is seen. In this figure, all the colors and lines seemingly can be seen at a glance, yet the presence of particular structures, such as one with four disks instead of three, or one with a blue, a yellow, and a red disk, is not immediately apparent. What makes attentional limits less intuitive than perceptual limits is that some version of "everything" can be seen clearly in this image. In this figure, the presence of a single purple

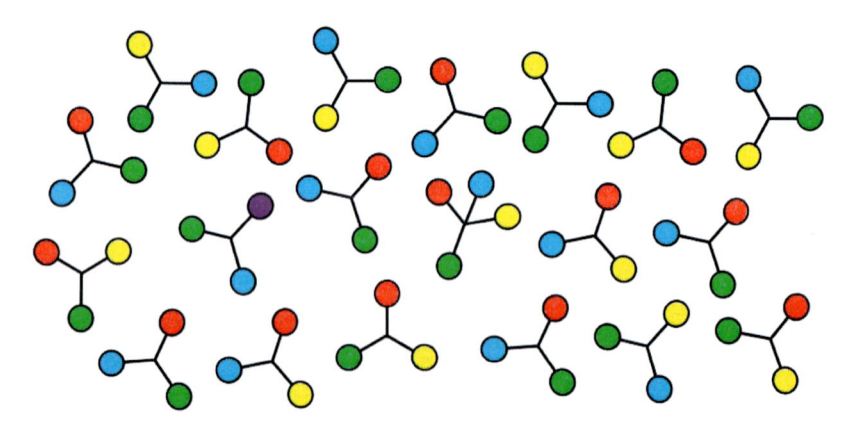

FIGURE 7-2 Attention and finding a target.
NOTE: This figure illustrates that some visual search tasks are easier than others. Finding the purple target is relatively easy because there is only one, and it is distinct. Finding a three-disk structure that includes blue, yellow, and red disks requires more effort, even though it is easy to confirm the correct colors once one has identified the right item. When the target is defined by a combination of colors, attentional scrutiny is required.
SOURCE: Redrawn from Wolfe (2003).

disk is immediately obvious because there is only one (although even in this case, one might not notice the purple disk until it became relevant). What is not obvious is that one needs to direct attention to a specific question to be sure of its specific features (its colors or orientation)—that is, attention is generally limited to one or maybe a few objects or locations at any moment. For the rest of what is presently in view, the visual system is generating something like a statistical statement. In this case, the statistical statement might be, "There are red, green, blue, and yellow circles, mostly in triangular structures (with one exception)." This estimate is surprisingly rough. For instance, only attentional scrutiny would identify whether there is a vertical line in the figure.

Interestingly, however, the perceptual experience is not so rough. Instead, people experience a "grand illusion" (Noë et al., 2000) that they are seeing a coherent visual world filled with meaningful, recognized objects. One way of conceptualizing this phenomenon is to say that people "see" their "unconscious inference" (Helmholtz, 1924) about the state of the world. This mismatch between the perceptual experience and what is actually held in attention is what leads people to miss something in plain sight.

Attention and memory are closely intertwined elements of cognitive performance, and there are related capacity limits in these domains. Failures of attention could be thought of as failures of memory as opposed to failures of attention. That is, the observer might have seen and recognized something, but then have simply failed to remember it for long enough to report it. Note that from a practical point of view, it matters little whether these errors are described as "blindness" or "amnesia" since versions of these errors (e.g., failure to see a tumor in a medical scan or a missile site in a satellite image) would have the same adverse consequences either way.

Limits to retention in long-term memory are familiar, but limits to short-term or working memory can feel more surprising (Cowan, 2001). There is considerable debate among researchers about whether the latter capacity should be understood as a continuous "resource" or a set of discrete "slots" (Suchow et al., 2014), but there is agreement that the capacity is small. Researchers have found a variety of ways to demonstrate the significant limits to what humans can successfully hold in short-term memory (e.g., see Pylyshyn and Storm, 1988; Vogel and Machizawa, 2004).

These findings could have implications for the design of a human–machine ecosystem, but additional foundational research is needed on the nature of the limits on attention and memory and their significance in IC contexts. Meanwhile, researchers pursuing the design of a human–machine ecosystem can use what is already known in developing technologies, systems, or processes that may augment these human capacities.

Managing Workload

The literature on workload demands, task switching, and interruptions and their effects on human performance is highly relevant to the design of communication protocols and priorities in a human–machine ecosystem. In this environment, the types of workload demands on individual analysts would be different than in the current analytic workflow. Many agents would likely be operating in the work environment, with other agents asynchronously providing new information to be assessed and possibly interrupting the task of another agent.

A promising research avenue is to seek ways to better characterize how and when the products of semiautonomous agents and supporting technologies can best be conveyed to human analysts. A large network of semiautonomous AI agents could generate notifications or push information to human analysts on a random, and sometimes rapid, schedule. From the point of view of the human, however, this capability could have costs as well as benefits. If the semiautonomous agents were to uncover evidence of unusually high-priority risks, this information likely should be pushed to the responsible human analysts as quickly as possible. Otherwise, in lower-risk situations, it would be important to schedule information transfer so as not to stress the human analyst and to increase the information's usability. Human analysts may also initiate searches for relevant data or inputs from other agents. Research questions of interest include how best to interrupt analysts to transfer information and how analysts would manage switching between tasks in a human–machine ecosystem.

Interruptions. The current literature on interruptions and work fragmentation suggests that people who are interrupted can sometimes compensate by working harder when they return to the interrupted task, though there may be costs in terms of stress and frustration (Bawden and Robinson, 2008; Mark et al., 2008). In other cases, interruptions simply degrade human performance. Interruption is a frequent occurrence for information workers in many work environments (for a review, see Mark et al. [2005]), but are all interruptions the same, and what are their costs? Do people spontaneously interrupt their work patterns, and if so, why? Can external cues help keep things on track (Smith et al., 2003)? These questions require new research.

Work fragmentation, with correspondingly short work episodes, may damage performance, especially on complex problems. Even when an interruption delivers task-relevant information, switching between tasks takes time (Braver et al., 2003; Monsell, 2003; Pashler, 2000). If the current task involves several complicated steps, an interruption may require going back several steps to reinstate context (Altman et al., 2014). Recursive interruptions, in which an interruption to handle a second task is in turn interrupted by a third, can pose high demands for recovery. On the other hand, some research has shown that multitasking can sometimes improve efficiency (Grier et al., 2008).

Researchers have coded the activities of individuals in their natural work environments and explored the costs of interruption and task switching (Mark et al., 2005, 2016). Such studies indicate that cycling between multiple tasks is common, and that interruptions are most detrimental if the interrupted task is complex, if the interruption does not occur at a natural breakpoint, and if the interruption requires a switch to a different work unit. Individuals who recover well following an interruption often note the current state of information within the interrupted task for later use or analysis (Mark et al., 2005). These observations have implications for the design of protocols for interaction between humans and machines.

Switching between tasks. A classic literature has examined when and how humans divide attention between tasks. Sometimes, tasks can be carried out concurrently without loss; more often, however, performance must be traded off between tasks (Sperling and Dosher, 1986; Sperling and Melcher, 1978; Wickens, 2008, 2010), and in overload situations, operators often carry out tasks and subtasks sequentially (Wickens et al., 2015). Some of the loss in performance caused by switching between tasks can be reduced with training or practice (Monsell, 2003; Strobach et al., 2012). Research in this area has focused on workload and task switching in laboratory tasks involving rapid stimulus classifications, such as alternating color or orientation judgments, where the switching to another task is triggered by the stimulus (Bailey and Konstan, 2006; Pashler, 2000). In voluntary task switching, also studied in laboratory settings (Arrington and Logan, 2004, 2005), operators who are instructed to switch between two tasks at their own rate generally prefer to avoid switch costs. However, research on factors that might be especially important for a human–machine ecosystem, such as the difficulty or priority of a task that might affect task choice, is sparse (Gutzwiller, 2014).

Task threading (a combination of concurrent and sequential task execution), task switching, and interruption have also been studied in human factors research, often using tasks related to flight deck or other complex operations scenarios. Such studies have consisted of observing how individual human agents (e.g., a pilot) facing a computer screen (e.g., on a flight deck) manage their duty cycle with two to four tasks, each with different incentives and time demands. Models predicting the pattern of switching between tasks include preferences for easy, interesting, or high-priority tasks (Gutzwiller et al., 2014; Wickens et al., 2015). These studies also have identified connections between task switching and the human agent's need for breaks (Helton and Russell, 2015). Other measured aspects of individual cognitive capacities or functions, such as working memory or perceptual abilities, and their interactions with task complexity or stress may be correlated with an individual's ability to perform in these complex environments (Kane and Engle, 2003; Kane et al., 2007; Oberlander et al., 2007; Unsworth and Engle, 2007).

When work cycles between tasks in relatively rapid episodes, the workload demands can be visible in various physiological measures, such as pupil diameter or other measures of workload or related stress, such as heart rate (Adamczyk and Bailey, 2004; Bailey and Konstan, 2006; Haapalainen et al., 2010; Iqbal et al., 2004, 2005). (See the discussion of applications of neuroscience later in this chapter.)

Research Directions

Identify how workload and task cycling would work in the more complex environment of a human–machine ecosystem.

Although the structure of the tasks studied in previous research on task management and the effects of interruption is relatively simple, the approaches used in this research provide a conceptual framework and set of research tools that could be used to address these questions in a human–machine ecosystem. Future research directions in this area include

- observational studies similar to those conducted in other work environments to characterize the work settings of the IC more accurately;
- research to evaluate the costs/benefits of work fragmentation and interruptions in tasks with more complex and longer work units (on the scale of minutes to hours as opposed to seconds in some of the laboratory studies conducted to date);
- research to identify guidelines for scheduling queries (i.e., the pushing and pulling of information) to best coordinate information sharing among multiple human agents, semiautonomous agents, and supporting technologies while best accommodating the needs of the human analyst; and
- research on the costs and benefits of ongoing monitoring of analytic work within a human–machine ecosystem, including issues of privacy and the need for control of the environment by the human analysts.

Human–Machine Interaction

Research dating back decades has explored human–machine interaction, focusing primarily on the respective strengths and weaknesses of humans and machines and means of assigning tasks accordingly (see, e.g., Endsley, 1987; Kaber et al., 2005; National Research Council, 1951; Parasuraman, 2000; Parasuraman et al., 2000). More recent frameworks for human–machine interaction are helping system designers think about the possibilities for collaboration between humans and machines (Chen and Barnes, 2014). As shown in Figure 7-3, for example, Cummings (2014) drew on Rasmussen's (1983) taxonomy of skills, rules, and knowledge-based behaviors to illustrate the synergy between computers and humans in relation to type of task and degree of uncertainty. Figure 7-3 shows that skills-based and rules-based tasks lend themselves to automation or execution by machines and that knowledge-based and expertise-based tasks are best performed by humans. However, the figure also indicates that the degree

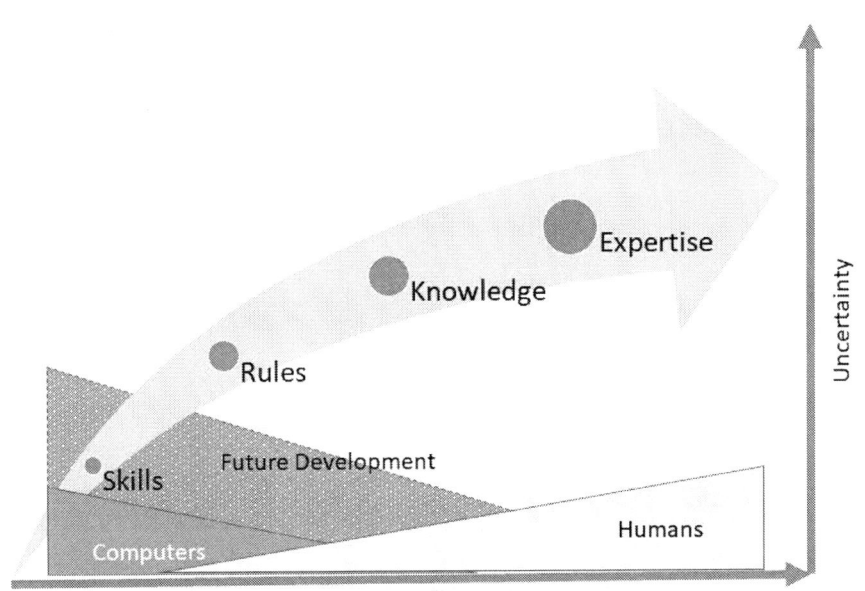

Relative strengths of computer vs. human information processing

FIGURE 7-3 Role allocation for information-processing behaviors.
NOTE: Skills-based tasks are defined as sensory–motor actions that can become highly automatic through training and practice. Rules-based tasks are actions guided by a set of procedures. Knowledge-based tasks are actions aided by mental models developed over time through repeated experience. Expertise-based tasks are actions predicated on previous knowledge-based tasks and dependent on significant experience in the presence of uncertainty.
SOURCE: Adapted from Cummings (2014).

of uncertainty inherent in the task at hand will help determine whether it can be fully automated, should be fully under human control, or can best be executed by human–machine interaction.

For repetitive or routine tasks, where the uncertainty is low and sensor reliability is high, machines have advantages over humans. For higher-level cognitive tasks, humans still outperform machines when judgment and intuition are key. However, current and projected advances in the reasoning capabilities of AI and machine learning show promise for enabling machines to take on more knowledge-based and even expertise-based tasks (Cummings, 2014; 2015 Study Panel of the One Hundred Year Study of Artificial Intelligence, 2016). With these advances, machines will be able to work alongside humans as teammates, changing the roles that both play and requiring a new understanding of how human–machine interactions can be most effective.

For intelligence analysis in the age of data overload, human analysts are likely to need assistance from machines in a number of ways. Examples include (1) providing decision support (e.g., helping to store critical information, search datasets, scan multiple images, monitor real-time data streams for anomalies, or recover situational awareness when switching between tasks); (2) generating data visualizations from large datasets in ways that help analysts discover patterns and critical information; and (3) augmenting forecasting capabilities to improve the IC's ability to anticipate events. This section explores some of the questions that need to be considered and research needed to improve human–machine interaction for intelligence analysis, including research on applications of neuroscience, a field that is advancing rapidly and providing tools and methods.

Decision Support

A wide range of research has investigated technologies that support decision making, much of it focused on medical decision support. Greenes (2014) provides an overview of the topic's scope within the medical field, which ranges from deep learning algorithms that support classification of images (e.g., Amir and Lehmann, 2016; Fraioli et al., 2010) to efforts to leverage big data methods so that genomic data on patients can be applied to support precision medical care (e.g., Hoffman et al., 2016). AI systems have also been developed to advise human decision makers. Examples of these applications include moving ships and cranes around a container port (Bierwirth and Meisel, 2015), moving energy around the grid (Ferruzzi et al., 2016), and maintaining supply chains (O'Rourke, 2014). At the level of individual consumers there are such applications as rules for conversing with one's car (Strayer et al., 2016) and even options for presenting online reviews that could shape one's choice of a restaurant (Zhang et al.,

2017). Efforts in the security realm include automating airport screening (Hättenschwiler et al., 2018).

For all of these applications, implementation requires making choices about the specific nature of the human–machine interactions involved, and the same will be true for applications of AI to intelligence analysis. Many different rules for transferring information between human and AI agents are possible. For example, does the AI offer its information before, during, or after the human's initial decision? Different rules will produce different outcomes. Moreover, the nature of the task influences rule decisions and outcomes. For instance, if the task is to detect or predict something rare, even a good AI system is likely to produce many more false-positive than true-positive findings. As discussed further below, the interaction rule on how these findings are presented and used can affect the human user's attitude toward and trust in the AI (Hoff and Bashir, 2015). Should the AI agent present only that information most likely to be useful, posing the risk of failing to draw attention to seemingly less important but actually critical pieces of information, or should the AI agent be programmed to deliver many possibilities to the human analyst, who would then have to separate out the useful material? Can the AI agent be programmed to base its behavior on the prior decision making of the human analyst? For instance, if the human agent were labeling all the information being provided by the AI agent as uninteresting, might the AI agent become more permissive in an effort to make the outputs of the task more comprehensive to increase its chances of providing useful information? There are no straightforward answers to such questions, and seeking those answers and developing ultimate rules for specific contexts will be a rich area for future research.

The remainder of this section reviews some of what is known about perception errors, rare events, biases, and trust to highlight the range of issues that need to be considered in developing the rules of interaction between humans and machines.

Perception errors. An error in perception might involve detecting something that is not present (a false-positive error) or failing to detect something that is present (a false-negative or miss error). Most existing research has focused on the latter class of errors. A useful taxonomy of such errors comes from work in medical image perception (Nodine and Kundel, 1987, p. 1):

- **Sampling errors** (also called "search" errors [Krupinski, 1996]) occur when experts fail to look in the right location or sample the right information. These are cases in which, in a world of too much information, the information that turned out to be relevant was simply never examined.

- **Recognition errors** are those in which the target was seen or the information reviewed, but no stimulus attracted any particular attention, and no action was taken. In these cases, the relevant information was examined but not regarded as important.
- **Decision errors** are those in which the observer recognizes that the stimulus or information might be important, but makes the wrong decision about what to do with that information.

Decisions depend on criteria (Macmillan and Creelman, 2005), either formally set by some standard or internally judged by the observer. A false-negative (or miss) error is made when the observer perceives a target and takes a conservative position by incorrectly concluding that it is not a target, whereas a false-positive error is made when the observer takes a more liberal position by incorrectly concluding that something is a target when it is not. The placement of a decision criterion is of particular importance for detection of rare events (see below). At an airport security checkpoint, for example, the same bag might pass through on one day but be sent for secondary inspection on another if the alert level were raised. The bag has not changed, but the decision criterion has. Signal detection theory (Green and Swets, 1966) makes it clear that shifting decision criteria simply changes the mix of errors made by observers and does not eliminate the possibility of errors.

Rare events. Many of the targets that intelligence analysts try to detect are rare events. It would be desirable, for example, to detect the warning signs of a terrorist's intentions or of a coup d'état. But, the likelihood that any individual will become a terrorist is very, very small, and coups d'état are also quite rare. Detecting events that are naturally rare is more complicated then detecting more common ones. Research has shown that the nature of human cognition predisposes a person to miss rare events. Humans are, at least in a rough sense, Bayesian decision makers (Maloney and Zhang, 2010): they take the prior probabilities of an event or stimulus into account when making decisions. Missing the signs of a rare event can therefore be considered a form of decision error because humans are typically biased against deciding that they are detecting a rare event (after all, it is rare).

Laboratory studies of rare events in the contexts of screening mammography (Evans et al., 2013) and baggage screening (Mitroff and Biggs, 2014; Wolfe et al., 2013) have shown that low-prevalence targets are more frequently missed (Wolfe et al., 2005) and that using more conservative decision criteria is an important factor in these cases. This research also has shown that observers more readily abandon the search for a rare than for a more common target (Cain et al., 2013; Tuddenham, 1962; Wolfe and Van Wert, 2010). Other research has demonstrated that observers are less vigilant in monitoring the world for rare events (Colquhoun and Baddeley, 1967; Mackworth, 1970; Thomson et al., 2015).

Rare events take different forms, falling on a continuum from predictable to unpredictable. The occurrence of breast cancer in a breast cancer screening program is an example of a predictable rare event: breast cancer will occur, but it will be rare (about 3 to 5 cases in 1,000 women screened in a North American population [Lee et al., 2016]). At the other end of the continuum are so-called "black swan" events.[4] Obviously, truly unpredictable events will by definition, be impossible to predict. Early detection of predictable rare events, from cancer to coups d'état, is a more tractable but still difficult problem.

Technology would appear to offer a solution to the problem of detecting rare events since a computer does not get bored. An algorithm's decision criteria can be set and will not drift to a more conservative value in the face of such events (Horsch et al., 2008). Yet even without a shift in the decision criteria, some false alarms will still occur. The extent of false alarms is one aspect of human–machine interaction that plays into human trust of technology, discussed further below.

Biases. Cognitive biases are thought processes that produce errors in decisions, as when an individual holds on to beliefs or ways of knowing in spite of contrary information (Gilovich and Griffin, 2002). Humans use information from prior experiences to understand current ones; they can often find connections and use related experience successfully in new applications. However, this ability to retrieve useful information from memory quickly is also subject to a number of biases. Individuals can, for example, be predisposed to search for information that is aligned with knowledge they already possess or that confirms a working hypothesis. While having hypotheses can be useful for sorting information, a person can become anchored to a particular working hypothesis and as a result, filter out discrepant information that may in fact be useful (Tversky and Kahneman, 1974; Yudkowsky, 2011).

Teams of people are just as susceptible to bias as individuals are. Consider the information-pooling bias—the tendency for a team to share and discuss information all members share over information known only to one team member (Stasser et al., 2000). In intelligence analysis, the capacity to consider other information that may be vital to the analysis is essential. Researchers have identified a number of simple cognitive prompts to guide

---

[4] A black swan event is a metaphor for something that was not predicted but happened nonetheless. For example, the Fukushima nuclear reactor accident in Japan has been called a black swan event since officials believed they had prepared for all extreme threats to the reactor (Achenbach, 2011).

people to think more strategically about their decisions (e.g., Heath et al., 1998; Klein, 2007; Wittenbaum et al., 2004). Further research is needed to determine whether such prompts could work for the tasks of intelligence analysis and whether interactions with machines can be optimized to ensure that additional information critical to the problem at hand is reviewed and shared among analysts as appropriate.

Like humans, moreover, machines and AI systems are subject to errors and decision biases. In an increasingly digitized world, data mining algorithms are used to make sense of emerging streams of behavioral and other data (Portmess and Tower, 2014). Machine learning algorithms are used to identify inaccurate information automatically at the source (e.g., fraud alerts on credit cards) (Mittelstadt et al., 2016), and personalization and filtering algorithms are used to facilitate access to particular information for users (Newell and Marabelli, 2015). The issue, however, is that developers and users of such algorithms may, intentionally or inadvertently, insert bias into the algorithms' operational parameters (Caliskan et al., 2017; Nakamura, 2013). Algorithms will reflect the gender, racial, socioeconomic, and other biases that are reflected in training data. For example, domestic U.S. criminal justice applications of machine learning and AI, such as facial recognition algorithms used in policing, have been found to be biased against African Americans (Garvie et al., 2016; Klare et al., 2012). (See Box 7-2 and Appendix D for more detail, and see Osoba and Welser [2017] and National Academies of Sciences, Engineering, and Medicine [2017a, 2018a] for further discussion of AI errors, bias, and associated risks.) This issue will continue to grow in importance as algorithms become more complex, and as they engage in semiautonomous interactions with other algorithms and are used to augment and/or replace analyses and decisions once the purview of humans.

Although research is under way to examine bias in training datasets and algorithms, one issue yet to be addressed is cultural bias, an issue of significance for the IC. Because data for training datasets are frequently collected in countries where relevant research is taking place, these algorithms are often biased to be more successful with certain cultures and geographic regions than others (Chen and Gomes, 2018). Analysts using computational models to assist in understanding and predicting the intent, behavior, and actions of adversaries may derive skewed results because of unrecognized cultural bias in the computational design process. Understanding of cultural nuances will be important in extending algorithmic applications to semantic and narrative analyses of use to the IC. For example, non-English data must be carefully defined and categorized for use in computational models to avoid mirror imaging and biasing the model toward one's own cultural norms.[5]

---

[5]Mirror imaging denotes analysts' assumption that people being studied think and act like the analysts themselves, including their gender, race, culture, and so on (Witlin, 2008).

> **BOX 7-2**
> **Bias in Machine Learning Algorithms**
>
> The "learning" in machine learning usually takes place through human agents' manual input in the classification of training data. It can also be driven by an algorithm itself, when it identifies best-fit models to make sense of new data. Once trained, the algorithm can process new data without the input of a human agent (Leese, 2014). However, large-scale training datasets are expensive to create, so only a small number are freely available for algorithm research and development, and these are overused. If the available training datasets contain biases, those biases will be propagated and incorporated into future prediction outcomes.
>
> There are several sources of bias in such training sets. One source is reliance on data collected in a particular site. For example, if the data were all collected in developed nations, the lack of data from developing countries may skew the results (Shankar et al., 2017); see Chapter 2. Another source of bias is a lack of strict parameters for data collection. Projects involving citizen science (also known as crowdsourced or networked science)[a] provide an effective and low-cost means of developing large datasets for noncommercial research (Siebert et al., 2017; Sullivan et al., 2014), but such projects may not include clear guidance for volunteers about where, when, and how to collect the data, which can introduce bias in the data. Unfortunately, uncovering the influence of human bias in algorithm design and use would require a lengthy investigation (Mittelstadt et al., 2016) that might still be unsuccessful at identifying the cause, particularly in the case of learning algorithms (Tutt, 2016).
>
> ---
>
> [a]Citizen science projects are those that typically involve nonscientists (i.e., people who are not professionally trained in project-relevant disciplines) in the processes, methods, and standards of research, with the intended goal of advancing scientific knowledge or application (NASEM, 2018b, p. 13).

Designers can take steps to address and mitigate machine-based biases before algorithms and technologies are put into use by incorporating SBS insights on complex cultural, political, and social phenomena into their designs.

Trust. Lack of trust on the part of human agents will limit the potential of a human–machine ecosystem. On the other hand, excessive trust can lead to complacency and failure to intervene when the performance of technology declines (Cummings et al., 2008) or it is used for circumstances beyond its design (Parasuraman and Riley, 1997; Lee and Moray, 1994; Hoffman et al., 2013). Machine-based biases and errors will likely affect a human's ability to trust machines completely, as demonstrated by the rare event example in Box 7-3.

The problem of low-prevalence events could adversely affect operations in a human–machine ecosystem. For example, an ecosystem's detection of

> **BOX 7-3**
> **Human Trust in Technology:**
> **The Case of Computer-Aided Detection Systems**
>
> An example of possible human responses to imperfect machine output comes from radiologists' use of computer-aided detection (CAD) systems in the detection of breast cancer—a rare event. A good CAD system might find 90 percent of cancers and yield false alarms in just 10 percent of cases. This performance is comparable to that of an expert radiologist. Thus the talented CAD is not quite good enough to perform the task on its own, but in principle, it should be a useful collaborator with a talented human. However, the low base rate or prevalence of breast cancer complicates this interaction, particularly when there are more false positives than true positives. In North America, as noted earlier, the average is 3 to 5 cases of breast cancer per 1,000 women screened. The CAD system will find 2.7 of those cases. If the system also yields false alarms for 10 percent of women screened, it will produce 100 false-positive reports. The positive predictive value of a CAD system (true-positive responses/total positive responses) is just 3 percent. A clinician can hardly be blamed for regarding such "advice" with skepticism. One study found that when a CAD system correctly detected a cancer not detected by a radiologist, the radiologist rejected that valid finding 70 percent of the time (Nishikawa et al., 2012). The source of these human responses is not yet known, but it appears reasonable to hypothesize that a lack of trust is an important contributing factor (Parasuraman and Manzey, 2010; Jorritsma et al., 2015).

two novel, otherwise undetected factors linking activities and information of the sort described earlier in Box 7-1 could be very useful. But if these two factors were embedded in a list of 100 spurious connections between activities, analysts might disregard the information. Given the vast number of possible interactions that might be uncovered by a human–machine ecosystem, the development of collaborative technologies capable of providing advice with high positive predictive value (i.e., number of correct conclusions/all conclusions) will be a daunting technical challenge.

Another challenge concerns the need to understand the reasoning behind the machine's connections or conclusions. This issue has been termed "explainable AI" and is being examined by a number of research programs.[6] In intelligence analysis or other types of decision making, it is not enough just to flag a connection or an anomaly; it would be useful if the machines could explain how they reached their findings.

The challenge for SBS research, then, is to understand how humans can make the best use of imperfect information from AI agents and supporting

---

[6] See more information on Defense Advanced Research Projects Agency's AI program at https://www.darpa.mil/program/explainable-artificial-intelligence [January 2019].

technologies. If the human–machine interactions are designed well, a feedback protocol will be in place to support both humans and machines in assessing any results critically, to allow more flexibility than human agents simply accepting or rejecting machine outputs.

Research Directions

Examine the most effective ways in which AI agents can bring information to the attention of human analysts that is both useful and trustworthy.

A number of researchable questions pertain to how AI agents can bring information to the attention of human analysts in a trustworthy manner. When AI agents detect information of interest, they will need to explain their findings to the analysts. The easier case is when the AI agent reads the same information read by the human analyst, looking for the same targets. For example, if the AI agent detects a potential threat (e.g., a missile launcher in search of satellite images), it can flag that stimulus, and the analyst can decide whether the finding is important. The more difficult case is when the AI agent makes a novel prediction about something the analyst has not considered. The AI agent will need to explain its reasoning to the human agent, and the exchange between the two will need to be concise (directed at information needed for a convincing explanation without going into detail that the human agent has already accepted), in a form that is meaningful to the analyst (see the discussion of data visualization below) and timely (see the earlier discussion of interruptions).

Existing research on human–human trust (Fetchenhauser and Dunning, 2009; Mayer et al., 1995; NASEM, 2018c) and direct studies of human–computer/technology interactions (Chen and Barnes, 2014; Defense Science Board, 2012; Goodrich and Schultz, 2007; Hancock et al., 2013) can provide valuable insights for understanding the development of human–machine trust. Additional research will be needed, however, to explore how the kind of trust needed in a human–machine ecosystem in which machines are teammates can be developed. Questions of interest include

- What makes for productive exchange and convincing explanations between human and AI agents?
- How does human–machine trust develop within a team of human and AI agents? How is it maintained? How does the nature of exchanges and level of detail in explanations change with evolving levels of trust?
- How can human–machine interaction be most effective so that AI agents learn from the feedback of human agents and progressively improve how they prioritize findings?
- How can human–machine interaction be most effective so that human agents receive information from AI agents in ways that improve their analyses and knowledge of what actions to take next?

Static and Dynamic Data Visualization

A human–machine ecosystem for intelligence analysis will use semi-autonomous AI agents and supporting technologies to process massive digital datasets as an aid in discovering relevant patterns, including many that change over time. Because human analysts will continue to play critical roles in analysis and decision making, it will be important to consider human characteristics in the design and selection of ways to perceive the data. Sophisticated data visualizations[7] are increasingly available in the public domain. Innovative new ways to present analyses of data are also likely to benefit the IC.

There are many approaches to data visualization. Textbooks and manuals have been written on the subject, many inspired by informal analysis of effectiveness, visual interest, and aesthetics (Tufte, 2003, 2006; Tufte and Graves-Morris, 2014; Tufte and Robins, 1997; Tufte et al., 1998). Visualization methods have been developed for statistical and computer applications (see, e.g., Rahlf, 2017). Indeed, the history of cartographic and visualization methods is long (Fayyad et al., 2002; Friendly and Denis, 2001; Fry, 2007; Keller et al., 1994; Steele and Iliinsky, 2010).

The volume and complexity of data available in the age of digital human behavior pose new challenges in analysis and visualization. Analyzing trends in time-varying multivariate data—that is, coding multiple variables at different times—creates special challenges for visualization and understanding, especially as large-scale time-varying simulations (Lee and Shen, 2009) are incorporated into analysis. As the volume of data potentially relevant both to research and to situations of interest to intelligence analysts increases, so do the challenges of how best to analyze and display these data for human interpretation and comprehension. Effectively conveying information to the human analyst may help support understanding, and therefore trust in the outputs of AI agents.

Researchers in the field of modern data visualization study how best to visualize data to support human perception and reasoning. An early literature on interpretation of simple graphs (e.g., Boy et al., 2014; Dujmović et al., 2010; Halford et al., 2005; Kosslyn, 1989; Wainer, 1992) focused on the distributions of single variables, differences in means, or interactive effects of variables. The aim of emerging work on data visualization is to support analysis and communication of more complex information. For example, researchers have proposed a rank ordering of different graphical formats to indicate how well they convey information about correlations

---

[7]The term "data visualization" refers to the representation of information or data analysis in the form of a chart, diagram, picture, etc.

among variables (Harrison et al., 2014; Kay and Heer, 2016). Other recent advances include the following:

- Research has been conducted on the relative effectiveness of different visual features, including the relative discriminability of different CIE colors[8] at different spatial scales (Stone et al., 2014); the effectiveness of coding by position, orientation, size, and color/luminance to reveal central tendencies, outliers, trends, and clusters in data (Healey, 1996; Szafir et al., 2016a); and how display size can influence the effectiveness of visualization (Shupp et al., 2009; Yost and North, 2006).
- Research has also been carried out on novel ways of visualizing word usage in text. Configurable color fields, such as clusters of color patterns, can help reveal patterns of word usage in documents, allowing comparison of those patterns across documents even when the relevant patterns may not be known a priori (Szafir et al., 2016b). In addition, complex word co-occurrence patterns based on frequently occurring words or word combinations can be used to derive the "topics" appearing in different bodies of text (Alexander et al., 2014; Dou et al., 2011). Keywords have been used to query financial transaction histories (Chang et al., 2007).
- Visualization of networks as graphs of connected points (nodes) or as points in multidimensional spaces in which distance conveys similarity has supported research on social networks. Study of the dynamics of social networks that change over time can potentially be aided by time animation displays or corresponding computer simulations of potential cascades of outcomes.

In practice, intelligence analysts will likely focus on the problems to be solved, not what can be accomplished with a specific visualization tool. Thus the most useful design focus will be on making the interactions with data tools natural, obvious, and transparent, permitting the analyst to move easily between different visualization applications (Shapiro, 2010; Steele and Iliinsky, 2010). Other predictable challenges may involve the fusion of multiple sources of data and treatment of missing data (Buja et al., 2008), both ongoing topics of study.

---

[8]The CIE color model is a color space model created by the International Commission on Illumination, known as the Commission Internationale de l'Elcairage (CIE).

> **Research Directions**
>
> ***Explore methods for enhancing data visualization capabilities within the context of a human–machine ecosystem.***
>
> Optimized visualizations of information are likely to be increasingly important in the complex work environment of a human–machine ecosystem. Improving data visualization tools and how the user interacts with those tools is an important area for future research. Such work is likely to leverage fast computing, new simulation methods, and behavioral testing involving vision science on the one hand and event and episode analysis on the other. Several areas seem promising:
>
> - evaluation of the effectiveness of specific visual cues for depicting properties beyond the simple measures of mean, variance, and first-order patterns, including the effective visualization of time-varying properties and more complex patterns and relations;
> - behavioral analysis and the development of new theories of knowledge discovery describing how analysts use visualization successfully to develop and test hypotheses and, equally important, how visualization can support collaboration among multiple analysts;
> - research to identify systems that can be used by human analysts or AI agents to query datasets for special-purpose visualizations with which to test hypotheses or look for specific patterns, with an emphasis on the naturalness and transparency of the query process; and
> - research to improve an AI agent's prediction of the data and/or analyses most likely to be needed by a human analyst, including the ability of an AI agent to predictively sample, preprocess, and/or precompute appropriate data visualizations.

A combination of research in the vision sciences, the behavioral sciences, and human factors has the potential to advance understanding of how people extract meaning from a data visualization, resulting in more effective techniques and design principles. Research on visual perception and attention can be mined to improve the functionality of data visualization. Relevant topics include studies of the perception of basic visual properties (e.g., color, shape), visual search, and working memory.

Forecasting Models and Tools

A well-designed human–machine ecosystem has the potential to transform predictive forecasting—a domain that has long been central to the IC. Forecasting (the so-called "Holy Grail" of intelligence analysis) is the reliable anticipation of future events. Large-scale data sources and the increasing complexity of intelligence problems will challenge the design of future forecasting systems. In addition, designers will have to determine how best to integrate information processed by semiautonomous AI agents and automated detection systems with human judgment. At present, forecasting methods with a 75–80 percent success rate are considered rather good, yet this success rate is often built on easy-to-moderate cases. Human analysts or algorithmic models may also score well on easy calls, but not so well on situations that are more difficult to predict. The IC needs forecasting methods that succeed with challenging problems. Recent SBS research has made significant progress toward (1) understanding how humans make predictions and improving the probability estimates of human forecasts and (2) incorporating human behavior into forecasting models. The next generation of forecasting research can build on this work to improve precision for those difficult problems with which the analyst most needs help.

Human forecasters. Human judgments and decisions, including the ability of humans to assess and manipulate probabilities, have been studied for decades, notably since the World War II era (Luce, 2005; Luce and Raiffa, 2012). Forecasting the future is a complex effort, though people do it often as they consider decisions in their personal lives (e.g., the likelihood of needing major medical treatment in the next year); in business (e.g., what kinds of dresses will sell); or in economic predictions (e.g., the economic consequences of a shift in monetary policy). The centrality of forecasting to intelligence analysis was recently highlighted by an Intelligence Advanced Research Projects Activity (IARPA) research initiative on geopolitical forecasting, which sponsored competitive forecasting tournaments.[9] These tournaments were focused on such questions as: How likely is it that unrest in region R will explode into violence, and on what time scale? Will country C develop enriched nuclear stockpiles of a critical size? Will a regional outbreak of infectious disease D be transmitted to the United States? Will the capacity to generate clean fresh water be outpaced by population growth in arid region Z?

The initial 4-year round of IARPA funding covered five academic research groups that participated in these tournaments, producing a wealth of research on potential approaches to improving geopolitical forecasting (Tetlock, 2017). The research groups focused directly on understanding the probability estimates made by humans and how best to aggregate them. The research topics included quantitative evaluation of probability estimation, the technical issues underlying the transformation and/or aggregation of probability estimates from several individuals, the characteristics of

---

[9]For more information on IARPA's Aggregative Contingent Estimation program, see https://www.iarpa.gov/index.php/research-programs/ace [November 2018].

individual forecasters who are very successful, and whether selection or training could improve the accuracy of forecasts. This research program yielded valuable information for the IC, predicting yes-or-no answers to geopolitical questions relevant to its work. For example: Will Italy's Silvio Berlusconi resign, lose reelection/confidence vote, or otherwise vacate office before October 1, 2011 (Satopää et al., 2014a)?[10]

The IARPA tournaments led to a number of key conclusions, resulting especially from the prominent work of one of the research groups—the Good Judgment Project (Mellers et al., 2014). This group may have outperformed others precisely because it focused on the training and selection of individuals and teams, as well as the use of technical models of probability estimation and aggregation.[11] The training directed individuals to recognize potential biases of human probability estimates and reasoning (Fischhoff et al., 1978; Fong et al., 1986; Slovic et al., 1980). The group showed that certain interventions—such as providing individual training, increasing the interchange within teams, and the selection of "superforecasters" (the top few percent of performers)—all can improve the performance of both individuals and teams[12] (Mellers et al., 2014).

One question for the next generation of research is how AI might be integrated into forecasting teams (see discussion of human–technology teaming below). To contribute effectively to team forecasts, AI and the automated models from which it would draw information would have to do a better job of incorporating human behavior into their predictions.

Incorporating human behavior into forecasting models. Research on human behavior, whether cognitive or social, has become increasingly relevant to forecasting. Many forecasting tools used in everyday life are based on physical models (e.g., forecasting of storm paths from weather models). Many of these physical models help predict impacts on humans but do not incorporate impacts of human behavior on the system. However, some tools have incorporated human behavior in their models. For example, a model used to predict the future geospatial distribution of valley fever—

---

[10] Each human forecaster participating in a tournament would provide a probability estimate—e.g., 0.70 for a yes-no event—with the event being coded as 1 or 0 for whether it was predicted to occur or not. Brier (1950) scoring was used to assess the calibration of the forecasted probability (e.g., $BS = E_{j=1}^{R}(f_i - o_i)^2$, where R is the number of outcomes—2 as the problems were binary, f_i is the forecasted probability, and o_i is the outcome).

[11] Other IARPA-funded groups focused on methods for aggregating and transforming probability estimates to correct for biases near the endpoints (i.e., underestimation near 1 and overestimation near 0) that may emerge from asymmetric noise distributions [Turner et al., 2014; Erev et al., 1994; Baron et al., 2014]).

[12] The team performance was measured by the median probability estimate of an interacting group of individuals.

which tends to expand north and east from its area of greatest incidence in the southwestern United States when air and soils become warmer—incorporates both the impacts of human behavior on soil disturbance and climate factors (Gorris et al., 2018).

Two relevant examples were highlighted in the workshops held for this study (NASEM, 2018d; see Chapter 1). One of these examples, parallel to the valley fever case, shows how physical models of Zika virus vectors based on seasonal wetness, temperature, and mosquito proliferation identify baseline risk, but can be made more accurate when such human factors as risk behaviors, the mobility of infected individuals, or the potential impacts of available sociopolitical responses are also modeled (Monaghan et al., 2016). Other inputs might include indicators derived from data mining of social messaging (Twitter, Facebook, etc.), used to provide online estimates of outbreak severity. In the second example, indicators of human behavior are introduced into analytic estimates of human water insecurity in regions of water scarcity and population increase identified by the United Nations, many in the Middle East. Researchers from the Massachusetts Institute of Technology (MIT) forecasted regional water poverty by estimating the likelihood of large-scale water infrastructure projects based on such observable human indicators as local decision making, permits, and funding (Siddiqi et al., 2016). This example illustrates the benefits of specifying the most useful human indicators to include in a forecasting model.

Both of these examples start with models based in physical or biological mechanisms that become more sophisticated in one of three ways: (1) by incorporating further model modules to account for important aspects of human behavior (e.g., population mobility, exposure epidemiology, physical consequences of policy initiatives); (2) by measuring key inputs based on associated aspects of human behavior (e.g., disease contagion or measures of social unrest harvested from social media); or (3) by incorporating new questions or new indicators based on deconstruction of a problem (e.g., physical precursors of water projects, analysis of the availability of precursor supplies in an economic supply chain).

Data analytics and statistical models are tools that underpin the majority of forecasting. Traditionally, empirical models have been built from intentional observational studies, using statistically designed data collections. The data revolution and the explosion of data science have opened up new data sources not traditionally used in empirical models (Keller et al., 2016, 2017; NASEM, 2017b). Today, access to administrative data (i.e., data collected to administer a program, business, or institution) and opportunity data (e.g., embedded sensors, social media, Internet entries) are routinely being accessed to support analyses, even within the IC and U.S. Department of Defense (DoD) contexts (NASEM, 2017b). New quantitative paradigms are being developed to manage the diversity of data and the challenges associated with repurposing massive amounts of non–statistically designed data sources for analysis (National Research Council, 2013). The IC has a growing program in open-source intelligence making use of such nontraditional data sources (Williams and Blum, 2018).

The IC has a long history of implementing and understanding engineering and physical systems modeling. The challenges highlighted in this report will require the IC to build corresponding competency in social systems modeling to support forecasting and sensemaking. The transition from physical/engineering-based modeling to social systems modeling is not straightforward (NASEM, 2016), however, for the following reasons:

- Physical systems often evolve according to well-known rules, so that uncertainties in predictions based on such models can be narrowed down to uncertainties in model parameters, initial conditions, and residual errors. By contrast, social systems often evolve according to rules that are not well understood, making the difference between such models and real life highly uncertain at times; quantifying this uncertainty can be challenging.
- A substantial amount of direct data is available for many physical systems with which to calibrate these models and estimate uncertainties in model-based predictions. Data for many social system models, on the other hand, are not readily available, and it may not be possible to produce those data directly (e.g., inducing strong emotions such as hatred in a human subject is unethical). Data may therefore need to be repurposed for use in supporting models of social systems.
- Engineered systems are often designed to operate so that their various subprocesses behave linearly, with minimal interaction, and operate within their designed specifications. Complex interactions and feedbacks are often the focus for many social systems, and the humans that are central to social systems do not have design specifications.
- Behavior mechanisms in physical systems can be modeled relatively easily because their effects are well known and independent (e.g., behavior of materials for yielding, fatigue, fracture, and creep). In contrast, mechanisms in human systems often interact (e.g., sadness, depression, addiction), making modeling more difficult.
- Extrapolation is difficult for physical and social systems. However, extrapolation is frequently required in many social system settings since the complexities of these systems often put them on a trajectory that is unlike previous experience.

Research Directions

Investigate ways of advancing the IC's forecasting capabilities.

The committee foresees that forecasting will increasingly be in the purview of systems of humans and machines working together, as a current IARPA project involving a hybrid human–machine design demonstrates.[13] Research is needed to support further progress in this area. Perhaps most obviously, many important forecasting questions are not naturally binary; that is, rather having yes-no answers, they call for distributed options (e.g., Will the Korean peninsula become nuclear free in 2018, in 2019, in 2020?). Forecasting of such questions is cumbersome and requires combining noisy probability estimates. Although multinomial (N outcome) problems have been discussed (Satopää et al., 2014b), less is known about biases and aggregation issues in such problems.[14] In addition, some forecasting challenges in the IC may involve a limited number of in-house analysts rather than a large number of forecasters whose forecasts can be aggregated for more precision. Important questions remain about how best to weight judgment from a small number of forecasters, or how to benefit from multiple sequential judgments or reforecasting.

Further, much work is needed to optimize approaches to forecasting for large-scale data mining or tracking of unformed artifacts of social media indicators. Other questions include whether and how human analysts may provide complementary and synergistic analyses or offer solutions to the challenges of machine learning and AI approaches.

Future forecasting will be affected by the availability of new forms of data and by improvements in integrated human–machine systems. Knowledge gleaned from SBS research—especially knowledge of human systems and behavior and the aggregation and interpretation of human predictions and probability assessments— can play an increasingly important role in forecasting efforts relevant to the IC. Recent research has provided many examples of human-augmented modeling and of human influences in forecasting. Yet many questions remain unanswered, including how forecasting can be optimized in more complex problem spaces using new computer algorithms and within the context of a human–machine ecosystem. Potential new directions for further research include

- developing, testing, and validating modes of forecasting that go beyond sets of binary questions, including N-alternative situations and attribution of probability distributions over timelines or events;
- identifying ways in which semiautonomous AI agents could detect and correct for human biases and patterns of reasoning; and
- finding the best mix of human and AI agents to use in solving complex forecasting problems.

---

[13]More information on IARPA's Hybrid Forecasting Competition can be found at https://www.iarpa.gov/index.php/research-programs/hfc?id=661 [November 2018].

[14]Also, strong claims have been made about the calibrating force of the proper scoring method, such as the Brier score (Brier, 1950; Mellers et al., 2015; Tetlock et al., 2014), and it is not clear whether training and calibration of human forecasters would be equally effective in multinomial or expanded probability assessment problems, or indeed how best to aggregate estimates from multiple sources.

Applications of Neuroscience

Projected progress in neuroscience could be particularly relevant to the development of human–machine ecosystems, optimizing human–machine interactions. Developing work on the neurobiological relationships that underlie emotion, motivation, and cognition and influence cognitive processes (e.g., decision making) and their determinants is yielding possibilities for identifying and tracking physiological responses that signal mental and emotional states and improving task performance. Related work on interfaces between the human brain and computer technology, while further from implementation, show promise for significantly increasing the efficiency of technology-supported work.

Monitoring physiological responses. As an example of the application of neuroscience, neurotechnologies such as functional neural imaging (functional magnetic resonance imaging [fMRI][15] and functional near-infrared spectroscopy [fNIRS][16]) provide tools with which to identify neural correlates of various dimensions of analytic thinking, such as inductive reasoning, pattern detection, cognitive flexibility, cognitive bias, open-mindedness, and even creativity. Mapping based on experimental results could produce a catalog of neural correlates of analytic thinking—that is, regions or networks of the brain that are active during a particular dimension of analytic thinking. Such mapping could provide a basis for vetting various human–machine interactions anticipated in a human–machine ecosystem.

Another important contribution of neuroscience is in the development of strategies and sensors designed to measure and potentially mitigate mental and physical fatigue in the workplace (see also the discussion of supports for the analytic workforce in Chapter 8). Recent advances have been made in developing tools for monitoring the physiological state of human agents and enhancing the interactions between humans and machines. Further developments in this area are likely to provide tools that can be used both in SBS research to study strategies for improving operations in a human–machine ecosystem and within the ecosystem itself as a way of monitoring the state of the environment and providing feedback to agents.

---

[15] fMRI is used to measure changes in blood flow across the brain as an indication of changes in neural activity. Used in hospitals and imaging facilities, it measures changes in neural activity with high spatial resolution, but the size of the device does not allow for deployment in field settings.

[16] fNIRS is used to measure changes in blood flow and changes in oxygenation of blood in discrete regions of the brain as an indication of neural activity. It measures changes in neural activity with moderate spatial resolution, and the size and portability of the device allow for deployment in field settings.

A wide range of portable, noninvasive biological sensors now available can monitor such physiological parameters as respiration and heart rate and a number of other biological signals.[17] Many of these parameters are highly sensitive to stress, and can serve as important markers of specific aspects of stress, performance, and fatigue in human agents. Output from a number of these sensors has been used in developing explicit measures of cognitive workload (Liu et al., 2018). Biological markers, for example, including emerging skin-sensor measures of metabolic and neuroendocrine status (Rohrbaugh, 2017), could be valuable in identifying workload effects and provide important tools for use in studies of strategies for mitigating fatigue.

Although direct contact between a human agent and the sensor is necessary for some of these measures, work on the development of remote sensors that do not have that limitation is under way. Such sensors could be used to monitor physiological parameters as diverse as heart rate and heart rate variability, respiration, electrodermal activity, and other responses in people who are moving and are at a distance from the sensor.[18]

The development and deployment of these technologies will pose a wide range of ethical, legal, and social challenges (discussed further below). The use of biological sensors without the consent of those whose responses were being measured would pose clear questions, for example, but their use could also foster various forms of dependence among those who consented. Individuals who relied on data from the sensors to monitor their states and regulate their activities might become overreliant on the technology and less skillful at monitoring their own physiological responses (Bhardwaj, 2013; Lu, 2016; Noah et al., 2018). And widespread use of biosensors would contribute to concerns about a state in which too many actions are under surveillance (Shell, 2018; Rosenbalt et al., 2014; Moore and Piwek, 2017), as well as raise questions about the "quantified self"—the idea that all understanding of human behaviors is reduced to the data being tracked (Swan, 2013).

Interfaces between the human brain and computers. Research in neurotechnology and human–machine interactions has also explored interfaces between the human brain and computers; current applications of this work tend to be limited to the laboratory and are not yet practical for general use (Nicolas-Alonso and Gomez-Gil, 2012). A human operator using a

---

[17]Other physiological parameters that can be monitored include heart rate variability; cardiovascular performance derived from impedance cardiography; sympathetic and parasympathetic activity indexed by pupillometry; localized cerebral blood flow revealed by near-infrared spectroscopy; and electrodermal, electroencephalographic, electromyographic, and neuroendocrine responses.

[18]Other responses include photoplethysmographic, pupillometric, oculometric (eye-tracking), and pneumographic (respiratory) responses (Rohrbaugh, 2017).

keyboard and perhaps a mouse to enter and receive information through visual displays and possibly auditory communications represents a rather cumbersome and inefficient mode of interaction. The ability of the computer to interpret the thoughts of an operator would have significant implications for intelligence analysis, especially in combination with AI. Indeed, developments in brain–computer interfaces are rapidly emerging, making "thoughts" available as input to software applications. Instead of using typing or voice to issue data, an operator can deliver commands or information to a computer program simply by thinking. Current applications of this technology include devices that monitor the attention an individual devotes to a task and those that detect a selection that currently would be indicated by a mouse click. Emerging applications interface with virtual reality to convey feedback of reactions to the system through thoughts. Eventually, the brain–computer communication could be two-way, allowing a computer to induce perception in the brain of an operator.

DoD and the broader scientific community are increasingly interested in enhancing such interfaces. In support of President Obama's BRAIN (Brain Research through Advancing Innovative Neurotechnologies) initiative, DoD sponsored the Systems-Based Neurotechnology for Emerging Therapies (SUBNETS) program.[19] This program entailed a multi-institutional effort (the University of California-San Francisco, Massachusetts General Hospital, Lawrence Livermore National Laboratory, and Medtronics) to develop and deploy brain–computer interfaces (including invasive procedures) to advance health. More recently, DARPA sponsored the Towards a High-Resolution, Implantable Neural Interface project in support of the 2016 Neural Engineering System Design program.[20] Although many of these efforts involve invasive methods, noninvasive approaches are increasingly viable and currently in development. One such system is envisioned as a wearable interactive smart system that can provide environmental and contextual information via multimodal sensory channels (visual, auditory, haptic); read the physiological, affective, and cognitive state of the operator; and assist in focusing attention on relevant items and facilitate decision making. Although this capability may be somewhat fanciful, and perhaps unrealistic with current technology and neurobiological understanding, ongoing interdisciplinary efforts are moving in this direction.

---

[19]See https://www.darpa.mil/program/systems-based-neurotechnology-for-emerging-therapies [July 2018].
[20]See https://www.darpa.mil/news-events/2017-07-10 [July 2018].

Human–Technology Teaming

Intelligence analysts generally work in analytic teams and collaborate regularly with their colleagues (see Chapter 4), and a key objective for a human–machine ecosystem is for analysts to work productively with technological teammates. A variety of research sheds light on the nature of teams in the workplace, some in the security context (see Box 7-4), and points to research directions for better understanding of human–machine teaming. This section reviews the science of teamwork and then explores its applications to teams involving autonomous or semiautonomous AI systems.

The Science of Teamwork

A rich literature describes research on teamwork and the factors that make human teams effective (Salas et al., 2008). The science of teams and teamwork gained impetus in July 1988 when the *USS Vincennes* accidentally took down an Iranian Airbus, killing 290 passengers. This incident was attributed in part to poor team decision making under stress. The Department of the Navy established a research program—TADMUS (Tactical Decision Making Under Stress)[21]—to identify research in human factors and training that could be useful in preventing such incidents. This program focused significant attention on team training (Cannon-Bowers and Salas, 1998). DoD subsequently supported significant research on

---

BOX 7-4
Teamwork and Cybersecurity

A 2017 study of teamwork among cybersecurity analysts illustrates the importance of research on teaming for the IC (Rajivan and Cooke, 2017). The researchers divided subjects into two groups: in one, responsibilities were allocated among analysts who were given incentives to work as a team, while members of the other group were given incentives to work alone. The analysts who worked in teams performed better at identifying the most difficult problems (cyberattacks). However, that group also demonstrated the information-pooling bias discussed earlier (a tendency to share information common to the team members and avoid sharing information unique to each analyst). The researchers later developed a collaboration tool designed to encourage the analysts on the team to share their unique information, which increased overall team performance (Rajivan and Cooke, 2018).

---

[21]See http://all.net/journal/deception/www-tadmus.spawar.navy.mil/www-tadmus.spawar.navy.mil/TADMUS_Program_Background.html [June 2018].

the science of teams (Goodwin et al., 2018). In 2016, for example, the Army Research Office funded a Multi-University Research Initiative on the network science of teams, and in 2018, the Army Research Laboratory announced its Strengthening Teamwork for Robust Operations in Novel Groups (STRONG) program, focused on human–agent teaming.

The research base in this area has grown as recognition of the importance of understanding and improving teamwork has spread to other sectors, including medicine, energy, and academia. Foundational work established the nature of a team: a special type of group whose members have different but interdependent roles on the team (Salas et al., 1992). The study of teams within academia has come to be known as team science, which focuses on examining such questions as which team features influence scientific productivity (e.g., number of publications) and scientific impact (e.g., number of citations) (for a review, see Hall et al. [2018]). A 2015 National Academies report, *Enhancing the Effectiveness of Team Science* (National Research Council, 2015) addresses collaboration among teams of scientists, which often operate across disciplines. The interdisciplinary field of computer-supported cooperative work (Grudin, 1994) has developed to address the integration of computing technologies into teams, and most recently, advances in AI have led to work on the teaming of humans and autonomous agents or robots (McNeese et al., 2017).

Individuals almost always are members of multiple teams concurrently (O'Leary et al., 2011). In some cases, this multiteam membership enriches the performance of all teams because individuals serve as conduits of best practices across teams (Lungeanu et al., 2018). Research also has examined teams of teams, treating them as multiteam systems (DeChurch et al., 2012). This research has focused on the dilemma that the overarching goals of the system (e.g., investing resources to share intelligence relevant to other teams) are often not well aligned with the local goals of each team (e.g., investing resources in collecting and acting on intelligence within a particular team), which makes for inherent tension. This research has led to conceptualizing multiteam systems as ecosystems of networked groups (Poole and Contractor, 2012).

Research has also yielded practical guidance on how best to assemble human teams, how to train and lead teams, and how such outside influences as stress influence teamwork (Cannon-Bowers and Salas, 1998; Contractor, 2013). Significant research has also been carried out in the area of team cognition (Salas and Fiore, 2004). This work indicates that teammates who share knowledge about the task and the team (what has been referred to as shared mental models) are better able to coordinate implicitly (Entin and Serfaty, 1999; Fiore et al., 2001). For large or spatially distributed teams, individual team members likely can hold only partial understandings of the tasks and teammates at any given time. In such situations, cognition at the team level has been observed to be fluid and heavily dependent on team interaction (Cooke et al., 2013). Considerable research also has focused on conceptualizing the effectiveness of a team in terms of its transactive memory (Wegner, 1987). That is, effective teams comprise individuals who each possess expertise in some of the areas required for the team to be effective, are aware of the expertise possessed by each of their team members, are able to retrieve that expertise as needed, and help expand those members' expertise by proactively providing them with information relevant to their areas of expertise.

Clarity about roles and the nature of communication and interaction are very important to team effectiveness because of the different contributions each member brings. These aspects of team functioning can be improved at minimal cost through attention to team composition, leadership, and training and the use of collaborative technologies (Salas et al., 2008). Training of team leaders is a particularly useful intervention for improving team functioning. Although groups can be trained to perform more effectively as teams, this poses a challenge for ad hoc teams that are formed to meet a particular need and may never function together again as a team. Trained leaders can address this challenge by training other team members, thereby improving overall team performance. This point is illustrated by a study of training strategy for effective code blue resuscitation (Hinski, 2017). The strategy used in this study was modeled after one developed by DoD in the context of an unmanned aerial system: the interactions among team member roles that are essential for an effective resuscitation were identified, and this model was studied by the leaders of the code blue exercises for as little as 5 minutes. Once on the code blue team, these leaders were taught to request information that did not come in a timely manner. Results later indicated that the trained leaders helped train the other team members, thereby improving team performance relative to that of teams with untrained leaders.

Teamwork and Autonomous Systems

Advances in AI and robotics have yielded computing technologies capable of collaboration on the level of a full-fledged teammate. SBS researchers are now exploring new types of human–machine interactions, including those among teams that include a mix of humans, autonomous AI, decision aids, wearable technologies, and robots. This research is examining optimal ways such teams can be assembled, developed, and led to be most effective. Building on a large body of knowledge about human teams, this work is considering the similarities and differences in teamwork characteristics and dynamics when teammates include technological agents. Human factors research has historically focused on human–machine interaction in relation to machines with automated functions but limited autonomy; today, however, machines have become increasingly intelligent and, in many ways, autonomous (Parasuraman et al., 2000). These machines do not require as much supervision, control, or oversight from humans relative to their less autonomous counterparts, and they function in many ways like human teammates. Thus they can take on those parts of a task that humans cannot or do not want to do, although in many circumstances, humans would need to maintain supervisory control even as their direct active control of machines decreased (Chen and Barnes, 2014).

Research in human factors has started to explore how this human–technology teaming relationship works in greater detail. Questions to be addressed include the following:

- How does the presence of an AI agent affect human team members?
- How should tasks be allocated to humans or machines?
- How are human trust, skill development, and situation awareness affected by AI systems?
- What form of interaction or communication is best suited to such heterogeneous teams?
- How much do the AI or robot team members need to know about their human counterparts? Can biometrics be used to sense human states?

Human factors research on such questions often requires multidisciplinary collaboration with the AI and robotics community. There is a body of research on human interaction with robots that possess autonomy. Most of this work has been at the dyadic level—between one human and a robot, and researchers are just starting to explore how the presence of a robot on the team affects human-to-human interaction (Jung et al., 2017). More research and theoretical advances are needed with respect to teaming contexts that include multiple humans and robots (Robert, 2018).

One outstanding question about the protocols for interaction within a human–machine ecosystem is the appropriate balance of control between the semiautonomous AI agents and the analysts (Chen and Barnes, 2014). Current findings from applied research and human factors analyses—albeit based on contexts other than intelligence analysis, such as aircraft navigation or production facilities—consistently reveal the need to retain one or more active human agents at the stage at which a system comes to a decision or chooses an action. This work indicates that, whereas using computer systems to perform analyses on input data at high rates may be necessary to support limited human capacities, overreliance on automated analyses (e.g., flight deck reliance on autopilot) is associated with an increased likelihood of failures (Parasuraman and Riley, 1997) and lack of situational awareness (Endsley and Kiris, 1995; Hancock et al., 2013; Parasuraman and Hancock, 2008; Wickens et al., 2016). Whether the same potential for error seen in these other operational environments applies to the more fluid environment of intelligence analysis, or in the same way, remains to be assessed (Holzer and Moses, 2015).

The IC is increasingly aware that its work is evolving from being carried out by analysts in fixed stable teams (or teams of teams) to what is described as teamwork on the fly, or "teaming" (Edmondson, 2012), whereby analysts dive in and out of teams as they are needed. These transient team memberships can improve performance, but require rapid identification of the human and AI agents with the requisite skills and resources. Traditionally, decisions about team composition have been made by humans. Recently, however, there have been preliminary attempts to use AI agents not only to participate on teams but also to assemble them (Tannenbaum et al., 2012). Some recent studies have investigated the use of AI agents to assemble "dream" or "flash" teams and even organizations on the fly (Gomez-Zara et al., 2018; Valentine et al., 2017).

Research Directions

Expand research on human–technology teaming to examine the challenges and opportunities that arise when technological agents serve as teammates.

Preliminary work focused on the development of collaborative technologies as effective team players has shown that subtle behaviors of humans that make them good teammates are absent in nonhuman agents. This research has found that AI agents failed to anticipate the information needs of their human teammates, whereas most human teammates do this naturally, and that limitations of AI agents as effective teammates can negatively affect the entire team (McNeese et al., 2017). Therefore, the development of semiautonomous AI agents for a human–machine ecosystem needs to be guided not only by research on effective teamwork but also by research on what makes an effective teammate.

Research is needed to extend theories and findings on human teamwork to teamwork among humans and AI agents, and more generally to the concept of human–technology teaming. Specific questions that require research include the following:

- How can teams or multiteam systems of humans and AI agents be assembled to work on specific intelligence problems?
- How do AI agents on multiple concurrent teams benefit or hinder performance?
- Can recommender systems or flash teams[22] facilitate rapid composition of multiagent teams?

---

[22]For more information on recommender systems and flash teams, see Contractor (2013) and Tannenbaum et al. (2012).

- Do multiagent teams, once assembled, require training, practice, or warm-up to be effective, and how can this be facilitated?
- How can multiagent teams best communicate or interact? To what extent do findings about single human–computer interactions apply to the effective distribution and coordination of information across the team as a whole?
- How can multiagent teams enhance their effectiveness by building accurate mental models of who (human or AI agent) knows what and who needs to know what?
- How can the effectiveness of multiagent teams in a human–machine ecosystem be assessed, and once assessed, how can effectiveness be improved?

Human–Systems Integration

In many industrial contexts, custom-developed technologies can go unused because in practice, they are either not useful for the task for which they are intended or are not usable by the intended user (Parasuraman and Riley, 1997). Technologies can even end up being disruptive to the task or have unintended consequences when they affect another part of the system in an unexpected way. Careful design and integration of system components is essential to realizing the vision of a human–machine ecosystem and to ensuring that the resulting system is an effective tool for analysis. The design of a human–machine ecosystem can leverage recent advances in social network theories[23] and methods (see Chapter 5), as well as in the field of human–systems integration, to address processes and outcomes within the ecosystem.

Researchers in the field of human–systems integration draw on a robust body of work from multiple SBS and other literatures (psychology, human factors, management, occupational health and safety, human–computer interaction) to develop well-integrated sociotechnical systems (dynamic systems in which people, tasks, technology, and the environment interact throughout the stages of the work being carried out). The goal of a human–systems integration approach is to develop a resilient and adaptive system and avoid unintended consequences (National Research Council, 2007), ensuring that operational solutions, like the human–machine ecosystem, address both the needs and the capabilities and limitations of human analysts. This kind of integration cannot be added on after a human–machine

---

[23]There is growing recognition in the research community that ecosystems can be characterized as multidimensional social networks of nodes representing both humans and nonhuman elements, such as AI agents. Networks of this sort are multirelational because they represent a wide variety of social (e.g., who knows or trusts whom) and cognitive (e.g., who thinks what others know) ties (Contractor et al., 2011).

ecosystem for the IC is developed. It needs to be a part of the process from the beginning of the ecosystem's development so that the resulting design allows for seamless coordination among analysts and available tools and technologies.

For each of the stages of design and integration, the full range of human dimensions would be considered in light of the larger system. New technology will create a need for new training, and possibly different selection methods and different task processes (see further discussion of the analytic workforce in Chapter 8). A human–systems integration approach has the potential to improve system performance while making unexpected negative outcomes less likely. Notably, many other industries and government agencies have required the use of this approach, often after a disaster occurs that can be partially attributed to poor integration of human behavior within a sociotechnical system (e.g., Three Mile Island, the *Piper Alpha*, the *Challenger* explosion). Such an approach is not costly relative to the potential costs of failing to undertake it: poor system performance, unintended consequences, or disaster.

Research Directions

Investigate the application of human–systems integration theories and methods to the development of a human–machine ecosystem.

This approach can help determine requirements for this ecosystem by addressing elements including

- the roles of human and machine agents and their relationships to one another in the system;
- analyst training and selection needs for the human–machine ecosystem; and
- iterative assessment of the design of the human–machine ecosystem to identify changes needed to improve the system's effectiveness.

CONCLUSIONS

The IC has for decades sought to exploit rapid technological changes in computer networking, data storage, supercomputing, and AI that could support intelligence analysis. Looking just at AI projects, the Central Intelligence Agency (CIA) reports that nearly 140 such efforts are under way.[24] Historically, as reported to the committee, the IC generally has added new technologies and tools on to a long-standing analytic process. The capabilities of AI are changing, and will continue to change, the way many industries do business. The committee believes that if the IC is to take advantage of advancing AI capabilities and adjust to evolving security threats, it will have to transform how it conducts intelligence analysis. This transformation will require not only understanding what capabilities are offered by new technologies but also understanding how analysts will function in collaboration with machines to make decisions.

CONCLUSION 7-1: To develop a human–machine ecosystem that functions effectively for intelligence analysis, it will be necessary to integrate findings from social and behavioral sciences research into the design and development of artificial intelligence and other technologies involved. A research program for this purpose would extend theory and findings from current research on human–machine interactions to new types of interactions involving multiple agents in a complex teaming environment.

The research described in this chapter will go a long way toward supporting the design of an effective human–machine ecosystem for intelligence analysis. If the IC pursues this objective, it will have to consider a number of issues. SBS research can provide answers to foundational questions necessary to support engineers and computer scientists in the design and development of such an ecosystem, including those related to the uses of technologies, measures, concepts of operation, and human–machine interaction and teaming. The use of such a system in the IC context would be unprecedented, and its responsible use will also require careful attention to a number of ethical questions. Since ethical considerations are so critical to such a system's development and ultimate implementation, we conclude this chapter with a discussion of some of these considerations.

---

[24]Presentation by Dawn Meyeriecks, CIA's Deputy Director for Science and Technology, at INSA-AFCEA Intelligence Summit in September 2017 (https://www.defenseone.com/technology/2017/09/cia-technology-director-artificial-intelligence/140801 [September 2018]). Projects, many involving collaboration with external software developers, range from algorithms that automatically tag objects in video to prediction models based on big data.

A Research Program to Support Design and Development

The development of a human–machine ecosystem for intelligence analysis will need to be carefully tailored to the unique needs of the IC, and the research described in this chapter will need to be applied to the complex tasks, processes, and contexts of intelligence analysis. The success of an SBS research program in accomplishing this will rest on collaboration between the IC and the broad SBS community.

The research needed to support the design and development of human–technology analytic teams crosses many disciplines. A successful research program will foster interdisciplinary work and, to the extent possible, remain open and unclassified. It will be important for a range of researchers with a broad set of expertise to contribute to the research efforts, share results with each other, and discuss improvements to the system's design and development. SBS researchers will also need to be able to collaborate with computer scientists and cognitive and human systems engineers to help translate research findings to practice.

The research needed will include basic, applied, and translational work and will need to be aimed at solving operational problems with strong connections to intelligence analysis. Researchers and members of the IC will need to collaborate to understand the needs the ecosystem should meet, the different functions the various team members (human and AI) should be able to perform, the kinds of interactions that will be possible, the forms of output, and many more features. The research program will also need to be an iterative one, in which findings from evaluations of results and assessments of evolving needs are continually fed into ongoing design work.

One mechanism for such a research program—particularly a program that requires the testing of hypotheses, tools, technologies, and designs in a realistic environment—is a testbed. Testbeds provide a way to test interactions at scale safely, accelerate the translation of findings from research and development to operations, and engage a wide range of researchers economically. They allow for early testing of concepts and the integration of humans and systems ahead of a finished human–machine ecosystem. However, they must be well managed to achieve such objectives. The most successful testbeds have been designed to address specific problems, and multiple testbeds might therefore be an option for carrying out all the research necessary to support the development and use of a human–machine ecosystem for intelligence analysis. For the types of human–machine interactions that need to be investigated, such a testbed could be virtual so that researchers from multiple institutions could be involved.

CONCLUSION 7-2: A social and behavioral sciences research agenda to support the development of technologies and systems for effective

human–machine teams for intelligence analysis should include, but not be limited to, the following goals:

- Apply methodologies from the vision sciences, the behavioral sciences, and human factors to advances in data visualization to improve understanding of how people extract meaning from visualizations and the functionality of tools designed to present information from large datasets.
- Use techniques from social network analysis to better understand how information can be transmitted effectively, as well as filtered among distributed teams of humans and machines, and how the need to use artificial intelligence (AI) to search and filter information can be balanced with the need to restrict access to certain information.
- Develop new modes of forecasting that incorporate human judgment with automated analyses by AI agents.
- Apply neuroscience-inspired strategies and tools to research on workload effects in a complex environment of networked human and AI agents.
- Examine the implications of ongoing system monitoring of work behaviors in terms of privacy issues, as well as potential interruptions to the intrinsic work habits of human analysts.
- Extend insights from the science of human teamwork to determine how to assemble and divide tasks among teams of humans and AI agents and measure performance in such teams.
- Identify guidelines for communication protocols for use in coordinating the sharing of information among multiple human and AI agents in ways that accommodate the needs and capabilities of human analysts and minimize disadvantages associated with interruption and multitasking in humans.

Ethical Considerations

For some, talk of machines and collaboration with AI agents can be somewhat chilling. Reasonable concerns include the prospect that, in restricted environments, there will be more opportunities for inadvertent disclosures of confidential information; that biases inherent in algorithms will negatively affect decision making; that machine-generated output may increase false positives and subsequent false alarms; and that too much trust may be placed in machines to find the emergent patterns and signals, perhaps usurping what should be functions of human analysts or occupying them with new oversight and management tasks that compete with their analytic work.

Such concerns can be addressed by systematic planning informed by research and attention to ethical considerations. As advanced as AI has become in the past few decades, it still cannot outperform humans in many regards. For cognitive tasks (e.g., chess), researchers are finding that a collaborative approach with humans and AI is far more effective than the best humans or AI agents on their own.

These important ethical issues need to be considered during the research and design phase, before a human–machine ecosystem is ready for implementation (see the discussion of standards for such research phases in Box 7-5). The primary ethical issues arise from the fact that the ecosystem would rely on semiautonomous AI agents, which, rather than being programmed to do a specific task, would be capable of performing multiple tasks of varying sophistication in an adaptive fashion. These agents would be goal-directed, respond to their environments in real time, and operate continuously (Brozek and Jakubiec, 2017), characteristics that would make them ethically distinct from more traditional machines, whose actions can be predicted based on their intended uses. AI agents in this system would

---

BOX 7-5
Research Standards

Before any new technology is adopted, research is needed to determine how it will affect the end user. Ideally, the IC will assess the applicable ethical questions raised by a human–machine ecosystem before analysts are expected to use the technology. Such assessments, conducted as research involving human subjects, will have to conform to the standard ethical requirements, spelled out in regulations, for any such work conducted using federal funding or in organizations that have agreed to conform to these requirements.[a] If analysts themselves are recruited to be part of the assessment, they should be clearly informed about whether the purpose of the activity is to contribute to generalizable knowledge, as would be the case in a systematic investigation (which would include research, development, testing, and evaluation, according to the definition in the Common Rule). If the research meets those criteria, the participating analysts will have to be considered research subjects entitled to all the usual protections, including prior protocol review by an institutional review board and provisions for informed consent. Included in that framework is the requirement that they not be coerced into participation or penalized if they decline to participate. Certain types of work conducted within the IC, such as some forms of program evaluation or quality improvement, might not be considered research in the sense specified in the federal regulations. In such cases, the individual participants would not be considered research subjects.

---

[a]45 CFR 46, Subpart A "Federal Policy for the Protection of Human Subjects" (the Common Rule) currently undergoing revisions (Chadwick, 2018).

need to adapt appropriately to challenges that designers might not have anticipated in advance.

Ethicists have examined the emerging problem of how AI agents with autonomy can be designed so they act safely and in accordance with the social and ethical requirements associated with their roles (e.g., Bostrom and Yudowsky, 2011; Campolo et al., 2017). Ethicists working in this area have not yet reached consensus about how this can be accomplished. The field of AI ethics is an emerging field that is, like AI itself, evolving rapidly and in a nonlinear fashion. Some ethicists argue that the problem is best addressed by involving experts in SBS fields, engineering, and ethics in the research and design of any autonomous agent. Some have suggested that to deploy such agents ethically, it is necessary to incorporate as part of their functionality the capacity to reason ethically and respond and adapt to changing ethical norms. Ethicists are still actively debating the fundamental question of whether AI systems themselves have moral status (Bostrom and Yudowsky, 2011; Brozek and Jakubiec, 2017; IEEE Standards Association, 2016). Some of the key questions are reviewed below.

Why Is It Important to Have Ethical AI?

Semiautonomous AI agents within a human–machine ecosystem will undoubtedly affect their environment in ways both predictable and unpredictable. Issues of human safety, justice, fairness, and the like will arise for AI agents that perform cognitive tasks once possible only for humans. Thus it is reasonable to consider that the agents must also take on the social responsibilities associated with the cognitive tasks they perform. For example, if an AI agent is entrusted with making decisions, it must be subject to the expectations that its decisions are fair as well as accurate (Bostrom and Yudowsky, 2011).

Semiautonomous agents in an IC context will need to operate according to the ethical requirements of their roles and the environment. The ethical requirements for an analyst are complex and may include responsibilities that require access to sensitive information and obligations to follow procedures for high-stakes decisions. It will also be necessary to consider the norms and values of the user community, in this case the client for intelligence—the policy maker or other decision maker who will use the analysis in taking actions (Benigni et al., 2017; IEEE Standards Association, 2016).

What Limits, If Any, Should Be Placed on AI Agency?

What kinds of tasks, decisions, or actions should be reserved only for people, on ethical and moral grounds? The potential need for such limits has received attention in the case of autonomous intelligent weapons (National

Research Council and National Academy of Engineering, 2014). While no consensus has yet emerged on criteria for the appropriate agency of AI agents in other types of computing systems, such as the ecosystem envisioned here, such questions are increasingly ubiquitous (National Research Council and National Academy of Engineering, 2014; van de Voort et al., 2015). Criteria specific to the IC context will be needed. For example, a semiautonomous AI agent might be permitted access to intelligence sources, but should it be permitted access to data from sensors monitoring human agents, or should that access be limited? For what purposes should an AI agent be permitted to forward information to another agent or party within the IC, to delete information it has determined is no longer valuable, or to initiate a new line of analysis? Answering these questions will require understanding of the norms and values of the analytical workplace and the moral benefits and limits of a human–machine ecosystem.

Including semiautonomous AI agents as team members in intelligence analysis raises further issues of accountability and control. When a team fails to identify a threat because of a failing on the part of the AI agent, who should be held responsible? If team members determine that the AI agent has begun producing unpredictable and potentially unreliable results or otherwise malfunctioning, who is responsible for determining whether that agent should be audited, taken offline, or trusted? These and other organizational and management questions will need careful consideration (Bohn et al., 2004; Bostrom and Yudowsky, 2011).

To What Degree Should Humans Rely on Autonomous Agents?

Designers and users of a human–machine ecosystem will also need to consider trade-offs associated with technological dependence on the system. The more computerized and automated the environment, the more individuals will rely on technical systems (Bohn et al., 2004). But this reliance may create problems when automated systems fail, leaving analysts unable to perform important tasks usually left to the system's AI agents. Ethical deployment of AI in a human–machine ecosystem will require attention to failsafe provisions and backup protocols.

Implementation of a human–machine ecosystem would also raise more familiar, but nonetheless important, issues of privacy and surveillance in the context of ubiquitous workplace and employee monitoring. The IC workforce is used to more workplace monitoring than is typical in most other professions. However, the use of technologies whose value rests in part on worker surveillance—for example, learning from analysts' inputs to increase the effectiveness of analyses or monitoring for signs of mental fatigue and stress to adjust interactions so as not to overload analysts' cognitive capacities—raises ethical concerns about privacy (Bohn et al.,

2004). It is important that such monitoring not be used for discriminatory purposes, that sensitive and confidential information be protected, and that the use of such systems not lower employee morale.

The development of appropriate limitations on the use of surveillance devices in the context of intelligence analysis will require further study. Answering questions about when and how sensor systems will be used will require careful ethical accounting to determine whether and when infringements on privacy are justified and on what grounds (Ajunwa et al., 2017).

Finally, some ethical challenges raised by human–machine ecosystems transcend the IC. Many employment sectors are already beginning to confront the challenge automation poses for workforces. The challenge of mitigating the consequences of any job loss and equipping workers with new skills in increasingly automated environments will not be unique to the IC.

CONCLUSION 7-3: The design, development, and implementation of a system of human–technology teams, which would include autonomous agents, for use in intelligence analysis raise important ethical questions regarding access to certain types of data; authority to modify, store, or transmit data; and accountability and protections when systems fail. The Intelligence Community (IC) could best ensure that such systems function in an ethical manner and prepare to address unforeseeable new ethical issues by

- from the start, incorporating into the design and development process collaborative research, involving both members of the IC and the social and behavioral sciences community, on the application of ethical principles developed in other human–technology contexts to the IC context;
- ensuring that all research supported by the IC adheres to the standards for ethical conduct of research; and
- establishing a structure for ongoing review of ethical issues that may arise as the technology develops and new circumstances arise.

REFERENCES

2015 Study Panel of the One Hundred Year Study of Artificial Intelligence. (2016). *Artificial Intelligence and Life in 2030*. Palo Alto, CA: Stanford University. Available: https://ai100.stanford.edu/sites/default/files/ai100report10032016fnl_singles.pdf [December 2018].

Achenbach, J. (2011). Japan's "black swan": Scientists ponder the unparalleled dangers of unlikely disasters. *The Washington Post*, March 17. Available: https://www.washingtonpost.com/national/japans-black-swan-scientists-ponder-the-unparalleled-dangers-of-unlikely-disasters/2011/03/17/ABj2wTn_story.html?utm_term=.c22f85fce8b7 [December 2018].

Adamczyk, P.D., and Bailey, B.P. (2004). If not now, when?: The effects of interruption at different moments within task execution. In *CHI '04 Proceedings of the SIGCHI Conference on Human Factors in Computing Systems* (pp. 271–278). New York: Association for Computing Machinery. doi:10.1145/985692.985727.

Ajunwa, I., Crawford, K., and Schultz, J. (2017). Limitless worker surveillance. *California Law Review*, 105(32017), 735–776.

Alexander, E., Kohlmann, J., Valenza, R., Witmore, M., and Gleicher, M. (2014). *Serendip: Topic Model-Driven Visual Exploration of Text Corpora*. Paris, France: Institute of Electrical and Electronics Engineers. Available: https://graphics.cs.wisc.edu/Papers/2014/AKVWG14/Preprint.pdf [December 2018].

Altmann, E.M., Trafton, J.G., and Hambrick, D.Z. (2014). Momentary interruptions can derail the train of thought. *Journal of Experimental Psychology*, 143(1), 215–266.

Amir, G.J., and Lehmann, H.P. (2016). After detection: The improved accuracy of lung cancer assessment using radiologic computer-aided diagnosis. *Academic Radiology*, 23(2), 186–191.

Arrington, C.M., and Logan, G.D. (2004). The cost of a voluntary task switch. *Psychological Science*, 15(9), 610–615.

Arrington, C.M., and Logan, G.D. (2005). Voluntary task switching: Chasing the elusive homunculus. *Journal of Experimental Psychology: Learning, Memory, and Cognition*, 31(4), 683–702.

Bailey, B.P., and Konstan, J.A. (2006). On the need for attention-aware systems: Measuring effects of interruption on task performance, error rate, and affective state. *Computers in Human Behavior*, 22(4), 685–708.

Baron, J., Mellers, B.A., Tetlock, P.E., Stone, E., and Ungar, L.H. (2014). Two reasons to make aggregated probability forecasts more extreme. *Decision Analysis*, 11(2), 133–145.

Bawden, D., and Robinson, L. (2008). The dark side of information: Overload, anxiety and other paradoxes and pathologies. *Journal of Information Science*, 35(2), 180–191.

Benigni, M.C., Joseph, K., and Carley, K.M. (2017). Online extremism and the communities that sustain it: Detecting the ISIS supporting community on Twitter. *PLoS ONE*, 12(12), e0181405. doi:10.1371/journal.pone.0181405.

Bhardwaj, S. (2013). Technology, and the up-skilling or deskilling conundrum. *WMU Journal of Maritime Affairs*, 12(2), 245–253.

Bierwirth, C., and Meisel, F. (2015). A follow-up survey of berth allocation and quay crane scheduling problems in container terminals. *European Journal of Operational Research*, 244(3), 675–689.

Bohn, J., Coroama, V., Langheinrich, M., Mattern, F., and Rohs, M. (2004). Living in a world of smart everyday objects—social, economic, and ethical implications. *Journal of Human and Ecological Risk Assessment*, 10(5), 763–786. Available: https://www.vs.inf.ethz.ch/publ/papers/hera.pdf [December 2018].

Bostrom, N., and Yudowsky, E. (2011). The ethics of artificial intelligence. In W. Ramsey, and K. Frankish (Eds.), *Cambridge Handbook of Artificial Intelligence* (pp. 316–334). Cambridge, UK: Cambridge University Press.

Boy, J., Rensink, R.A., Bertini, E., and Fekete, J-D. (2014). A principled way of assessing visualization literacy. *IEEE Transactions on Visualization and Computer Graphics*, 20(12), 1963–1972.

Braver, T.S., Reynolds, J.R., and Donaldson, D.I. (2003). Neural mechanisms of transient and sustained cognitive control during task switching. *Neuron*, 39(4), 713–726.

Brier, G.W. (1950). Verification of forecasts expressed in terms of probability. *Monthey Weather Review*, 78(1), 1–3.

Brozek, B., and Jakubiec, M. (2017). On the legal responsibility of autonomous machines. *Artificial Intelligence Law*, 25(3), 293–304.

Buja, A., Swayne, D.F., Littman, M.L., Dean, N., Hofmann, H., and Chen, L. (2008). Data visualization with multidimensional scaling. *Journal of Computational and Graphical Statistics, 17*(2), 444–472.

Cain, M.S., Adamo, S.H., and Mitroff, S.R. (2013). A taxonomy of errors in multiple-target visual search. *Visual Cognition, 21*(7), 899–921. doi:10.1080/13506285.2013.843627.

Caliskan, A., Bryson, J.J., and Narayanan, A. (2017). Semantics derived automatically from language corpa contain human-like biases. *Science, 356*(6334), 183–186.

Campolo, A., Sanfillippo, M., Whittaker, M., and Crawford, K. (2017). *AI Now 2017 Report*. New York: New York University. Available: https://assets.ctfassets.net/8wprh-hvnpfc0/1A9c3ZTCZa2KEYM64Wsc2a/8636557c5fb14f2b74b2be64c3ce0c78/_AI_Now_Institute_2017_Report_.pdf [October 2018].

Cannon-Bowers, J.A., and Salas, E. (Eds.). (1998). *Making Decisions Under Stress: Implications for Individual and Team Training*. Washington, DC: American Psychological Association.

Chadwick, G.L. (2018). *Final Rule Material: New and Revised Definitions*. Available: https://about.citiprogram.org/wp-content/uploads/2018/07/Final-Rule-Material-New-and-Revised-Definitions.pdf [October 2018].

Chang, R., Ghoniem, M., Kosara, R., Ribarsky, W., Yang, J., Suma, E., Ziemkiewicz, C., Kern, D., and Sudjianto, A. (2007). WireVis: Visualization of categorical, time-varying data from financial transactions. In *VAST '07 Proceedings of the 2007 IEEE Symposium on Visual Analytics Science and Technology* (pp. 155–162). Washington, DC: IEEE Computer Society. doi:10.1109/VAST.2007.4389009.

Chen, J.Y.C., and Barnes, M.J. (2014). Human–agent teaming for multirobot control: A review of human factors issues. *IEEE Transactions on Human-Machine Systems, 44*(1), 13–29.

Chen, D., and Gomes, C.P. (2018). *Bias Reduction via End-to-End Shift Learning: Application to Citizen Science*. arXiv preprint arXiv:1811.00458v2.

Cohen, M.A., Dennett, D.C., and Kanwisher, N. (2016). What is the bandwidth of perceptual experience? *Trends in Cognitive Science, 20*(5), 324–335.

Colquhoun, W.P., and Baddeley, A.D. (1967). Influence of signal probability during pretraining on vigilance decrement. *Journal of Experimental Psychology, 73*(1), 153–155.

Contractor, N. (2013). Some assembly required: Leveraging Web science to understand and enable team assembly. *Philosophical Transactions of the Royal Society: Mathematical, Physical and Engineering Sciences, 371*(1987), 20120385. doi:10.1098/rsta.2012.0385.

Contractor, N., Monge, P.R., and Leonardi, P. (2011). Multidimensional networks and the dynamics of sociomateriality: Bringing technology inside the network. *International Journal of Communication, 5*, 682–720. Available: https://ijoc.org/index.php/ijoc/article/view/1131/550 [December 2018].

Cooke, N.J., Gorman, J.C., Myers, C.W., and Duran, J.L. (2013). Interactive team cognition. *Cognitive Science, 37*(2), 255–285. doi:10.1111/cogs.12009.

Cowan, N. (2001). The magical number 4 in short-term memory: A reconsideration of mental storage capacity. *Behavioral Brain Science, 24*(1), 87–114; discussion 114–185.

Cummings, M. (2014). Man versus machine or man + machine? *IEEE Intelligent Systems*, 62–69. Available: https://hal.pratt.duke.edu/sites/hal.pratt.duke.edu/files/u10/IS-29-05-Expert%20Opinion%5B1%5D_0.pdf [December 2018].

Cummings, M.L., Pina, P., and Crandall, J.W. (2008). *A Metric Taxonomy for Human Supervisory Control of Unmanned Vehicles*. San Diego, CA: Association for Unmanned Vehicle Systems International. Available: https://pdfs.semanticscholar.org/d696/e4deea76c6165ad36e0bcde113b3c5f6d309.pdf [December 2018].

DeChurch, L.A., Marks, M.A., and Zaccaro, S.J. (Eds.). (2012). *Multiteam Systems: An Organization Form for Dynamic and Complex Environments*. New York: Routledge.

Defense Science Board. (2012). *The Role of Autonomy in DoD Systems*. Washington, DC: U.S. Department of Defense.

Dien, J., Kogut, P., Gwizdka, J., Hatfield, B., Gentili, R.J., Oh, H., Lo, L-C., and Jaquess, K.J. (2017). *Cognitive Augmentation for Coping with Open-Source Intelligence (OSINT) Overload* [White Paper]. Available: http://sites.nationalacademies.org/cs/groups/dbassesite/documents/webpage/dbasse_177283.pdf [November 2018].

Dou, W., Wang, X., Chang, R., and Ribarsky, W. (2011). ParallelTopics: A probabilistic approach to exploring document collections. In *Proceedings of the IEEE Conference on Visual Analytics Science and Technology* (pp. 231–240). Washington, DC: IEEE Computer Society. doi:10.1109/VAST.2011.6102461.

Dujmovi, V., Gudmundsson, J., Morin, P., and Wolle, T. (2010). Notes on large angle crossing graphs. *Proceedings of the Sixteenth Symposium on Computing: The Australasian Theory, 109,* 19–24.

Edmondson, A.C. (2012). *Teaming: How Organizations Learn, Innovate, and Compete in the Knowledge Economy.* San Francisco, CA: John Wiley & Sons.

Endsley, M. (1987). The application of human factors to the development of expert systems for advanced cockpits. *Proceedings of the Human Factors and Ergonomics Society Annual Meeting, 31*(12), 1388–1392. doi:10.1177/154193128703101219.

Endsley, M.R., and Kiris, E.O. (1995). The out-of-the-loop performance problem and level of control in automation. *Human Factors, 37*(2), 381–394.

Entin, E.E., and Serfaty, D. (1999). Adaptive team coordination. *Human Factors, 41*(2), 312–325. doi:10.1518/001872099779591196.

Erev, I., Wallsten, T.S., and Budescu, D.V. (1994). Simultaneous over- and underconfidence: The role of error in judgment processes. *Psychological Review, 101*(3), 519–527. doi:10.1037/0033-295X.101.3.519.

Evans, K.K., Birdwell, R.L., and Wolfe, J.M. (2013). If you don't find it often, you often don't find it: Why some cancers are missed in breast cancer screening. *PLoS ONE, 8*(5), e64366. doi:10.1371/journal.pone.0064366.

Fayyad, U.M., Wierse, A., and Grinstein, G.G. (2002). *Information Visualization in Data Mining and Knowledge Discovery.* San Francisco, CA: Morgan Kaufmann Publishers.

Ferruzzi, G., Cervone, G., Delle Monache, L., Graditi, G., and Jacobone, F. (2016). Optimal bidding in a Day-Ahead energy market for Micro Grid under uncertainty in renewable energy production. *Energy, 106,* 194–202. doi:10.1016/j.energy.2016.02.166.

Fetchenhauser, D., and Dunning, D. (2009). Do people trust too much or too little? *Journal of Economic Psychology, 30*(3), 263–276. doi:10.1016/j.joep.2008.04.006.

Fiore, S.M., Salas, E., and Cannon-Bowers, J.A. (2001). Group dynamics and shared mental model development. In M. London (Ed.), *Applied in Psychology: How People Evaluate Others in Organizations* (pp. 309–336). Mahwah, NJ: Lawrence Erlbaum Associates.

Fischhoff, B., Slovic, P., and Lichtenstein, S. (1978). Fault trees: Sensitivity of estimated failure probabilities to problem representation. *Journal of Experimental Psychology: Human Perception and Performance, 4*(2), 330–344. Available: https://www.gwern.net/docs/predictions/1978-fischhoff.pdf [December 2018].

Fong, G.T., Krantz, D.H., and Nisbett, R.E. (1986). The effects of statistical training on thinking about everyday problems. *Cognitive Psychology, 18*(3), 253–292.

Fraioli, F., Serra, G., and Passariello, R. (2010). CAD (computed-aided detection) and CADx (computer aided diagnosis) systems in identifying and characterising lung nodules on chest CT: Overview of research, developments and new prospects. *La Radiologia Medica, 115*(3), 385–402. doi:10.1007/s11547-010-0507-2.

Friendly, M., and Denis, D.J. (2001). *Milestones in the History of Thematic Cartography, Statistical Graphics, and Data Visualization.* Available: http://www.datavis.ca/milestones [July 2018].

Fry, B. (2007). *Visualizing Data: Exploring and Explaining Data with the Processing Environment* (1st ed.). Sebastopol, CA: O'Reilly Media, Inc.

Garvie, C., Bedoya, A., and Frankle, J. (2016). *The Perpetual Line-Up: Unregulated Police Face Recognition in America*. Georgetown Law Center on Privacy and Technology. Available: https://www.perpetuallineup.org [January 2019].

Gilovich, T., and Griffin, D.W. (2002). Heuristics and biases: Then and now. In D.G.T. Gilovich, and D. Kahneman (Eds.), *Heuristics and Biases: The Psychology of Intuitive Judgment* (pp. 1–18). Cambridge, UK: Cambridge University Press.

Gomez-Zara, D.A., Paras, M., Twyman, M., Ng, J., Dechurch, L., and Contractor, N. (2018). Who would you like to work with? In *CHI 2018 Proceedings of the 2018 CHI Conference on Human Factors in Computing Systems*. New York: Association for Computing Machinery.

Goodrich, M.A., and Schultz, A.C. (2007). Human–robot interaction: A survey. *Human–Computer Interaction*, 1(3), 203–275.

Goodwin, G.F., Blacksmith, N., and Coats, M.R. (2018). The science of teams in the military: Contributions from over 60 years of research. *American Psychologist*, 73(4), 322–333.

Gorris, M.E., Cat, L.A., Zender, C.S., Treseder, K.K., and Randerson, J.T. (2018). Coccidioidomycosis dynamics in relation to climate in the southwestern United States. *GeoHealth*, 2(1), 6–24.

Green, D.M., and Swets, J.A. (1966). *Signal Detection Theory and Psychophysics*. New York: Wiley.

Greenes, R.A. (2014). A brief history of clinical decision support: Technical, social, cultural, economic, and governmental perspectives. In *Clinical Decision Support* (2nd ed.) (pp. 49–109). Oxford, UK: Elsevier. doi:10.1016/B978-0-12-398476-0.00002-6.

Grier, R., Wickens, C., Kaber, D., Strayer, D., Boehm-Davis, D., Trafton, J.G., and St. John, M. (2008). The red-line of workload: Theory, research, and design. In *Proceedings of the Human Factors and Ergonomics Society Annual Meeting*, 52(18), 1204–1208. Los Angeles, CA: SAGE Publications.

Grudin, J. (1994). Computer-supported cooperative work: History and focus. *Journal Computer*, 27(5), 19–26.

Gutzwiller, R. (2014). *Applied Multi-Task Management*. Ph.D. Thesis. Colorado State University.

Gutzwiller, R.S., Wickens, C.D., and Clegg, B.A. (2014). Workload overload modeling: An experiment with MATB II to inform a computational model of task management. *Proceedings of the Human Factors and Ergonomics Society Annual Meeting*, 58(1), 849–853.

Haapalainen, E., Kim, S., Forlizzi, J.F., and Dey, A.K. (2010). Psycho-physiological measures for assessing cognitive load. In *UbiComp '10 Proceedings of the 12th ACM International Conference on Ubiquitous Computing* (pp. 301–310). New York: Association for Computing Machinery. doi:10.1145/1864349.1864395.

Halford, G.S., Baker, R., McCredden, J.E., and Bain, J.D. (2005). How many variables can humans process? *Psychological Science*, 16(1), 70–76.

Hall, K.L., Vogel, A.L., Huang, G.C., Serrano, K.J., Rice, E.L., Tsakraklides, S., and Fiore, S.M. (2018). The science of team science: A review of the empirical evidence and research gaps on collaboration in science. *The American Psychologist*, 73(4), 532–548. doi:10.1037/amp0000319.

Hancock, P.A., Jagacinski, R. J., Parasuraman, R., Wickens, C.D., Wilson, G.F., and Kaber, D.B. (2013). Human-automation interaction research: Past, present, and future. *Ergonomics in Design*, 21(2), 9–14.

Harrison, L., Yang, F., Franconeri, S., and Chang, R. (2014). Ranking visualizations of correlation using Weber's law. *IEEE Transactions on Visualization and Computer Graphics*, 20(12), 1943–1952.

Hättenschwiler, N., Sterchi, Y., Mendes, M., and Schwaninger, A. (2018). Automation in airport security X-ray screening of cabin baggage: Examining benefits and possible implementations of automated explosives detection. *Applied Ergonomics*, 72, 58–68. doi:10.1016/j.apergo.2018.05.003.

Healey, C.G. (1996). Choosing effective colours for data visualization. In *VIS '96 Proceedings of the 7th Conference on Visualization '96* (pp. 263–271). Los Alamitos, CA: IEEE Computer Society Press. Available: http://www.diliaranasirova.com/assets/PSYC579/pdfs/02.1-Healey.pdf [December 2018].

Heath, C., Larrick, R.P., and Klayman, J. (1998). Cognitive repairs: How organizational practices can compensate for individual shortcomings. *Review of Organizational Behavior, 20*, 1–37.

Helmholtz, H.V. (1924). *Treatise on Physiological Optics* (Translation from 3rd German ed.). J.P.C. Southall, (Ed.). Rochester, NY: The Optical Society of America.

Helton, W.S., and Russell, P.N. (2015). Rest is best: The role of rest and task interruptions on vigilance. *Cognition, 134*, 165–173. doi:10.1016/j.cognition.2014.10.001.

Hinski, S. (2017). *Training the Code Team Leader as a Forcing Function to Improve Overall Team Performance During Simulated Code Blue Events.* Ph.D. Thesis, Human Systems Engineering, Arizona State University. Available: https://repository.asu.edu/attachments/194035/content/Hinski_asu_0010E_17454.pdf [December 2018].

Hoff, K., and Bashir, M. (2015). Trust in automation: Integrating empirical evidence on factors that influence trust. *Human Factors, 57*(3), 407–434.

Hoffman, R.R., Johnson, M., Bradshaw, J.M., and Underbrink, A. (2013). Trust in automation. *IEEE Intelligent Systems, 28*(1), 84–88.

Hoffman, J.M., Dunnenberger, H.M., Hicks, J.K., Caudle, K.E., Carrillo, M.W., Freimuth, R.R., Williams, M.S., Klein, T.E., and Peterson, J.F. (2016). Developing knowledge resources to support precision medicine: Principles from the Clinical Pharmacogenetics Implementation Consortium (CPIC). *Journal of the American Medical Informatics Association, 23*(4), 796–801.

Holzer, J.R., and Moses, F.L. (2015). Autonomous systems in the intelligence community: Many possibilities and challenges. *Studies in Intelligence, 59*(1), Extracts. Available: https://www.cia.gov/library/center-for-the-study-of-intelligence/csi-publications/csi-studies/studies/vol-59-no-1/pdfs/Autonomous-Systems.pdf [December 2018].

Horsch, K., Giger, M.L., and Metz, C.E. (2008). Potential effect of different radiologist reporting methods on studies showing benefit of CAD. *Academic Radiologist, 15*(2), 139–152.

IEEE Standards Association. (2016). *The IEEE Global Initiative for Ethical Considerations in Artificial Intelligence and Autonomous Systems. Ethically Aligned Design: A Vision for Prioritizing Wellbeing with Artificial Intelligence and Autonomous Systems, Version 1.* IEEE. Available: http://standards.ieee.org/develop/indconn/ec/autonomous_systems.html [November 2018].

Iqbal, S.T., Zheng, X.S., and Bailey, B.P. (2004). Task-evoked pupillary response to mental workload in human–computer interaction. In *CHI '04 Extended Abstracts on Human Factors in Computing Systems* (pp. 1477–1480). New York: Association for Computing Machinery. doi:10.1145/985921.986094.

Iqbal, S.T., Adamczyk, P.D., Zheng, X.S., and Bailey, B.P. (2005). Towards an index of opportunity: Understanding changes in mental workload during task execution. In *CHI '05 Proceedings of the SIGCHI Conference on Human Factors in Computing Systems* (pp. 311–320). New York: Association for Computing Machinery. doi:10.1145/1054972.1055016.

Jorritsma, W., Cnossen, F., and van Ooijen, P.M. (2015). Improving the radiologist–CAD interaction: Designing for appropriate trust. *Clinical Radiologist, 70*(2), 114–122.

Jung, M.F., Beane, M., Forlizzi, J., Murphy, R., and Vertesi, J. (2017). Robots in group context: Rethinking design, development and deployment. In *Proceedings of the 2017 CHI Conference Extended Abstracts on Human Factors in Computing Systems* (pp. 1283–1288). New York: Association for Computing Machinery. doi:10.1145/3027063.3051136.

Kaber, D.B., Wright, M.C., Prinzel, L.J. III, and Clamann, M.P. (2005). Adaptive automation of human–machine system information-processing functions. *Human Factors, 47*(4), 730–741.

Kane, M.J., and Engle, R.W. (2003). Working-memory capacity and the control of attention: The contributions of goal neglect, response competition, and task set to Stroop interference. *Journal of Experimental Psychology: General, 132*(1), 47–70.

Kane, M.J., Conway, A.R.A., Hambrick, D.Z., and Engle, R.W. (2007). Variation in working memory capacity as variation in executive attention and control. In A.R.A. Conway, C. Jarrold, M.J. Kane, A. Miyake, and J.N. Towse (Eds.), *Variation in Working Memory* (pp. 21–48). New York: Oxford University Press.

Kay, M., and Heer, J. (2016). Beyond Weber's law: A second look at ranking visualizations of correlation. IEEE *Transactions on Visualization and Computer Graphics, 22*(1), 469–478.

Keller, P.R., Keller, M.M., Markel, S., Mallinckrodt, A.J., and McKay, S. (1994). Visual cues: Practical data visualization. *Computers in Physics, 8*(3), 297–298.

Keller, S.A., Shipp, S., and Schroeder, A. (2016). Does big data change the privacy landscape? A review of the issues. *Annual Review of Statistics and Its Application, 3*, 161–180. doi:10.1146/annurev-statistics-041715-033453.

Keller, S.A., Korkmaz, G., Orr, M., Schroeder, A., and Shipp, S. (2017). The evolution of data quality: Understanding the transdisciplinary origins of data quality concepts and approaches. *Annual Review of Statistics and Its Application, 4*, 85–108. doi:10.1146/annurev-statistics-060116-054114.

Klare, B.F., Burge, M.J., Klontz, J.C., Vorder Bruegge, R.W., and Jain, A.K. (2012). Face recognition performance: Role of demographic information. *IEEE Transactions on Information Forensics and Security, 7*(6), 1789–1801. doi:10.1109/TIFS.2012.2214212.

Klein, G. (2007). Performing a project premortem. *Harvard Business Review, 85*, 18–19. Available: https://hbr.org/2007/09/performing-a-project-premortem [February 2019].

Kosslyn, S.M. (1989). Understanding charts and graphs. *Applied Cognitive Psychology, 3*(3), 185–225.

Krupinski, E.A. (1996). Visual scanning patterns of radiologists searching mammograms. *Academic Radiology, 3*(2), 137–144.

Lee, J., and Moray, N. (1994). Trust, self-confidence, and operators' adaptation to automation. *International Journal of Human–Computer Studies, 40*(1), 153–184.

Lee, T-Y., and Shen, H-W. (2009). Visualization and exploration of temporal trend relationships in multivariate time-varying data. *IEEE Transactions on Visualization and Computer Graphics, 15*(6), 1359–1366. doi:10.1109/TVCG.2009.200.

Lee, C.S., Bhargavan-Chatfield, M., Burnside, E.S., Nagy, P., and Sickles, E.A. (2016). The National Mammography Database: Preliminary data. *American Journal of Roentgenology, 206*(4), 883–890.

Leese, M. (2014). The new profiling: Algorithms, black boxes, and the failure of anti-discriminatory safeguards in the European Union. *Security Dialogue, 45*(5), 494–511.

Liu, Y., Ayaz, H., and Shewokis, P. (2017). Multisubject "learning" for mental workload classification using concurrent EEG, fNIRS, and physiological measures. *Frontiers in Human Neuroscience, 11*, 389. doi:10.3389/fnhum.2017.00389.

Lu, J. (2016). Will medical technology deskill doctors? *International Education Studies, 9*(7), 130–134.

Luce, R.D. (2005). *Individual Choice Behavior: A Theoretical Analysis.* Mineola, NY: Dover Publications.

Luce, R.D., and Raiffa, H. (2012). *Games and Decisions: Introduction and Critical Survey.* New York: John Wiley & Sons.

Lungeanu, A., Carter, D.R., DeChurch, L.A., and Contractor, N.S. (2018). How team interlock ecosystems shape the assembly of scientific teams: A hypergraph approach. *Communication Methods and Measures, 12*(2–3), 174–198. doi:10.1080/19312458.2018.1430756.

Mackworth, J. (1970). *Vigilance and Attention.* Harmondsworth, UK: Penguin Books.

Macmillan, N.A., and Creelman, C.D. (2005). *Detection Theory.* Mahwah, NJ: Lawrence Erlbaum Associates.

Maloney, L.T., and Zhang, H. (2010). Decision-theoretic models of visual perception and action. *Vision Research, 50*(23), 2362–2374.

Mark, G., Gonzalez, V.M., and Harris, J. (2005). No task left behind? Examining the nature of fragmented work. In *CHI '05 Proceedings of the SIGCHI Conference on Human Factors in Computing Systems* (pp. 321–330). New York: Association for Computing Machinery. doi:10.1145/1054972.1055017.

Mark, G., Gudith, D., and Klocke, U. (2008). The cost of interrupted work: More speed and stress. In *CHI '08 Proceedings of the SIGCHI Conference on Human Factors in Computing Systems* (pp. 107–110). New York: Association for Computing Machinery. doi:10.1145/1357054.1357072.

Mark, G., Iqbal, S.T., Czerwinski, M., Johns, P., Sano, A., and Lutchyn, Y. (2016). Email duration, batching and self-interruption: Patterns of email use on productivity and stress. In *CHI '16 Proceedings of the 2016 CHI Conference on Human Factors in Computing Systems* (pp. 1717–1728). New York: Association for Computing Machinery.

Mayer, R.C., Davis, J.H., and Schoorman, F.D. (1995). An integrative model of organizational trust. *The Academy of Management Review, 20*(3), 709–734.

McCorduck, P. (2004). *Machines Who Think: A Personal Inquiry into the History and Prospects of Artificial Intelligence* (2nd ed.). Natick, MA: A. K. Peters, Ltd.

McNeese, N.J., Demir, M, Cooke, N.J., and Myers, C. (2017). Teaming with a synthetic teammate: Insights into human–autonomy teaming. *Human Factors, 60*(2), 262–273. doi:10.1177/0018720817743223.

Mellers, B., Ungar, L., Baron, J., Ramos, J., Gurcay, B., Fincher, K., Scott, S.E., Moore, D., Atanasov, P., Swift, S.A., Murray, T., Stone, E., and Tetlock, P.E. (2014). Psychological strategies for winning a geopolitical forecasting tournament. *Psychological Science, 25*(5), 1106–1115. doi:10.1177/0956797614524255.

Mellers, B., Stone, E., Atanasov, P., Rohrbaugh, N., Metz, S.E., Ungar, L., Bishop, M.M., Horowitz, M., Merkle, E., and Tetlock, P. (2015). The psychology of intelligence analysis: Drivers of prediction accuracy in world politics. *Journal of Experimental Psychology: Applied, 21*(1), 1–14. Available: https://www.apa.org/pubs/journals/releases/xap-0000040.pdf [December 2018].

Mitroff, S.R., and Biggs, A.T. (2014). The ultra-rare-item effect: Visual search for exceedingly rare items is highly susceptible to error. *Psychology Science, 25*(1), 284–289.

Mittelstadt, B.D., Allo, P., Taddeo, M., Wachter, S., and Floridi, L. (2016). The ethics of algorithms: Mapping the debate. *Big Data & Society,* 1–21. doi:10.1177/2053951716679679.

Monaghan, A.J., Morin, C.W., Steinhoff, D.F., Wilhelmi, O., Hayden, M., Quattrochi, D.A., Reiskind, M., Lloyd, A.L., Smith, K., Schmidt, C.A., Scalf, P.E., and Ernst K. (2016). On the seasonal occurrence and abundance of the Zika virus vector mosquito Aedes aegypti in the contiguous United States. *PLoS Currents, 8.* doi:10.1371/currents.outbreaks.50dfc7f46798675fc63e7d7da563da76.

Monsell, S. (2003). Task switching. *Trends in Cognitive Sciences, 7*(3), 134–140.

Moore, P., and Piwek, L. (2017). Regulating wellbeing in the brave new quantified workplace. *Employee Relations, 39*(3), 308–316.

Nakamura, L. (2013). *Cybertypes: Race, Ethnicity, and Identity on the Internet.* New York: Routledge.

National Academies of Sciences, Engineering, and Medicine (NASEM). (2016). *From Maps to Models: Augmenting the Nation's Geospatial Intelligence Capabilities.* Washington, DC: The National Academies Press. doi:10.17226/23650.

NASEM. (2017a). *Challenges in Machine Generation of Analytic Products from Multi-Source Data: Proceedings of a Workshop.* Washington, DC: The National Academies Press. doi:10.17226/24900.

NASEM. (2017b). *Strengthening Data Science Methods for Department of Defense Personnel and Readiness Missions*. Washington, DC: The National Academies Press. doi:10.17226/23670.
NASEM. (2018a). *Artificial Intelligence and Machine Learning to Accelerate Translational Research: Proceedings of a Workshop—in Brief*. Washington, DC: The National Academies Press. doi:10.17226/25197.
NASEM. (2018b). *Learning Through Citizen Science: Enhancing Opportunities by Design*. Washington, DC: The National Academies Press.
NASEM. (2018c). *Learning from the Science of Cognition and Perception for Decision Making: Proceedings of a Workshop*. Washington, DC: The National Academies Press. doi:10.17226/25118.
NASEM. (2018d). *Emerging Trends and Methods in International Security: Proceedings of a Workshop*. Washington, DC: The National Academies Press. doi:10.17226/25058.
National Research Council. (1951). *Human Engineering for an Effective Air Navigation and Traffic Control System*. Washington, DC: National Academy Press. Available: https://apps.dtic.mil/dtic/tr/fulltext/u2/b815893.pdf [February 2019].
National Research Council. (2007). *Human–System Integration in the System Development Process: A New Look*. Washington, DC: National Academies Press. doi:10.17226/11893.
National Research Council. (2013). *Frontiers in Massive Data Analysis*. Washington, DC: The National Academies Press. doi:10.17226/18374.
National Research Council. (2014). *Complex Operational Decision Making in Networked Systems of Humans and Machines: A Multidisciplinary Approach*. Washington, DC: The National Academies Press. doi:10.17226/18844.
National Research Council. (2015). *Enhancing the Effectiveness of Team Science*. Washington, DC: The National Academies Press. doi:10.17226/19007.
National Research Council and National Academy of Engineering. (2014). *Emerging and Readily Available Technologies and National Security: A Framework for Addressing Ethical, Legal, and Societal Issues*. Washington, DC: The National Academies Press. doi:10.17226/18512.
Newell, S., and Marabelli, M. (2015). Strategic opportunities (and challenges) of algorithmic decision-making: A call for action on the long-term societal effects of "datification". *The Journal of Strategic Information Systems*, 24(1), 3–14.
Nicolas-Alonso, L.F., and Gomez-Gil, J. (2012). Brain computer interfaces: A review. *Sensors*, 12(2), 1211–1279. doi:10.3390/s120201211.
Nishikawa, R.M., Schmidt, R.A., Linver, M.N., Edwards, A.V., Papaioannou, J., and Stull, M.A. (2012). Clinically missed cancer: How effectively can radiologists use computer-aided detection? *American Journal of Roentgenology*, 198(3), 708–716. doi:10.2214/AJR.11.6423.
Noah, B., Keller, M.S., Mosadeghi, S., Stein, L., Johl, S., Delshad, S., Tashjian, V.C., Lew, D., Kwan, J.T., Jusufagic, A., and Spiegel, B.M.R. (2018). Impact of remote patient monitoring on clinical outcomes: An updated meta-analysis of randomized controlled trials. *npj Digital Medicine*, 1(1), 20172.
Nodine, C.F., and Kundel, H.L. (1987). Using eye movements to study visual search and to improve tumor detection. *RadioGraphics*, 7(6), 1241–1250. doi:10.1148/radiographics.7.6.3423330.
Noë, A., Pessoa, L., and Thompson, E. (2000). Beyond the grand illusion: What change blindness really teaches us about vision. *Visual Cognition*, 7(1), 93–106.
Oberlander, E.M., Oswald, F.L., Hambrick, D.Z., and Jones, L.A. (2007). *Individual Difference Variables as Predictors of Error during Multitasking*. No. NPRST-TN-07-9. Millington, TN: Navy Personnel Research Studies and Technology.

O'Leary, M.B., Mortensen, M., and Woolley, A.W. (2011). Multiple team membership: A theoretical model of its effects on productivity and learning for individuals and teams. *Academy of Management Review, 36*(3), 461–478.

O'Rourke, D. (2014). The science of sustainable supply chains. *Science, 344*(6188), 1124–1127.

Osoba, O., and Welser, IV, W. (2017). *An Intelligence in Our Image: The Risks of Bias and Errors in Artificial Intelligence*. Santa Monica, CA: RAND Corporation.

Parasuraman, R. (2000). Designing automation for human use: Empirical studies and quantitative models. *Ergonomics, 43*(7), 931–951.

Parasuraman, R., and Manzey, D.H. (2010). Complacency and bias in human use of automation: An attentional integration. *Human Factors, 52*(3), 381–410.

Parasuraman, R., and Hancock, P.A. (2008). Mitigating the adverse effects of workload, stress, and fatigue with adaptive automation. In P.A. Hancock, and J.L. Szalma (Eds.), *Performance Under Stress* (pp. 45–58). Burlington, VT: Ashgate.

Parasuraman, R., and Riley, V. (1997). Humans and automation: Use, misuse, disuse, abuse. *Human Factors, 39*(2), 230–253.

Parasuraman, R., Sheridan, T.B., and Wickens, C.D. (2000). A model for types and levels of human interaction with automation. *IEEE Transactions on Systems, Man, and Cybernetics—Part A: Systems and Humans, 30*(3), 286–297. doi:10.1109/3468.844354.

Pashler, H. (2000). Task switching and multitask performance. In S. Monsell, and J. Driver (Eds.), *Attention and Performance XVIII: Control of Mental Processes* (Ch. 12) (pp. 277–307). Cambridge, MA: MIT Press. Available: http://citeseerx.ist.psu.edu/viewdoc/download?doi=10.1.1.408.7509&rep=rep1&type=pdf [December 2018].

Phillips, C., Wood, T., and Lewis, S. (2017). *An Integrated Approach to Language Capabilities in Humans and Technology* [White Paper]. Available: http://sites.nationalacademies.org/cs/groups/dbassesite/documents/webpage/dbasse_179909.pdf [December 2018].

Poole, M.S., and Contractor, N.S. (2012). Conceptualizing the multiteam system as an ecosystem of networked groups. In S.J. Zaccaro, M.A. Marks, and L.A. DeChurch (Eds.), *Multiteam Systems: An Organizational Form for Dynamic and Complex Environments* (pp. 193–224). New York: Routledge Academic.

Portmess, L., and Tower, S. (2014). Data barns, ambient intelligence and cloud computing: The tacit epistemology and linguistic representation of Big Data. *Ethics and Information Technology, 17*(1), 1–9.

Puma, S., Matton, N., Paubel, P.V., Raufaste, É., and El-Yagoubi, R. (2018). Using theta and alpha band power to assess cognitive workload in multitasking environments. *International Journal of Psychophysiology, 123*, 111–120. doi:10.1016/j.ijpsycho.2017.10.004.

Pylyshyn, Z., and Storm, R.W. (1988). Tracking multiple independent targets: Evidence for a parallel tracking mechanism. *Spatial Vision, 3*(3), 179–197.

Rahlf, T. (2017). *Data Visualization with R: 100 Examples*. Cham, Switzerland: Springer International. doi:10.1007/978-3-319-49751-8.

Rajivan, P., and Cooke, N.J. (2017). Impact of team collaboration on cybersecurity situational awareness. In P. Liu, S. Jajodia, and C. Wang (Eds.), *Theory and Models for Cyber Situation Awareness* (pp. 203–226). Cham, Switzerland: Springer International Publishing. doi:10.1007/978-3-319-61152-5.

Rajivan, P., and Cooke, N.J. (2018). Information pooling bias in collaborative security incident correlation analysis. *Human Factors, 60*(5), 626–639. doi:10.1177/0018720818769249.

Rasmussen, J. (1983). Skills, rules, and knowledge: Signals, signs, and symbols, and other distinctions in human performance models. *IEEE Transactions on Systems, Man, and Cybernetics, 13*(3), 257–266.

Robert, L.P. (2018). Motivational theory of human robot teamwork. *International Robotics & Automation Journal, 4*(4), 248–251.

Rohrbaugh, J.W. (2017). Ambulatory and non-contact recording methods. In J.T. Cacioppo, L.G. Tassinary, and G.G. Berntson (Eds.), *Handbook of Psychophysiology* (4th ed.) (pp. 300–338). New York: Cambridge University Press.

Rosenbalt, A., Kneese, T., and Boyd, D. (2014). *Workplace Surveillance*. Data & Society Research Institute. Available: https://datasociety.net/pubs/fow/WorkplaceSurveillance.pdf [December 2018].

Russell, S., and Norvig, P. (2010). *Artificial Intelligence, A Modern Approach* (3rd ed.). Upper Saddle River, NJ: Pearson Education, Inc.

Sagan, P., and McCormick, H.W. (2017). *Multi-Disciplinary Studies of Probability Perception Contribute to Engineering & Exploiting Predictive Analytic Technologies* [White Paper]. Available: http://sites.nationalacademies.org/cs/groups/dbassesite/documents/webpage/dbasse_176650.pdf [February 2019].

Salas, E., and Fiore, S.M. (Eds.) (2004). *Team Cognition: Understanding the Factors That Drive Process and Performance*. Washington DC: American Psychological Association.

Salas, E., Dickinson, T.L., Converse, S.A., and Tannenbaum, S.I. (1992). Toward an understanding of team performance and training. In R.W. Swezey and E. Salas (Eds.), *Teams: Their Training and Performance* (pp. 3–29). Norwood, NJ: Ablex.

Salas, E., Cooke, N.J., and Rosen, M.A. (2008). On teams, teamwork and team performance: Discoveries and developments. *Human Factors: Golden Anniversary Special Issue, 50*(3), 540–547. doi:10.1518/001872008X288457.

Satopää, V.A., Baron, J., Foster, D.P., Mellers, B.A., Tetlock, P.E., and Ungar, L.H. (2014a). Combining multiple probability predictions using a simple logit model. *International Journal of Forecasting, 30*(2), 344–356.

Satopää, V.A., Jensen, S.T., Mellers, B.A., Tetlock, P.E., and Ungar, L.H. (2014b). Probability aggregation in time-series: Dynamic hierarchical modeling of sparse expert beliefs. *The Annals of Applied Statistics, 8*(2), 1256–1280.

Shankar, S., Halpern, Y., Breck, E., Atwood, J., Wilson, J., and Sculley, D. (2017). *No Classification without Representation: Assessing Geodiversity Issues in Open Data Sets for the Developing World*. arXiv preprint arXiv:1711.08536. Available: https://ai.google/research/pubs/pub46553 [December 2018].

Shapiro, M. (2010). Once upon a stacked time series. In J. Steele and N. Iliinsky (Eds.), *Beautiful Visualization: Looking at Data through the Eyes of Experts* (pp. 15–36). Sebastopol, CA: O'Reilly Media.

Shell, E.R. (2018). The employer-surveillance state. *The Atlantic*, October 15.

Shupp, L., Andrews, C., Dickey-Kurdziolek, M., Yost, B., and North, C. (2009). Shaping the display of the future: The effects of display size and curvature on user performance and insights. *Human–Computer Interaction, 24*(1-2), 230–272.

Siddiqi, A., Ereiqat, F., and Anadon, L.D. (2016). Formulating expectations for future water availability through infrastructure development decisions in arid regions. *Systems Engineering, 19*(2), 101–110.

Siebert, J., Strobl, B., Etter, S., Vis, M., Ewen, T., and van Meerveld, H. (2017). Engaging the public in hydrological observations-first experiences from the CrowdWater project. *EGU General Assembly Conference Abstracts, 19*, 11592.

Simons, D.J., and Chabris, C.F. (1999). Gorillas in our midst: Sustained inattentional blindness for dynamic events. *Perception, 28*(9), 1059–1074.

Simons, D.J., and Levin, D.T. (1998). Failure to detect changes to people during a real-world interaction. *Psychonomic Bulletin & Review, 5*(4), 644–649.

Slovic, P., Fischhoff, B., and Lichtenstein, S. (1980). Facts and fears: Understanding perceived risk. In *Societal Risk Assessment* (pp. 181–216). Boston, MA: Springer.

Smith, G., Baudisch, P., Robertson, G., Czerwinski, M., Meyers, B., Robbins, D., and Andrews, D. (2003). *GroupBar: The TaskBar Evolved*. Available: http://rajatorrent.com.patrickbaudisch.com/publications/2003-Smith-OZCHI03-GroupBar.pdf [November 2018].

Sperling, G., and Dosher, B.A. (1986). Strategy and optimization in human information processing. In *Basic Sensory Process I* (pp. 2.1–2.65). Available: https://pdfs.semanticscholar.org/ba80/4c88813e27bcb225475054f947eb0ef3a934.pdf [December 2018].

Sperling, G., and Melchner, M.J. (1978). The attention operating characteristic: Examples from visual search. *Science*, 202(4365), 315–318.

Stasser, G., Vaughan, S., and Stewart, D. (2000). Pooling unshared information: The benefits of knowing how access to information is distributed among group members. *Organizational Behavior and Human Decision Processes*, 82(1), 102–116.

Steele, J., and Iliinsky, N. (2010). *Beautiful Visualization: Looking at Data through the Eyes of Experts*. Sebastopol, CA: O'Reilly Media.

Stone, M., Szafir, D.A., and Setlur, V. (2014). *An Engineering Model for Color Difference as a Function of Size*. Available: https://graphics.cs.wisc.edu/Papers/2014/SAS14/2014CIC_48_Stone_v3.pdf [December 2018].

Strayer, D.L., Cooper, J.M., Turrill, J., Coleman, J.R., and Hopman, R.J. (2016). Talking to your car can drive you to distraction. *Cognitive Research: Principles and Implications*, 1(16). doi:10.1186/s41235-016-0018-3.

Strobach, T., Liepelt, R., Schubert, T., and Kiesel, A. (2012). Task switching: Effects of practice on switch and mixing costs. *Psychological Research*, 76(1), 74–83.

Suchow, J.W., Fougnie, D., Brady, T.F., and Alvarez, G.A. (2014). Terms of the debate on the format and structure of visual memory. *Attention, Perception & Psychophysics*, 76(7), 2071–2079. doi:10.3758/s13414-014-0690-7.

Sullivan, B.L., Aycrigg, J.L., Barry, J.H., Bonney, R.E., Bruns, N., Cooper, C.B., Damoulas, T., Dohndt, A.A., Dietterich, T., Farnsworth, A., Fink, D., Fitzpatrick, J.W., Fredericks, T., Gerbracht, J., Gomes, C., Hochachka, W.M., Iliff, M.J., Lagoze, C., La Sorte, F.A., Merrifield, M., Morris, W., Phillips, T.B., Reynolds, M., Rodewald, A.D., Rosenberg, K.V., Trautmann, N.M., Wiggins, A., Winkler, D.W., Wong, W-K., Wood, C.L., Yu, J., and Kelling, S. (2014). The eBird enterprise: An integrated approach to development and application of citizen science. *Biological Conservation*, 169, 31–40. doi:10.1016/j.biocon.2013.11.003.

Swan, M. (2013). The quantified self: Fundamental disruption in big data science and biological discovery. *Big Data*, 1(2), 85–110.

Szafir, D.A., Haroz, S., Gleicher, M., and Franconeri, S. (2016a). Four types of ensemble coding in data visualizations. *Journal of Vision*, 16(5), 11. doi:10.1167/16.5.11.

Szafir, D.A., Stuffer, D., Sohail, Y., and Gleicher, M. (2016b). *TextDNA: Visualizing Word Usage with Configurable Colorfields*. Available: https://graphics.cs.wisc.edu/Papers/2016/ASSG16/TextDNA.pdf [December 2018].

Tannenbaum, S.I., Mathieu, J.E., Salas, E., and Cohen, D. (2012). Teams are changing: Are research and practice evolving fast enough? *Industrial and Organizational Psychology*, 5(1), 2–24. doi:10.1111/j.1754-9434.2011.01396.x.

Tetlock, P.E. (2017). *Expert Political Judgment: How Good Is It? How Can We Know?* Princeton, NJ: Princeton University Press.

Tetlock, P.E., Mellers, B.A., Rohrbaugh, N., and Chen, E. (2014). Forecasting tournaments: Tools for increasing transparency and improving the quality of debate. *Current Directions in Psychological Science*, 23(4), 290–295.

Thomson, D.R., Smilek, D., and Besner, D. (2015). Reducing the vigilance decrement: The effects of perceptual variability. *Conscious Cognition*, 33, 386–397. doi:10.1016/j.concog.2015.02.010.

Tuddenham, W.J. (1962). Visual search, image organization, and reader error in roentgen diagnosis: Studies of the psycho-physiology of roentgen image perception. *Radiology, 78*, 694–704. doi:10.1148/78.5.694.
Tufte, E.R. (2003). *The Cognitive Style of PowerPoint*. Cheshire, CT: Graphics Press.
Tufte, E.R. (2006). *Beautiful Evidence* (Vol. 1). Cheshire, CT: Graphics Press.
Tufte, E.R., and Graves-Morris, P. (2014). *The Visual Display of Quantitative Information*. Cheshire, CT: Graphics Press.
Tufte, E.R., and Robins D. (1997). *Visual Explanations*. Cheshire, CT: Graphics Press.
Tufte, E.R., McKay, S.R., Christian W., and Matey, J.R. (1998). Visual explanations: Images and quantities, evidence and narrative. *Computers in Physics, 12*, 146. doi:10.1063/1.168637.
Turner, B.M., Steyvers, M., Merkle, E.C., Budescu, D.V., and Wallsten, T.S. (2014). Forecast aggregation via recalibration. *Machine Learning, 95*(3), 261–289.
Tutt, A. (2016). *An FDA for Algorithms*. SSRN Scholarly Paper. Rochester, NY: Social Science Research Network. Available: http://papers.ssrn.com/abstract=2747994 [December 2018].
Tversky, A., and Kahneman, D. (1974). Judgment under uncertainty: Heuristics and biases. *Science, 185*(4157), 1124–1131.
Unsworth, N., and Engle, R.W. (2007). The nature of individual differences in working memory capacity: Active maintenance in primary memory and controlled search from secondary memory. *Psychological Review, 114*(1), 104–132. doi:10.1037/0033-295X.114.1.104.
Valentine, M.A., Retelny, D., To, A., Rahmati, N., Doshi, T., and Bernstein, M.S. (2017). Flash organizations: Crowdsourcing complex work by structuring crowds as organizations. In *CHI '17 Proceedings of the 2017 CHI Conference on Human Factors in Computing Systems* (pp. 3523–3537). New York: Association for Computing Machinery. Available: https://hci.stanford.edu/publications/2017/flashorgs/flash-orgs-chi-2017.pdf [December 2018].
van de Voort, M., Pieters, W., and Consoli, L. (2015). Refining the ethics of computer-made decisions: A classification of moral mediation by ubiquitous machines. *Ethics of Information Technology, 17*(1), 41–56. doi:10.1007/s10676-015-9360-2.
Vogel, E.K., and Machizawa, M.G. (2004). Neural activity predicts individual differences in visual working memory capacity. *Nature, 428*(6984), 748–751.
Wainer, H. (1992). Understanding graphs and tables. *Educational Researcher, 21*(1), 14–23.
Wegner, D.M. (1987). Transactive memory: A contemporary analysis of the group mind. In B. Mullen and G.R. Goethals (Eds.), *Theories of Group Behavior* (pp. 185–208). New York: Springer-Verlag.
Wickens, C.D. (2008). Multiple resources and mental workload. *Human Factors, 50*(3), 449–455.
Wickens, C.D. (2010). Multiple resources and performance prediction. *Theoretical Issues in Ergonomics Science, 3*(2), 159–177. doi:10.1080/14639220210123806.
Wickens, C.D., Gutzwiller, R.S., and Santamaria, A. (2015). Discrete task switching in overload: A meta-analyses and a model. *International Journal of Human–Computer Studies, 79*, 79–84. doi:10.1016/j.ijhcs.2015.01.002.
Wickens, C.D., Gutzwiller, R.S., Vieane, A., Clegg, B.A., Sebok, A., and Janes, J. (2016). Time sharing between robotics and process control: Validating a model of attention switching. *Human Factors, 58*(2), 322–343.
Williams, H.J., and Blum, I. (2018). *Defining Second Generation Open Source Intelligence (OSINT) for the Defense Enterprise*. Santa Monica, CA: RAND Corporation. Available: https://www.rand.org/pubs/research_reports/RR1964.html [December 2018].
Witlin, L. (2008). Of note: Mirror-imaging and its dangers. *SAIS Review of International Affairs 28*(1), 89–90.

Wittenbaum, G.M, Hollingshead, A.B., and Botero, I.C. (2004). From cooperative to motivated information sharing in groups: Moving beyond the hidden profile paradigm. *Communication Monographs, 71*(3), 286–310. doi:10.1080/0363452042000299894.

Wolfe, J.M. (2003). Moving towards solutions to some enduring controversies in visual search. *Trends in Cognitive Sciences, 7*(2), 70–76.

Wolfe, J.M., and Van Wert, M. (2010). Varying target prevalence reveals two dissociable decision criteria in visual search. *Current Biology, 20*(2), 121–124. doi:10.1016/j.cub.2009.11.066.

Wolfe, J.M., Horowitz, T.S., and Kenner, N.M. (2005). Rare targets are often missed in visual search. *Nature, 435*(7041), 439–440.

Wolfe, J.M., Brunelli, D.N., Rubinstein, J., and Horowitz, T.S. (2013). Prevalence effects in newly trained airport checkpoint screeners: Trained observers miss rare targets, too. *Journal of Vision, 13*(3), 33. doi:10.1167/13.3.33.

Yost, B., and North C. (2006). The perceptual scalability of visualization. *IEEE Transactions on Visualization and Computer Graphics, 12*(5), 837–844.

Yudkowsky, E. (2011). Cognitive biases potentially affecting judgment of global risks. In N. Bostrom, and M. Cirkovic (Eds.), *Global Catastrophic Risks* (pp. 91–119). New York: Oxford University Press.

Zhang, H.Y., Ji, P., Wang, J.Q., and Chen, X.H. (2017). A novel decision support model for satisfactory restaurants utilizing social information: A case study of TripAdvisor.com. *Tourism Management, 59*, 281–297. doi:10.1016/j.tourman.2016.08.010.

8

Strengthening the Analytic Workforce for Future Challenges

The Intelligence Community (IC) has always needed a workforce that is responsive, flexible, effective, and well equipped to learn and adapt to change. This workforce will surely be influenced in the coming decade by factors that will drive change across most industries, including "ubiquitous high-speed mobile internet; artificial intelligence (AI); widespread adoption of big data analytics; and cloud technology" (World Economic Forum, 2018, p. vii). The opportunities discussed in this report are ways in which these technologies and other developments can bring fundamental changes in the way intelligence analysis is conducted. In a decade or less, for example, analysts may have the capacity to obtain sophisticated analysis of a months-long narrative stream on social media sites, compare it with activities from that period identified through geospatial imaging, and develop a graphical representation of the intersections between the two—as part of a day's work.

To leverage these opportunities, the analytic workforce will need new skills: developments in such areas as network science, complex systems models, statistics, and data analytics of all kinds will likely add new methods and tools to the analyst's toolbox.[1] In areas in which intelligence analysts are expert—qualitative analysis of text and narrative, for example—new developments such as improved quantitative methods for text analysis,

---

[1] Many of the challenges facing analysts are documented in the National Research Council (2011) report *Intelligence Analysis for Tomorrow: Advances from the Behavioral and Social Sciences*.

including methods for analyzing social media, offer possibilities that may not yet have been integrated into common practice within the IC.

The analytic workforce already reflects diverse and valuable technical and academic skills and experience. Today, intelligence analysts typically join the workforce with specific disciplinary subject matter knowledge; Box 8-1 suggests the range of expertise analysts bring to the job. As analysts mature in their careers, they gain deep regional expertise (e.g., China, Russia, the Middle East) and become functional experts in such topics as fighter aircraft, naval systems, nuclear issues, missile technology, counterterrorism, counterproliferation, or counterintelligence. As discussed in Chapter 4, day-to-day analysis is typically core task-based, with analysts culling volumes of classified and unclassified intelligence information to build analyses associated with their region of interest or the function being surveilled. Analysts need critical thinking skills, and they also need strong writing and communication skills because the quality of their writing is vital to the effectiveness of the briefings they provide.

The IC will need to continue building on the expertise of the analytic workforce as it integrates new tools into the workflow, and may need to compete with the private sector for individuals with the expertise needed, though this is not a new challenge. Analysts of the future will need to build on the skills they have always had, including technical skills, domain-specific knowledge, social intelligence, strong communication skills, and the capacity for continued learning (Dawson and Thomson, 2018). But they will also need to function in new ways. In particular the innovations in the integration of human–machine systems discussed in Chapter 7 are likely to provide new working environments and methodologies that expand analysts' capacity and productivity. Survey results indicate that human–machine systems of some sort are likely to become increasingly common, and that the percentage of task hours performed by machines is likely to increase across industries (Schwartz et al., 2017; World Economic Forum, 2018). Research in contexts other than the IC has emphasized that the rapid influx of AI and automation into the workplace has intensified the demand for such "human" skills as complex problem solving and social skills (Agrawal et al., 2018). As discussed in Chapter 7, the optimal integration of human and machine skills for intelligence analysis will require careful research; it will also require close attention to the management and structure of the workplace and the workforce.

As in any large organization, the agencies of the IC pay attention to means of identifying, recruiting, and selecting individuals likely to excel as intelligence analysts; providing training and using other means to develop their skills and abilities; obtaining optimal performance from the workforce; and retaining effective employees. Researchers in the fields of industrial-

> **BOX 8-1**
> **Current Central Intelligence Agency (CIA)**
> **Position Posting for Analysts**
>
> **Analysis:** Collaborative. Problem-solvers. Critical thinkers. These are the qualities needed for CIA analytic positions. The ability to study and evaluate sometimes inconsistent and incomplete information and provide unique insights that help inform decisions is a key aspect of these positions.
>
> - Analytic Methodologist
> - Counterintelligence Threat Analyst
> - Counterterrorism Analyst
> - Cyber Exploitation Officer
> - Cyber Threat Analyst
> - Directorate of Operations Targeting Officer
> - Economic Analyst
> - Human Resources Analyst
> - Intelligence Collection Analyst
> - Leadership Analyst
> - Military Analyst
> - Multi-Discipline Security Officer
> - Political Analyst
> - Resource Analyst
> - Science, Technology, and Weapons Analyst
> - Targeting Analyst
> - Technical Targeting Analyst
>
> SOURCE: Available: https://www.cia.gov/careers/opportunities/cia-jobs/index.html [October 2018].

organizational psychology and human resource development have produced a robust body of work on ways to pursue most of these objectives. Applying this work for the IC context, however, requires translational research on the precise applications of well-established findings in the unique context of intelligence analysis.

This chapter provides a review of the state of the foundational research in industrial-organizational psychology and human resource development that is relevant to the evolving needs of the IC. It highlights developments in a few areas that hold particular promise for supporting the IC in meeting four key workforce challenges: selecting applicants likely to be effective in analytic roles, retaining effective analysts, developing skills on the job through both formal training and informal learning, and providing support for a potentially stressed and fatigued workforce.

SELECTING INDIVIDUALS TO SUCCEED IN INTELLIGENCE ANALYST ROLES

The research base on workforce selection is robust. Researchers in psychology and other fields have been working for more than a century to develop empirically based approaches to selecting those workers most likely to be effective, long-term employees in a particular context. They have explored the use of psychological measures to predict how well individuals will perform aspects of particular jobs. They also have developed psychological tests of cognitive abilities, personality traits, interests, values, and work styles, as well as other selection tools, such as interviews, situational judgment tests, and assessment centers (see Ployhart et al. [2017] for a review of work on the development of selection systems and Sackett et al. [2017b] for a review of work on the study of individuals' personal attributes that influence job performance).

This work has provided the basis for approaches with a strong record of effectiveness in predicting job performance and improving the quality of the selected workforce. It has led to the development of measures commonly used in personnel selection that include tests of knowledge, skill, and abilities; personality inventories; structured interviews; situational judgment tests; and job samples and simulations (National Academies of Sciences, Engineering, and Medicine, 2018b). Here we explore advances in measurement tools designed to predict the performance of potential employees, outcomes of interest in evaluating the effectiveness of a system for selecting new hires, approaches to evaluating the effectiveness and utility of a selection system, and the implications of these findings for the IC.

Advances in Measurement

Testing to predict how well an individual is likely to perform in a particular job has obvious utility for employers, including IC agencies that must sort through large numbers of applicants. While the well-established and well-researched selection methods outlined above are obvious starting points for thinking about selection in the IC context, new approaches are emerging, particularly new testing formats made possible by computer technology that have expanded the kinds of information that can be collected and assessed. For instance, researchers have investigated how well information about such psychological constructs as the ability to address multiple competing demands in an environment can be extracted from individuals' performance in carefully designed computer games. Likewise, big data analytics (see Chapter 2) have made it possible to develop predictive algorithms based on large numbers of individual bits of data that can be used in the selection process.

These big data approaches have led to the emergence of people analytics as an approach to addressing human resource issues such as recruitment, selection, and retention and predicting satisfaction and performance (Bersin, 2015). With people analytics, individual words or phrases used in a resumé or interview can be evaluated for predictive relationships with the outcome(s) of interest (e.g., subsequent job performance) (see the discussion below). Digitally captured information such as voice patterns, perhaps collected during interviews, can also be examined. Information about job applicants gleaned from online information (e.g., social media) can also be used in the selection process—either in an informal, ad hoc way, as in the case of a hiring manager who looks online for information about a job candidate, or using more systematic, automated approaches.

The emergence of these approaches has led firms such as Google to create a people analytics division (Bock, 2015). Google was among the first to recognize the potential for using big data to infer individual attributes of individuals (such as their personality traits), as well as their knowledge capital (such as specific skills). More recently, as part of Project Aristotle, Google used people analytics to understand drivers of individual and team performance. Digital trace data captured passively from the workforce's use of social media and enterprise social media channels can also be used to assess individuals' social capital, based on their position in the network. The result has been a growing interest in relational analytics (or the interplay or interactions among people) (Leonardi and Contractor, 2018). A key remaining challenge is the development of techniques for aggregating various digital trace activities (such as posting a message, "liking" a post, "following" a person or project, or "@mentioning" a person in a post) across multiple enterprise social media digital platforms (those that have been developed and used for communication and social interaction within organizations, such as e-mail, Slack, Jive, and IBM Connections) to provide meaningful relational data, such as who trusts whom, who seeks advice from whom, and who is likely to be an innovator or influencer or leave the organization.

While much work is ongoing in the development of these new approaches, many questions remain. Much of the work is proprietary, conducted by firms marketing services to organizations; relatively little has been subjected to the traditional peer review process. In some cases, marketing claims go beyond what can be supported by solid research. Some of these new approaches involve applying different analytic methods to information collected in traditional ways (e.g., interviews, resumés), while others involve new types of information (e.g., evaluation of candidates based on data gleaned from social media). These latter approaches raise significant ethical and privacy issues. With traditional approaches, for example, the candidate chooses whether to provide information (e.g., to submit a resumé, to participate in an interview or test), but this may not be the case when online information is extracted.

Privacy concerns arise in the security clearance process as well. Employment in the IC is contingent on a potential employee's ability to successfully obtain a security clearance at a level that is appropriate for the position. The requirements for enhanced security review include collection of information from "government, publicly available and commercial data sources, consumer reporting agencies, social media and such other sources."[2] In other words, the IC can collect publicly available information on U.S. citizens for the purposes of employment. The number of possible data points collected in such searches can easily stretch into the billions, so computational algorithms are used to identify relevant information for both prospective and current employees. Bias and other issues may affect the output of such algorithms, so their use for personnel matters must be considered with care (see Chapter 7).

The selection approaches we have discussed offer both opportunities and challenges. There are tensions between the behavioral scientist's orientation toward careful measurement of well-defined constructs (e.g., combining multiple items into scales, with careful evaluation of the contribution of each item to the scale score) and the application of the big data approach, where it may be difficult to identify how and why the algorithm produces scores that appear to predict performance. The possibility that conscious or unconscious bias against certain subgroups (e.g., based on racial, ethnic, or gender identity) may affect outcomes is a significant issue, particularly in the case of algorithmic approaches of a "black box" nature (see Chapter 7). While these new approaches merit attention, they also warrant a cautious and critical stance (Society for Industrial and Organizational Psychology, 2018). Novel approaches may or may not prove superior to tried-and-true, established selection procedures.

Outcomes of Interest

Industrial-organizational researchers use the performance of employees once hired (i.e., outcomes) as the basis for evaluating how well a system for selecting new hires has functioned. Recognizing the limitations of definitions of job performance, researchers have recently focused on developing more nuanced understanding of what characterizes effective performance. Once viewed as an undifferentiated phenomenon, performance is best understood in terms of various components that contribute to an employee's effectiveness. Researchers have identified such measurable elements of

---

[2]*Consolidated Appropriations Act of 2016.* Public Law No. 114-113, § 11001, 129 Stat. 673 (2015) (p. 673).

job performance as (1) performing core tasks; (2) being a "good citizen" of the organization (i.e., behaving in a way that benefits the organization by contributing to its social and psychological environment, such as persisting to complete a time-consuming job, providing personal support to coworkers, or representing the organization in a professional manner [Sackett and Walmsley, 2014]); and (3) avoiding various forms of counterproductive behavior (e.g., theft, sexual harassment, violations of company policy, drug and alcohol abuse). Specifying such elements has provided the basis for developing both tools for identifying facets of performance that are of greatest interest in a particular situation and predictors of these facets (Rotundo and Sackett, 2002; Campbell et al., 1993).

Cognitive ability testing is an example of how this new insight into the multidimensionality of job performance has influenced thinking and practice in personnel selection. Before this differentiated perspective emerged, it was generally accepted that cognitive ability tests were the best single predictor of job performance. Now, however, it has become clear that while such tests forecast certain aspects of performance well, they are of little to no value in forecasting others. A meta-analysis of studies on the relationship between cognitive ability and other aspects of task performance revealed strong relationships for task performance, more modest relationships for citizenship, and a near-zero relationship for counterproductive behavior (Gonzalez-Mulé et al., 2014).

These developments in the evaluation of potential job performance make it possible for organizations to identify the facets of performance in which they have the greatest interest and design selection systems accordingly. One likely outcome of this approach is a more elaborate selection system, with different predictors targeting different facets of performance. These developments have clear utility for the IC. For example, although 2007 Intelligence Community Directive (ICD) Number 203 set standards regarding the production and evaluation of intelligence analysis and analytical products in order to improve the critical thinking and writing skills of analysts across the IC (Miles, 2016), some note that one of the largest issues in analysis is the hiring of new employees who lack adequate critical thinking and writing skills (Gentry, 2015). While the committee did not have access to complete information on selection practices within the agencies of the IC, the input we received indicated that the primary focus is on selecting for the cognitive aspects of the analyst's job: obtaining, evaluating, and synthesizing information and presenting one's findings, commonly in written form.

The cognitive demand on analysts is surely considerable—the analytic workforce performs widely varying functions in an often fast-paced, unpredictable, high-stress, and largely classified environment (Pirolli et al., 2004), as demonstrated by the discussion of global challenges and the role of the analyst in Chapters 3 and 4, respectively. Analysts are also under persistent pressure not to miss critical signals (Connors et al., 2004). When a surprise occurs, it is often considered to be an "intelligence failure," most often a failure in analysis; the terrorist attacks of September 11, 2001, and the claim that Iraq possessed weapons of mass destruction are two examples often cited (Johnston, 2005; Lowenthal and Marks, 2015).

In addition to core tasks associated with their fields of expertise and assigned accounts, analysts must coordinate and collaborate with peers and supervisors. They must carefully weigh the best and most accurate way to present complex assessments in situations that may be momentous, urgent, and politically charged. And they must shepherd an analytic report through a review process in which they must defend their analysis while being open to useful changes. These are but a few examples of a broader view of the analyst's job, with implications for the attributes to be assessed in a selection system. It is critical to clarify from the outset which facets of performance are of interest, and to design a selection system accordingly.

The Effectiveness and Utility of a Selection System

Perfect prediction of performance is an unattainable ideal. Performance is affected by a large number of factors—such as the support and mentoring available from supervisors and peers within the workplace and life circumstances (e.g., marital difficulties, child- or eldercare issues)—some of which are unknowable when individuals are hired and all of which can significantly influence a worker's performance. Thus the effectiveness of a selection system is best viewed in terms of improvement over a baseline level: a well-developed selection system might, for example, allow an employer to move from having 50 percent up to 70 percent of hires meet expectations. Without knowing what percentage of the IC analytic workforce meets expectations or their rate of turnover, the committee assumes that improvement in this regard is an objective.

Both initial development costs and per-person administration costs for sophisticated selection systems with multiple components can be substantial, but these costs must be evaluated relative to potential benefits. What is the value to the organization of, say, a 20 percent increase in the number of high-performing employees? Utility analysis is an approach used by industrial-organizational psychologists and human resources specialists to systematically balance multiple possible benefits and costs. Utility models express the benefits of selection systems using a variety of metrics, from percentage improvement in the proportion of hires reaching a specified performance threshold to increase in the dollar value of performance per employee per year resulting from the implementation of a selection system. Pushback against the initial costs of developing a selection system is not uncommon, and utility analysis is a useful tool for identifying benefits an improved workforce can bring. (See Cascio [1991] and Cascio and Scott [2017] for discussion of utility analyses applied to selection systems.)

Researchers studying selection have recently focused on troubling findings that are difficult to reconcile with expectations. For example, elaborate job simulations have been developed for use in evaluating job candidates, yet a meta-analytic comparison found that a brief multiple-choice test of cognitive ability had greater predictive power than a lengthy (e.g., 1- to 2-day) set of simulation-based assessments known as an assessment center (Schmidt and Hunter, 1998). A recent study has shed new light on this unexpected finding. Sackett and colleagues (2017a) note that meta-analytic comparisons of the validity of two predictors are questionable unless both predictors are compared using the same job and the same facet(s) of job performance. They found that in head-to-head comparisons in which both predictors were used with the same sample with the goal of predicting the same criteria, the assessment center had twice the predictive power of the short ability test. This evidence supports the utility of complex job simulations.

Workforce Selection: Implications for the Intelligence Community

There is strong evidence that the quality of selection decisions in virtually any organization can be improved with the use of scientifically based selection systems. Many organizations still rely on more casual and informal approaches to selection, using, for example, some form of resumé screening to reduce the applicant pool to a manageable size and then basing decisions primarily on interviews. The committee did not have access to information that would indicate where IC entities would fall on a continuum from informal to sophisticated selection approaches. Individuals who made presentations to the committee[3] did, however, describe the selection strategies used in some IC agencies and offered their suggestions for improvement. Among the attributes suggested for inclusion in a selection system were critical thinking skills, the ability to write, and the ability to prepare effective briefings; teamwork skills; openness to feedback; curiosity; a proactive personality; an orientation toward learning goals; the courage to deliver an unwanted message when necessary; the intellectual humility to consider that one's conclusions may be in error; and a willingness to stand one's ground under pressure.

---

[3]The committee held a workshop on workforce issues pertaining to national security on January 24, 2018; a summary of the workshop presentations and discussions can be found at http://sites.nationalacademies.org/DBASSE/BBCSS/DBASSE_183502. See also http://sites.nationalacademies.org/DBASSE/BBCSS/DBASSE_178412 for white papers on this topic.

> **Research Directions**
>
> *Investigate approaches for selecting those individuals likely to succeed in intelligence analyst roles, including the key attributes of such individuals and ways in which those attributes can best be measured.*
>
> The committee views these ideas about ways to improve selection within the IC as hypotheses in need of testing. The IC workforce leadership could conduct a systematic assessment of the intelligence analyst's job to determine whether these proposed attributes reflect an idiosyncratic view of what is needed for the job or there is in fact agreement among subject matter experts as to their relevance and importance. Existing measures may be available with which to select for attributes that survive such a review, or new measures for this purpose might be developed. The final step would be to develop hypotheses about the relationship of these measures to conceptually relevant job performance measures within the agencies.
>
> The committee also notes that while individual agencies may develop their selection systems independently, there may be merit in more cooperative efforts. An initial step would be job-analytic assessments to identify similarities and differences in the analyst's role across agencies. Once similarities had been identified, participating agencies could collaborate on the development and evaluation of potential new selection measures (Tippins and Macey, 2007). A cross-agency effort could have several benefits. First, if participating agencies shared the costs of the effort, they could likely accomplish more. Second, if researchers had access to more robust research samples—drawn from across the IC—they could better refine and improve selection processes. Finally, sharing of successes and failures in the development of selection systems would have obvious benefits for all the agencies.

RETAINING EFFECTIVE ANALYSTS

The research literature on employee turnover and retention is vast and nuanced. This is a topic that attracts a broad range of scholars, from psychologists to labor economists, and research has focused on issues affecting individual employees as well as their collective workgroups and organizations. Here we summarize findings from key research domains that could be applied to the job of the intelligence analyst, ranging from classic findings to modern advances.

Dissatisfaction and the Desirability of Movement

Although employee turnover has been an active research topic since the early 20th century, early investigations were largely atheoretical: only in the 1950s did researchers begin to articulate formalized theories about why people leave their jobs. The first attempt at a comprehensive theory of turnover was offered by James March and Nobel Prize winner Herbert Simon (1958) in their seminal book *Organizations*. The authors posited that turnover is influenced by (1) the desirability of movement (e.g., job dissatisfaction makes other jobs appear more attractive) and (2) ease of movement (e.g., perceptions of job opportunities).

The March–Simon model sparked both research on predictors of turnover and efforts to develop conceptual models of its determinants. Perhaps most notably, Mobley (1977) identified intermediate psychological processes that could explain how employees arrive at the decision to leave their jobs. Mobley proposed that turnover decisions result from a chain of cognitions and emotions in a process of (1) evaluating one's job, (2) experiencing (dis)satisfaction, (3) thinking of quitting, (4) considering the costs and benefits of quitting, (5) developing an intention to search for alternatives, (6) following through with a search, (7) evaluating alternatives, (8) comparing alternatives with one's present job, (9) developing an intention to quit or stay, and (10) choosing to quit or stay. Although he posed this as a linear process, Mobley noted that the strict progression of options need not occur in all cases and that choices might also be influenced by nonjob factors (e.g., relocating because of family members), the availability of unsolicited opportunities, or impulsive decisions to quit. Elaborations on this model included more processes and predictors of turnover. Mobley and colleagues (1979), for example, emphasized the role of expected utility judgments (i.e., evaluations regarding the likelihood that opportunities will provide desired outcomes) in turnover decisions.

The many predictive variables identified during the early days of research on turnover have been summarized in several meta-analyses over the past two decades. Of particular note is the work of Griffeth and colleagues (2000), who showed that turnover is not reliably predicted by such individual characteristics as cognitive ability, education, training, tenure, or demographic factors, but is predicted by variables from the work context. These authors found, for example, that employees were *less* likely to leave their jobs when they reported more job satisfaction, supervisory satisfaction, coworker satisfaction, role clarity, participation, and organizational commitment. Turnover also was less likely among employees with more tenure (but only in samples with an average age under 40), as well as among those who exhibited high performance within a year of the performance assessment. On the other hand, employees were more likely to leave their jobs when they reported greater role overload, role conflict, overall stress, alternative job opportunities, comparisons of alternatives with their present jobs, and turnover intentions/cognitions (e.g., search intentions, intention to quit, thinking of quitting, withdrawal cognitions, expected utility of withdrawal). Withdrawal behaviors such as lateness and absenteeism were also predictive of turnover.

An Unfolding Model of Turnover Decisions

Research on employee turnover underwent a transformation in response to a highly influential paper by Lee and Mitchell (1994) describing an "unfolding" model of turnover. In contrast with earlier researchers, who focused on job attitudes and utility judgments as predictors of turnover, these authors used qualitative methods to describe the types of events that precipitated workers' job searches. They described how disruptive events they called "shocks" can lead employees to quit and described four paths, or sequences of events and cognitions, that can lead to stay/quit decisions. One path is similar to the one established in the earlier turnover research (e.g., Mobley, 1977), in which job satisfaction and searches for alternatives predict turnover decisions. The other three paths are initiated by shocks that prompt workers to evaluate their options and determine which option best matches their mental image of a preferred job situation. Path 1 is activated by an event that prompts action on a preexisting turnover plan (e.g., a pregnancy prompts a worker to quit in order to devote time to parenting, consistent with an existing plan to quit upon becoming pregnant). Path 2 is activated when a negative event prompts a reevaluation of the worker's fit with the job, which leads to quitting if there is a misfit (e.g., a request to falsify financial records prompts a worker to quit because of misalignment between the worker's and manager's morals). Here the "shock" is so severe that the worker quits before initiating a search for alternatives. Finally, path 3 is activated when an event prompts a worker to actively seek out and evaluate alternative job opportunities; if the search turns up an alternative that fits with the worker's preferred job image, the worker is inclined to quit his or her current job.

Shifting the Focus from Who Leaves to Who Stays

After introducing their unfolding model, Mitchell and colleagues (2001) again changed the direction of the field by shifting the focus from determinants of leaving to determinants of staying. They introduced the concept of "job embeddedness," which represents a collection of work and nonwork factors that encourage people to remain in their jobs. They proposed three general categories of embeddedness mechanisms that can predict staying: (1) links (i.e., connections with people, teams, and groups, both at and outside of work); (2) fit (i.e., workers' compatibility with their job, organization, and community); and (3) sacrifices (i.e., things one would have to give up if one took another job). The authors also posited that embeddedness helps predict both turnover intentions and voluntary turnover, even after accounting for the predictive power of job attitudes, job alternatives, and job search behaviors.

Job embeddedness can be combined with the unfolding model for a more comprehensive explanation of job turnover. According to Hom and colleagues (2012), a simple stay/leave dichotomy is not always useful because "everyone eventually leaves; no one stays with an organization forever" (p. 831). They identified different types of people who stay and who leave and broadened the range of turnover criteria that researchers should consider. In this paradigm, it is not enough simply to know whether an employee quits. It is also valuable to know (1) whether the employee wants to leave or stay, (2) whether the employer is exerting pressure for the employee to leave or stay, and (3) whether extrinsic factors (e.g., pay, benefits, perks) exert pressure for the employee to leave or stay. The combination of these three factors, along with the decision to stay or quit, gives rise to four general "proximal withdrawal states": (1) enthusiastic stayers, (2) reluctant stayers, (3) reluctant leavers, and (4) enthusiastic leavers (i.e., the type of leaver who is of interest in most historical turnover research). These general categories can be further broken down to understand workers' motives. Workers from different categories are motivated by different forces, demonstrate different types of attitudes and behaviors in response to their work situations, take different amounts of time to exit the organization, and exit for different reasons (e.g., another job, retirement, disability). This model emphasizes that not all turnover is bad turnover: some employees exit an organization as a result of pressure from the organization to leave, in reaction to a poor performance appraisal, or because of low perceived fit. Similarly, not all turnover, such as that due to retirement, disability, or familial relocation, is avoidable. By clarifying whether turnover is functional/dysfunctional and avoidable/unavoidable, the taxonomy of proximal withdrawal states is useful for making sense of how, why, and when employees leave an organization.

Social Influences in the Turnover Process

A relatively recent development in research on turnover is the study of "turnover contagion," which occurs when an individual's turnover is influenced by that of coworkers. Felps and colleagues (2009) proposed that workers' job search behaviors can be influenced by coworkers through social comparison processes. When workers observe colleagues updating resumés, searching for job postings, or taking time off from work for interviews, they can be provoked to begin engaging in their own turnover cognitions (e.g., "If so-and-so is trying to leave, should I start looking for other opportunities, too?"). In support of the theory of turnover contagion, Felps and colleagues (2009) found that coworkers' job search behaviors predicted individual turnover above and beyond individual job attitudes, coworker job attitudes, and other individual- and group-level predictors. In terms of the unfolding model, seeing coworkers engage in job search activities could be viewed as a "shock" that initiates an individual's own evaluation of present and alternative opportunities.

Unmet Expectations and the Value of Realistic Job Previews

The notion that turnover is driven by unmet expectations has driven a large body of work on ways to give potential new employees a realistic job preview to limit inaccurate expectations. Work on such previews has explored the association between their use and both affective and behavioral consequences on the job, including turnover. Meta-analyses of the relevant research have identified small but statistically reliable associations between the use of previews and lower turnover (Earnest et al., 2011; Phillips, 1998; Premack and Wanous, 1985). Experiments in the use of previews have been conducted in a variety of settings with varying degrees of fidelity, so it is particularly valuable to note that the association between previews and turnover is slightly stronger in field than in laboratory studies (Earnest et al., 2011). While previews have shown benefit when presented both before and after hiring (Earnest et al., 2011; Phillips, 1998), the most recent meta-analytic evidence suggests that the effect of posthire previews is slightly stronger (Earnest et al., 2011).

Although it has been presumed that previews are effective because they increase the likelihood that new hires' expectations will be met, recent work suggests that the primary mechanism may be perceptions of employers' honesty. Earnest and colleagues (2011) meta-analytically tested met expectations, role clarity, perceptions of honesty, and attraction as mediators between previews and turnover. These researchers found that previews had a significant effect on turnover through perceptions of honesty, but not through the other mechanisms.

Collective Turnover

We have focused thus far on research examining what prompts individuals to stay or leave. But researchers have also explored the issue on the aggregate level, examining "collective turnover," where the unit of analysis is the group or organization (Hausknecht, 2017). Here the outcome is the rate of turnover in the group or organization, and aggregate-level variables (e.g., human resources practices) are examined as predictors of turnover rates. In their meta-analysis, Hancock and colleagues (2017) found less collective turnover in units with high-commitment human resources systems (i.e., those whose practices increase employees' sense of investment in the organization); more personnel changes; and lower turnover intentions. Less turnover also is seen in units with stronger perceptions of cohesiveness and teamwork, management and leadership quality, satisfaction, commitment, climate and culture, and justice and fairness.

Retaining Effective Analysts: Implications for the Intelligence Community

Keeping employees in the organization once they have joined is a focus of the retention literature, but a related important issue is whether the pool of recruits persists through the application process or drops out along the way. Observers have noted that while the IC identifies and attracts highly qualified individuals, many candidates opt not to join the IC workforce because of the lengthy and difficult hiring process (Miles, 2016). A prospective employee may wait as long as 20 weeks after submitting an application before receiving approval for a position at the Office of the Director of National Intelligence (ODNI).[4]

Despite decades of research on turnover and a large volume of published findings on the subject, it remains unclear whether those findings generalize to the IC. Many turnover studies are conducted in high-volume employment settings (e.g., fast food restaurants, retail stores, call centers), and meta-analyses on turnover have not explored effects at the level of specific industries/occupations/jobs with confidence because of the limited availability of data points. Thus, the relationships described above may or may not generalize to the IC setting. However, the literature can certainly provide a set of testable hypotheses that could be examined in the IC context.

---

[4] See "Application Timeline" at https://www.intelligencecareers.gov/icapply.html [February 2019].

> **Research Directions**
>
> *Examine the applicability of key practical insights from research on employee turnover to the intelligence analyst workforce.*
>
> Research suggests the potential diagnostic/intervention value of tracking employee metrics over time and attending to trajectories in individuals' job attitudes (e.g., engagement, job satisfaction, organizational commitment), performance, and withdrawal behaviors (e.g., lateness, absenteeism) to identify those at risk of attrition. Negative job attitudes are associated with turnover, and those who quit voluntarily tend to exhibit worse performance in the year leading up to their exit (Griffeth et al., 2000). Intervening with employees who show declines in attitudes, attendance, and/or performance could help identify and resolve workplace concerns that would otherwise lead to turnover. Research also shows the role of job embeddedness in employee retention, and it therefore appears plausible that interventions might be designed to develop and strengthen embeddedness.
>
> There is also evidence that retention can be boosted by transparent and realistic job previews that can calibrate newcomers' job expectations, promote perceptions of organizational honesty, and help those with low perceived fit with the job self-select out of the recruitment/selection process (Earnest et al., 2011). Helping candidates make an informed choice about pursuing the job can help reduce the organizational burden associated with dysfunctional avoidable turnover.
>
> The IC could benefit from translational research to assess the application of these findings for the analytic workforce.

DEVELOPING SKILLS THROUGH FORMAL TRAINING AND INFORMAL LEARNING

Further developing existing knowledge and skills and acquiring new ones are key objectives for most workers, including intelligence analysts. IC leadership has identified "improved opportunities for achieving and maintaining mastery in their chosen career fields" as important for IC leaders and staff and for maintaining and sustaining "current and emerging mission success" (Office of the Director of National Intelligence, 2014, p. 7). These opportunities include acquiring new knowledge and skills to increase effectiveness in one's current role, as well as to advance to a broader career path. Organizations commonly invest effort in helping workers acquire and develop knowledge and skills that are relevant to their current roles or progression to new roles within the organization (rather than learning that would help individuals pursue a change of career and/or organization).

Organizations foster learning by providing training, whether formal (e.g., classroom-based) or informal (e.g., offered by mentors), as well as by supporting autonomous learning, in which the individual identifies the need for new knowledge and/or skills and a mechanism for acquiring them. All of these types of learning will be increasingly critical for intelligence analysts as new technologies become available and must be quickly assimilated into their workflow and as the nature of technologically based conflict evolves. Indeed, the analyst's job by its very nature requires constant adaptation and learning.

Formal training, which is provided by most organizations, has been studied extensively (see, e.g., Aguinis and Kraiger, 2009; Salas and Cannon-Bowers, 2001). However, informal training is increasingly widespread: according to one study, it accounts for up to 75 percent of learning in organizations (Bear et al., 2008). Formal training is common for new employees who may not be fully ready to step immediately into the job, but is also used to help employees remain current and/or become more effective as the job and work environment change. This type of formal training may be a one-time occurrence (e.g., a change in technology requires updating skills), but the nature of the work may call for continuous learning, an ongoing process of updating and developing skills. Some employees are predisposed to orient themselves toward continuous learning, while others are not. A continuous learning orientation is also influenced by organizational values, and organizations use various measures to create incentives for and otherwise support such an orientation.

The IC has identified continuous learning as an important component in developing the analytic workforce. ODNI's *Human Capital Vision 2020* (Office of the Director of National Intelligence, 2014) identifies continuous learning as one of three focus areas for the IC, with the stated goal that "leaders and staff will have improved opportunities for achieving and maintaining mastery in their chosen career fields, resulting in a workforce better able to maintain and sustain current and emerging mission success" (p. 7).

Organizations and researchers have focused on formal means of providing continuous learning, but autonomous learning, also termed "informal" or "self-directed" learning, is an emerging research frontier (see Ellingson and Noe, 2017). Among the questions researchers have begun to explore is which organizational factors facilitate autonomous learning. For example, Tannenbaum and colleagues (2010) identify as a key factor an organizational climate that signals to employees that learning is a valued activity. A considerable body of research documents the importance of this factor with respect to formal training, and while the same might be hypothesized for autonomous learning, more empirical research on this linkage is needed. Other key organizational factors identified by Tannenbaum and colleagues (2010) include the opportunity to obtain feedback, tolerance of error as employees attempt to use new skills, support and encouragement from supervisors and peers, and the allocation of time for autonomous learning.

Tannenbaum and colleagues (2010) also identify individual factors that facilitate autonomous learning. One such factor is learning motivation, which has multiple facets—motivation to improve and learn (i.e., setting learning goals), motivation to take action in pursuit of these goals, motivation to seek feedback, and motivation to reflect upon one's learning experiences (see NASEM [2018a] for more on motivation and learning). Other facets include an internal locus of control (i.e., to what extent a person attributes outcomes to his or her own efforts and abilities), higher self-esteem, a feedback-seeking orientation, and a learning goal orientation (as opposed to a performance orientation, which does not facilitate the needed exploration and trial and error).

Other research delves more deeply into motivational processes underlying autonomous learning. For example, Vancouver and colleagues (2017) explored the application of self-regulatory theories[5] to goal setting in autonomous learning. The authors highlight the importance of the concept of self-efficacy, which encompasses an individual's assessment of (1) her current capability for the task in question, (2) the potential level of capability she might attain with investment in learning, (3) the likelihood that she will reach this potential, and (4) her ability to regulate the processes needed for this learning to take place. Other researchers focus on the distinction between a current state (e.g., current skill level) and a desired state (e.g., desired skill level). The central mechanism in these theories is a feedback loop between the current and desired states, with the discrepancy between the two driving action.

Self-regulatory frameworks have been used to examine a variety of questions relevant to autonomous learning. While much of the research examines pursuit of a single goal, an increasing number of researchers are recognizing that in many settings, individuals face competing goals. Autonomous learning in an organization is a classic example because time devoted to new learning is time not spent on current tasks. The process used to allocate effort in the face of competing goals is illuminated by a combination of research (e.g., Schmidt and DeShon, 2007) and computational modeling (Vancouver et al., 2010). This work has revealed that initial effort commonly is allocated to the task that is characterized by the greatest discrepancy between the current and desired states, and that this allocation shifts as performance deadlines approach. Halper (2015) provides another example, explicitly in the learning context, by examining the choice of whether to allocate learning effort to further build a strength or address a weakness. She found that if individuals were going to be evaluated in both areas, learning effort would focus on the weakness, whereas if individuals

---

[5]Self-regulatory theories describe the processes or consequences of establishing, planning, and revising goals (Austin and Vancouver, 1996; Kanfer, 1990).

could choose the area in which to be evaluated, they would choose the area of strength and allocate their learning effort to that area.

Research Directions

Explore organizational and individual factors that can facilitate autonomous learning in the IC context.

Autonomous learning is important for the work of the intelligence analyst. In a demanding job, there is tension between the need to allocate effort to meeting current task demands and a desire to invest in new knowledge and skill. Research suggests organizational features that influence this allocation, and an investigation into these features in the IC context appears promising. At the individual level, better understanding of how individuals choose to invest in learning would be useful.

SUPPORTING THE ANALYTIC WORKFORCE

As discussed in Chapter 7, fundamental capacity limits affect all humans. The tempo and complexity of intelligence analysis, including the need to assess large amounts of information, can tax or overload the processing capacity of the human agent. Mental and physical fatigue can in turn markedly reduce attention, leading to impaired performance and decreased efficiency (Grandjean, 1979). It is worth noting that these forms of fatigue—mental and physical—are at least partially independent; mental fatigue as manifested by performance deficits, for example, can occur in the absence of muscular or physiological fatigue (e.g., Van Custem et al., 2017). The ability to recognize the cause of and possibly mitigate cognitive decline related to mental fatigue would have clear benefits for the intelligence analyst, who often works under substantial time pressure and whose work may have life-and-death implications. There are many ways to reduce mental fatigue (e.g., promoting sleep, improving diet, increasing exercise), but the focus here is on methods based in neuroscience (including psychopharmacology), as they have the greatest potential to bring new benefits to the IC in the coming decade.

The study of neuroergonomics integrates theories and principles of ergonomics[6] and neuroscience to provide insights into brain function and behavior in a variety of settings, including at work (Parasuraman, 2011). The field of ergonomics originally focused on ways to increase productivity, particularly within physical work environments, but has expanded to encompass interactions between humans and the work ecosystem and

---

[6]The terms "ergonomics" and "human factors" are synonymous and used interchangeably.

ways to improve human well-being and overall ecosystem performance (Karwowski et al., 2003). One of the most widely studied topics in ergonomics is mental—not physical—workload (Wickens and McCarley, 2008).[7] Although neuroergonomics and neuroscience are distinct fields, studies and assessments in neuroergonomics rely heavily on current neuroimaging methods (see Box 8-2).

Researchers who work on resource theory have also contributed to understanding of the importance of cognitive workload for workforce performance. Study in this area has shown that, for tasks that are not highly automatic, performance is directly proportional to the use of attentional resources. Multiple cognitive resources are available and may be recruited in varying combinations when two or more tasks, such as driving and texting, are performed simultaneously (Wickens, 1984, 2002; see also Wickens and McCarley, 2008; Mehta and Parasuraman, 2013). Attentional distractions can be external (e.g., from the environment) or internal (e.g., mind wandering), and both can hinder vigilance and performance, particularly

---

**BOX 8-2
Neuroimaging Techniques Used in Neuroergonomics**

Neuroimaging techniques are used in research (e.g., to identify neural correlates with cognition) but can also be used to monitor brain function and to support the identification of interventions for use in the workplace and other contexts. Most brain imaging studies have focused on individuals, but such approaches could also be used to explore social dynamics and other attributes of teams. Neuroergonomics uses two categories of neuroimaging techniques for workplace assessments and interventions: those that detect or measure (1) direct neuronal activity in response to a stimulus or action (e.g., electroencephalography [EEG] or event-related potentials [ERPs]) and (2) indirect neuronal activity measured via metabolic indicators (e.g., functional magnetic resonance imaging [fMRI], positron emission tomography [PET], functional near infrared spectroscopy [fNIRS]) (Mehta and Parasuraman, 2013). Which neuroimaging method to use in neuroergonomic assessments depends on the question of interest, which will determine the necessary resolution (both temporal and spatial) and degree of immobility needed. Less technology-heavy methods, such as measuring blink rate (Caffier et al., 2003), heart rate (Jiao et al., 2004), and heart rate variability (De Rivecourt et al., 2008), have also been used to evaluate cognitive workload.

---

[7] Mental workload that is too high or too low can cause the human–system performance to decline, so workload assessments are conducted on existing systems and during the design phases of new systems, such as those described in Chapter 7.

in terms of perceptual sensitivity (Braboszcz and Delorme, 2011; Chun et al., 2011).

Cognitive workload is directly related to human agents' vigilance and their cognitive fatigue in work environments. Vigilance on critical tasks decreases with time spent on the task because cognitive resources get depleted (Davies and Parasuraman, 1982; Warm et al., 2008). A number of mitigation strategies can be used to address this decline in vigilance, depending on the nature of work tasks and settings. While loss of vigilance can be mitigated by reduced work hours and more frequent breaks, for example, these strategies may not be appropriate for time-sensitive intelligence analysis.

The use of "cueing" has been shown to improve performance on tasks that require vigilance (such as detecting particular phenomena), while also reducing or eliminating the decline in vigilance associated with time spent on the task (Wiener and Attwood, 1968). Cueing allows human agents to manage their information-processing (cognitive) resources by reducing the time during which they must remain vigilant. With cueing, the agent is prompted to monitor a display for the arrival of a signal, whereas without cueing, the agent must monitor the display at all times in anticipation of a signal, thereby using more cognitive resources. Cueing may therefore be an appropriate strategy for mitigating cognitive load on such tasks as monitoring input from human–machine teaming or input from sensors and other sources (see Chapter 7).

The use of a visual or auditory warning signal to refocus the human agent has been studied extensively in the context of driving. This work has shown, for example, that auditory warnings improve performance in drivers experiencing fatigue (and thus cognitive decline) (Lin et al., 2009, 2010). In these studies, however, the auditory feedback is provided after cognitive lapses (e.g., nonresponsiveness to simulated lane departures), and such delays in warning could have catastrophic results depending on the task at hand. To implement more timely warnings, Wang and colleagues (2014) proposed a smartphone-based system that would first detect and track the human agent's cognitive state and then deliver an arousing signal should cognitive fatigue be detected. Other researchers are pursuing mobile brain imaging techniques for workload and fatigue assessment. Gramann and colleagues (2011) identified two critical requirements of such systems: (1) robust mobile sensor technology to measure brain activity and (2) powerful computational software to process and analyze the data. The committee recognizes the potential security issues posed by wireless and mobile technologies in classified environments, but nevertheless notes the possibilities afforded by these technologies, which will continue to be refined and will likely be implemented in non-IC workforces over the next decade.

Another possible approach to mitigating decreased vigilance and cognitive fatigue is the use of noninvasive[8] brain stimulation. Noninvasive stimulation of the peripheral parasympathetic vagus nerve, for example, yields a specific pattern of brain activation and has been shown to have mood-elevating effects (Hein et al., 2013; Kraus et al., 2013). In this regard, the U.S. Department of Defense (specifically the Defense Advanced Research Projects Agency [DARPA]) has sponsored a program, Targeted Neuroplasticity Training, aimed at determining whether peripheral nerve stimulation can enhance learning and the development of cognitive skills. Research has also indicated that noninvasive transcutaneous direct current stimulation of the brain improves performance in professional athletes (e.g., Okano et al., 2015). Noninvasive stimulation techniques have been used as well to modulate brain activity in order to improve performance on cognitive or motor tasks and to reduce or eliminate normally occurring performance declines in tasks requiring vigilance (Coffman et al., 2014). Follow-up work (e.g., Nelson et al., 2014) has explored questions about the most effective timing for applying noninvasive stimulation techniques and other questions, some in a military context (Nelson et al., 2016).

This line of research suggests that enhancement of attentional performance in the absence of sleep deprivation or other fatigue-inducing factors can be effective, but additional research is needed to examine the long-term effectiveness of noninvasive brain stimulation as a strategy for mitigating decreased task vigilance and cognitive fatigue. Further, because noninvasive brain stimulation methods require the application of either magnetic pulses or a small electric current to the scalp, careful consideration of the ethical use of such devices to improve work performance is needed.

Pharmacological solutions to cognitive fatigue have also been investigated. Examples include a mouth rinse with caffeine and maltodextrin (uningested) to counter mental fatigue (Van Cutsem et al., 2018) and Modafinil (a weak dopamine reuptake inhibitor and neuropeptide activator) to keep sleep-deprived individuals awake (Fernández et al., 2015). Further research on the efficacy of such approaches in an IC context is needed.

Physiologically based methods for cognitive enhancement are not limited to the neuroscience/neuroimaging and pharmacological domains. Any procedure capable of enhancing ongoing neural processing may have performance-enhancing effects in some domains or contexts. Further, neuroscience-based interventions do not necessarily require sophisticated instrumentation. One ongoing line of research concerns the effects of the circadian rhythm on behavior and cognition, an active area of investigation in the basic science community as well as the military (see, e.g., the

---

[8]Noninvasive in this context refers to a technique that entails no incisions or insertions in the body.

Military Health System Research Symposium [MHSRS], August 2017). Even relatively simple manipulation of aspects of the environment, such as illumination levels and light frequencies, may hold potential for enhancing performance (Zakerian et al., 2018).

Likewise, researchers have noted a number of possible cognitive benefits of automation in the workplace, including a reduction in workload, fatigue, and stress induced by high-stakes situations. Automation can free attentional resources that can be allocated to other tasks, decrease the occurrence of human errors, and improve data monitoring and analytic capabilities (Breton and Bossé, 2003). The use of adaptive automation (such as that described in Chapter 7) may reduce the cognitive load for the human agent, particularly during emergencies, time-sensitive tasks, and other circumstances that increase task load. In adaptive automation, the workload assigned to human and machine agents becomes flexible to allow for greater use of automation during conditions of high task load (e.g., emergencies) and less use during normal operations (Lintern, 2012). Researchers have investigated neuroergonomic assessments and other measures that could be used to incorporate such adaptive systems into the workflow (Byrne and Parasuraman, 1996; Ting et al., 2010) by assessing the agent's state in real (or near real) time. The accuracy rates of statistical and machine learning techniques (e.g., discriminant analysis, artificial neural networks, Bayesian networks, fuzzy logic) implemented in real time for this purpose has been approximately 62–85 percent (Baldwin and Penaranda, 2012; Berka et al., 2004; Borghetti et al., 2017; Ting et al., 2010; Wang et al., 2011).

Despite the evidence of potential benefits, the utility of automation in the workplace depends on a number of factors, such as the nature of tasks that are automated, the human oversight required, the age and experience of the workforce, and the accuracy of the automation. Automation can even have a counterintuitive effect on human workload. Automation does decrease workload, but it can also increase workload because the automation itself must be monitored, a task added to the human workload (Parasuraman, 1987). Other research indicates that task performance, situational awareness, and workload effects are dependent on the level of automation and the length of time a task is automated (Kaber and Endsley, 2004).[9] When designing complex human–machine systems as a mitigation strategy for cognitive fatigue, then, it is important to evaluate both human and machine abilities and limitations, as well as the appropriate levels of

---

[9] In dual-task situations, low levels of automation lead to improved performance, and intermediate levels of automation lead to improved situational awareness on the primary task. But when a greater percentage of the primary task is automated, the human agent is able to shift resources, which leads to improved performance on the secondary task.

automation. Not doing so can lead to safety, security, and performance issues (Habib et al., 2017).

Potentially viable neuroergonomic, pharmacological, and neuroscience methods, as well as biologically based interventions, for assessing attention and arousal, workload and workload capacity, and stress and fatigue hold potential for application in the IC. However, this area is in need of further research.

Biological interventions for cognitive enhancement, be they behavioral, electrical, mechanical, or pharmacological (e.g., nootropic agents) may have the potential for negative or adverse outcomes. Any such approach to performance enhancement must be considered from the standpoint of the risk–reward trade-off. Some of the approaches mentioned here have been studied extensively for safety. For example, transcranial brain stimulation has been the subject of numerous safety reviews that have shown no serious adverse events in tens of thousands of patients and subjects across varying health spectrums (Antal et al., 2017; Bikson et al., 2016). Other interventions, however, need to be carefully evaluated for efficacy and safety.

Clear guidelines for the ethical application of such methods in the IC workforce are needed. Moreover, workers' acceptance of and compliance with their use will depend on input from the intended users into the design of methods for monitoring cognitive workload/fatigue and potential interventions (including adaptive systems) (Mehta and Parasuraman, 2013).

Research Directions

Investigate the challenges and ethical concerns associated with neuroergonomic methods for combating fatigue and cognitive decline in the workplace.

A number of challenges remain with respect to implementing neuroergonomic-based adaptive systems in the workplace. Supervisors need to be cautious regarding the accuracy of assessment measures and the use of neuroergonomic interventions for cognitive fatigue until these challenges have been addressed. One technical issue is the detection and removal of artifacts from the neuroimaging data used to assess and implement a mitigation strategy, which is difficult to do in real time and requires additional research. Likewise, the reliability, real-world validity, and stability of neuroergonomic measures need to be further assessed both within and between individual analyses (Wang et al., 2011). Practically speaking, the implementation of neuroergonomic assessments in the workforce requires that individuals be willing to have their brain activity monitored, either continuously or periodically. Otherwise, the use of such methods could lead to an inability to fill open positions, disaffection among the existing workforce, and employees' development of counterassessment strategies to work around the monitoring.

> More important, a number of ethical questions and issues need to be addressed before neuroergonomic assessments and interventions are implemented (see Keebler et al. [2010] for a summary of neuroethics in neuroergonomics). For example, concerns about basic human subjects protection and privacy concerns are raised by the sensitive data collected through neuroergonomic/neuroimaging methods, as these data are not collected explicitly from individuals but through their brain activity. Further, the potential for misuse of these data, as well as related neuromodulation interventions, is of critical concern. Although such interventions are generally classified as noninvasive, risks are associated with their use. Thus, potential ethical issues include the remote possibility of an adverse medical event associated with neuromodulatory (as well as pharmacological) interventions and the possibility of an unanticipated finding from the monitoring/assessment carried out as part of these interventions.

CONCLUSIONS

Both relatively settled and emerging findings from the fields of industrial-organizational psychology and human resource development suggest the value of significant modifications and adaptations in the management of the analytic workforce, the selection of candidates, and the way organizations and workflow are structured. While the committee was unable to gather systematic information about current analytic approaches across the IC, it is likely that agencies make use of some of these methods. Thus at least some IC agencies may rightly conclude that they have already incorporated the ideas and approaches discussed in this chapter. It is also likely, however, that at least some agencies have not implemented these ideas and approaches at the scale and with the complexity that are possible, and so would be well served by a more in-depth understanding of the benefits of the existing and emerging research presented here.

The research highlighted in this chapter includes some ideas and approaches that could be integrated immediately into the intelligence analysis workforce, as well as others that will be increasingly applicable as they evolve. The findings, methods, and tools described in this chapter can be used to strengthen the analyst workforce and prepare it to meet emerging security challenges, make optimal use of available technologies, and collaborate with others who are instrumental to analytic success (including machines). The committee sees both (1) opportunities that can be exploited regardless of whether or how quickly innovations in methods for sensemaking and human–machine interactions may occur, and (2) opportunities to transform the workforce to compete with the intelligence efforts of other nations as they also innovate and exploit new technologies.

Translational research is needed, however, to identify specific ways the IC can take advantage of these opportunities. Moreover, the nature of analytic work is a moving target. In the next 10 years, new work challenges, new analytic technologies, and new work practices can be expected to emerge, and new collaborations will become necessary. Selection practices, training regimes, and teamwork requirements will need to be adapted to the new work requirements that will result. Therefore, additional research will be needed to translate the opportunities discussed in this chapter accordingly.

This chapter has reviewed three domains—employee selection, training, and retention—in which well-developed bodies of knowledge can support effective translational research for the IC environment. It has also reviewed a fourth domain—mitigating cognitive fatigue—in which research is still at a relative early stage, and in which more work is needed and ethical challenges must be addressed before conclusions about applicability to the IC can be drawn. Systematic attention to all of these issues will be essential for the IC to ensure that its workforce is optimized for the future.

Important questions also remain for which research has not yet provided clear answers. An important example is how the IC can most profitably recruit potential employees likely to be interested in—and to succeed at—intelligence analysis. Nor have questions about, for example, factors that may attract or repel promising young people and generational differences that may call for an array of approaches yet been systematically addressed. Similarly, the use of gaming and simulation in a training context may hold promise for intelligence analysis, but no body of research sufficient to guide the IC in this area currently exists. Answers to these and other questions will be important to the intelligence analysis enterprise moving forward, and the IC will need a mechanism for monitoring ongoing developments in potentially applicable research.

CONCLUSION 8-1: A range of personal attributes—including skills in critical evaluation, writing and presentation, and teamwork; openness to feedback; and a continuous learning orientation—contribute to successful job performance as an intelligence analyst. To strengthen its capacity to select individuals well suited to work as an intelligence analyst, the Intelligence Community (IC) would benefit from

- regularly updating its assessment of the facets of the analyst's job performance that are of greatest value to the IC and the attributes most useful for selection of personnel for intelligence analysis roles;
- having the capacity to measure a broad range of attributes for use in selecting individuals who possess those attributes; and
- evaluating the predictive power and potential ethical implications of such assessment devices as digital games, gleaning information

about candidates from social media, and using machine learning approaches to extract information from interviews and resumes and develop scoring algorithms.

CONCLUSION 8-2: A large body of social and behavioral sciences research identifies individual and organizational factors linked to employee retention, including employees' attitudes and engagement, unit cohesiveness, and leader quality, but these factors have not been examined in the Intelligence Community (IC) context. Translational work examining the role of these potential influencing factors could aid in managing retention in the IC.

CONCLUSION 8-3: A systematic review of the degree to which the organizational culture within the agencies of the Intelligence Community supports both organizationally directing training and autonomous learning could provide valuable information that could be used to promote these means of enhancing the skills of the analytic workforce. This review could focus on practices that promote such a culture, including

- opportunities for workers to receive feedback;
- tolerance for error as employees attempt to use new skills;
- support and encouragement from supervisors and peers; and
- allocation of time for autonomous learning.

CONCLUSION 8-4: Emerging research indicates that developing tools and methods could be used to assess and mitigate issues related to the effects of work in the high-stress environment of intelligence analysis, including cognitive fatigue, reduced attention, impaired performance, and decreased efficiency. Possibilities include the application of neuroergonomics (e.g., cueing, visual or auditory warning signals, automation); neuroscience (e.g., noninvasive brain stimulation); and neuropharmacology. The development of effective and safe tools and methods ready for implementation would require (1) research on the utility and applicability of these methods in the Intelligence Community environment, and (2) careful consideration of safety and ethical issues related to their use.

CONCLUSION 8-5: To fully benefit from research findings relevant to the development of an optimal analytic workforce, the Intelligence Community (IC) would need to invest in research and evaluation to guide their application in the context of intelligence analysis. Translating key insights about selection, training, retention of, and support for the IC analytic workforce will in itself require a team approach in which members of the IC, SBS researchers, applied scientists, and others collaborate to help translate the approaches discussed here for the IC context and assess their effectiveness.

REFERENCES

Agrawal, D., Bersin, J., Lahiri, G., Schwartz, J., and Volini, E. (2018). Introduction: The rose of the social enterprise. *Deloitte Insights,* March 28. Available: https://www2.deloitte.com/insights/us/en/focus/human-capital-trends/2018/introduction.html [December 2018].

Aguinis, H., and Kraiger, K. (2009). Benefits of training and development for individuals and teams, organizations, and society. *Annual Review of Psychology, 60,* 451–474. doi:10.1146/annurev.psych.60.110707.163505.

Antal, A., Alekseichuk, I., Bikson, M., Brockmöller, J., Brunoni, A.R., Chen, R., Cohen, L.G., Dowthwaite, G., Ellrich, J., Flöel, A., Fregni, F., George, M.S., Hamilton, R., Haueisen, J., Herrmann, C.S., Hummel, F.C., Lefaucheur, J.P., Liebetanz, D., Loo, C.K., McCaig, C.D., Miniussi, C., Miranda, P.C., Moliadze, V., Nitsche, M.A., Nowak, R., Padberg, F., Pascual-Leone, A., Poppendieck, W., Priori, A., Rossi, S., Rossini, P.M., Rothwell, J., Rueger, M.A., Ruffini, G., Schellhorn, K., Siebner, H.R., Ugawa, Y., Wexler, A., Ziemann, U., Hallett, M., and Paulus, W. (2017). Low intensity transcranial electric stimulation: Safety, ethical, legal, regulatory and application guidelines. *Clinical Neurophysiology, 128*(9), 1774–1809. doi:10.1016/j.clinph.2017.06.001.

Austin, J.T., and Vancouver, J.B. (1996). Goal constructs in psychology: Structure, process, and content. *Psychological Bulletin, 120*(3), 338–375. doi:10.1037/0033-2909.120.3.338.

Baldwin, C.L., and Penaranda, B. (2012). Adaptive training using an artificial neural network and EEG metrics for within- and cross-task workload classification. *Neuroimage, 59*(1), 48–56. doi:10.1016/j.neuroimage.2011.07.047.

Bear, D.J., Thompson, H.B., Morrison, C.L., Vickers, M., Paradise, A., Czarnowsky, M., Soyars, M., and King, K. (2008). *Tapping the Potential of Informal Learning: An ASTD Research Study.* Alexandria, VA: American Society for Training and Development.

Berka, C., Levendowski, D.J., Cvetinovic, M.M., Petrovic, M.M., Davis, G., Lumicao, M.N., Zivkovic, V.T., Popovic, M.V., and Olmstead, R. (2004). Real-time analysis of EEG indexes of alertness, cognition, and memory acquired with a wireless EEG headset. *International Journal of Human–Computer Interactions, 17*(2), 150–171. doi:10.1207/s15327590ijhc172_3.

Bersin, J. (2015). The geeks arrive in HR: People analytics is here. *Forbes,* February 1. Available: https://www.forbes.com/sites/joshbersin/2015/02/01/geeks-arrive-in-hr-people-analytics-is-here/#24d8463373b4 [December 2018].

Bikson, M., Grossman, P., Thomas, C., Zannou, A.L., Jiang, J., Adnan, T., Mourdoukoutas, A.P., Kronberg, G., Truong, D., Boggio, P., Brunoni, A.R., Charvet, L., Fregni, F., Fritsch, B., Gillick, B., Hamilton, R.H., Hampstead, B.M., Jankord, R., Kirton, A., Knotkova, H., Liebetanz, D., Liu, A., Loo, C., Nitsche, M.A., Reis, J., Richardson, J.D., Rotenberg, A., Turkeltaub, P.E., and Woods, A. (2016). Safety of transcranial direct current stimulation: Evidence-based update 2016. *Brain Stimulation, 9*(5), 641–661. doi:10.1016/j.brs.2016.06.004.

Bock, L. (2015). *Work Rules: Insights from Inside Google That Will Transform How You Live and Lead.* Boston, MA: Twelve.

Borghetti, B.J., Giametta, J.J., and Rusnock, C.F. (2017). Assessing continuous operator workload with a hybrid scaffolded neuroergonomic modeling approach. *Human Factors, 59*(1), 134–146. doi:10.1177/0018720816672308.

Braboszcz, C., and Delorme, A. (2011). Lost in thoughts: Neural markers of low alertness during mind wandering. *Neuroimage*, 54(4), 3040–3047. doi:10.1016/j.neuroimage.2010.10.008.

Breton, R., and Bossé, E. (2003). The cognitive costs and benefits of automation. In *The Role of Humans in Intelligent and Automated Systems* (RTO-MP-088). France: Research and Technology Organisation/North Atlantic Treaty Organisation. doi:10.14339/RTO-MP-088.

Byrne, E.A., and Parasuraman, R. (1996). Psychophysiology and adaptive automation. *Biological Psychology*, 42(3), 249–268. doi:10.1016/0301-0511(95)05161-9.

Caffier, P.P., Erdmann, U., and Ullsperger, P. (2003). Experimental evaluation of eye-blink parameters as a drowsiness measure. *European Journal of Applied Physiology*, 89(3-4), 319–325.

Campbell, J.P., McCloy, R.A., Oppler, S.H., and Sager, C.E. (1993). A theory of performance. In N. Schmitt, and C.W. Borman (Eds.), *Personnel Selection in Organizations* (pp. 35–70). San Francisco, CA: Jossey-Bass.

Cascio, W.F. (1991). *Costing Human Resources: The Financial Impact of Behavior in Organizations* (3rd ed.). Boston, MA: Kent.

Cascio, W., and Scott, J. (2017). The business value of employee selection. In J.L. Farr and N.T. Tippins (Eds.), *Handbook of Employee Selection* (pp. 226–248). New York: Taylor and Francis.

Chun, M.M., Golomb, J.D, and Turk-Browne, N.T. (2011). A taxonomy of external and internal attention. *Annual Review of Psychology*, 62, 73–101. doi:10.11496/annurev.psych.093008.100427.

Coffman, B.A., Clark, V.P., and Parasuraman, R. (2014). Battery powered thought: Enhancement of attention, learning, and memory in healthy adults using transcranial direct simulation. *Neuroimage*, 85(Pt. 3), 895–908. doi:10.1016/j.neuroimage.2013.07.083.

Connors, E.S., Craven, P.L., McNeese, M.D., Jefferson, T., Jr., Bains, P., and Hall, D.L. (2004). An application of the Akadam approach to intelligence analyst work. *Proceedings of the Human Factors and Ergonomics Society 48th Annual Meeting*, 627–628. Available: https://pdfs.semanticscholar.org/93ff/40b52a54d919bbe3295c4590fced7730dc9a.pdf [February 2019].

Davies, D.R., and Parasuraman, R. (1982). *The Psychology of Vigilance*. London, UK: Academic Press.

Dawson, J., and Thomson, R. (2018). The future cybersecurity workforce: Going beyond technical skills for successful cyber performance. *Frontiers in Psychology*, 9, 744. doi:10.3389/fpsyg.2018.00744.

De Rivecourt, M., Kuperus, M.N., Post, W.J., and Mulder L.J.M. (2008). Cardiovascular and eye activity measures as indices for momentary changes in mental effort during simulated flight. *Ergonomics*, 51(9), 1295–1319. doi:10.1080/00140130802120267.

Earnest, D.R., Allen, D.G., and Landis, R.S. (2011). Mechanisms linking realistic job previews with turnover: A meta-analytic path analysis. *Personnel Psychology*, 64(4), 865–897. doi:10.1111/j.1744-6570.2011.01230.x.

Ellingson, J.E., and Noe, R.A. (2017). *Autonomous Learning in the Workplace*. New York: Routledge.

Felps, W., Mitchell, T.R., Hekman, D.R., Lee, T.W., Holtom, B.C., and Harman, W.S. (2009). Turnover contagion: How coworkers' job embeddedness and job search behaviors influence quitting. *Academy of Management Journal*, 52(3), 545–561. doi:10.5465/AMJ.2009.41331075.

Fernández, A., Mascayano, F., Lips, W., Painel, A., Norambuena, J., and Madrid, E. (2015). Effects of modafinil on attention performance, short-term memory and executive function in university students: A randomized trial. *Medwave*, 25(5), e6166. doi:10.5867/medwave.2015.05.6166.

Gentry, J. (2015). Has the ODNI improved U.S. intelligence analysis? *International Journal of Intelligence and Counterintelligence*, 28(4), 637–661.

Gonzalez-Mulé, E., Mount, M.K., and Oh, I.-S. (2014). A meta-analysis of the relationship between general mental ability and nontask performance. *Journal of Applied Psychology*, 99(6), 1222–1243. doi:10.1037/a0037547.

Gramann, K., Gwin, J.T., Ferris, D.P., Oie, J., Jung, T.P., Lin, C.T., Liao, L.D., and Makeig, S. (2011). Cognition in action: Imaging brain/body dynamics in mobile humans. *Review of Neuroscience*, 22(6), 593–608. doi:10.1515/RNS.2011.047.

Grandjean, E. (1979). Fatigue in industry. *British Journal of Industrial Medicine*, 36(3), 175–186.

Griffeth, R.W., Hom, P.W., and Gaertner, S. (2000). A meta-analysis of antecedents and correlates of employee turnover: Update, moderator tests, and research implications for the next millennium. *Journal of Management*, 26(3), 463–488. doi:10.1177/014920630002600305.

Habib, L., Pacaux-Lemoine, M.-P., and Millot, P. (2017). A method for designing levels of automation based on a human–machine cooperation model. *IFAC-PapersOnLine*, 50(1), 1327–1377. doi:10.1016/j.ifacol.2017.08.235.

Halper, L. (2015). *Continuous Learning: Choosing and Allocating Resources to Strengths and Weaknesses* (Electronic Thesis or Dissertation). Available: https://etd.ohiolink.edu/!etd.send_file?accession=ohiou1427828223&disposition=inline [February 2019].

Hancock, J.I., Allen, D.G., and Soelberg, C. (2017). Collective turnover: An expanded meta-analytic exploration and comparison. *Human Resource Management Review*, 27(1), 61–86. doi:10.1016/j.hrmr.2016.06.003.

Hausknecht, J.P. (2017). Collective turnover. *Annual Review of Organizational Psychology and Organizational Behavior*, 4(1), 527–544. doi:10.1146/annurev-orgpsych-032516-113139.

Hein, E., Nowak, M., Kiess, O., Biermann, T., Bayerlein, K., Kornhuber, J., and Kraus, T. (2013). Auricular transcutaneous electrical nerve stimulation in depressed patients: A randomized controlled pilot study. *Journal of Neural Transmission*, 120(5), 821–827. doi:10.1007/s00702-012-0908-6.

Hom, P.W., Mitchell, T.R., Lee, T.W., and Griffeth, R.W. (2012). Reviewing employee turnover: Focusing on proximal withdrawal states and an expanded criterion. *Psychological Bulletin*, 138(5), 831–858.

Jiao, K., Li, Z., Chen, M., Wang, C., and Qi, S. (2004). Effect of different vibration frequencies on heart rate variability and driving fatigue in healthy drivers. *International Archives of Occupational and Environmental Health*, 77(3), 205–212.

Johnston, R. (2005). *Analytic Culture in the U.S. Intelligence Community: An Ethnographic Study*. Washington, DC: Center for the Study of Intelligence.

Kaber, D.B., and Endsley, M.R. (2004). The effects of level of automation and adaptive automation on human performance, situation awareness and workload in a dynamic control task. *Theoretical Issues in Ergonomics Science*, 5(2), 113–153. doi:10.1080/1463922021000054335.

Kanfer, R. (1990). Motivation theory and industrial and organizational psychology. In M.D. Dunnette and L.M. Hough (Eds.), *Handbook of Industrial and Organizational Psychology* (Vol. 1) (pp. 75–170). Palo Alto, CA: Consulting Psychologists Press.

Karwowski, W., Siemionow, W., and Gielo-Perczak, K. (2003). Physical neuroergonomics: The human brain in control of physical work activities. *Theoretical Issues in Ergonomic Science*, 4(1-2), 175–199. doi:10.1080/1463922021000032339.

Keebler, J.R., Ososky, S., Taylor, G., Sciarini, W.L., and Jentsch, F. (2010). Neuroethics and neuroergonomics: Protecting the private brain. In T. Marek, W. Karwowski, and V. Rice (Eds.), *Advances in Understanding Human Performance Neuroergonomics, Human Factors Design, and Special Populations*. Boca Raton, FL: CRC Press.

Kraus, T., Kiess, O., Hösl, K., Terekhin, P., Kornhuber, J., and Forster, C. (2013). CNS BOLD fMRI effects of sham-controlled transcutaneous electrical nerve stimulation in the left outer auditory canal—a pilot study. *Brain Stimulation*, 6(5), 798–804. doi:10.1016/j.brs.2013.01.011.

Lee, T.W., and Mitchell, T.R. (1994). An alternative approach: The unfolding model of voluntary employee turnover. *Academy of Management Review*, 19(1), 51–89. doi:10.5465/AMR.1994.9410122008.

Leonardi, P., and Contractor, N.S. (2018). Better people analytics: Measure who they know, not just who they are. *Harvard Business Review*, November–December. Available: https://hbr.org/2018/11/better-people-analytics [December 2018].

Lin, C.T., Chiu, T.T., Huang, T.Y., Chao, C.F., Liang, W.C., Hsu, S.H., and Ko, L.W. (2009). Assessing effectiveness of various auditory warning signals in maintaining drivers' attention in virtual reality-based driving environments. *Perceptual and Motor Skills*, 108(3), 825–835.

Lin, C.T., Huang, K.C., Chao, C.F., Chen, J.A., Chiu, T.W., Ko, L.W., and Jung, T.P. (2010). Tonic and phasic EEG and behavioral changes induced by arousing feedback. *Neuroimage*, 52(2), 633–642.

Lintern, G. (2012). Work-focused analysis and design. *Cognition, Technology, and Work*, 14(1), 71–81. doi:10.1007/s10111-010-0167-y.

Lowenthal, M., and Marks, R. (2015). Intelligence analysis: Is it as good as it gets? *International Journal of Intelligence and Counterintelligence*, 28(4), 662–665.

March, J.G., and Simon, H.A. (1958). *Organizations*. Oxford, UK: Wiley.

Mehta, R.K., and Parasuraman, R. (2013). Neuroergonomics: A review of applications to physical and cognitive work. *Frontiers in Human Neuroscience*, 7, 889. doi:10.3389/fnhum.2013.00889.

Miles, A.D. (2016). *The U.S. Intelligence Community: Selected Cross-Cutting Issues*. Washington, DC: Congressional Research Service.

Mitchell, T.R., Holtom, B.C., Lee, T.W., Sablynski, C.J., and Erez, M. (2001). Why people stay: Using job embeddedness to predict voluntary turnover. *Academy of Management Journal*, 44(6), 1102–1121. doi:10.2307/3069391.

Mobley, W.H. (1977). Intermediate linkages in the relationship between job satisfaction and employee turnover. *Journal of Applied Psychology*, 62(2), 237–240.

Mobley, W.H., Griffeth, R.W., Hand, H.H., and Meglino, B.M. (1979). Review and conceptual analysis of the employee turnover process. *Psychological Bulletin*, 86(3), 493–522.

National Academies of Sciences, Engineering, and Medicine (NASEM). (2018a). *How People Learn II: Learners, Contexts, and Cultures*. Washington, DC: The National Academies Press. doi:10.17226/24783.

NASEM. (2018b). *Workforce Development and Intelligence Analysis for National Security Purposes: Proceedings of a Workshop*. Washington, DC: The National Academies Press. doi:10.17226/25117.

National Research Council. (2011). *Intelligence Analysis for Tomorrow: Advances from the Behavioral and Social Sciences*. Washington, DC: The National Academies Press. doi:10.17226/13040.

Nelson, J.T., Mckinley, R.A., Golog, E.J., Warm, J.S., and Parasuraman, R. (2014). Enhanced vigilance in operators with prefrontal cortex transcranial direct stimulation. *Neuroimage*, 85(Pt. 3), 907–917. doi:10.1016/j.neuroimage.2012.11.061.

Nelson, J., McKinley, R.A., Phillips, C., McIntire, L., Goodyear, C., Kreiner, A., and Monforton, L. (2016). The effects of transcranial direct current stimulation (tDCS) on multitasking throughput capacity. *Frontiers in Human Neuroscience*, 10, 589. doi:10.3389/fnhum.2016.00589.

Office of the Director of National Intelligence. (2014). *Human Capital Vision 2020.* Available: https://www.dni.gov/files/documents/CHCO/US_IC_Human_Capital_Vision_2020_Strategy%202020_5_March_2014_U.pdf [December 2018].

Okano, A.H., Fontes, E.B., Montenegro, R.A., Farinatti, P.T., Cyrino, E.S., Li, L.M., Bikson, M., and Noakes, T.D. (2015). Brain stimulation modulates the autonomic nervous system, rating of perceived exertion and performance during maximal exercise. *British Journal of Sports Medicine, 49*(18), 1213–1218. doi:10.1136/bjsports-2012-091658.

Parasuraman, R. (1987). Human–computer monitoring. *Human Factors, 29*(6), 695–706. doi:10.1177/001872088702900609.

Parasuraman, R. (2011). Neuroergonomics: Brain, cognition, and performance at work. *Current Directions in Psychological Science, 20*(3), 181–186. doi:10.1177/0963721411409176.

Phillips, J.M. (1998). Effects of realistic job previews on multiple organizational outcomes: A meta-analysis. *Academy of Management Journal, 41*(6), 673–690. doi:10.2307/256964.

Pirolli, P., Lee, T., and Card, S.K. (2004). *Leverage Points for Analyst Technology Identified through Cognitive Task Analysis.* Palo Alto, CA: Palo Alto Research Center.

Ployhart, R.E., Schmitt, N., and Tippins, N.T. (2017). Solving the supreme problem: 100 years of selection and recruitment at the *Journal of Applied Psychology. Applied Psychology, 102*(3), 291–304. doi:10.1037/apl0000081.

Premack, S.L., and Wanous, J.P. (1985). A meta-analysis of realistic job preview experiments. *Journal of Applied Psychology, 70*(4), 706–719.

Rotundo, M., and Sackett, P.R. (2002). The relative importance of task, citizenship, and counterproductive performance to global ratings of job performance: A policy-capturing approach. *Journal of Applied Psychology, 87*(1), 66–80. doi:10.1037/0021-9010.87.1.66.

Sackett, P.R., and Walmsley, P.T. (2014). Which personality attributes are most important in the workplace?. *Perspectives on Psychological Science, 9*(5), 538–551.

Sackett, P.R., Shewach, O.R., and Keiser, H.N. (2017a). Assessment centers versus cognitive ability tests: Challenging the conventional wisdom on criterion-related validity. *Journal of Applied Psychology, 102*(10), 1435–1447. doi:10.1037/apl0000236.

Sackett, P., Lievens, F., Van Iddekinge, C.H., and Kuncel, N.R. (2017b). Individual differences and their measurement: A review of 100 years of research. *Applied Psychology, 102*(3), 254–273. doi:10.1037/apl0000151.

Salas, E., and Cannon-Bowers, J.A. (2001). The science of training: A decade of progress. *Annual Review of Psychology, 52*(1), 471–499.

Schmidt, A.M., and DeShon, R.P. (2007). What to do? The effects of discrepancies, incentives, and time on dynamic goal prioritization. *Journal of Applied Psychology, 92*(4), 928–942.

Schmidt, F.L., and Hunter, J.E. (1998). The validity and utility of selection methods in personnel psychology: Practical and theoretical implications of 85 years of research findings. *Psychological Bulletin, 124*(2), 262–274. doi:10.1037/0033-2909.124.2.262.

Schwartz, J., Collins, L., Stockton, H., Wagner, D., and Walsh, B. (2017). The future of work: The augmented workforce. *Deloitte Insights,* February 28. Available: https://www2.deloitte.com/insights/us/en/focus/human-capital-trends/2017/future-workforce-changing-nature-of-work.html [December 2018].

Society for Industrial and Organizational Psychology. (2018). *Principles for the Validation and Use of Personnel Selection Procedures* (5th ed.). Cambridge, MA: Cambridge University Press.

Tannenbaum, S.I., Beard, R.L., McNall, L.A., and Salas, E. (2010). Informal learning and development in organizations. In S.W.J. Kozlowski and E. Salas (Eds.), *Learning, Training, and Development in Organizations* (pp. 303–332). New York: Routledge.

Ting, C.H., Mahfouf, M., Nassef, A., Linkens, D.A., Panoutsos, G., Nickel, P., Roberts, A.C., and Hockey, G.R.J. (2010). Real-time adaptive automation system based on identification of operator functional state in simulated process control operations. *IEEE Transactions on Systems, Man, and Cybernetics. Part A: Systems and Humans*, 40(2), 251–262. doi:10.1109/TMSCA.2009.2035301.

Tippins, N.T., and Macey, W.H. (2007). Consortium studies. In S.M. McPhail (Ed.), *Alternative Validation Strategies: Developing New and Leveraging Existing Validation Evidence* (pp. 233–251). San Francisco, CA: Jossey-Bass.

Van Cutsem, J., Marcora, S., De Pauw, K., Bailey, S., Meeusen, R., and Roelands, B. (2017). The effects of mental fatigue on physical performance: A systematic review. *Sports Medicine*, 47(8), 1569–1588. doi:10.1007/s40279-016-0672-0.

Van Cutsem, J., De Pauw, K,. Marcora, S., Meeusen, R., and Roelands, B. (2018). A caffeine-maltodextrin mouth rinse counters mental fatigue. *Psychopharmacology*, 235(4), 947–958.

Vancouver, J.B., Halper, L.R., and Bayes, K.A. (2017). Regulating our own learning: Stuff you did not realize you needed to know. In J.E. Ellingson and R.A. Noe (Eds.), *Autonomous Learning in the Workplace* (pp. 95–116). New York: Routledge.

Vancouver, J.B., Weinhardt, J., and Schmidt, A.M. (2010). A formal, computational theory of multiple-goal pursuit: Integrating goal-choice and goal-striving processes. *Journal of Applied Psychology*, 95(6), 985–1008. doi:10.1037/a0020628.

Wang, Z., Hope, R.M., Wang, Z.Ji, Q., and Gray, W.D. (2011). Cross-subject workload classification with a hierarchical Bayes model. *Neuroimage*, 59(1), 64–69. doi:10.1016/j.neuroimage.2011.07.094.

Wang, Y.T., Huang, K.C., Wei, C.S., Huang, T.Y, Ko, L.W., Lin, C.T., Cheng, C.K., and Jung, T.P. (2014). Developing an EEG-based on-line closed-loop lapse detection and mitigation system. *Frontiers in Neuroscience*, 8, 321. doi:10.3389/fnins.2014.00321.

Warm, J.S., Parasuraman, R., and Matthews, G. (2008). Cerebral hemodynamics and vigilance. In R. Parasuraman and M. Rizzo (Eds.), *Neuroergonomics: The Brain at Work* (pp. 146–158). New York: Oxford University Press.

Wickens, C.D. (1984). Processing resources in attention. In R. Parasuraman and R. Davies (Eds.), *Varieties of Attention* (pp. 63–101). Orlando, FL: Academic Press.

Wickens, C.D. (2002). Multiple resources and performance prediction. *Theoretical Issues in Ergonomic Science*, 3(2), 159–177. doi:10.1080/14639220210123806.

Wickens, C.D., and McCarley, J.S. (2008). *Applied Attention Theory*. London, UK: CRC Press.

Wiener, E.L., and Attwood, D.A. (1968). Training for vigilance: Combined cueing and knowledge of results. *Journal of Applied Psychology*, 52(6, Pt.1), 474–479. doi:10.1037/h0026444.

World Economic Forum. (2018). *The Future of Jobs Report*. Available: http://www3.weforum.org/docs/WEF_Future_of_Jobs_2018.pdf [December 2018].

Zakerian S.A., Yazdanirad, S., Gharib, S., Azam, K., and Zare, A. (2018). The effect of increasing the illumination on operators' visual performance in the control-room of a combined cycle power plant. *Annals of Occupational and Environmental Medicine*, 30, 56. doi:10.1186/s40557-018-0267-3.

PART III

LOOKING FORWARD

We turn next to the question of how the Intelligence Community (IC) can position itself to take optimal advantage of the opportunities described in Part II and others like them. Collaboration and coordination—not only interdisciplinary approaches to research within the academic community, but also a multitude of ways researchers and IC agencies can work together and learn from one another—will be essential. In Chapter 9, we explore lessons learned in conducting this study and broaden the discussion to consider lessons that can be drawn from the history of collaboration between the IC and the research community. Chapter 10 summarizes the opportunities the committee sees for the IC in this collaborative work and describes our ideas about how the IC can capitalize on them most effectively.

9

Strengthening Ties Between the Two Communities

An important part of this committee's charge was to propose ways to "facilitate productive interchange between the security community and the external social science research community" (refer to Box 1-1 in Chapter 1). In this chapter, we offer reflections on how these ties can be strengthened. We begin with reflections on what we learned about the relationship between these two communities from the process of conducting this decadal survey, and then explore past collaborations between the two communities, drawing lessons from both successful and less-successful experiences and offering our conclusions about ways to strengthen these ties.

LESSONS FROM CONDUCTING THE DECADAL SURVEY

The committee was asked to reflect on the process of conducting this decadal survey and identify insights and practices that could be useful for any future such studies in social and behavioral sciences (SBS) fields. As noted in Chapter 1, this study marked the first time the National Academies of Sciences, Engineering, and Medicine's decadal process was applied to SBS fields. The decadal process was chosen because the Office of the Director of National Intelligence (ODNI) recognized the need for a comprehensive look across this research landscape: the process offered a way to address the urgency of integrating SBS research into intelligence analysis while also opening the door to a wide array of ideas. Our observations about this process may bear on planning for any future decadal studies in this universe but may also help ODNI to continue capitalizing on SBS research in a systematic and continuous way, apart from any future decadal surveys.

Challenges and Benefits of a Broad Charge

The committee's charge did not identify a precise objective to be met within 10 years, akin to the development of a space telescope. Rather, it directed us to look for opportunities that would "contribute to the IC's analytic responsibilities," a task that by its nature is ongoing, not one that might be complete at the end of 10 years. The breadth of this charge, which required us to look across a very wide research landscape, initially appeared to be the greatest challenge, but it turned out to have significant advantages.

It was clear from the start that the processes used in prior decadal surveys would be valuable but not easy to apply to this committee's work.[1] In particular, we recognized that, while surveying the research community for ideas was a key element of the process for this study, there was no practical way to survey such a broad community systematically. Indeed, although there is in a sense a community of SBS researchers—in that researchers in these fields share many common interests—SBS is by no means a single discipline. No institution or entity links all members of this set of disciplines; rather, the various SBS disciplines form an abstract community that encompasses a wide range of theories and methods. Further, the breadth of our charge and the importance of representing such a diverse array of work had a cost in terms of the level of depth with which we could explore particular research areas. The product of our deliberations, then, certainly is not exhaustive, and it would be impossible to forecast precisely which areas of research across all SBS fields will make the most important contributions to the IC in the coming decade.

Despite these constraints, however, there were distinct benefits to casting a wide net in seeking intersections between the needs of the IC and the available SBS research. One benefit was that, because a multidisciplinary approach was necessary, our work was not driven by the perspectives of a single discipline, and we had no preconceptions about where to look for relevant work. The process we developed to pursue understanding of the needs of the IC and merge that understanding with input on potentially relevant research exposed us to new ideas while also supporting some of our hypotheses.

---

[1] For example, prior decadal committees relied on the work of subpanels, designated from the start of the project to gather information in particular relevant disciplines. This approach was not practicable for our decadal study because we could not assume that a particular set of individual disciplines would have the most important contributions to make to fulfill our charge. See Chapter 1 and Appendix B for description of the process used for this study.

Challenges in Integrating Social and Behavioral Sciences and Other Research

Although the committee's charge was to examine SBS research, exploiting most of the opportunities identified in this report will depend on integrating research from SBS fields as disparate as neuroscience, engineering, and computer science. There are always challenges when researchers from different fields work together. Researchers from different domains may each sometimes view their counterparts as naïve, but here we focus on some errors that might occur when technically based research is conducted without the benefit of deep SBS knowledge.

One potential problem is rediscovery, or the reinvention of wheels. For example, early roboticists interested in the coordination of groups of agents "discovered" a finding already well established by organizational science—that teams adapt more rapidly than do hierarchies (Bersin, 2017). Of greater concern are cases in which researchers unaware of well-established findings make significant errors. An example is when claims about networks based on mathematical analysis (Barabási and Bonabeau, 2003) contradicted earlier work in sociology and demography (Heathcote et al., 2000; Jones and Handcock, 2003) and were later disproved (Broido and Clauset, 2018). Such errors can be serious. For instance, when artificial intelligence (AI) techniques not based in results of computational models driven by SBS theory are used in ways that have concrete impacts for individuals, the result can be unintended discrimination or other harms (Hauch et al., 2015; Siegel, 2018).

SBS researchers and engineers, computer scientists, and physicists take different approaches even when addressing the same phenomena (Borgatti et al., 2009), and the benefit of integrating SBS methods and findings has been noted in such realms as health care delivery (Burger, 2017) and the marketing of technology (Brookey, 2007; Grindley, 1990). More generally, technological developments occur in a social and economic context, and SBS research is essential to understanding technology's potential applications and benefits, risks, and long-term effects (Smith and Stirling, 2007). The industrial revolution was not driven by improvements in manufacturing and engineering alone; SBS research was needed to support the development of applications of these advances (Porter, 1986). As discussed throughout this report, SBS perspectives are essential to the development of sound research and applications involving sophisticated technology, and direct collaboration across SBS and technological fields is necessary for that to happen.

Obstacles to Collaboration Between Researchers and the Intelligence Community

Adapting the decadal process to a new context also required that the committee simultaneously conduct this study and continuously take stock of the effectiveness of the study process. Doing so allowed us to see firsthand some of the obstacles to integration and collaboration between the two communities on which we were focusing. One such obstacle is that even within the IC, and in the context of the numerous mechanisms it already has in place for drawing specifically on SBS research, there appears to be less coordination between the two than would be optimal. Existing IC entities were developed to pursue particular missions, not necessarily with the goal of advancing the integration of SBS knowledge. This reality, along with the need to keep some projects or information classified, is likely to work against coordination of these communities, to say nothing of funding and political considerations that were beyond our purview.

Another obstacle to integration is that awareness of potential applications of research to IC needs is highly uneven across relevant SBS fields. It is notable, for example, that this report contains little discussion of developments in such fields as political science and international relations. These fields make extremely important contributions to national security, and have done so for decades. Yet there was little need to address them here because for the most part, scholars in these fields are highly attuned to security issues, and the IC is highly attuned to their findings. Methodological and technological breakthroughs of which the IC may not be fully aware seemed far more likely in other areas of the SBS terrain.

Applying the decadal survey process to the IC context had another significant benefit. The committee cast the widest possible net in seeking white papers and other input from the SBS community (refer to Chapter 1 and Appendix B). The results, while valuable and intriguing, also clearly demonstrate that there is a long way to go in building awareness within the SBS research community of the potential application of its work to national security. However, our iterative process did reveal elements that would likely have emerged even if a different, parallel set of committee members had embarked on this study and devised a different method for applying the decadal survey process in the IC context. Without a doubt, for example, any attempt to fulfill our charge would highlight the importance of learning more about human–machine interactions. Likewise, emerging research in data science has many potential applications to national security work that would surely be included in any report such as this in some form. It is similarly difficult to imagine that the critical importance of integrating insights about human behavior and group functioning into the pursuit of cybersecurity would not have been recognized.

Finally, an issue that was a key challenge for this committee may be relevant to any future efforts to cull information from this broad research landscape. We struggled to find the best way to take stock of the diverse knowledge and expertise brought by the 16 committee members, and to find an optimal way to take advantage of our own knowledge base while also extending our reach widely in areas not well known to any of us. Our own knowledge base was a valuable foundation, but it was also limited, as were our resources for supplementing it. The rapid project schedule required us to quickly assess promising areas in order to make decisions about how to use our six workshops and other information-gathering strategies; there was no established process on which we could rely for this purpose. This procedural challenge mirrors a challenge faced by the IC: to systematically utilize an ever-expanding base of foundational SBS research while also identifying new work in unexpected areas that may prove equally valuable.

BUILDING ON PAST COLLABORATIONS

As noted in the overview of the SBS community and the IC in Chapter 2, the objectives and perspectives of these two communities are not always aligned, but the two have always had much to learn from one another. The relevance of SBS research to national security challenges has been apparent to both communities at least since researchers first worked with the U.S. military during World War I.[2] The first division of the National Academy of Sciences devoted to SBS research, the Division of Anthropology and Psychology, formed committees to explore military issues as early as 1919. Collaborations between the security and SBS communities began to play a critical and sustained role in military operations, and to expand to intelligence issues beyond military concerns, once the United States became involved in World War II. Since then, research partnerships between the two communities have generated important scientific insights and provided valuable support for intelligence and security activities, although the relationship has not always been smooth.

---

[2]In 1916, the leadership of the National Academy of Sciences formally "place[d] itself at the disposal of the Government for any services within its scope." This involvement led directly to the establishment of the National Research Council, the operating arm of the Academy, which would "advise the nation on matters of science and engineering." For more information about this history, see https://sites.nationalacademies.org/PGA/PGA_180900 [November 2018] and http://www.nasonline.org/about-nas/history/archives/milestones-in-NAS-history/organization-of-the-nrc.htm [November 2018]. The institution formally changed its name to the National Academies of Sciences, Engineering, and Medicine in 2015.

Working Together: A Brief History

Successful collaborations between SBS researchers and the IC have run the gamut from fundamental research into human–computer teaming and human cognition to applied work that facilitates cross-cultural and wartime operations. During World War II, the Office of Strategic Services—the nation's first foreign intelligence agency and the precursor to the Central Intelligence Agency (CIA)—hired political scientists, psychologists, anthropologists, sociologists, and economists to support such functions as analyzing foreign intelligence, assessing enemy and allied morale, screening and training intelligence operatives, calculating the enemy's military capacity, and identifying optimal bombing routes and payloads (O'Rand, 1992). Similarly, anthropologists and psychologists working at the Office of War Information (OWI) provided insights into the cultures and values of foreign populations relevant to the war effort. Anthropologist Ruth Benedict's groundbreaking and best-selling study of Japanese culture, *The Chrysanthemum and the Sword*, which began as an OWI report, influenced the values and design of the United Nations when it was established at war's end (Mandler, 2013).

Wartime projects benefited SBS scholarship even as they served national security. For example, political scientist Harold Lasswell's studies of international political opinion and morale for the Wartime Communications Research Project were widely recognized as proving the value of large-scale, quantitative methods for studying communication (Backhouse and Fontaine, 2010; Rohde, 2013). Likewise, during and after World War II, the Office of Naval Research helped support the development of field theory in sociology through its financial support for the Massachusetts Institute of Technology (MIT) because it hoped to learn about group dynamics and the ways people identify with each other as members of a particular group (O'Rand, 1992, p. 190).

Federal investments in SBS research expanded in scale and scope in the second half of the 20th century. These investments demonstrate that the intelligence and security communities have consistently supported a spectrum of SBS research, from fundamental scientific investigations to scholarship with direct applications to intelligence and related security activities. In the applied domains, for example, research at the RAND Corporation facilitated new understandings of human decision making derived from game theory, social psychology, and systems analysis. These insights fostered and supported nuclear deterrence strategies that helped keep the Cold War cold in the United States and Europe.

Such efforts have parallels today. For example, SBS researchers work in partnership with intelligence and military agencies to enhance cultural and linguistic knowledge. Drawing on basic research in communications, cultural anthropology, political science, social psychology, and sociology, for instance, the Marine Corps Center for Advanced Operational Culture and Language provides the security community with concepts and skills that facilitate cross-cultural understanding (National Academies of Sciences, Engineering, and Medicine, 2017, p. 23).

Recognizing a need for more sustained investment in SBS research relevant to counterterrorism and counterinsurgency in the 21st century, the secretary of defense created the Minerva Research Initiative in 2008. This initiative bridges basic and applied SBS research by supporting unclassified social science research that improves "basic understanding of the social, cultural, behavioral, and political forces that shape" strategically important regions of the globe.[3] Funded projects include studies of social, cultural, economic, and psychological factors that affect radicalization; the role of cybermedia in state stability; and the impacts of environmental, economic, social, and political factors on conflict and instability among both state and nonstate actors.

The Defense Advanced Research Projects Agency (DARPA) began funding research on machine-aided cognition and human–computer communication in the early 1960s. The first director of DARPA's behavioral sciences and computer science division, psychologist and computer scientist J.C.R. Licklider, articulated a vision of human–computer symbiosis in 1960 that is still relevant today. He wrote, "in not too many years, human brains and computing machines will be coupled together very tightly . . . the resulting partnership will think as no human brain has ever thought" (Licklider, 1960, p. 4; Norberg et al., 1996). DARPA has funded research that has produced major advances. For example, its funds contributed to the creation of PLATO (Programmed Logic for Automatic Teaching Operations), which, first released in 1972, harnessed research in psychology to revolutionize computer-based education (Dear, 2017). More recently, IC investments in social network analysis have generated methodological breakthroughs.

Together with the Intelligence Advanced Research Projects Activity (IARPA)—created by ODNI in 2006—DARPA continues to support research that combines computational tools with SBS knowledge to develop social forecasting techniques and other approaches to improved human and organizational decision making. This research has been foundational to the development of such systems as the Worldwide Integrated Crisis Early Warning system, which uses natural language processing, modeling, and other methods to track international events and forecast political instability (NASEM, 2017, p. 22).

The research portfolios of DARPA and IARPA also include support for research in the decision sciences, cognitive science, and other SBS areas

---

[3]Available: https://basicresearch.defense.gov/minerva [February 2019].

with the potential to enhance basic and applied knowledge that can contribute to both national security and scientific knowledge (Defense Advanced Research Projects Agency, 2018; Office of the Director of National Intelligence, 2018). In addition to providing new computational tools for monitoring and forecasting of global events, these research portfolios advance SBS knowledge about human judgment and decision making in high-stakes and rapidly changing environments.

One recent example of such contributions, discussed in Chapter 7, is the Good Judgment Project (Office of the Director of National Intelligence, 2015). Developed by scholars at the University of Pennsylvania and the University of California, Berkeley as part of IARPA's forecasting tournaments (which ran annually from 2011 to 2015), the project generated results valued by both IARPA and SBS researchers and has been adopted by the National Intelligence Council. The project demonstrated the validity of forecasting tournaments as predictive tools and provided IARPA with insights into best practices for designing and running such tournaments. It also produced results directly relevant to the SBS research community broadly, including the identification of mechanisms for quantifying good judgment and methods for facilitating it, such as cognitive debiasing, providing incentives for accuracy, and designing predictive questions that facilitate accuracy. Notably, both researchers and project managers have been careful not to oversell the results of their findings (Rohde, 2017, pp. 792–813). Previous predictive projects had claimed more accuracy and foresight than they were able to provide. By contrast, researchers involved in the Good Judgment Project have stressed that their work shows that prediction is currently most accurate for approximately 1 year into the future, rather than longer timespans (Chen, 2015; Tetlock et al., 2014, pp. 290–295).

The above research investments run parallel to research in other high-stakes professional domains, such as medicine and finance, in yielding promising insights that can improve judgment and performance. SBS research has shown that human cognitive fallibilities, such as hindsight bias (the unsubstantiated belief that one could have predicted an event) and outcome bias (the tendency to judge decisions by how they turned out rather than by how thoughtfully they were made) hinder learning in workforces. These findings have led to the development of new methods for facilitating the reduction of biases in thinking in high-stakes situations by better identifying sources of failure in judgment and decision making (National Research Council, 2012, pp. 15–16).

Lessons for Productive Collaboration

The examples of productive collaboration discussed in this report demonstrate that the partnership between the IC and the SBS community has often been successful when research, whether basic or applied, has advanced knowledge of mutual interest to both communities. The relationship between SBS researchers and the national security community has not always operated as smoothly as in these examples, however. We examine here a few cases in which problems arose so as to draw lessons for future collaborations.

Careful attention to transparency in funding relationships on both sides has helped restore the public reputation of joint efforts, as well as protect the integrity of the products of joint research.

During the early years of the Cold War, the need for research-based information was great, but security concerns were also heightened. On some occasions, normal protocols for transparency and accountability were not observed, and financial and other ties between SBS researchers and the IC were hidden from the public (Rohde, 2013). This lack of transparency caused problems within both communities, as illustrated by the experience of MIT's prestigious Center for International Studies. The center, which had the mission of applying "social science to problems bearing on the peace and development of the world community" (Gilman, 2004, p. 159), was established in 1951 in large part with secret CIA funds. For the next 15 years, the center's researchers produced some of the most influential work in modernization theory, international communications, and development studies without disclosing their relationship to the IC. Despite being questioned, they denied any ties to the CIA until investigative journalists produced unequivocal proof in 1966, at which time MIT terminated its relationship with the agency (Rohde, 2013). The American Political Science Association's integrity was similarly compromised when social scientists learned that the association's longtime executive director disguised ideological statements as scholarship and founded a private research corporation that secretly took CIA money (Oren, 2002).

While less common, programs that used or appeared to use SBS as a cover for IC programs also contributed to public suspicion of SBS–IC collaboration. From 1955 to 1962, for example, a Michigan State University program that allegedly provided public administration training in South Vietnam served as cover for a CIA-funded counterespionage training program that was implicated in accusations of torture and assassination in South Vietnam.

SBS researchers and the IC have taken these experiences to heart. It has been decades since collaborations between the two communities have been marred by evidence of covert funding.

Explicit attention to balancing scientific norms and procedures with the need to protect security in the design and execution of research benefits both the researchers and security agencies involved.

The agencies that fund and use SBS research face the challenge of balancing their own needs with the desire of academic researchers to advance intellectual developments in their fields. As noted in a recent report by the Institute for Defense Analyses, when the goals of a research program are ambiguous, or when the uses to which funding agencies will put the research are unclear, particularly in relation to the program's security or intelligence mission, the program is more likely "to sow seeds of mistrust" between the two communities (Koonin et al., 2013, p. 12). While the Good Judgment Project, discussed above, provides an example of successful balancing of agency and SBS needs and interests, examples of failure provide instructive lessons for future collaboration.

One such example is Project Camelot, an ambitious, unclassified, multidisciplinary study of political revolution in Latin America during the Cold War. The project, funded by the U.S. Army and DARPA, was designed to identify the causes of communist insurgency to facilitate prediction of the onset of revolution. The project attracted international criticism in 1965 when press accounts in several Latin American countries where the work was being carried out revealed that researchers affiliated with the work had misrepresented it to potential research partners in those countries as a foundation-supported effort. Journalists in several of the countries involved argued that these events proved that the U.S. government used SBS research as a cover for intelligence gathering and espionage (Rohde, 2013).

The National Research Council concluded that Project Camelot demonstrated "that military sponsorship of social science research pertaining to the internal politics of other nations may have adverse repercussions on American foreign policy" (National Research Council, 1971, p. 7). The accusations directed at the project triggered congressional hearings into the military's research programs, prompting the Army to cancel the project abruptly so as to avoid further scrutiny and embarrassment (Rohde, 2013; Zehfuss, 2012).

Project Camelot also was emblematic of the failure of SBS researchers and their sponsors to balance scientific and national security goals. Critics in the SBS community argued that the project's core problem was that its researchers converted SBS research to militarized language and goals, thereby subverting the natural direction of research and introducing politics into science. Critics argued that researchers and their sponsors had brought "the whole of social sciences under the heading of counter-insurgency" by framing the research questions in military terms—as studies of counter-insurgency, guerrilla warfare, and the like (Rohde, 2013, p. 84). As the National Academy of Sciences concluded at the time, government agencies and researchers could improve their relationship by assuming more responsibility for stating needs in terms that are meaningful to the investigator rather than the military (National Research Council, 1971).

The funders of Project Camelot had reasons to be critical of their SBS partners as well. For example, they had to intervene during the study's planning phase when social scientists proposed including studies of the French Canadian separatist movement in their investigation (Rohde, 2013, pp. 70–71). Experts on counterinsurgency research at DARPA and members of the Defense Science Board pointed out that the project would likely have failed on its own merits. Months before it attracted public attention, government officials worried that the researchers directing the project had not produced a clear research plan, but instead listed only "generalities ... about research hypotheses" and "vague and formless" descriptions of the project's methodology (Deitchman, 1976, p. 146).

SBS research projects during the Vietnam War era also include cases in which government funders were let down by SBS researchers who failed to provide rigorous and relevant expertise. In 1967, for example, DARPA hired the research group Simulmatics Corporation—which was led by an MIT political scientist and staffed by reputable SBS scholars—to study social relationships in South Vietnamese hamlets and determine what motivated support for the North and South Vietnamese causes. Government experts found that the studies seemed as if "someone had taken a book of rules about scientific methodology, then systematically violated each one" (Weinberger, 2017, p. 179). A study of communications and propaganda, for example, yielded results that DARPA officials found were riddled with contaminated variables and violations of basic rules of inference.

Camelot and Simulmatics were military-sponsored, not IC, projects. Nevertheless, their histories point to the fact that the partnership between the SBS community and the IC may be weakened when research priorities, methods, and administration fail to meet the needs, standards, and values of both collaborators. Achieving that balance is difficult even when research is carried out with sufficient scholarly integrity and careful management.

Recent examples indicate that members of both communities have become more successful in balancing their mutual needs, standards, and values. For example, SBS researchers criticized the U.S. Department of Defense (DoD)–funded Minerva Research Initiative in its first year for defining research areas that leaned too heavily toward national security concerns, which thus failed to appeal to many relevant researchers (Gearty, 2008). They also criticized the program for its grant review process, which initially was performed internally within DoD rather than through peer review. In subsequent years, Minerva program managers responded to these concerns and incorporated substantial scholarly input into the processes for setting research priorities and reviewing grants (Krebs, 2008).

Relationships between research universities and the IC can be complicated in other ways as well. A 2017 book documents cases in which members of the IC have enrolled in university programs in an undercover capacity—so that at least their fellow students were not aware of their official role—and of cases where students who were foreign nationals took advantage of access to research for the benefit of their governments (Golden, 2017).

It is important to recognize that not all SBS researchers view partnerships between their community and the IC in the same way. Researchers may have differing expectations for fundamental and applied research conducted in this context, or for classified as opposed to unclassified research. Furthermore, researchers' interpretation of the appropriate balance between scholarship and application can differ across and within scholarly disciplines. While many scholars see DARPA and Minerva programs as well balanced, some criticize such efforts for implicitly favoring narrow and short-term American interests and unwittingly supporting "non-democratic actions or governments" (Koonin et al., 2013, p. 11). Scholars in the fields of anthropology, political science, and international relations have been particularly critical of security-funded research, while scholars in other fields have embraced collaboration more fully (Zehfuss, 2012).

The SBS–IC relationship can become strained when clarity or consensus with respect to values and the ethics of research projects and programs is lacking. Respecting ethical norms for research will require that members of the SBS community and the IC engage in ongoing dialogue concerning research ethics in new research domains.

Research endeavors in which both academics and members of the IC take part or have a stake can highlight differences between the two cultures (see Chapter 2) and raise sometimes challenging questions. The development of complex and sophisticated technologies adds another layer of complexity to many questions about research protocols and ethics. We look briefly here at three key issues: ethics and values in a research context, emerging ethical standards in a world of big data, and the reproducibility of research findings.

Ethics and Values in a Research Context

Neither SBS research nor intelligence analysis is a value-free enterprise. Like all researchers, those in SBS fields must be aware of and articulate the influence of values in their work. The values of scientific objectivity and rigor are paramount for most researchers, but values come into play as well in the selection and definition of research questions to pursue. Scholars investigating the effects of poverty on children, for example, recognize that they regard promoting children's welfare as an undisputed good, just as medical researchers regard protecting or restoring health as a noncontroversial objective.

More complex and subtle values and assumptions may arise in research that is relevant to national security issues. For example, researchers working on national security issues agree that protecting democracy is a positive good, but they may disagree about whether certain research programs or policies embody those values. Social scientists who assisted stability operations of the U.S. military in Iraq and Afghanistan, for instance, argued that their research made Americans, Iraqis, and Afghanis safer, but other social scientists argued that the research only facilitated military operations and did not serve science or democracy (Zehfuss, 2012). While researchers will likely continue to disagree about national security policy, clear and open communication about objectives and the relationship between research and application may help build and maintain trust between SBS researchers and the IC even in the face of policy disagreement.

If history is a good indicator, scrutiny of SBS research and its relationship to government is more likely to arise in contexts of heightened political and other sensitivities. During some periods—the 1940s and 1950s, for example—Americans have largely shared a public consensus as to American strategic and security interests. At such times, collaborations between the SBS community and the IC have attracted very little attention or concern. During the 1960s, however, especially as dissent related to U.S. policies in Vietnam grew, the IC–SBS collaboration faced greater public scrutiny. During congressional hearings in 1968, for example, Senator William J. Fulbright linked U.S. failures in the Vietnam War to the security community's SBS research investments. As a result, congressional appropriations for security community–funded SBS research dropped from $40 million in 1967 to $13.7 million in 1969 (Rohde, 2013).

Similar challenges are apparent today. Revelations about controversial intelligence practices in the first decade of the 21st century—from extraordinary rendition;[4] to the National Security Agency's bulk data collection programs; to harsh interrogation methods, including methods based in psychological research (Voosen, 2015)—also have fostered concerns about intelligence and security practices among the public. While these practices do not pertain directly to research relevant to the capabilities of intelligence analysts, they may seed mistrust in or heightened scrutiny of the SBS–security community relationship (Goolsby, 2005; National Research

---

[4]Extraordinary rendition is a policy first used by the United States in the early 1990s in which foreign nationals who are suspected of involvement in terrorist-related activities are detained on foreign soil for interrogation in U.S. facilities or those of another country; see https://www.aclu.org/other/fact-sheet-extraordinary-rendition [January 2019].

Council and National Academy of Engineering, 2014; Zehfuss, 2012) This report appears at a time when questions related to terrorism, immigration, cybersecurity, and many other issues keep those concerns very current. Practices that build trust, including transparency in funding and clarity about research methods, goals, and applications, may help mitigate such concerns and strengthen ties. Examination of the relationship between academics and the IC has prompted several social science disciplines to embrace the recommendation that unless a national emergency presents an overriding need, the following activities should be avoided (Johnson, 2019, p. 17):

- agency covert recruitment on campus;
- covert research relationships;
- the use of academic cover by intelligence officers;
- the tasking of faculty and students to collect intelligence; and
- the tapping of academicians for counterintelligence or covert action operations.

It is also important to recognize that SBS research is valuable to the IC, as well as to other sectors, including education, finance, and medicine, to name but a few, because of its capacity to expand analytic understanding of human emotions, motivations, and actions. But because that understanding can facilitate the shaping and perhaps even the manipulation of emotional responses and perceptions, government-funded SBS research may generate public concern.

One example of such concern arises from the dramatic development of new data sources, such as social media mining and new computational social science techniques that can be used to analyze and possibly shape population sentiments. In 2018, controversy was sparked by revelations that the private research firm Cambridge Analytica was improperly obtaining data on Facebook users and deploying nontransparent and proprietary behavioral technologies to design information campaigns intended to influence human attitudes and actions. Whether Cambridge Analytica's psychographic techniques are scientifically sound or effective is an open question (Gibney, 2018). But scholars, journalists, and public officials have expressed grave concern that the firm's services were or could be purchased by governmental and nongovernmental clients (Cadwalladr and Harrison-Graham, 2018; Lewis et al., 2018; Shaw, 2018; Wildermuth, 2018). This episode demonstrates sensitivities that can accompany the deployment of behavioral technologies. These concerns are likely to remain salient with the growth of computational social science and big data research, including some of the research areas endorsed in this report, because of their valuable applications for protecting security.

Changing norms with regard to research ethics also require attention from SBS researchers and their partners in the IC. The U.S. military's aboveground nuclear exercises, carried out in Nevada from 1951 to 1957 and code-named Desert Rock, illustrate the way changing norms have complicated the relationship. As part of this effort, psychologists seeking to understand soldiers' ability to function in the tactical atomic environment and gauge the risk of panic on the atomic battlefield studied 600 soldiers to assess the psychological impact of witnessing an atomic explosion. While the soldiers were informed of the risks of radiation exposure and reassured that the exercises were systematic, the research design and scientific utility of the tests were the subject of internal disagreement among military officials. Military officials also disagreed about an emerging ethical question: whether the test subjects should be considered volunteers to whom risks were disclosed or soldiers involved in training (Advisory Committee on Human Radiation Experiments, 1995).

At the time of this research, the 1950s, attitudes in the country with respect to large institutions, including both the military and scientific establishments, were in a state of transition. There was little public comment on this research at the time. Public controversy about the physical effects of the blasts on the "atomic soldiers" emerged only decades later as norms for human subjects protections changed.

A more contemporary example is DARPA's Brain Machine Interface program, which has generated debate among neuroscientists (Moreno, 2012). Some pointed to the program's potential medical benefits, including treatments for degenerative neurological diseases. Other researchers argued that DARPA-funded researchers were conducting research that would support the development of human enhancements, such as "brain–machine interfaces," that would be used to enhance performance on the battlefield, which many regard as unethical (Hoag, 2003; National Research Council, 2008, 2009; Rudolph, 2003; Silence of the Neuroengineers, 2003). Another example is so-called enhanced interrogation: in the wake of the September 11, 2001, attacks, psychologists helped the CIA establish and carry out a program of interrogation of suspected terrorists that included methods regarded by many as torture, which led to a highly critical investigation by the Senate Select Committee on Intelligence (U.S. Senate Select Committee on Intelligence, 2014; see also Pfiffner, 2010), as well as policy statements by the American Psychological Association. One of the methods, waterboarding, was used by Japanese soldiers interrogating captured U.S. soldiers during World War II, for which they later went to prison (Johnson, 2018).

Such examples demonstrate how important it is that research sponsors consider researchers' positions and evolving perspectives so as to avoid proposing and supporting projects that cross ethical lines. Clear statements of mission intent also help sponsors and researchers avoid misunderstandings about the implications or goals of research programs (Moreno, 2012). SBS researchers are concerned about ensuring that their research does not cause unnecessary harm, but the relationship between research and potential harm is often unclear—and itself is the subject of unresolved debate. These episodes are instructive because this report is emerging at a time when the ethics of research using big data are also under scrutiny and in flux.

Emerging Ethical Standards in a World of Big Data

Advances in computational social science are offering exciting new possibilities for IC-related SBS research, including enhanced analysis of open-source intelligence such as social media data, data collected from sensors, and other digital information produced by routine human actions and behaviors (Harman, 2015). This information is often granular, is durable, and can be shared across institutional and national borders at high speeds. Research conducted using such data has the potential to cause harm to the individuals whose information or attributes are collected, including the loss of privacy and of individuals' autonomous control over their personal information.

While SBS researchers have long been accustomed to addressing research ethics via the Common Rule (a federal policy statement regarding the protection of human subjects involved in research), computational social science research transcends traditional human subjects protections and raises a number of new ethical questions. For example: Are data subjects the same as human subjects, or are they different? What reasonable expectations of privacy do people have with respect to their digital traces, and how do those expectations change in different digital venues? Is informed consent possible, realistic, or required in big data research? Researchers and ethicists stress that these questions do not have straightforward answers (Buchanan, 2017; Zook et al., 2017). Furthermore, because digital collection tools are proliferating, because digital methods are changing rapidly, and because machine learning tools create decision rules that may not be transparent or intuitive, digital research may generate new and unexpected ethical questions.

These issues are discussed in detail in Appendix D, but we note here that they are especially salient when data are collected or analyzed in a national security context. Internet users typically do not know what traces of their everyday lives are monitored; what happens to their information; or what, if anything, happens because of it. The potential for surveillance by the security community afforded by digital data compounds the power imbalances already present in digital spaces. As discussed above, failure to address ethical concerns can have a chilling effect on research; the public may lose its trust in the SBS research community, as well as in the government agencies that sponsor such research, including the security community. In the digital context, widespread concern that the Internet is a space where actions are monitored, stored, and analyzed rather than a site of free information exchange also may cause people to censor their online behavior, with a chilling effect on Internet use itself (Brunton and Nissenbaum, 2015; Mayer-Schönberger, 2011; Penny, 2016). Researchers and the IC will continue to grapple with the need to balance privacy and autonomy on the one hand and security on the other (Walsh and Miller, 2016). These domains both overlap and conflict, and navigating this terrain will require careful attention to evolving ethical norms and values.

Reproducibility of Research Findings

Questions about the reproducibility of research results, not only in SBS fields but also across the sciences, have implications for intelligence analysis. The reproducibility of results and testing for generality are key ways in which researchers confirm that their findings are valid; these steps are regarded as keystones of the scientific method. Studies completed over the past decade, however, have pointed to the widespread difficulty of replicating results in numerous fields, such as medicine, big data and computation, and biometrics and behavior metrics. In science, as in national security, any index or finding may fail to replicate precisely because of intrinsic limits in measurement; in some cases, more valid conclusions may be derived from measures other than those originally used. The research community is focused on identifying best practices for enhancing both reproducibility and validity (see Appendix C for a more detailed discussion).

A consensus committee of the National Academies has examined this issue,[5] but it is clear that the importance of understanding and quantifying the reliability of information and of determining how best to process and display the information and integrate or aggregate information from multiple sources will influence emerging SBS research in the coming decade. The robustness and validity of new data, modeling, and theory development are also important in answering researchable questions related to national security, and it will therefore be important for the IC to consider these issues carefully in planning its own empirical efforts.

---

[5]Information about the study can be found at http://sites.nationalacademies.org/dbasse/bbcss/reproducibility_and_replicability_in_science/index.htm [December 2018].

CONCLUSIONS

The committee saw ample evidence of the productive potential of collaboration between the IC and the SBS research community. We offer three conclusions regarding the elements needed for productive collaboration.

CONCLUSION 9-1: Explicit attention to the respective intellectual goals, values, and perspectives of members of the Intelligence Community (IC) and academic researchers is a prerequisite for productive collaboration. Collaborations between the two have yielded important scientific and analytic insights, and have functioned well when funding sources and agency goals have been transparent, when social and behavioral sciences research questions and agency missions and goals have been harmonized and clear, and when ethical and value-based concerns have been treated with sufficient care. Conversely, the relationship has fractured in the past when funding sources have been kept secret or misrepresented, researchers and government agencies have struggled to balance research and agency needs, and research has touched on broader ethical or value-based disagreements.

CONCLUSION 9-2: Ethical issues may arise at all steps of the research process, from planning, to dissemination of findings, to the operationalization of digital tools in analytic contexts. Because standards with respect to some ethical issues—particularly those concerning the use of large-scale digital datasets—are developing, and because these issues are context-sensitive, ethical assessments require careful attention throughout the research process.

CONCLUSION 9-3: Meticulous clarity and openness about the approaches taken to ensure the reproducibility and validity of the evidence generated in the course of research conducted by or with the support of the Intelligence Community (IC) are critical to the utility of the research results. The IC can promote this standard by requiring researchers to identify project components that incorporate assessments of reproducibility, replication, and validity.

REFERENCES

Advisory Committee on Human Radiation Experiments. (1995). *Final Report of the Advisory Committee on Human Radiation Experiments* (No. 061-000-00-848-9). Washington, DC: U.S. Government Printing Office. Available: https://www.osti.gov/opennet/servlets/purl/120931/120931.pdf [December 2018].

Backhouse, R., and Fontaine, P. (2010). *The History of the Social Sciences since 1945.* Cambridge, UK: Cambridge University Press.

Barabási, A.L., and Bonabeau, E. (2003). Scale-free networks. *Scientific American, 288*(5), 60–69.
Bersin, J. (2017). Robotics, AI and cognitive computing are changing organizations even faster than we thought. *Forbes*, March 9. Available: https://www.forbes.com/sites/joshbersin/2017/03/09/robotics-ai-and-cognitive-computing-are-changing-organizations-even-faster-than-we-thought/#2b7db67fa3f4 [December 2018].
Borgatti, S.P., Mehra, A., Brass, D.J., and Labianca, G. (2009). Network analysis in the social sciences. *Science, 323*(5916), 892–895.
Broido, A.D., and Clauset, A. (2018). Scale-Free Networks Are Rare. *arXiv:1801.03400*. Available: https://arxiv.org/abs/1801.03400v1 [December 2018].
Brookey, R.A. (2007). The format wars: Drawing the battle lines for the next DVD. *Convergence: The International Journal of Research into New Media Technologies, 13*(2), 199–211.
Brunton, F., and Nissenbaum, H. (2015). *Obfuscation: A User's Guide for Privacy and Protest*. Cambridge, MA: MIT Press.
Buchanan, L. (2017). *Brief Overview of the Revised Common Rule and Subpart B—Pregnant Women*. Washington, DC: Office for the Human Research Protections. Available: https://www.nichd.nih.gov/sites/default/files/2017-11/4-OverviewNew_Rule_SubpartB.pdf [December 2018].
Burger, J. (2017). *The Health of People: How the Social Sciences Can Improve Population Health*. London, UK: SAGE Publications.
Cadwalladr, C., and Harrison-Graham, E. (2018). 50 million Facebook profiles harvested for Cambridge Analytica in major data breach. *The Guardian*, March 17. Available: https://www.theguardian.com/news/2018/mar/17/cambridge-analytica-facebook-influence-us-election [December 2018].
Chen, A. (2015). Seeing into the future: Does Philip Tetlock hold the key to accurate predictions? *The Chronicle Review*, October 5. Available: https://www.chronicle.com/article/Philip-Tetlock-s-Tomorrows/233507 [December 2018].
Dear, B. (2017). *The Friendly Orange Glow: The Untold Story of the Rise of Cyberculture*. New York: Penguin Random House
Defense Advanced Research Projects Agency. (2018). *Our Research*. Available: https://www.darpa.mil/our-research [December 2018].
Deitchman, S. (1976). *The Best-Laid Schemes: A Tale of Social Research and Bureaucracy*. Cambridge, MA: The MIT Press.
Gearty, C. (2008). Skewing scholarship. *The Social Science Research Council*, October 9. Available: http://essays.ssrc.org/minerva/2008/10/09/gearty [November 2018].
Gibney, E. (2018). The scant science behind Cambridge Analytica's controversial marketing techniques. *Nature News Explainer*, March 29. Available: https://www.nature.com/articles/d41586-018-03880-4?utm_source=twt_nnc&utm_medium=social&utm_campaign=naturenews&sf185785067=1 [November 2018].
Gilman, N. (2004). *Mandarins of the Future: Modernization Theory in Cold War America*. Baltimore, MD: Johns Hopkins University Press.
Golden, D. (2017). *Spy Schools: How the CIA, FBI, and Foreign Intelligence Secretly Exploit America's Universities*. New York: Henry Holt and Company.
Goolsby, R. (2005). Ethics and defense agency funding: Some considerations. *Social Networks, 27*(2), 95–106.
Grindley, P. (1990). Winning standards contests: Using product standards in business strategy. *Business Strategy Review, 1*(1), 71–84.
Harman, J. (2015). Disrupting the Intelligence Community: America's spy agencies need an upgrade. *Foreign Affairs*, March/April. Available: https://www.foreignaffairs.com/articles/united-states/2015-03-01/disrupting-intelligence-community [November 2018].

Hauch, V., Blandón-Gitlin, I., Masip, J., and Sporer, S.L. (2015). Are computers effective lie detectors? A meta-analysis of linguistic cues to deception. *Personality and Social Psychology Review, 19*(4), 307–342.

Heathcote, A., Brown, S., and Mewhort, D.J.K. (2000). The power law repealed: The case for an exponential law of practice. *Psychonomic Bulletin and Review, 7*(2), 185–207.

Hoag, H. (2003). Remote control. *Nature, 423*(6942), 796–798. doi:10.1038/423796a.

Johnson, L.K. (2018). *Spy Watching: Intelligence Accountability in the United States.* New York: Oxford University Press.

Johnson, L.K. (2019). Spies and scholars in the United States: Winds of ambivalence in the groves of academe. *Intelligence and National Security, 34*(1), 1–21. doi:10.1080/02684527.2018.1517429.

Jones, J.H., and Handcock, M.S. (2003). Sexual contacts and epidemic thresholds. *Nature, 423*(6940), 605–606.

Koonin, S., Keller, S.A., Shipp, S.S., Allen, T.W., and Walejko, G.K. (2013). *Pathways to Cooperation between the Intelligence Community and the Social and Behavioral Science Communities* (Analyses Paper P-5000). Alexandria, VA: Institute of Defense.

Krebs, R.R. (2008). Minerva: Unclipping the owl's wings. *The Social Science Reseach Council,* November 19. Available: http://essays.ssrc.org/minerva/2008/11/19/krebs [November 2018].

Lewis, P., Grierson, J., and Weaver, M. (2018). Cambridge Analytica academic's work upset university colleagues. *The Guardian,* March 24. Available: https://www.theguardian.com/education/2018/mar/24/cambridge-analytica-academics-work-upset-university-colleagues [December 2018].

Licklider, J.C.R. (1960). Man–computer symbiosis. *IRE Transactions on Human Factors in Electronics, HFE-1*(1), 4–11. doi:10.1109/THFE2.1960.4503259.

Mandler, P. (2013). *Return from the Natives: How Margaret Mead Won the Second World War and Lost the Cold War.* New Haven, CT: Yale University Press.

Mayer-Schönberger, V. (2011). *Delete: The Virtue of Forgetting in the Digital Age.* Princeton, NJ: Princeton University Press.

Minerva Research Initiative. (2018). *Minerva Research Initiative.* Available: https://minerva.defense.gov [November 2018].

Moreno, J. (2012). *Mind Wars: Brain Science and the Military in the 21st Century.* New York: Bellevue Literary Press.

National Academies of Sciences, Engineering, and Medicine. (2017). *The Value of Social, Behavioral, and Economic Sciences to National Priorities: A Report for the National Science Foundation.* Washington, DC: The National Academies Press.

National Research Council. (1971). *Behavioral and Social Science Research in the Department of Defense: A Framework for Management.* Washington, DC: The National Academies Press.

National Research Council. (2008). *Emerging Cognitive Neuroscience and Related Technologies.* Washington, DC: The National Academies Press.

National Research Council. (2009). *Opportunities in Neuroscience for Future Army Applications.* Washington, DC: The National Academies Press.

National Research Council. (2012). *Using Science as Evidence in Public Policy.* Washington, DC: The National Academies Press.

National Research Council and National Academy of Engineering. (2014). *Emerging and Readily Available Technologies and National Security: A Framework for Addressing Ethical, Legal, and Societal Issues.* Washington, DC: The National Academies Press. doi:10.17226/18512.

Norberg, A.L., O'Neill, J.E., and Freedman, K. (1996). *Transforming Computer Technology: Information Processing for the Pentagon, 1962–1986.* Baltimore, MD: Johns Hopkins University Press.

O'Rand, A.M. (1992). Mathematizing social science in the 1950s: The early development and diffusion of game gheory. *History of Political Economy,* 24, 177–204.
Office of the Director of National Intelligence. (2015). *The Good Judgment Project.* Available: https://www.iarpa.gov/index.php/newsroom/iarpa-in-the-news/2015/439-the-good-judgment-project [November 2018].
Office of the Director of National Intelligence. (2018). *Getting Started with IARPA.* Available: https://www.iarpa.gov/index.php [November 2018].
Oren, I. (2002). *Our Enemies and Us: America's Rivalries and the Making of Political Science.* Ithaca, NY: Cornell University Press.
Penny, J.W. (2016). Chilling effects: Online surveillance and Wikipedia use. *Berkeley Technology Law Journal,* 31(1), 117. doi:10.15779/Z38SS13.
Pfiffner, J.P. (2010). *Torture as Public Policy: Restoring U.S. Credibility on the World Stage.* Boulder, CO: Paradigm.
Porter, T.M. (1986). *The Rise of Statistical Thinking, 1820–1900.* Princeton, NJ: Princeton University Press.
Rohde, J. (2013). *Armed with Expertise: The Militarization of American Social Research During the Cold War.* Ithaca, NY: Cornell University Press.
Rohde, J. (2017). Pax Technologica: Computers, international affairs, and human reason in the Cold War. *ISIS,* 108(4), 792–813.
Rudolph, A. (2003). Military: Brain machine could benefit millions. *Nature,* 424(6947), 369. doi:10.1038/424369b.
Shaw, T. (2018). The new military-industrial complex of big data psy-ops. *The New York Review of Books,* March 21. Available: https://www.nybooks.com/daily/2018/03/21/the-digital-military-industrial-complex [December 2018].
Siegel, E. (2018). Blatantly discriminatory machines: When algorithms explicitly penalize. *Predictive Analytics World,* September 25. Available: https://www.predictiveanalyticsworld.com/patimes/blatantly-discriminatory-machines-when-algorithms-explicitly-penalize/9697 [December 2018].
Silence of the Neuroengineers. (2003). *Nature,* 423, 787. doi:10.1038/423787b.
Smith, A., and Stirling, A. (2007). Moving outside or inside? Objectification and reflexivity in the governance of socio-technical systems. *Journal of Environmental Policy and Planning,* 9(3-4), 351–373.
Tetlock, P.E., Mellers, B.A., Rohrbaugh, N., and Chen, E. (2014). Forecasting tournaments: Tools for increasing transparency and improving the quality of debate. *Current Directions in Psychological Science,* 23(4), 290–295.
U.S. Senate, Select Committee on Intelligence. (2014). *Committee Study of the Central Intelligence Agency's Detention and Interrogation Program,* 113th Cong., 2d Sess., December 3, 2014.
Voosen, P. (2015). Damning revelations prompt social science to rethink its ties to the military. *Chronicle of Higher Education,* July 15. Available: https://www.chronicle.com/article/Damning-Revelations-Prompt/231591 [July 2018].
Walsh, P.F., and Miller, S. (2016). Rethinking 'five eyes' security intelligence collection policies and practice post Snowden. *Intelligence and National Security,* 31(3), 345–368.
Weinberger, S. (2017). *The Imagineers of War: The Untold Story of DARPA, the Pentagon Agency That Changed the World.* New York: Knopf Doubleday.
Wildermuth, J. (2018). California elected officials dismayed at use of Facebook data. *San Francisco Chronicle,* March 20. Available: https://www.sfchronicle.com/politics/article/California-elected-officials-dismayed-at-use-of-12769078.php [December 2018].
Zehfuss, M. (2012). Culturally sensitive war? The human terrain system and the seduction of ethics. *Security Dialogue,* 43(2), 175–190.
Zook, M., Barocas, S., Boyd, D., Crawford, K., Keller, E., Gangadharan, S.P., Goodman, A., Hollander, R., Koenig, B.A., Metcalf, J., Narayanan, A., Nelson, A., and Pasquale, F. (2017). Ten simple rules for responsible big data research. *PLoS Computational Biology,* 13(3), e1005399. doi:10.1371/journal.pcbi.1005399.

10

Capitalizing on Opportunities in Social and Behavioral Sciences (SBS) Research: A 10-Year Vision

Ten years from now the job of the intelligence analyst will have been transformed. Technological changes—both new technologies that can be used to conduct analysis and risks related to technologically based activities and communications around the world—are virtually inevitable. What is not inevitable is that the Intelligence Community (IC) will adapt to these changes in the most productive ways. The central argument of this report is that integrating the understanding of human beings and social processes that comes from social and behavioral sciences (SBS) research into the analyst's work as it evolves in the coming decade will be critical. It is this knowledge base that will enable the IC to develop technological supports that are both proactive and interactive and can effectively augment the capacities of human analysts and, more broadly, to respond effectively to the security threats of the coming decades. Capitalizing on the power of research that integrates the insights from SBS research with what technology makes possible will require a fundamental commitment by the IC.

INTELLIGENCE ANALYSIS IN 10 YEARS

Consider the daily activities of an individual analyst. An analyst's workday begins with an inventory of key questions for which she is responsible (see Chapter 4), and that is not likely to change. Today, an analyst may have a running list of such questions, supplemented each day through a review of news feeds, emails, conversations, or written messages. Ten years from now, an individual analyst will likely work with an artificial intelligence (AI) agent that will continuously monitor sources of information relevant to the analyst's inventory of questions and identify anomalies that may indicate new areas about which inquiry is warranted. This technological support will enable the analyst to spend much less time getting updated on current events, and more time looking for emergent trends in data and identifying optimal intervention points and policy opportunities for decision makers.

The key questions of the day for an analyst frequently include specific queries from policy makers about developing events. In the future, White House officials and other national security experts are also likely to have AI agents that highlight key developments based on priorities set by algorithms that reflect the concerns for which those individuals, in turn, are responsible. These AI agents will uncover connections and circumstances that sharpen the questions they relay to analysts.

The analyst of the future who participates in the scenario presented in Chapter 4 receives questions from the White House about the activities of terrorist group Z in country Y, located in the region for which she is responsible. The questions from the White House suggest a direction that needs exploration, so the analyst and colleagues identify particular aspects of current social media traffic about which further analysis is needed.

Through AI real-time processing of large amounts of data, the analyst has access to a continuously updated compilation of emergent narrative themes in the flow of social media information with potential relevance to her account, but it is up to her and her human colleagues to identify the most intriguing themes, those worthy of further exploration and analysis. This analysis comes in the form of an interactive graphic display; the analysis team has requested highlights from new narrative threads, the emotional intensity of the dialogue about threads that have been flagged, and the source of those threads. The interactive graphical display shows connections between the relatively closed network of chat rooms associated with terrorist group X and other networks. The analyst can click on links to learn more about the nature of the other networks, the geographic range of their members, how the connections were forged, and the key narratives being promulgated by each network.

The analyst's personal AI agent, which has already stored a significant amount of information about her responsibilities and mode of working, notifies her that another analytic team has requested a similar analysis, and suggests contact with that group. It also offers her data maintained by a third team, whose account has to do with monitoring of weapons shipments around the globe, because that group has recently logged a change in transit points, bringing a particular supply chain closer to the region she monitors. The system also prompts her on whether it would be helpful to have an analysis of recent news coverage of elections in country X, which borders country Y. The system notes that the amount of Internet chatter from one of the terrorist networks in her region of responsibility has escalated and may signal an impending threat. Her AI agent reminds her of her most persistent cognitive biases and blind spots, and recommends involving colleagues who complement her cognitive profile.

When the analyst brainstorms with her team of colleagues, they determine that the political developments are not likely relevant to the question about terrorist group Z's current activities, applying deep knowledge and instincts that only human beings could have. One colleague who was recently stationed in the region knows that the elections are tightly controlled by the ruling regime, which is separate from the terrorist group. Because a serious and years-long drought in the area may be contributing to instability, the analytic team begins to investigate whether terrorist group Z may have become involved in black market activities associated with the water supply. The AI agent identifies recent published anthropological field research about the region that might guide the development of new lines of research and analysis. Social media analytics reveals that some of the narratives being promoted by the terrorist group are aimed at undermining the current regime; the terrorist group is using sophisticated bots to spread images and stories suggesting that the regime is denying water to particular groups.

The analyst realizes that the new line of analysis that has emerged is important enough that others in the national security community should be alerted. After a first-draft assessment of the situation has been generated by the AI agent, she refines the text and adds software-generated visualizations that are easier for her colleagues and clients to digest. The creation of the assessment triggers automated processes that elevate the warnings associated with terrorist group Z and provides clients with a visual cue that new analytic assessments are forthcoming.

OPPORTUNITIES TO SHAPE THE FUTURE OF INTELLIGENCE ANALYSIS

Reliance on SBS research is embedded is almost every line of this portrait of the future, which is based on the premise that the IC has taken advantage of research discussed in this report. There is little doubt that the IC can expect new tools and types of data—and new security challenges—to alter the way intelligence analysis is carried out. SBS research offers the IC important opportunities to shape the way it responds to these changes. The opportunities described in this report offer the potential for

- stronger intelligence assessments;
- tools and technologies optimally designed for human use and human–machine interaction; and
- strengthened readiness to confront evolving security threats.

Stronger Intelligence Assessments

The research described in this report can support the development of intelligence assessments that will be **richer** 10 years from now because of the capacity to make use of new types of information and analyze existing types of information in new ways. For example, the analyst may be able to draw on new types of information—such as digital trace data that simultaneously reveal patterns in social media discourse and live interactions, models of interactions between social networks and political ideology, and analysis using natural language processing—which will improve his capacity to conceptualize and quantify cultural phenomena. Technology is making it possible to identify patterns in large datasets and integrate different sorts of data, including video and audio data and other visual representations; SBS research is providing the essential theoretical and empirical basis for designing and using these sophisticated methodologies to make the data meaningful and enrich the analyst's understanding of the social and political worlds.

Assessments may be **more nuanced**. Technology that is grounded in foundational SBS research may enable analysts to identify intersections and see connections that humans alone could not have detected. Analysts may be able to assess complex phenomena and developments more systematically, for example, and to discern more easily the way an incident or piece of information fits—or may influence—a larger context. This technological augmentation of a human's capacity to synthesize multiple types of data and to visualize and communicate complex findings may facilitate more nuanced understanding of the developments analysts track, and also support forecasting from a sociocultural perspective to facilitate more robust assessments of future possibilities.

Assessments may be **more accurate and efficient**. The methodologies and tools described in this report may allow for faster processing of large volumes of data, integration of multiple kinds of data, and other forms of analysis and tracking that would be beyond the capacity of human analysts. These capabilities can make it possible to efficiently track regions, populations, groups, and sources of information, from news coverage and social media discourse to satellite imagery of troop movements. The analyst may have improved capacity to address probabilistic events and to anticipate a range of possible outcomes. Indicators useful for gauging changes in a political leader's behavior, the developing strength of minority group's influence, or the cohesiveness of networks within which toxic narratives are spreading may aid the analyst in avoiding surprises and lead him more swiftly to developments requiring attention. Advances in cognitive science and neuroscience may provide more reliable indications of whether someone is being persuaded than could be gleaned from that person's self-report.

Advances in social cybersecurity may decrease the time needed to assess the veracity of narratives, making earlier identification of threats possible and allowing for more reliable assessments of how populations respond to events of interest.

Tools and Technologies Optimally Designed for Human Use and Human–Machine Interaction

Technologies that become operational in the coming decade and beyond will augment the capacities of the human in vital ways, which will necessarily change how human analysts use and interact with them. Insights from SBS fields are essential to the design and development of tools and technologies that

- take advantage of the strengths of both humans and machines;
- allow humans to collaborate productively with machine partners;
- support more rapid assessment and forecasting of human activity; and
- avoid serious unintended practical and ethical consequences.

SBS research offers insights on human capacities and limitations, how humans can interact effectively with machines, how humans and machines can collaborate as teams, and how machines can mimic and manipulate humans. These insights will be needed in the design of tools that use AI and machine learning in conjunction with social network analysis, which will likely be an important component of analysis. This work could also support the development of an ecosystem for intelligence analysis composed of human analysts and semiautonomous AI agents, operating on and through diverse social media and supported by other technologies. Such a team could, proactively and securely, reach across controlled-access networks and develop enhanced intelligence analyses by identifying patterns and associations in data more rapidly than humans alone could, doing so in real time and uncovering connections that previously would not have been detectable.

Whatever directions the IC takes in developing and procuring technologies to support intelligence analysis in the coming decade, it will surely rely on researchers and other experts, both those working within the IC and outside contractors; commercially available software programs; and other resources. The extent to which both basic and emerging SBS research is being incorporated into the planning, design, and use of the tools and methods used and purchased by the IC is not publicly known. Emphasis on this aspect of design is critical, however, because the technology used for analysis is only as strong as the understanding of the human behavior it is being used to model or explain; insights from SBS fields will provide essential support for the procurement of valid and effective products from the private sector to support the analyst's work.

Strengthened Readiness to Confront Evolving Security Threats

In the coming decade, the United States will face security challenges that include complex shifts in political dynamics; threats to international structures that have been a force for stability; and new types of weapons, including weaponized uses of information—all in the context of the effects of global climate change (see Chapter 3). Insights from SBS research discussed in this report—including improved understanding of the nature of social networks and complex systems, emerging sociotechnical responses to social cybersecurity threats, evolving ways of influencing hearts and minds, and the development of radicalization and extremism—represent but a few of the SBS contributions that will be vital to the U.S. capacity to react effectively to these evolving threats.

The emergence of new threats in cyberspace—cyber-mediated changes in individual, group, societal, and political behaviors and outcomes—is already a profound challenge for the IC, one that can be expected to grow in scale and urgency in the coming decade. The developing field of social cybersecurity, which integrates methods from the social sciences, most notably social network analysis, with machine learning, natural language processing, and other technologies, is offering tools, tactics, procedures, and policies with which to assess, predict, and mitigate the impact of adversarial social cyberattacks. Further research in this area can augment the significant approaches to cybersecurity already in place within the IC by integrating SBS-based understanding of individual and social processes and supporting the development of a new set of techniques for open-source assessment and forecasting that are grounded in understanding of social processes and phenomena.

Finally, the IC can use research from the fields of industrial-organizational psychology and human resource development in strengthening the readiness of its workforce to meet the challenges of the coming decade. The IC's procedures with respect to the selection and retention of its analytic workforce, analysts' skill development, and other aspects of workforce management are classified. However, translational research is needed to identify the applications of a well-developed body of research and practice to strengthening the analyst workforce. Such work could, for example, yield detailed descriptions of those attributes most useful for the selection of individuals likely to be effective analysts; strengthen agencies' capacity to retain the most effective analysts; foster an organizational climate conducive to trust, collaboration, and learning; and provide support for a workforce exposed to significant stresses in both offline and cyber-mediated environments.

CAPITALIZING ON THESE OPPORTUNITIES

The ideas discussed in this report highlight the reality that technological and other developments in intelligence analysis that proceed without the benefit of SBS research are likely to be limited in their effectiveness or worse, to result in misleading or distorted analysis. We close the report with our broad conclusion about the research opportunities that show promise for the coming decade and a recommendation for strengthening ties between the IC and the research community.

Research Opportunities

We have described both specific ideas and broad areas of opportunity for the IC to consider as it sets priorities for research in the coming decade that can support growth and development in how the analyst workforce performs its functions and in how that workforce itself is nurtured. There are many important areas—such as linguistics, cultural anthropology, behavioral economics, and learning science—that we were unable to address in this decadal survey, which by its nature could highlight only a few among many promising ideas. It is only through sustained attention to the integration of SBS research into its work that the IC can begin to more systematically take advantage of the full range of what SBS research has to offer. The following conclusion expresses our key message to IC leadership as they set specific priorities for research in the coming decade.

CONCLUSION 10-1: Social and behavioral sciences (SBS) research offers a fundamental—indeed essential—contribution to the mission of the Intelligence Community (IC), a mission that requires understanding of what human beings do, how, and why. The research described in this report amply demonstrates the critical importance of

- interdisciplinary research—both foundational and applied and domestic and international—designed to take advantage of and integrate theory, methodology, and data from across SBS fields to yield new insights into human behavioral and social processes with relevance to national security;
- the integration of basic science and developing research on human behavior and social processes, as well as advances in computational methods for large-scale data analysis, with the expertise of the IC on analytic methods and challenges;

- the incorporation of a deep understanding of the IC's challenges into the identification of research questions and hypotheses to be tested, as well as the design and execution of research;
- the integration of SBS insights into the design and engineering of technologically based analytic tools; and
- translational and applied work to establish the direct utility of SBS research findings for the IC.

Strengthening Ties Between the IC and the Research Community

This chapter's overview of the research examined in this report demonstrates both the power of the opportunities SBS research offers for the IC and the extent of the challenge of fully taking advantage of these opportunities. These ideas come from an extremely diverse set of academic disciplines: there is no "field" of SBS. This long report addresses only a sampling of potentially relevant SBS research; the contributions to intelligence analysis represented by these opportunities—and the landscape of opportunities we could not discuss here—cannot be realized simply by adding features to existing programs. If SBS perspectives are not fully integrated into the IC's thinking, they will bring limited benefit.

This report has described clear evidence of the IC's attention to SBS research, and valuable mechanisms, such as the Defense Advanced Research Projects Agency (DARPA) and the Intelligence Advanced Research Projects Activity (IARPA) are in place that can sponsor, facilitate, and help the IC utilize this research. However, these efforts remain ad hoc in important ways. While many of the mechanisms in place are stable, others come and go; many valuable efforts are "one-offs." The IC as a whole has not yet developed a means of systematically identifying opportunities in SBS research and ensuring that the potential applications of these opportunities to intelligence analysis are pursued.

Scholars have taken note of the gap between the information, ideas, and theories produced by academic researchers and the exigencies of applying that knowledge in the context of government service.[1] This gap is evident across domains, but some work has addressed its significance for the production and use of intelligence analysis. Literature produced under the umbrella of intelligence studies has produced conclusions about the practice of analysis (see Chapter 4) but has had only limited influence because

---

[1] An influential book that addresses these issues documents problems with the U.S. strategy in Iraq between 1988 and 1991 and suggests ways in which scholars might develop information that is easier to apply, and policy makers might make better use of available research (George, 1993; see also Desch, 2019).

of the distinct difference between the cultures of the IC and academia (see Chapter 2.) (Marrin, 2012; see also Hare and Coghill, 2016).

Strengthening the relationship between the SBS community and the IC is a broad-based challenge that has no single solution, and we recognize that we are by no means the first group to focus on this important challenge. Chapter 9 reviews lessons to be drawn from past collaborations between academic researchers and the IC. Capitalizing on the research opportunities discussed in this report will require the IC to abandon procedures and ways of doing business that have been in place for a long time; we close the report with our suggestions regarding ways the IC can proactively build collaboration with SBS researchers into its work.

RECOMMENDATION 10-1: The leadership of the Intelligence Community should make sustained collaboration with researchers in the social and behavioral sciences a key priority as it develops research objectives for the coming decade. A multipronged effort to integrate the knowledge and perspectives of researchers from these fields into the planning and design of efforts to support intelligence analysis is most likely to reap the potential benefits described in this report.

As the key coordinator of the IC, the Office of the Director of National Intelligence (ODNI) can continue to play an important leadership role in fostering the critical ties. The committee had no empirical foundation on which to base specific recommendations about institutional structures within the IC, and future efforts will need to be considered in light of particular efforts currently under way. Whatever structures are chosen, effective interchange is likely to involve four key ingredients:

1. Identifying and building on successful examples
2. Strengthening bridges between the two communities
3. Providing opportunities for analytic staff to build their knowledge of SBS research
4. Drawing on the principles of human–systems integration

Identify and Build on Successful Examples

As early as 1968, the National Academies noted that bringing SBS research to bear on national problems required bridging the divide between the specialized expertise of researchers and the broad problems faced by government (National Research Council Advisory Committee on Government Programs in the Behavioral Sciences, 1968, p. 46). The Intelligence Community Associates program brings academic specialists together and provides a natural bridge to the SBS community. Other valuable efforts to bridge the gap between the IC and academia have included the Future of Intelligence Analysis Project, a cooperative effort involving the University of Maryland's Center for International and Security Studies and ODNI, which yielded a two-volume report (Lahneman, 2006). Scholars have made broad recommendations for improving understanding and cooperation, such as encouraging scholars to spend time working in agencies and also encouraging analysts to spend time in academia; boosting the contributions of think tanks, which play a useful role in linking research to practice; and redesigning academic programs focused on intelligence (Marrin, 2012).

There is, however, no one office within the IC whose primary function is to survey the SBS landscape for promising research. The Intelligence Community Associates program and other efforts to support collaboration are a valuable resource for the IC and provide the platform on which to build stronger collaboration. One promising approach is the development of communities of practice by "finding junctures where the interests of the communities overlap sufficiently to create significant benefits for both," an objective recommended in a recent Institute for Defense Analyses report (Koonin et al., 2013). A few examples are highlighted in Boxes 10-1, 10-2, 10-3, and 10-4.

**BOX 10-1
Community of Practice:
The Defense Science Study Group (DSSG)**

Sponsored by the Defense Advanced Research Projects Agency (DARPA), the DSSG identifies new cohorts of talented researchers in the sciences and technology every 2 years. The group meets periodically to confer about research and development challenges facing the national security community. Many DSSG alumni maintain their ties to government, serving as advisors, consultants, and members of special task forces and boards (Koonin et al., 2013; http://dssg.ida.org). While the DSSG has focused primarily on the physical sciences and engineering, a similar program targeted at the SBS community might facilitate translation across the two communities.

> **BOX 10-2**
> **Community of Practice: The MEDEA Project**
>
> A collaboration between the IC and scholars in the environmental sciences offers one model for fostering a community of practice. Through the MEDEA (Measurement of Earth for Environmental Analysis) Project, the IC gave more than 60 environmental scientists access to classified images and data for use in environmental analysis. The project resulted in a number of successes, including the generation of new scientific insights and the public release of more than 860,000 satellite photographs. Perhaps most notably, the project built trust between the research communities and IC. This example suggests that big data research provides a set of problems well suited to facilitating IC–SBS collaboration (Koonin et al., 2013).[a]
>
> ---
> [a]For more information about the MEDEA Project, see Johnson (2000).

> **BOX 10-3**
> **Community of Practice: The Political Instability Task Force**
>
> The Central Intelligence Agency (CIA) established the Political Instability Task Force in 1994 in response to the request of senior U.S. policy makers for more social science–based information about the problems of state failure. For more than 15 years, the task force—a collection of mainly university-based social scientists—created quantitative databases, statistical models, and forecasting tools that deepened scholars' and policy officials' understanding of the causes of revolution, ethnic conflict, violent regime change, and genocide (Adler, 2001; McMurtrie, 2014). The work produced by these scholars appeared in dozens of academic research publications and has contributed to social scientific theories about state stability, as well as to methodological advances in international relations (Goldstone, 2001; Goldstone et al., 2010). At the same time, members of the IC have found the task force's forecasts of instability valuable: data collected by the group have, for example, been used to develop the National Intelligence Council's warning list of weak and failing states.[a]
>
> ---
> [a]This list has been prepared twice a year since 2005 (Wyler, 2008).

> **BOX 10-4**
> **Community of Practice:**
> **Laboratory for Analytic Sciences (LAS)**
>
> The LAS at North Carolina State University is a successful model of a directly applied research collaboration between the IC and the SBS community. Founded in 2013 by the National Security Agency, the LAS is "a mission-oriented, translational research laboratory" that seeks to "develop new analytic tradecraft, techniques, and technology" for users in the intelligence and defense communities (https://ncsu-las.org/about). This partnership is led by a team that combines deep expertise in both SBS fields and intelligence analysis (https://ncsu-las.org/about). LAS's research has contributed to social scientific knowledge about interdisciplinary research collaborations; it has also created a number of prototypes to facilitate intelligence analysis, including programs that automatically generate textual and visual explanations of incoming data (https://ncsu-las.org/about/accomplishments). Its research programs address important scholarly questions about human cognition, biases, and visualization, as well as research challenges in computational social science, while simultaneously providing translational tools for the intelligence and defense communities.

Strengthen Bridges Between the Two Communities

As discussed in Chapter 2, profound differences between the cultures of the IC and the SBS community reflect their differing missions. One prominent difference is in openness: academic researchers are accustomed to making their data and methods available to other researchers, having their hypotheses and work tested and reviewed, and so on. By contrast, intelligence analysts must work around the need for varying levels of classification.

Some SBS researchers have been reluctant to work on classified projects, which they perceive as placing restrictions on academic freedom, because of their scholarly commitment to open dissemination of research results, and universities have varying policies regarding the acceptance of contracts involving classified research (Goolsby, 2005). The IC worries about classified projects for other reasons, most notably because any expansion of access to classified materials creates the "potential for unintentional disclosure of sensitive intelligence or information about sources and methods" (National Research Council, 2011, p. 23, note 42). Some members of the IC have argued that making the most of open-source intelligence (OSINT) sources and SBS knowledge requires a culture shift, including addressing the problem of classification (Fingar, 2007). One specific illustration of the problem is the requirement that many agencies have for prepublication review and approval of publications derived from research funded by these agencies, which can inhibit collaboration with SBS academics and may even cause grant proposals to be rejected by university institutional review boards.

Several approaches may be of use in addressing this challenge. For some research purposes, it may be as effective to use a parallel but unclassified source of data. For example, data that once were classified but were later declassified could be made available to the entire SBS research community for comparison of methods and results. It may also be that a review of classification policies by the IC, in consultation with scholars, regarding research needs and objectives could identify policies that could be modified in particular cases.

Apart from issues of classification, means of facilitating productive interactions can play a key role. Possibilities include regular meetings at which members of the two communities share thinking about connections between research issues of concern to the IC, increased funding for unclassified research relating to such issues, and means of continuously soliciting input from researchers and providing incentives for them to pursue topics of interest to the IC. Testbeds, such as the one described in Chapter 7, offer another possibility for forging connections. One advantage to this model, in which researchers and members of the IC collaborate to design, test, and evaluate new projects, is that it can allow researchers access to analysts and their data and tools. Such collaborations can be a venue for research that targets important aspects of the work of the analyst without requiring outside access to classified material.

Provide Opportunities for Analytic Staff to Build SBS Knowledge

Members of the analytic workforce bring a wide range of educational and other experiences when they join the IC. While many have studied or earned degrees in SBS fields, others have not. The nature of their job allows them little time for keeping up with developments in even a single academic field, and little of the classified training they receive is likely to focus on basic SBS research. The committee heard anecdotally of valuable opportunities for analysts to deepen their knowledge of SBS work, including opportunities to take college courses periodically, attend training seminars at conferences, take short courses offered by universities, and participate in training offered by the agencies.

Nevertheless, there is a need for mechanisms through which analysts can keep current on SBS research relevant to their work in focused ways. The volume of relevant SBS research increases continuously, and keeping up even with a single subspecialty relevant to IC concerns could be a full-time job. While individual analysts and institutional units pursue the objective of staying current, we are not aware of any process for ensuring that analysts working in a particular area can remain abreast of research developments. Possibilities for the IC to consider include working groups developed for the purpose of addressing a particular problem set or theme with SBS dimensions that could allow analysts the opportunity to develop expertise in that area over time. By focusing on such a problem set or theme, the working group could both identify relevant work and pursue individual interests while collaborating with others to build the expertise of the group, establishing themselves as a resource for others. The use of challenge problems, datasets, and artificial social media environments could, for example, support the development and testing of new theories and technologies for cybersecurity.

Other options include the use of such arrangements as the Intergovernmental Personnel Act (IPA) Mobility Program[2] and internship opportunities for Ph.D. candidates that would allow SBS researchers to spend time in the IC and analysts to spend time in academic settings. Such options would require that onerous clearance and classification review constraints be relaxed.

The development of expertise in relevant SBS research could be treated as a core responsibility, and rewarded accordingly. All of these efforts would have the additional benefit of helping researchers build their understanding of the IC.

Draw on the Principles of Human–Systems Integration

Finally, the SBS research identified in this report as relevant to national security is in different stages of operational readiness. Some is still in the basic science stage; some (e.g., many of the ideas for the analyst workforce) is close to translation; and early versions of other research (e.g., social network methods) are in use by the IC. In some cases, new research conducted in the IC context will be needed to assess interventions found to improve teamwork in other settings. Evidence from other contexts for the effectiveness of various interventions can be used as a starting point for the development of interventions for the security community that will need to be tested in the security context.

Once basic research has been evaluated for its applicability in the IC context, it can be translated into operational procedures, methods, or pol-

---

[2] The IPA program allows for the temporary assignment of personnel between the federal government and outside organizations (e.g., state/local governments, universities, federally funded research and development centers). The Office of Personnel Management notes that although federal agencies do not take full advantage of the IPA program, it is particularly useful in filling positions that require special expertise (e.g., research scientists). The personnel are on detail to the federal agencies and remain employees of their home institutions. See https://www.opm.gov/policy-data-oversight/hiring-information/intergovernment-personnel-act/#url=Assignment for more information on the IPA program.

icies. This translation requires collaboration among scientists, engineers, analysts, and applied scientists who are adept at the process. The nature of some SBS research (e.g., that in social networks and social cybersecurity) is such that the basic research involves the codevelopment of operational procedures, methods, and theories. In such cases, translational research takes a very different form from that in other areas, such as team science and psychology. Moreover, much of the research that will need to be translated for the IC context in the coming decade will involve interactions among humans and machines, often through social media.

Human–systems integration, an approach developed in the early 20th century, draws on research from numerous SBS domains, including psychology, human factors, management, occupational health and safety, and human–computer interaction, to improve the development of sociotechnical systems (dynamic systems in which people, tasks, technology, and the environment interact throughout the stages of the work the system is to carry out). The goal of this approach is to develop a resilient and adaptive system and avoid unintended consequences (National Research Council, 2007). A human–systems integration approach helps ensure that operational solutions address the needs as well as the capabilities and limitations of the analyst, including limitations that derive from policy decisions.

CLOSING THOUGHTS

Addressing the barriers that interfere with productive collaboration between the IC and the SBS community will require that both communities have realistic expectations; a shared understanding of what SBS research can offer; and an understanding of "the inherent limitations in providing simple, universally applicable answers to complex social science questions," in the words of another National Academies committee, charged with examining the integration of SBS research into the weather enterprise (National Academies of Sciences, Engineering, and Medicine, 2017, p. 6). In 1968, the National Academies argued that bridging the gap between the behavioral sciences and the federal government "requires identifying positions of responsibility in the government where an understanding of the behavioral sciences is essential" (National Research Council Advisory Committee on Government Programs in the Behavioral Sciences, 1968, p. 47).

The IC has unmistakably recognized the importance of SBS research, as its request for the present study demonstrates. Such efforts as the inventory of in-house SBS expertise conducted by ODNI in the wake of the 9/11 Commission Report are further evidence of that commitment (Fingar, 2011). Most recently, the director of national intelligence released a formal strategy for taking advantage of AI and other technologies to augment intelligence, which addresses the importance of "basic research focused on sense-making" and strengthening collaboration between the IC and research institutions (Office of the Director of National Intelligence, 2019, pp. v and 12). Academic institutions could contribute to the IC–SBS collaboration by devoting greater attention to translational research, supporting the operationalization of tools from the SBS community, and applying SBS research findings to national security needs. The continued strengthening of the IC workforce and the technological systems it needs will depend on interdisciplinary approaches in which the insights and ideas of SBS researchers are fully integrated with the needs and objectives of the IC.

REFERENCES

Adler, R. (2001). The crystal ball of chaos. *Nature, 414*(6863), 480–481.

Desch, M.C. (2019). *Cult of the Irrelevant: The Waning Influence of Social Science on National Security*. Princeton, NJ: Princeton University Press.

Fingar, T. (2007). *Remarks and Q&A by the Deputy Director of National Intelligence for Analysis & Chairman, National Intelligence Council*. Available: https://www.dni.gov/files/documents/Newsroom/Speeches%20and%20Interviews/20070717_speech_3.pdf [December 2018].

Fingar, T. (2011). Analysis in the U.S. Intelligence Community: Missions, masters, and methods. In B. Fischhoff and C. Chauvin (Eds.), *Intelligence Analysis: Behavioral and Social Scientific Foundations* (pp. 21–22). Washington, DC: The National Academies Press.

George, A.L. (1993). *Bridging the Gap: Theory and Practice in Foreign Policy*. Washington, DC: United States Institute of Peace Press.

Goldstone, J.A. (2001). Toward a fourth generation of revolutionary theory. *Annual Review of Political Science, 4*, 139–187. doi:10.1146/annurev.polisci.4.1.139.

Goldstone, J.A., Bates, R.H., Epstein, D.L., Gurr, T.R., Lustik, M.B., Marshall, M.G., Ulfelder, J., and Woodward, M. (2010). A global model for forecasting political instability. *American Journal of Political Science, 54*(1), 190–208.

Goolsby, R. (2005). Ethics and defense agency funding: Some considerations. *Social Networks, 27*(2), 95–106.

Hare, N., and Coghill, P. (2016). The future of the intelligence analysis task. *Intelligence and National Security, 31*(6), 858–870. doi:10.1080/02684527.2015.1115238.

Johnson, L.K. (2000). *Bombs, Bugs, Drugs, and Thugs: Intelligence and America's Quest for Security*. New York: New York University Press.

Koonin, S.E., Keller, S.A., Shipp, S.S., Allen, T.W., and Walejko, G.K. (2013). *Pathways to Cooperation Between the Intelligence Community and the Social and Behavioral Science Communities*. IDA Paper P-5000. Arlington, VA: Institute for Defense Analyses.

Lahneman, W.J. (2006). *The Future of Intelligence Analysis, Volume I. Final Report*. College Park: The Center for International and Security Studies at Maryland.

Marrin, S. (2012). Is intelligence analysis an art or a science? *International Journal of Intelligence and Counterintelligence, 25*(3), 529–545. doi: 10.1080/08850607.2012.678690.

McMurtrie, B. (2014). Scoping out the future. *Chronicle of Higher Education*, October 13. Available: https://www.chronicle.com/article/Scoping-Out-the-Future/149271 [December 2018].

National Academies of Sciences, Engineering, and Medicine. (2017). *Integrating Social and Behavioral Sciences within the Weather Enterprise*. Washington, DC: The National Academies Press. doi:10.17226/24865.

National Research Council Advisory Committee on Government Programs in the Behavioral Sciences. (1968). *The Behavioral Sciences and the Federal Government*. Washington, DC: National Academy of Sciences.

National Research Council. (2007). *Human–System Integration in the System Development Process: A New Look*. Washington, DC: The National Academies Press. doi:10.17226/11893.

National Research Council. (2011). *Intelligence Analysis: Behavioral and Social Scientific Foundations*. Washington, DC: The National Academies Press.

Office of the Director of National Intelligence. (2019). *The AIM Initiative—A Strategy for Augmenting Intelligence Using Machines*. Available: https://www.dni.gov/files/ODNI/documents/AIM-Strategy.pdf [February 2019].

Wyler, L.S. (2008). *Weak and Failing States: Evolving Security Threats and U.S. Policy* (Order Code RL34253). Washington, DC: Congressional Research Service. Available: https://fas.org/sgp/crs/row/RL34253.pdf [December 2018].

Appendix A

Summary of National Security-Related Research Programs

The federal government supports work in the social and behavioral sciences (SBS) through many of its agencies and programs, including those responsible for national security and defense. The National Science Foundation (NSF), for example, provides funding to support partners that include the Army Research Laboratory, the U.S. Department of Homeland Security (DHS), the Office of Naval Research, and the Air Force Research Laboratory. This funding is used for basic research that contributes to the development of mission-specific tools and applications, including work from SBS fields (National Academies of Sciences, Engineering, and Medicine, 2017). There are several entities whose missions specifically include a focus on SBS research related to security and intelligence. The best known are the Minerva Research Initiative (Minerva), the Defense Advanced Research Projects Agency (DARPA), and the Intelligence Advanced Research Projects Activity (IARPA), but other entities also make contributions. The committee examined publicly available descriptions of the work of these three entities and invited federal officials to make presentations and answer questions about these programs during public portions of its meetings. This appendix provides an overview of the SBS work sponsored by these entities, as well as other relevant programs within the U.S. Department of Defense (DoD); it does not represent all relevant research sponsored by the Intelligence Community (IC) or other federal entities.

MINERVA RESEARCH INITIATIVE

The goal of the Minerva Research Initiative is to improve DoD's "basic understanding of the social, cultural, behavioral, and political forces that shape regions of the world of strategic importance to the U.S."[1] Minerva does so primarily by funding basic SBS research conducted at universities within the United States and around the world. None of the research is classified, and Minerva encourages and supports data sharing. Minerva coordinates its research efforts with work at other government entities that sponsor SBS research, including DARPA, IARPA, DHS, NSF, and the U.S. Department of Justice, as well as with research entities in the United Kingdom. Minerva researchers provide expertise to the Office of the Joint Chiefs of Staff, DoD and the IC, the U.S. Department of State, and the U.S. Agency for International Development.

Each year, Minerva specifies topics of particular interest to DoD to guide researchers seeking funding. For 2018, the Minerva Topics of Interest were as follows:[2]

- Topic 1: Sociopolitical (In)Stability, Resilience, and Recovery
- Topic 2: Economic Interdependence and Security
- Topic 3: Alliances and Burden Sharing
- Topic 4: Fundamental Dynamics of Scientific Discovery
- Topic 5: Adversarial Information Campaigns
- Topic 6: Automated Cyber Vulnerability Analysis
- Topic 7: Power, Deterrence, Influence, and Escalation Management for Shaping Operations
- Topic 8: Security Risks in Ungoverned and Semi-Governed Spaces

For that year, Minerva indicated a particular interest in "proposals that align with and support the National Defense Strategy" (see Ch. 3, this volume) (Minerva Research Initiative, 2018, p. 1).

Researchers from more than 40 SBS disciplines have been involved in Minerva research initiatives. In addition to those that might be expected, such as international studies, anthropology, demography, and political science, specialized fields such as religious studies, mathematical social science, and cyber law are also represented. A sampling of topics addressed by Minerva projects in the past suggests the range of areas covered; see Box A-1.

---

[1] For more information on Minerva, see https://minerva.defense.gov [February 2019].
[2] Available: https://minerva.defense.gov/Research/Research-Priorities [January 2019].

BOX A-1
Examples of Recently Funded Minerva Projects

Terrorism, Governance, and Development: The "Terrorism, Governance, and Development" project has focused on understanding how efforts to rebuild social and economic order in conflict and post-conflict regions can effectively reduce violence. Demonstrating the value of rigorous analysis of microlevel data on conflict and the policies implemented to prevent or resolve them, the project brings game-theoretic models—an approach of proven utility to the analysis of non-violent social systems—to the study of conflict.

Documenting the Virtual Caliphate: ISIS propaganda, which is produced at an ever-increasing level of sophistication, has not been systematically logged and archived, by governments, academia, or other think tanks. Distinct from all other studies of ISIS media, this project will produce an updated, searchable database for future research.

Institutional Reform, Social Change, & Stability in Sahelian Africa: This project seeks answers to questions about the factors affecting stability and instability in six African countries—Senegal, Mauritania, Mali, Burkina Faso, Niger, and Chad—stretching across the arid Sahelian region. It focuses comparatively on factors influencing the capacity of these states to manage pressures—such as radical jihadi movements, endemic underdevelopment, and significant demographic changes—and hence maintain stability and ensure the social order and effective governance that serves as a bulwark against radical movements.

Measuring and Counting Social Influence and Persuasion: A dominant focus of the proposed work consists of information cascades (ICs), wherein large numbers of individuals participate to spread information and opinions across the globe, oftentimes producing significant changes in attitudes and behaviors. We will develop automated approaches informed by social science to determine what types of information "goes viral" and under what circumstances. We will develop novel measurement and analytic technologies for detecting ICs and understanding the ideological orientations of participating communities.

The Social Ecology of Radicalization: This project proposes to capitalize on knowledge and methods accrued in criminology to investigate (1) the characteristics of radicalizing settings (places where individuals undergo all or part of the process of radicalization, both geographic and virtual); (2) the processes of self- and social selection through which individuals end up exposed to these radicalizing settings; and (3) the systemic processes that promote (or suppress) the emergence of radicalizing settings and, hence, a social ecology favorable (or unfavorable) to radicalization.

SOURCE: Excerpted from project descriptions posted on the Minerva website at https://minerva.defense.gov/Research/Funded-Projects [January 2019].

DARPA AND IARPA

DARPA and IARPA (together with the Advanced Research Projects Agency of the U.S. Department of Energy[3]) function as the primary federal research and development (R&D) agencies supporting national security and intelligence. Both agencies fund research from a wide variety of academic and scientific disciplines, not exclusively SBS fields. These agencies have been described as sharing "an ambitious innovation organization model" because they serve as intermediaries between the research community and industry and the needs of the federal government; both seek to fund and oversee research programs conducted by university researchers, as well as outside contractors (Bonvillian, 2018). Both agencies are charged with identifying and fostering research that is intended to achieve transformative change rather than incremental advances.[4]

DARPA was founded in 1958, in the wake of the USSR's launch of the Sputnik satellite, to help the U.S. government "spur innovation through its R&D investments," with a specific focus on the needs of the U.S. military (Gallo, 2018, p. 4). It was designed to operate flexibly, relatively unfettered by rules and regulations that tend to retard the functioning of federal agencies. Its program managers were accorded levels of trust recognized as "unique across the federal government" (Gallo, 2018, p. 4).

DARPA regularly updates its criteria for identifying the highest-priority projects to support. The current criteria are as follows:[5]

- To rethink complex military systems
- To master the information explosion
- To harness biology as technology
- To expand the technological frontier

Much of DARPA's work is highly technical, but the agency also supports research in SBS fields. The Next Generation Social Science (NGS2) Program, for example, was designed to foster social science research that takes advantage of large digital datasets.[6] Another DARPA program with a social science focus is Ground Truth, focused on research using social science modeling and simulation methods.[7]

IARPA, which was established in 2007 to apply the DARPA model specifically to intelligence, uses models including funded research programs, seedling studies to foster emerging ideas, prize challenges, and technical

---

[3] See https://arpa-e.energy.gov [January 2019].
[4] Available: https://www.darpa.mil/about-us/about-darpa [January 2019].
[5] Available: https://www.darpa.mil/program/our-research/more [February 2019].
[6] See https://www.darpa.mil/program/next-generation-social-science [January 2019].
[7] See https://www.darpa.mil/program/ground-truth [January 2019].

workshops to explore promising ideas. The products of many of its projects are applied by federal agencies.[8]

IARPA is well known for supporting work in highly technical areas including quantum computing and superconducting computing, as well as topics in physics, chemistry, biology, and other fields. Partly in response to the recommendations in a National Research Council (2011) report, IARPA leadership has focused greater attention on SBS research. Recent IARPA-sponsored projects in fields including cognitive psychology, organizational psychology, economics, geography, sociology, sociophysiology, behavioral epidemiology, sociolinguistics, computational linguistics, and political science demonstrate this focus. IARPA organizes its work through four "research thrusts":[9] analysis, anticipatory intelligence, collection, and computing. A list of IARPA's research programs can be found at https://www.iarpa.gov/index.php/research-programs [January 2019].

OTHER DOD PROGRAMS

The committee did not do a comprehensive survey of all entities that sponsor or conduct SBS-related research with relevance to security and intelligence, but we note that other programs within DoD play a role.

The Office of Naval Research (ONR) (2018) established the Multidisciplinary University Research Initiatives (MURI) Program with goals similar to those of DARPA and IARPA, with an emphasis on seeking significant breakthroughs through research that involves multiple disciplines.[10] A subset of the work supported by MURI is drawn from SBS fields. Six of the 24 projects funded in 2018 include SBS components; the topics addressed were the following:[11]

1. Coevolution of Neural, Cognitive, and Social Networks: Mind-Body-Community Connections
2. Network Games
3. Modeling Interdependence among Natural Systems and Human Population Dynamics
4. Advanced Mean-Field Game Theory for Complex Physical and Socioeconomic Systems
5. Automated Technical Document Comprehension
6. Self-Assessment of Proficiency for Autonomous and Intelligent Systems

---

[8]See https://www.iarpa.gov/index.php/about-iarpa/2017-year-in-review [February 2019].
[9]See https://www.iarpa.gov/index.php/about-iarpa [February 2019].
[10]See https://www.onr.navy.mil/Science-Technology/Directorates/office-research-discovery-invention/Sponsored-Research/University-Research-Initiatives/MURI.aspx [January 2019].
[11]See https://media.defense.gov/2018/Apr/02/2001898337/-1/-1/1/MURI-2018-AWARDS-ANNOUNCEMENT.PDF [January 2019]).

ONR also fosters research to enhance the performance of its personnel through the Warfighter Performance Department, which sponsors work in bioengineered and biorobotics systems, medical technologies, improved manpower, personnel, training, and system design.[12] Another ONR project is the Cognitive Science for Naval Adaptive Training Program, focused on the design of training devices, simulations, and materials for naval personnel.[13]

Similarly, the U.S. Army sponsors and uses SBS research through numerous projects. The Department of Human Research and Engineering conducts basic and applied research focused on "future technologies to enhance Soldier performance and Soldier-system interactions."[14] The U.S. Army Research Institute for the Behavioral and Social Sciences also conducts its own SBS research, with an emphasis on maximizing individual and unit performance and readiness to meet Army operational requirements through advances in the SBS.[15] Another example is the Human Sciences Campaign, which pursues advances and technological innovations that can support the warfighter in three areas: human behavior, human capability enhancement, and integration of humans and systems.[16] The U.S. Air Force also has a unit devoted to research to enhance performance, the 711th Human Performance Wing.[17]

REFERENCES

Bonvillian, W.B. (2018). DARPA and its ARPA-E and IARPA clones: A unique innovation organization model. *Industrial and Corporate Change*, 27(5), 897–914. Available: https://academic.oup.com/icc/article-abstract/27/5/897/5096003?redirectedFrom=PDF [February 2019].

Gallo, M.A. (2018). *Defense Advanced Research Projects Agency: Overview and Issues for Congress.* Washington, DC: Congressional Research Service. Available: https://fas.org/sgp/crs/natsec/R45088.pdf [February 2019].

Minerva Research Initiative. (2018). *2018 Minerva Research Initiative Topics of Interest.* Available: https://minerva.defense.gov/Portals/47/documents/Research_Topics/Minerva%20FOA%202018%20topics%20file.pdf?ver=2018-06-04-163439-463 [February 2019].

National Academies of Sciences, Engineering, and Medicine. (2017). *The Value of Social, Behavioral, and Economic Sciences to National Priorities: A Report for the National Science Foundation.* Washington, DC: The National Academies Press. doi: 10.17226/24790.

---

[12] See https://www.onr.navy.mil/en/Science-Technology/Departments/Code-34 [January 2019].
[13] See https://www.onr.navy.mil/Science-Technology/Departments/Code-34/All-Programs/human-bioengineered-systems-341/cognitive-science-for-naval-adaptive-training [January 2019].
[14] See https://www.arl.army.mil/www/default.cfm?page=31 [January 2019].
[15] See https://www.consortium-research-fellows.org/work-sites/agencyid/3 [January 2019].
[16] See https://www.arl.army.mil/www/default.cfm?page=2519 [January 2019].
[17] See https://www.wpafb.af.mil/afrl/711hpw.aspx [January 2019].

National Research Council. (2011). *Intelligence Analysis for Tomorrow: Advances from the Behavioral and Social Sciences*. Committee on Behavioral and Social Science Research to Improve Intelligence Analysis for National Security. Board on Behavioral, Cognitive, and Sensory Sciences; Division of Behavioral and Social Sciences and Education. Washington, DC: The National Academies Press. doi:10.17226/13040.

Office of Naval Research. (2018). *Fiscal Year (FY) 2018 Department of Defense Multidisciplinary Research Program for the University Research Initiative* (ONR Announcement #N00014-17-S-F006). Available: https://micde.umich.edu/wp-content/uploads/sites/6/2017/04/2018-MURI-N00014-17-S-F006.pdf [February 2019].

Appendix B

Summary of the Committee's Information Gathering

The purpose of a decadal survey is to gather ideas from researchers and the community interested in the subject of the study that can be used to support future research initiatives. Following on the successful approach used in previous decadal surveys of the National Academies of Sciences, Engineering, and Medicine, this committee used a number of mechanisms to solicit input from relevant communities. Its efforts included public meetings, calls for white papers, public workshops, and other forums for gathering research ideas.

PUBLIC MEETINGS

Prior to the nomination of the decadal survey committee, a separate steering committee was appointed to plan and carry out a Summit on Social and Behavioral Sciences for National Security. The purposes of this summit, held October 4–5, 2016, in Washington, D.C., were to explore issues likely to be relevant and encourage members of the social and behavioral sciences (SBS) community to participate in the survey process.[1] The summit brought together academics, members of the Intelligence Community (IC), and representatives from the government to explore cutting-edge SBS research, the relevance of such work to intelligence analysis, and future directions for research. Presenters described relevant trends in their disciplines (e.g., brain research and neuroscience; the study of social interaction, behavioral

---

[1]Proceedings of the Summit can be found at http://www.nap.edu/catalog/24710/social-and-behavioral-sciences-for-national-security-proceedings-of-a [June 2019].

genetics, and risk and decision making). Representatives from the IC discussed objectives for the decadal survey and highlighted recurring issues and long-term strategic challenges (see Box B-1 for a list of presentations/speakers). In addition to the steering committee and staff, there were 130 in-person attendees and 226 webcast viewers from across the United States and Canada. The product of this summit provided valuable background as the committee was formed and began its work.

The decadal survey committee also invited researchers and members of the IC to make public presentations at two of its six meetings.[2] One panel included scholars in linguistics, political psychology, and political science. The second panel included representatives of federal research programs supporting SBS research for national security purposes who discussed accomplishments and objectives of such programs. Both sessions were accessible to in-person attendees (33, including speakers) and via webcast (98 individuals from across the United States and Argentina). See Box B-2 for a list of presenters.

WHITE PAPERS

The committee issued two separate calls for white papers. The first, open from November 2016 to February 2017, sought information on the needs and challenges facing the IC that might relate to SBS research. This call sought input from SBS academics and researchers with IC experience and/or knowledge to provide insights into the IC's needs and challenges. Authors were asked to address the following questions: (1) What are some of the key challenges, questions, and needs facing the IC regarding social and behavioral developments (see below)? (2) What makes these challenges and questions important at this time and in the foreseeable future? and (3) What are the anticipated national security benefits from addressing these challenges and questions? The committee received 36 papers in response to this first call. Table B-1 lists the papers; all white papers received are available on the study website at http://sites.nationalacademies.org/DBASSE/BBCSS/DBASSE_175673 [June 2019].

---

[2]See the study website for meeting agendas, speaker biographies, and select presentations at http://sites.nationalacademies.org/DBASSE/BBCSS/DBASSE_177475 [June 2019].

BOX B-1
Individuals Who Made Presentations at the Summit

The Past, Present, and Future: The Intelligence Community Needs of the Social and Behavioral Sciences
Charles Gaukel, National Intelligence Council
George Gerliczy, Central Intelligence Agency
Geoffrey Strayer, Defense Intelligence Agency

Brain and Neuroscience
Paul Glimcher, New York University, Synoptic data for integrating the social, behavioral, and biological sciences: The Kavli HUMAN project
Read Montague, Virginia Polytechnic Institute and State University, The new, new neuroscience: Extending the reach of modern approaches to brain and mind
Elizabeth Phelps, New York University, Emotion and decision making

Social Interaction
Joshua Epstein, Johns Hopkins University, Agent Zero and generative social science
Susan Fiske, Princeton University, Stereotyping and national security: Inequality and conflict—or peace
Mathew Burrows, Atlantic Council, What kind of future world?

Behavioral Genetics
Benjamin Neale, Harvard Medical School, Behavioral genetics and polygenic inheritance
David Cesarini, New York University, Predicating behavioral traits from genomic data

Decision Sciences and Risk
David Broniatowski, George Washington University, Communication strategies for behavior change on social media: Implications for public trust in government in the face of conspiracy theories
Paul Slovic, University of Oregon, Psychological perspectives on terrorism, national security and human rights: Research findings and future directions
Jeremy Wolfe, Harvard Medical School, How the heck did I miss that? How visual attention limits visual perception

Summative Comments
Robert Fein, Intelligence Community Studies Board, National Academies of Science, Engineering, and Medicine

> **BOX B-2**
> **Individuals Who Made Presentations to the Committee**
>
> *Meeting 1:*
> David Honey, Office of the Director of National Intelligence
> Sallie Keller, Virginia Polytechnic Institute and State University
> Roger Blandford, Stanford University
> Rita Bush, National Security Agency
> Charles Gaukel, National Intelligence Council
> George Gerliczy, Central Intelligence Agency
> Nancy Hayden, Sandia National Laboratories
> Emma Barrett, Centre for Research and Evidence on Security Threats
> Bear Braumoeller, The Ohio State University
> Sarah Croco, University of Maryland
> Michael Desch, The University of Notre Dame
> Ian McCulloh, Johns Hopkins University
> Leah Windsor, University of Memphis
>
> *Meeting 3:*
> Howard C. Nusbaum, National Science Foundation
> Adam Russell, Defense Advanced Research Projects Agency
> Lisa Troyer, Army Research Office/Minerva Research Initiative
> Jason Matheny, Intelligence Advanced Research Projects Activity

The second call for white papers, open May to June 2017, focused on possibilities in SBS research (concepts, methods, tools, techniques, and new ideas that could advance knowledge) for addressing analytic challenges and needs. This call sought input from researchers across a broad range of SBS fields, beyond those normally associated with national security and international relations. Authors were asked to identify recent advances and accomplishments in SBS research or consider new lines of investigation and to highlight possibilities for advancing fundamental knowledge in an SBS research domain. The committee received 62 papers in response to this second call; see Table B-2.

APPENDIX B

TABLE B-1 First Call White Papers

Principal Author and Institution	Paper (title)
Amir Kamel, King's College London	Economics and Security: The Ignored Relationship
Anna Duran, Avatar Research Institute	The Case for Sociocultural Situational Analysis in Intelligence Assessments
Dana Perkins, U.S. Department of Health and Human Services (HHS)	Mitigating Insider Threats through Strengthening Organizations' Culture of Biosafety, Biosecurity, and Responsible Conduct
David Broniatowski, George Washington University (GWU)	Combating Misinformation and Disinformation Online: The Battle of the Narrative
David Delaney, University of Maryland (UMd)	Behavioral Public Choice and National Security Decision Making
Elizabeth O'Hare, Society for Industrial and Organizational Psychology (SIOP)	Using Industrial-Organizational Psychology to Strengthen the National Security Workforce
Francisco Parra-Luna, Universidad Complutense de Madrid	Could We Speak of a "Social Sin" of Political Science?: A Critical Look from the Systemic Perspective
Herman Aguinis, GWU, School of Business	Early Identification of Outstanding Performers
Jason Spitaletta, Johns Hopkins University-Applied Physics Laboratory (JHU-APL)	The Role of Test and Evaluation in Intelligence Community Sponsored Social and Behavioral Science Research
Jennifer Webster, Pacific Northwest National Laboratory	Mathematical Lacks in Network Analysis
John Hoven	Business Schools: Context-Specific Social Science for an Operational Purpose
John Hummel, Argonne National Laboratory	Challenges in Incorporating Social and Behavioral Aspects into Intelligence Community Assessments
Joseph Dien, UMd, College Park	Cognitive Augmentation for Coping with Open-Source Intelligence (OSINT) Overload
Josiah Dykstra, National Security Agency (NSA)	Cyber Issues Related to Social and Behavioral Sciences for National Security
Kent Myers, Office of the Director of National Intelligence (ODNI)	Government Workshop on Decadal Questions
Kent Myers, ODNI	A Security Community Challenge: System Effects

continued

TABLE B-1 Continued

Principal Author and Institution	Paper (title)
Kent Myers, ODNI	Social and Behavioral Science for National Security: A Government Workshop held at the National Academy of Sciences, January 31, 2017
Kent Myers, ODNI	Social Science Research Needed to Help the IC Identify and Counter Deception-Related Threats
Leah Windsor, University of Memphis	The Predictive Potential of Political Discourse
Lucien Randazzese, SRI International	Social, Behavioral, and Economic Influences in Security Decision Making: Lessons from Early Work in Cybersecurity
Mark Wilson, North Carolina State University	Development of Key Variance Visualizations of Analytic Workflow for the Support of Data-Based Discussions
Mica Endsley, Human Factors and Ergonomics Society	HFES Comments on Social and Behavioral Sciences for National Security
Michael Fundator, Rutgers University	Combining Academic and Intelligence Knowledge and Methods in Finding Optimal Strategy for Health Policy and Cyber Security
Michael Lissack, American Society for Cybernetics (ASC)	The Role of UnCritically Examined Presuppositions (UCEP's) in SBS
Michael Lissack, ASC	We Need SBS to Embrace Its Subjectivity Not Hide It
Michael Mousseau, University of Central Florida (UCF)	The Promise of Economic Norms Theory
Morris Bosin	Proposed Threat Assessment and Mitigation Framework
Philip Sagan, Sagan Consulting, LLC	Multi-Disciplinary Studies of Probability Perception Contribute to Engineering and Exploiting Predictive Analytic Technologies
Robert Knisely	The Need for a Discipline of Program Design, Between Those of Public Policy ("What needs to change?") and Public Administration ("How did that work?")
Stuart Umpleby, GWU	Two Systems of Ethical Cognition
Stuart Umpleby, GWU	Reconsidering Cybernetics
Stuart Umpleby, GWU	Action Research

TABLE B-1 Continued

Principal Author and Institution	Paper (title)
Teodora Ivanuša, University of Maribor	Systemic Behavior via Social Responsibility: A Way Toward a More Holistic, Reliable, and Efficient Intelligence and Counterintelligence
Theodore J. Gordon, Millennium Project	New Analysis Tools for Pre-Detecting Terrorist Intent
Tom Pike, US Army/George Mason University (GMU)	The Foreign Population Analytic Framework
Vladimir Krylov, State Educational Institution of Higher Education of the Republic of Crimea "Crimean Engineering and Pedagogical University" (GBOUVO RK "CEPU")	RUSSIAN WORLD: Qualitative Analysis in PARADIGM Object-Oriented Design

TABLE B-2 Second Call White Papers

Principal Author and Institution	Paper (title)
Aleksandra Bielska, VALCRI Project	The Psychology of Intelligence Analysis: Where Are We and Where Should We Be?
Andrew Peterson, GMU	Developing Ethical, Legal, and Policy Analyses Relevant to the Use of Machine Learning Algorithms in National Security
Ashley Richter	Towards Ubiquitous Sensing: Staking Out the Best Paths to and Through the Upcoming 3D Data Avalanche
Aude Oliva, Massachusetts Institute of Technology (MIT)	The Cognitive Envelope
Bear Braumoeller, The Ohio State University (OSU)	International Order and Armed Conflict
Bear Braumoeller, OSU	Statistical Methods for Evidence-Based National Security Policy
Brad Allenby, Arizona State University (ASU)	White Paper on Weaponized Narrative
Cameron MacKenzie, Iowa State University	Better Models for National Security Strategic Decision Making
Can Uslay, Rutgers University	Security and Paton Satisfaction: Issues and Recommendations

continued

TABLE B-2 Continued

Principal Author and Institution	Paper (title)
Colin Phillips, UMd	An Integrated Approach to Language Capabilities in Humans and Technology
Curtis Rasmussen, Department of Homeland Security, National Protection and Programs Directorate, Office of Cyber and Infrastructure Analysis	Intellectual Styles as a Predictor of Intelligence Analyst Job Performance
David Berube, NCSU	The State of the Social Science of Nanoscience
Diane Maye, Embry-Riddle Aeronautical University	Artificial Intelligence in Shaping Preferences and Countering the Radicalization Process
Fred Roberts, Rutgers University	Big Data, Social and Behavioral Sciences, and National Security
Fritz Allhoff, University of Alaska, Anchorage	The New Arctic: National and Indigenous Security, Infrastructure, and Climate Change
Gary Berntson, OSU	Predicting Violent Behavior: Collectively vs. Individually
Giuseppe Labianca, University of Kentucky	The Political Independence Index: Ranking Actors' Power in Signed Social Network Graphs
Irene Wu, Georgetown University (GU)	Measuring Soft Power with Conventional and Unconventional Data
James Giordano, GU Medical Center	Development and Employment of Neurocognitive Science in Intelligence Operations
Jason Spitaletta, JHU-APL	The Need for Intelligence Community Sponsored Influence Research
Jennifer Lerner, Harvard University	Improving National Security through Research on Emotion and Decision Making
Joel Kulesza, Los Alamos National Laboratory	Standardization of Color Palettes for Scientific Visualization
Jonathan Herrmann, National Intelligence University (NIU)	Resilience against the Weaponized Narrative and Disinformation
Jonathan Victor, Weill Cornell Medical College	A response to the Decadal Survey of Social and Behavioral Sciences and Applications to National Security
Joseph Fargnoli, RITRE Corporation	The Root Causes of National Security and the Opportunities for the Application of the Principle of the Oneness of Humanity in a New Framework of Action

TABLE B-2 Continued

Principal Author and Institution	Paper (title)
J.B. Spencer, J.A. Kulesza, and A. Sood, Los Alamos National Laboratory	3D Geometry Visualization Capability for MCNP
Judi See, Sandia National Laboratories (Sandia)	First Principles Analogs for the Behavioral Sciences
Judi See, Sandia	Multimedia Instructional Resources for Nonpractitioners
Judi See, Sandia	Developing a Predictive Model for Vigilance Performance
Julie Mendosa, National Intelligence University and DEA	Transnational Organized Crime: An Evolving OCEA Challenge
Laura Steckman, The MITRE Corporation	Cultural and Linguistic Influences on Sociotechnical Space: Some General Challenges and Opportunities
Laura Steckman, The MITRE Corporation	Combining Narratology and Psychology to Examine Multinational Cultural Motivators, Expression, and Perceptions
Leah Windsor, University of Memphis	Language, Nonverbal, and Audiovisual Cues: Multimodal Approaches to Understanding Political Behavior
Lisa Pearl, University of California	Large-Scale Sophisticated Linguistic Monitoring
Mark Frankel, International Neuroethics Society	Response to the National Academy of Sciences Decadal Survey of Social and Behavioral Sciences for Applications to National Security Nine Areas of Neuroethical Importance
Michael Franz, Loyola University, Maryland	Analyzing the Mindset of Religiously Inspired Terrorists
Michael Fundator, Rutgers University	Impact of Behavioral and Social Sciences on Medical and Intelligence Studies
Michael Maxwell, University of Maryland Center for Advanced Study of Language (UMd-CASL)	The Role of Test and Evaluation in Social and Behavioral Sciences
Michael Tennison	White Paper adapted from Security Threats Versus Aggregated Truths: Ethical Issues in the Use of Neuroscience and Neurotechnology for National Security
Olusegun Owotomo, University of Texas at Austin	Opioid Epidemic and Homeland Security: An Integrative Framework of Intricacies and Proposed Solutions

continued

TABLE B-2 Continued

Principal Author and Institution	Paper (title)
Paul Kantor, Rutgers University	A Program for Better Human Computer Collaboration to Counter Terrorism
Petra Bradley, UMd-CASL	A National Research Agenda on Insider Threat
Polinpapilinho Katina, Old Dominion University	Complex System Governance: Implications and Research Directions
R. Bowen Loftin, University of Missouri	Increasing the Analyst's Bandwidth for Perception and Understanding of Large, Multivariate Collections of Data
Reeshad Dalal, GMU	Enhancing Decision Making by Cybersecurity Employees
Richard Cincotta, Stimson Center	Assessing Political Demography's Potential Application to Foreign Policy, Defense, and Intelligence Analyses
Robert Horn, Stanford University	Information Murals for Intelligence Analysis
Robert Hubal, University of North Carolina	Professional Social Competency Identification, Assessment, and Training
Robert West, DePauw University	A Social Cognitive Neuroscience Approach to Information Security
Robin Gregory, Decision Research	Decision Making to Prevent Genocide: National Security vs. Saving Lives?
Ronald Rensink, University of British Columbia	Applying Vision Science to Improve Data Visualization
Shann Turnbull, International Institute for Self-governance	Assessing Risk and Resilience in Governance
Stephen Cimbala, Pennsylvania State University, Brandywine	Nuclear Crisis Management in the Information Age
Stephen Marrin, James Madison University	Intelligence Studies, Intelligence Analysis, and Multidisciplinary Learning
Susan Aaronson, GWU	The Silent Erosion of Freedom of Association and Collective Bargaining (FACB) and Its Implications for Social, Political, and Economic Instability
Valerie Hudson, Texas A&M University	Women and National Security; Kin Groups, Environments, and Security
Vincent Alcazar	Needed: A Framework to Succeed the OODA Loop
Vladimir Krylov, CEPU	The Inauguration of Donald Trump Ended the Epoch of Submissional Leaders
Vladimir Krylov, CEPU	Donald Trump Is America's Response to the Challenge of History

TABLE B-2 Continued

Principal Author and Institution	Paper (title)
Wendy Chambers, UMd-CASL	Predicting Terrorist Attacks by Automating Integrative Complexity
William Shelby, Purdue University	Considerations for the Study of Combat-Capable Robots
Zlatan Krizan, Iowa State University	Identifying How Sleep Shapes Human Intelligence Gathering and Diagnosticity

PUBLIC WORKSHOPS

Building on the insights gained through the public discussions and white papers, the committee identified a range of issues and questions for further exploration. Separate steering committees, which each included members of the parent committee and outside experts, were appointed to plan six 1-day public workshops to explore some of these issues. Experts were invited to make presentations, answer questions, and engage in discussion with members of the committee and external participants (academics, members of the IC, and government representatives). The topics for these workshops were

1. Changing sociocultural dynamics and implications for national security
2. Emerging trends and methods in international security
3. Leveraging advances in social network thinking for national security
4. Learning from the science of cognition and perception for decision making
5. Workforce development and intelligence analysis
6. Understanding narratives for national security purposes

The first three workshops were held concurrently on October 11, 2017; 78 in-person registrants and 251 webcast viewers from the United States, Canada, Sweden, and the United Kingdom participated. Box B-3 provides an overview of these three workshops. The second three workshops were held concurrently on January 24, 2017; 111 in-person attendees and 230 webcast viewers from the United States, the United Kingdom, Brazil, The Netherlands, Mexico, and Canada participated. Box B-4 provides an overview of these three workshops. Documents describing the proceedings of all six workshops can be found at http://sites.nationalacademies.org/DBASSE/BBCSS/SBS_for_National_Security-Decadal_Survey/index.htm [June 2019].

BOX B-3
October 11, 2017, Workshops

Changing Sociocultural Dynamics and Implications for National Security

Summary

The workshop explored the current state of the science regarding culture, language, and behavior for national security contexts. Themes included the following:

- How research using big data can shed light on culture, language, and behavior, and links between recent developments in the quantitative measurement of culture and the work of experts in social computing and computational social science
- Strategies for linking different types of research that can contribute to understanding these phenomena in multiple-methods (or triangulation) and multiple-site (replication) research designs
- The challenge of working across multiple levels of analysis

Speakers

Joy Rohde, University of Michigan, *Ethical Considerations for Digital SBS Research in Support of National Security*

Susan Weller, University of Texas Medical Branch, *Moderator*

Dan Kahan, Yale University, *What Does Cultural Cognition Imply for National Security Risk Perceptions? You Tell Me*

William Dressler, University of Alabama, *Cultural Consonance and Health: An Overview with Special Reference to Measurement*

Dhiraj Murthy, University of Texas at Austin, *Small Data to Big Data: Coding and Culture with Social Media Data*

Mark Liberman, University of Pennsylvania, *Moderator*

Giuseppe (Joe) Labianca, University of Kentucky, *Identifying Positive and Negative Ties in Social Networks Through Triangulated Data*

David Broniatowski, George Washington University, *Surveys, Laboratory Experiments, and Social Media: Better Together*

Philip Resnik, University of Maryland, *The (in)ability to Triangulate in Data-Driven Healthcare Research*

David Matsumoto, San Francisco State University, *Moderator*

Gwyneth Sutherlin, Geographic Services, Inc., *Levels of Influence*

Michele Gelfand, University of Maryland, *Tightness-Looseness: A Fractal Pattern of Cultural Variation*

Jesse A. Egbert, Northern Arizona University, *Meaningful Levels of Analysis in (corpus) Linguistics*

Emerging Trends and Methods in International Security

Summary: The workshop explored the current state of research on political and strategic reasoning, with a focus on examining the role of political or economic actors, structures, and/or contexts within which they exist (e.g., domestic, international, transnational). Themes included the following:

- The strategic use of information in cyber-enabled information warfare and influence operations, authoritarian governments, and use of strategic cyber persistence
- Forecasting methods and topics
- Trends in social science methods relevant to intelligence analysis

Speakers
Jeffrey Taliaferro, Tufts University, *Opening Remarks and Moderator*
Steven Ward, Cornell University, *Status and International Security*
Deborah Larson, University of California, Los Angeles, *Shifting Power and the Legitimacy of the International Pecking Order*
Amanda Murdie, University of Georgia, *Beyond States: Measuring Reputation, Power, and Status in Nonstate Actors*
Sumit Ganguly, Indiana University, *Moderator*
Herb Lin, Stanford University, *On Cyber-Enabled Information Warfare and Influence Operations*
Jacklyn Kerr, Stanford University, *Authoritarian Soft Powers? Internet Content, Information Conflict, and the Future of Free Expression*
Richard J. Harknett, University of Cincinnati, *Cyber Persistence: Rethinking Security and Seizing the Strategic Cyber Initiative*
Suzanne Fry, National Intelligence Council, *Moderator*
Kacey Ernst, University of Arizona, *From Prediction to Practice: Integrating Forecasting Models into Public Health Education and Response*
Afreen Siddiqui, Massachusetts Institute of Technology, *Formulating Expectations for Future Water Availability in Arid Regions*
Jennifer Dresden, Georgetown University, *Authoritarian Backsliding: Drivers, Trends, and Implications*
Christopher Gelpi, The Ohio State University, *Connecting Theory to Policy with Forecasting*
Andrew Bennett, Georgetown University, *Moderator*
James Goldeiger, American University, *Panel discussant*
Sean Lynn-Jones, Harvard University, *Panel discussant*
William R. Thompson, Indiana University, *Panel discussant*

Leveraging Advances in Social Network Thinking for National Security

Summary: The workshop explored how network thinking will evolve and transform the IC in the next 10 years. Themes included the following:

continued

BOX B-3 Continued

- External influences on networks, including assembling analytic team supersynthesizers, team organization, urban network research, and the use of crowdsourced data
- The individual and internal factors of networks such as brain functioning and social networks and emotional artificial intelligence and the study of social identities
- Multilevel, high-dimensional, evolving, and emerging networks via the examination of dark networks, robust summary statistics for networks, and the future of complex networks
- Collaboration networks in the IC, areas for further research on networks and network thinking, data needs, and ethical considerations in conducting research on social networks.

Speakers
Kathleen Carley, Carnegie Mellon University, *Opening Remarks and Moderator*
Matthew Brashears, University of South Carolina, *Moderator*
Leslie DeChurch, Northwestern University, *Organizing in Teams*
Zachary Neal, Michigan State University, *The Future of Urban Network Research*
Regina Joseph, New York University, *Supersynthesizers: Confronting the Coming Analytical Crisis in an Age of Influence*

BOX B-4
January 24, Workshop Summaries

Learning from the Science of Cognition and Perception for Decision Making

Summary: The workshop featured invited presentations and discussions to review the current state of the science to consider (1) the aspects of sensory, cognitive, and decision sciences that are relevant to the work of intelligence analysts and (2) what intelligence analysts and managers should know about the limits and capabilities of human cognition in order to improve their effectiveness. Themes included the following:

- The nature of data and analysis in the IC
- The challenges of forecasting and preparing for events that impact national security and opportunities to improve the performance of intelligence analysts who make sense of data on possible events

Guido Cervone, Pennsylvania State University, *Use of Crowdsourced Data during Emergencies*
Randolph H. Pherson, Pherson Associates, LLC, *Respondent*
Noshir Contractor, Northwestern University, *Moderator*
Emily Falk, University of Pennsylvania, *Moderator, Brain and Social Networks: Fundamental Building Blocks of Human Experience*
Carolyn Parkinson, University of California, Los Angeles, *The Brain in the Social World: Integrating Approaches from Social Neuroscience, Psychology, and Social Network Analysis*
Jesse Hoey, University of Waterloo, *Emotional Artificial Intelligence in Sociotechnical Systems*
Kenneth Joseph, Northeastern University, *Studying Identities and Their Impact on Networks Using Social Media Data*
Markus Mobius, Microsoft, *Moderator*
Hsinchun Chen, University of Arizona, *Exploring Dark Networks: From the Surface Web to the Dark Web*
Benjamin Golub, Harvard University, *Robust Summary Statistics for Strategic and Social Process in Networks*
Alexander Volfovsky, Duke University, *The Future of Complex Networks: Statistics, Algorithms, and Causality*

- Individual trust and trends in interdisciplinary and computational research and insights on how individuals trust data, automated analyses, and sources of research findings
- Perceptual and cognitive constraints of both humans and machines to derive insights on models and tools for effective human–machine interactions

Speakers
Jeremy Wolfe, Harvard Medical School, *Opening Remarks*
Thomas Fingar, Stanford University, *Data and Analysis in the Intelligence Community*
Sallie Keller, Virginia Polytechnic Institute and State University, *Moderator*
Barbara Mellers, University of Pennsylvania, *Returns to Precision*
Gary Klein, MacroCognition, LLC, *Challenges for Engaging in Anticipatory Thinking*

continued

BOX B-4 Continued

Alyson Wilson, North Carolina State University, *Prediction and Anticipatory Thinking*
Fran Moore, CENTRA Technology, Inc., *Moderator*
David Dunning, University of Michigan, *Interpersonal Trust: Current Findings and Mysteries*
Roger Mayer, North Carolina State University, *The Importance of Interpersonal Trust: Now More Than Ever*
Adam Waytz, Northwestern University, *Humans and Machines*
Victoria Stodden, University of Illinois at Urbana–Champaign, *Trust in Research Findings*
Barbara Dosher (NAS), University of California, Irvine, *Moderator*
Edward Awh, University of Chicago, *Capacity Limits in Online Memory and Attention*
Danielle Albers Szafir, University of Colorado, Boulder, *Visualization and Perception Across Scales*
Remco Chang, Tufts University, *From Vision Science to Data Science: Applying Perception to Problems in Big Data*
Peter L.T. Pirolli, Florida Institute for Human & Machine Cognition, *Integrated Cognitive Models for Collaborative Human–AI Sensemaking*

Workforce Development and Intelligence Analysis

Summary: The workshop focused on the current state of the science on workforce development with a focus on identifying individual and organizational factors that influence analyst performance, including barriers to skill adoption. Themes included the following:

- The building and professionalization of the analytic workforce including topics from recruitment and selection, to leadership contribution, to skill acquisition
- The state of the science regarding current challenges facing the analytic workforce, such as the increased use of technology (and the need for human–systems integration) and three challenges faced when working in teams—team building, collaborative knowledge building, and communication
- Challenges and trends in workforce development such as fundamental transformations affecting the workforce at an accelerated pace, with automation and "thinking machines" replacing human tasks and jobs and changing the skills organizations seek in their workforces

Speakers
Noshir Contractor, Northwestern University, *Opening Remarks and Moderator*
Ted Clark, CENTRA Technology, Inc., *Intelligence Analysis: Characteristics of the Workforce and Workload*

APPENDIX B

Nancy Tippins, CEB Valtera, *Recruiting and Selecting the Analytic Workforce*
Jill Ellingson, University of Kansas, *Training the Workforce: Learning Autonomously*
Steve Zaccaro, George Mason University, *Motivating the Workforce: The Role of Leadership*
Jonathan Moreno (NAM), University of Pennsylvania, *Moderator*
Nancy Cooke, Arizona State University, *Integrating the Workforce into the National Security System*
Steve Fiore, University of Central Florida, *Developing Team Cognitive Computing to Augment Collaborative Knowledge Building*
Kara Hall, National Cancer Institute, *Supporting Individuals and Enhancing Teams*
Eric Eisenberg, University of South Florida, *Intelligence Analysts as Communicators*
Gerald (Jay) Goodwin, Army Research Institute, *Moderator*
Scott E. Page, University of Michigan, *What Do We Mean by Diverse Talent, and How Do We Leverage It?*
Andrew Ysursa, Salesforce, Inc., *Evolution of Work: Thriving in an Age of Automation*
Brian Uzzi, Northwestern University, *Scientists Get a Brain Boost: AI Mind + Machine Partnership and the Reproducibility Problem in Science*

Understanding Narratives for National Security

Summary: The workshop focused on the nature and role of narratives as causes, effects, and transformers of cultures and people, with particular attention to the following:

- Cutting-edge SBS narrative research
- The science of communication
- Emerging technologies and the role of human–computer interactions on the flow of narrative reflections by intelligence analysts on the workshop presentations

Speakers
Carmen Medina, MedinAnalytics, LLC, *Opening Remarks and Moderator*
Jeffrey Johnson, University of Florida, *Moderator*
Betty Sue Flowers, University of Texas at Austin, *Moderator*
Roberto Franzosi, Emory University, *Panel Discussant: Introduction to Narrative Research in the Social and Behavioral Sciences*
Mark Turner, Case Western Reserve University, *Panel Discussant: Introduction to Narrative Research in the Social and Behavioral Sciences*
James Pennebaker, University of Texas at Austin, *Panel Discussant: Introduction to Narrative Research in the Social and Behavioral Sciences*
Michael Bamberg, Clark University, *Panel Discussant: Introduction to Narrative Research in the Social and Behavioral Sciences and Panel Discussant: Narrative and Power, Mobilization/Intervention, and the Clash of Narratives*

continued

> **BOX B-4 Continued**
>
> David Matsumoto, San Francisco State University, *Moderator*
> Michael Dahlstrom, Iowa State University, *Panel Discussant: Why Study Narratives for National Security and How to Study Narratives in Real Time?*
> Pauline Cheong, Arizona State University, *Panel Discussant: Why Study Narratives for National Security and How to Study Narratives in Real Time?*
> Mark Turner, Case Western Reserve University, *Panel Discussant: Why Study Narratives for National Security and How to Study Narratives in Real Time?*
> Sarah Cobb, George Mason University, *Moderator*
> Douglas Randall, Protagonist, *Moderator*

TOWN HALLS

Another mechanism used in past decadal studies to engage scientists and gather input is participation in town halls, forums usually held in conjunction with meetings of professional societies. Because of the exceptionally broad range of academic disciplines with potential relevance to this study, the committee had to balance the possible benefits of such meetings against the risk of hearing more from some disciplines than others because resources were limited. The committee held a roundtable December 11, 2017, at the Society for Risk Analysis in Arlington, Virginia, but also elected to host a 6-month virtual town hall through which ideas could be sought from across disciplines.

The committee used the online platform IdeaBuzz to host its virtual town hall. IdeaBuzz allowed users to submit information via short summaries of their ideas in response to the committee's questions and criteria. Contributors could enter a few sentences or attach a white paper describing their ideas in greater detail. Alternatively, contributors could vote for ideas and/or comment on other ideas.

The SBS Decadal Survey IdeaBuzz Challenge website was open for public input from October 2017 to March 2018. The IdeaBuzz Challenge announcement was distributed to 95 academic associations and universities, publicized via Twitter, and shared through six National Academy of Sciences (NAS) member section liaisons and various Boards within NAS (see list below). At the beginning of the Challenge, seven white papers from our first and second calls for white papers were uploaded to the platform

> Michael Young, University of Utah, *Panel Discussant: Artificial Intelligence, Emerging Technologies, Social Media, and Narratives*
> Catherine Tejeda, Parenthetic, *Panel Discussant: Artificial Intelligence, Emerging Technologies, Social Media, and Narratives*
> James Phelan, The Ohio State University, *Panel Discussant: Narrative and Power, Mobilization/Intervention, and the Clash of Narratives*
> Debra Louison Lavoy, Narrative Builders, *Panel Discussant: Narrative and Power, Mobilization/Intervention, and the Clash of Narratives*
> Karen Monaghan, Central Intelligence Agency (retired), *Summative Comments*
> Josh Kerbel, National Intelligence University, *Summative Comments*

to encourage comments. In addition to comments and votes, the committee received seven original submissions (see Table B-3).[3]

To elicit input from the scientific community, the study staff and committee reached out to a number of professional organizations, university departments, NAS section liaisons, and other electronic databases. Although it is difficult to know the exact number of individuals reached, we estimate roughly that our requests were sent to more than 10,000 researchers across our outreach groups. We asked the following groups to help distribute notices for our second call for white papers and IdeaBuzz Challenge:

- professional organizations in the SBSSBS: 41;
- NAS section liaisons: 6;
- deans of schools of SBSSBS (Consortium of Social Science Association's members, contacted by Bill Maurer, dean of the School of Social Sciences, University of California, Irvine): 54;
- Division of Behavioral and Social Sciences and Education listserv: 3,130 individuals;
- National Academies of Sciences, Engineering, and Medicine social media feed: 53,000 individuals; and
- SBS Decadal Survey listserv.

---

[3] An archive of the committee's challenge is available at https://ideabuzz.com/a/buzz/nasem-bbcss/sbsdecadalsurvey [February 2019].

TABLE B-3 Ideas Received from IdeaBuzz Challenge

Author/Institution	Idea Title
University of Miami Miller School of Medicine	Supports for Immigrant Families and Adolescent Rebellion
Adrian James	The Isolationism/Interactivity Continuum: Vehicle for Assessing Barriers to Intelligence Sharing
Arne Norlander, Norlander Science and Engineering Consulting (NORSECON)	Human-Systems Integration in Cognitive Theatre of Operations
Bruce Crawford	A Quick Peek Under the Hood: National Security Research Needs
Christopher Soren and Shann Turnbull, International Institute of Self-Governance	Research How to Define, Evaluate, and Create Sound Governance
Gavrill Michas	Remarks Following January Workshop
Lisa Miller, University of California, Davis	Science Literacy
Michael Ramirez	Change Tactics
Michael Snelgrove, Former USAF Intelligence Officer	There's a Person on the Other Side of This Chat
Valerie Hudson	Women and National Security
Vladimir Krylov	On the National Security Criteria for a Post-Monetary Society

Appendix C

Reproducibility and Validity

The essence of the scientific method is the drawing of sound conclusions from carefully collected evidence. Scientific progress occurs when questions that expand the boundaries of knowledge are explored with the best available experiments, assessments, and analytic tools, but key to progress is what comes next. In assessing the merits of new work, the scientific community must consider the reliability of the evidence and whether the research approach was suitable to the inquiry. Scientists ask such questions as: Could these results be reproduced by remeasuring the same kind of evidence a second time, by broadening the evidence considered, or by expanding and triangulating the sources of evidence? Was the relevant evidence collected and interpreted in an objective manner, or was the work toward a desired conclusion? How can biased interpretations be avoided? Can the research be reproduced? Can the results be generalized to other people or contexts?

Within scientific fields, particularly including branches of psychology and the life sciences and computer science, there has been a growing recognition that many studies cannot be replicated—an issue that has attracted significant attention and is referred to as the replicability crisis. Advances in computational power, the collection of vast datasets, and the plurality of statistical methods have raised additional challenges associated with issues of the reproducibility, validity, and generalizability of results.

The National Academies recently conducted a congressionally mandated study of the issues and practices of reproducibility and replication across scientific and engineering research domains (National Academies of

Sciences, Engineering, and Medicine, 2019).[1] Major journals and agencies have published editorials and commentaries on the issues (Baker, 2016a; Collins and Tabak, 2014; McNutt, 2014a, 2014b). Ongoing discussion of reproducibility in social and behavioral sciences (SBS) fields, in allied fields that use big data and computation, and in biometrics and behavior metrics is likely to continue, but in this appendix, we review the main components of reproducibility and describe three ideas that have been suggested for ensuring that research is reproducible.

COMPONENTS OF REPRODUCIBILITY

When researchers report the results of an experimental or computational study, another researcher or laboratory will ideally be able to carry out the same or a similar experiment and analysis, and derive similar findings and conclusions. But there are irreducible sources of randomness or variation in any experiment or observational data sample. Since subjects, organisms, or digital traces are samples from a larger group, each observational dataset is a sample that may differ from other samples. The result is unavoidable statistical and sampling variation, especially for designs with smaller datasets. There is also inevitable or intentional randomness in experimental protocols. The problem may be further exacerbated by "publication bias"—the implicit or explicit policy of journals to publish statistically significant findings, favoring them over studies that fail to find an effect. Rarely, such failures of reproducibility result from intentional selection of evidence.

These issues of reproducibility occur in all domains of science: examples have been seen with topics as disparate as measuring and calculating physical properties (Lejaeghere et al., 2016); growing the same cell lines in different laboratories (Hines et al., 2014); impacts of housing practices on the physiology and behavior of animal models (Voelkl et al., 2018; Vogt et al., 2016); biometric measurement devices (Hamill et al., 2009); and the code used to generate research products or clean or filter data (Baker, 2016b; Stodden, 2015; Stodden et al., 2013, 2014). Yet debates about how best to address these issues are especially vigorous in the SBS, where there have been high-profile research efforts aimed at replicating a sample of experiments and a systematic focus on statistical analysis of data (Open Science Collaboration, 2015; Pashler and Wagenmakers, 2012).

---

[1] Information about workshops conducted as part of this project is also available. Topics included reproducibility in federal statistics, see https://sites.nationalacademies.org/DBASSE/CNSTAT/DBASSE_070786 [October 2018]); research with animals and animal models (see NASEM, 2015); and statistical challenges in assessing and fostering reproducibility in scientific results (NASEM, 2016).

The language used to describe reproducibility is itself in flux. Scholars have defined components of reproducibility from different perspectives. Those focusing on the design of the experiment have identified the reproducibility of methods, results, and inferences as primary targets (Goodman et al., 2016). Those focusing on the computation carried out as part of the work identify empirical, statistical, and computational reproducibility as key (Stodden, 2017). And some consider the robustness or generalizability of findings with respect to variations in procedures, stimuli, or sampling and the validity of research approaches for the domain of application of equal or perhaps greater importance (see Table C-1).

Validation refers to matching the design of the research to the inquiry, whether the approach entails collecting appropriate and applicable observa-

TABLE C-1 Key Components of Reproducibility

Component	Definition
Experimentation	
Reproducibility of methods ("transparency")	Providing sufficient detail to enable the same procedures to be repeated by others
Reproducibility of results ("replication")	An independent study with procedures or methods matched as closely as possible yields the same results, subject to statistical variation in samples
Inferential reproducibility	Equivalent inferences from the same data with independently conceived analyses
Computation	
Empirical reproducibility	Replication enabled by providing details of data methods and data collection and the data themselves being available
Statistical reproducibility	Specifying the models and statistical tests used and their parameters to enable independent replication
Computational reproducibility	Making the codes, software, hardware, and implementation details used to conduct the original research freely available
Validation	
Surface validity	Experimental procedures, results, and inferences are appropriate for the domain of application
Model validation	Methods for evaluating the match between the results of a model and data from the real-world system
Robustness or generalizability	Similar results and inferences obtain even with some variation in procedures or samples

SOURCE: Generated by the committee drawing on Goodman et al. (2016), Stodden (2017), and Babuska and Oden (2004).

tional or experimental data or developing computational models or methods. To obtain results that support valid interpretations, a researcher must carefully consider the theory and assumptions that drive the experimental design or model for collecting evidence that can provide information about the questions to be answered or hypothesis to be tested. The determination of validity is complex, perhaps more so in SBS fields because human systems are particularly subject to variation and change. Methods for validation generally have focused on whether the same conclusions would have followed from a different subsampling of data.

Validation techniques used for mechanical and physical systems often test a model against historical data. Some classical treatments of verification and validation methods in computer science and engineering can be found in Law and Kelton (1991) and Babuska and Oden (2004). These techniques often assume a constant system, whereas social situations may be more complex and changeable (e.g., new leadership, new technologies), raising questions about whether models based on historical data will be appropriate for forecasting future outcomes. One approach might be the generation of several different models that triangulate a target domain, followed by generation of a narrative description of possibilities that may be more persuasive to the end consumer.

The proper approach to assessing the validity and generalizability of research for more complex situations remains an open question. It is likely that different approaches may be appropriate for distinct scientific domains or problems. Over the next decade, developing policies on reproducibility in science will likely suggest nuanced standards adapted to the respective fields and to the nature of the research questions.

The issues of reproducibility, generalizability, and validity will need to be addressed in appropriate and potentially different ways in undertaking the varied opportunities presented in this report. The recommendations of the National Academies committee and discussions of standards and practices in specific field domains should support future research practices and implementations.

PRACTICES

Certain fields have embarked on systematic efforts to improve replication of experiments, while others have argued that replication may slow science by diverting resources (Bissell, 2013). Some are advocates of preregistration of studies, whereby researchers submit their research rationale, hypotheses, design, and analytic strategy to a scientific journal for peer review prior to beginning the study (Munafò et al., 2017; Wagenmakers et al., 2012). Preregistration would allow studies to be rejected and/or revised and resubmitted before the data collection begins. Proponents of preregistration argue that the process will result in improved use of theory and stronger research methods, and ultimately better studies, as well as a decrease in false-positive publications (Chambers, 2014). Others (e.g., Scott, 2013) have noted that preregistration may reduce support for exploratory research. The process does not allow for use of the research results as an indicator of the value of the study, potentially leaving editors and reviewers to rely on the prestige of the researchers and accepted methods—an outcome that would disproportionately affect graduate students and early-career researchers.

Another approach is to build heterogeneity explicitly into research programs, and proposals to this end have been developed in a number of domains. These proposals focus on heterogeneity of materials, subjects, or laboratories. For example, in the context of research on animal models in medical and physiological discovery, advocates of heterogeneity have proposed introducing explicit variation into subject samples, housing variables, and other factors (Vogt et al., 2016). Similar ideas have been suggested for work involving tracking of human movement and behavior (Pantic et al., 2007; Pentland and Liu, 1999). Cognitive scientists have proposed "meta-studies" for robust tests of theory (Baribault et al., 2017), coupled with Bayesian analysis (Etz and Vandekerckhove, 2016).[2] These meta-studies purposely include variations in potentially important experimental variables to test theories or applications and increase the likelihood that conclusions will be generalizable within the relevant domain, supporting robust conclusions. Notably, this practice of introducing purposeful yet randomized variations may work successfully in some research domains but not others.

For large-scale datasets and the associated data mining computations used to understand patterns in those data, the issues of reproducibility arise in the context of statistical reproducibility and computational reproducibility. One initiative in these domains has focused on a broad call for open publication of statistical and computational code so that others can repeat and test the products (Baker, 2016b; Stodden, 2015; Stodden et al., 2013, 2014). While the call for publication of databases, code, and statistical products would raise privacy and ethical considerations, the principle of independent validation and targeted replication tests could be prioritized, at least for a subset of study conditions.

---

[2]Bayesian analysis addresses research questions about unknown parameters using probability statements. Bayesian approaches allow researchers to incorporate background knowledge into their analyses, taking into account the issues of reproducibility and replication. Because the statistical model incorporates background knowledge, new data can be evaluated against the plausibility of previous research findings (van de Schoot et al., 2014).

REFERENCES

Babuska, I.M., and Oden, J.T. (2004). Verification and validation in computational engineering and science: Basic concepts. *Computer Methods in Applied Mechanics and Engineering, 193*(36-38), 4057-4066.

Baker, M. (2016a). Reproducibility crisis? *Nature, 533*(26).

Baker, M. (2016b). Why scientists must share their research code. *Nature News*, September 13. Available: https://www.nature.com/news/why-scientists-must-share-their-research-code-1.20504 [December 2018].

Baribault, B., Donkin, C., Little, D.R., Trueblood, J.S., Oravecz, Z., van Ravenzwaaij, D., White, C.N., De Boeck, P., and Vandekerckhove, J. (2017). Meta-studies for robust tests of theory. *Proceedings of the National Academy of Sciences of the United States of America, 115*(11), 2607-2612.

Bissell, M. (2013). Reproducibility: The risks of the replication drive. *Nature News, 503*(7476), 333-334. Available: https://www.nature.com/news/reproducibility-the-risks-of-the-replication-drive-1.14184 [December 2018].

Chambers, C. (2014). Psychology's "registration revolution." *The Guardian*, May 20. Available: http://www.theguardian.com/science/head-quarters/2014/may/20/psychology-registration-revolution [November 2018].

Collins, F.S., and Tabak, L.A. (2014). NIH plans to enhance reproducibility. *Nature, 505*(7485), 612-613.

Etz, A., and Vandekerckhove, J.A. (2016). Bayesian perspective on the reproducibility project: Psychology. *PLoS One, 11*(2), e0149794. doi:10.1371/journal.pone.0149794.

Goodman, S.N., Fanelli, D., and Ioannidis, J.P. (2016). What does research reproducibility mean? *Science Translational Medicine, 8*(341). doi:10.1126/scitranslmed.aaf5027.

Hamill, N., Romero, R., Hassan, S.S., Lee, W., Myers, S.A., Mittal, P., Kusanovic, J.P., Chaiworapongsa, T., Vaisbuch, E., Espinoza, J., Gotsch, F., Carletti, A., Gonçalves, L.F., and Yeo, L. (2009). Repeatability and reproducibility of fetal cardiac ventricular volume calculations using spatiotemporal image correlation and virtual organ computer-aided analysis. *Journal of Ultrasound in Medicine, 28*(10), 1301-1311.

Hines, W.C., Su, Y., Kuhn, I., Polyak, K., and Bissell, M.J. (2014). Sorting out the FACS: A devil in the details. *Cell Reports, 6*(5), 779-781.

Law, A.M., and Kelton, W.D. (1991). *Simulation Modelling and Analysis* (2nd ed.). New York: McGraw-Hill.

Lejaeghere, K., Bihlmayer, G., Björkman, T., Blaha, P., Blügel, S., Blum, V., Caliste, D., Castelli, I.E., Clark, S.J., Dal Corso, A., de Gironcoli, S., Deutsch, T., Dewhurst, J.K., Di Marco, I., Draxl, C., Dułak, M., Eriksson, O., Flores-Livas, J.A., Garrity, K.F., Genovese, L., Giannozzi, P., Giantomassi, M., Goedecker, S., Gonze, X., Grånäs, O., Gross, E.K., Gulans, A., Gygi, F., Hamann, D.R., Hasnip, P.J., Holzwarth, N.A., Iuşan, D., Jochym, D.B., Jollet, F., Jones, D., Kresse, G., Koepernik, K., Küçükbenli, E., Kvashnin, Y.O., Locht, I.L., Lubeck, S., Marsman, M., Marzari, N., Nitzsche, U., Nordström, L., Ozaki, T., Paulatto, L., Pickard, C.J., Poelmans, W., Probert, M.I., Refson, K., Richter, M., Rignanese, G.M., Saha, S., Scheffler, M., Schlipf, M., Schwarz, K., Sharma, S., Tavazza, F., Thunström, P., Tkatchenko, A., Torrent, M., Vanderbilt, D., van Setten, M.J., Van Speybroeck, V., Wills, J.M., Yates, J.R., Zhang, G.X., and Cottenier, S. (2016). Reproducibility in density functional theory calculations of solids. *Science, 351*(6280), aad3000. doi:10.1126/science.aad3000.

McNutt, M. (2014a). Journals unite for reproducibility. *Science, 346*(6210), 679. doi:10.1126/science.aaa1724.

McNutt, M. (2014b). Reproducibility. *Science, 343*(6168), 229. doi:10.1126/science.1250475.

Munafò, M.R., Nosek, B.A., Bishop, D.V., Button, K.S., Chambers, C.D., du Sert, N.P., Simonsohn, U., Wagenmakers, E.-J., Ware, J.J., and Ioannidis, J.P.A. (2017). A manifesto for reproducible science. *Nature Human Behaviour, 1,* 0021. Available: https://www.nature.com/articles/s41562-016-0021 [December 2018].

National Academies of Sciences, Engineering, and Medicine (NASEM). (2015). *Reproducibility Issues in Research with Animals and Animal Models: Workshop in Brief.* Washington, DC: The National Academies Press.

NASEM. (2016). *Statistical Challenges in Assessing and Fostering the Reproducibility of Scientific Results: Summary of a Workshop.* Washington, DC: The National Academies Press.

NASEM. (2019). *Reproducibility and Replicability in Science.* Washington, DC: The National Academies Press.

Open Science Collaboration. (2015). Estimating the reproducibility of psychological science. *Science, 349*(6251), aac4716. doi:10.1126/science.aac4716.

Pantic, M., Pentland, A., Nijholt, A., and Huang, T.S. (2007). Human computing and machine understanding of human behavior: A survey. In *Artificial Intelligence for Human Computing* (pp. 47–71). Berlin/Heidelberg, Germany: Springer-Verlag.

Pashler, H., and Wagenmakers, E.J. (2012). Editors' introduction to the special section on replicability in psychological science: A crisis of confidence? *Perspectives on Psychological Science, 7*(6), 528–530.

Pentland, A., and Liu, A. (1999). Modeling and prediction of human behavior. *Neural Computation, 11*(1), 229–242.

Scott, S. (2013). Pre-registration would put science in chains. *Time Higher Education,* July 25. Available: http://www.timeshighereducation.co.uk/comment/opinion/pre-registration-would-put-science-in-chains/2005954.article [December 2018].

Stodden, V. (2015). Reproducing statistical results. *Annual Review of Statistics and Its Application, 2,* 1–19. doi:10.1146/annurev-statistics-010814-020127.

Stodden, V. (2017). *Framing the Issues: Reproducibility in Many Forms.* Available: https://web.stanford.edu/~vcs/talks/NASSacklerMar82017-STODDEN.pdf [December 2018].

Stodden, V., Guo, P., and Ma, Z. (2013). Toward reproducible computational research: An empirical analysis of data and code policy adoption by journals. *PLoS One, 8*(6), e67111. doi:10.1371/journal.pone.0067111.

Stodden, V., Leisch, F., and Peng, R.D. (2014). *Implementing Reproducible Research.* Boca Raton, FL: CRC Press.

van de Schoot, R., Kaplan, D., Denissen, J., Asendorpf, J.B., Neyer, F.J., and van Aken, M.A. (2014). A gentle introduction to Bayesian analysis: Applications to developmental research. *Child Development, 85*(3), 842–860.

Voelkl, B., Vogt, L., Sena, E., and Würbel, H. (2018). Reproducibility of preclinical animal research improves with heterogeneity of study samples. *PLoS Biology, 16*(2), e2003693. doi:10.1371/journal.pbio.2003693.

Vogt, L., Reichlin, T.S., Nathues, C., and Würbel, H. (2016). Authorization of animal experiments is based on confidence rather than evidence of scientific rigor. *PLoS Biology, 14*(12), e2000598. doi:10.1371/journal.pbio.2000598.

Wagenmakers, E.-J., Wetzels, R., Borsboom, D., van der Maas, H.L., and Kievit, R.A. (2012). An agenda for purely confirmatory research. *Perspectives on Psychological Science, 7*(6), 632–638.

Appendix D

New Data, New Research Tools, New Ethical Questions

Advances in computational social science provide new ways to understand human behaviors, generating insights that may facilitate intelligence analysis and provide decision support. Many researchers in the social and behavioral sciences (SBS) and public officials are excited about the possibilities that big data and computational social science hold for enhanced analysis of open-source intelligence in particular, including intelligence gleaned from social media, sensor data, and other digital information produced by routine human actions and behaviors (Harman, 2015). But many of the qualities that make big data exciting and accessible to researchers may risk causing harm. Big datasets are not just large in volume. They also often contain sensitive information at a grain size that could allow individual identities to be uncovered. These data are durable and can be shared across institutional and national borders at scale and at high speeds.

As more people live more of their lives online and as sensor technologies proliferate, the volume and range of sensitive digital data will grow. These factors increase the potential for harms from research, including loss of privacy and autonomous control over personal information for the individuals who, knowingly or not, are the sources of the data. The reach of big data and its shareability also increase the potential for larger numbers of people to be harmed. A Department of Homeland Security report emphasizes that "the relative ease in engaging multitudes of distributed human subjects (or data about them) through intermediating systems speeds the potential for harms to arise and extends the range of stakeholders who may be impacted" (Boyd and Crawford, 2012; Dittrich and Kenneally, 2012, p. 3).

Although big data traces may appear as disembodied points of information, it is important to bear in mind that data are generated by people. The Council for Big Data, Ethics, and Society notes that "the scope, scale, and complexity of many forms of big data creates a rich ecosystem in which human participants and their communities are deeply embedded and susceptible to harm" (Zook et al., 2017, p. 1). In this appendix, we note some of the challenges that have emerged, and consider their particular implications in the national security context.

NEW ETHICAL CHALLENGES

One primary issue for researchers who use large datasets is that these datasets raise new ethical questions that have not yet been systematically addressed. While SBS researchers have long been accustomed to addressing research ethics via the Common Rule, computational social science research transcends traditional human subjects protections and raises a number of new ethical questions. To name but a few: Are data subjects the same as human subjects, or are they different? What reasonable expectations of privacy do people have for their digital traces, and how do those expectations change in different digital venues? Is informed consent possible, realistic, or required in big data research?

Researchers and ethicists stress that there are no straightforward answers to these questions (Buchanan, 2017; Zook et al., 2017). Because digital research affords more distance between researchers and their human subjects, researchers and ethicists also note that such research is susceptible to ethical distancing (Dittrick and Kenneally, 2012; Lyon, 2001). Furthermore, because digital research methods are advancing rapidly, and because machine-learning tools create decision rules that may not be transparent or intuitive, the applications of these methods and tools may lead to unanticipated ethical questions. The multidisciplinary nature of digital research further complicates the landscape of digital research ethics. While SBS researchers have experience dealing with research ethics challenges, their collaborators in computer science traditionally have had less training in ethical reasoning (Salganik, 2017).

A second key complication is the involvement of new stakeholders in the research process. Stakeholders such as individuals whose data are collected online may have different expectations than researchers have regarding what privacy protections, practices for informed consent, and other approaches to research ethics are reasonable; this further complicates the ethical landscape of digital research (Association of Internet Researchers Ethics Working Committee, 2012). For example, in a recent study demonstrating the power of social network analysis to identify and analyze online extremist networks, Benigni and colleagues (2017) note that social media users may not be comfortable with knowing that their online behavior was used to support diplomacy, military operations, or intelligence analysis. Yet digital researchers are not required to obtain consent for such research as long as they respect platforms' terms of service and privacy policies and afford appropriate privacy protections, including deidentification.

In part because of the risks to individuals' privacy, governing agencies in the United States and elsewhere have a voice as well. For example, the European Union recently enacted a General Data Protection Regulation to address privacy and other issues. Some legal scholars have argued, however, that despite the intentions for this regulation, it facilitates rather than hinders the conduct of computational social science research (Forgó et al., 2017). At present, the most robust consensus is that digital research ethics is not "one size fits all." Researchers and ethicists take a variety of positions on what expectations should govern digital research, in part because there is no clear consensus on what the threshold for risk of harm should be in this research area. While some analysts argue that ethical practices must account for the potential for indirect harms, others disagree (Bellaby, 2010). Many researchers and ethicists stress the importance of examining questions of privacy, autonomy, harm, and justice in the context of each dataset, research methodology, and intended use of research outcomes (Benigni et al., 2017). Below, we discuss in greater detail some of the most common ethical concerns and issues that arise in digital research and some commonly proposed ways to address them.

PRIVACY

Traditional norms of privacy that are relevant to research ethics are oriented toward protecting individuals by ensuring that neither personally identifying information nor sensitive personal information will be exposed. Digital researchers typically deidentify individuals attached to digital datasets, but even this approach does not guarantee that the subjects of digital research will remain fully anonymous, as a National Research Council (2008) report on the subject stresses. A number of studies have shown that the scale, granularity, and durability of data make reidentification possible: it is possible to stitch databases together to identify specific people despite deidentification (Acquisti and Gross, 2009; Lewis et al., 2008). This breach of privacy may be particularly problematic when the identified individuals are members of vulnerable or stigmatized groups (see, e.g., Lee, 2014).

Some researchers argue that Internet users should have no or little expectation of privacy for digital information shared on such public sites as Twitter, Facebook, and YouTube (Walsh and Miller, 2016). But others argue that it is important to think of privacy not in binary terms—where information is either public or private—but instead as a situational and contextual category (Association of Internet Researchers Ethics Working Committee, 2012; Keller et al., 2016; Zook et al., 2017). According to this view, the public accessibility of data does not necessarily make use of the data ethical. Rather, users' expectations of privacy vary across different cultural, national, and digital contexts. Ethical challenges may arise when researchers inadvertently violate user expectations and norms in the course of their research. Facebook's study of emotional contagion, in which the emotional content of the newsfeeds of more than 600,000 users was altered without their knowledge to investigate the relationships between social media exposure and emotion, sparked controversy for this reason (Boyd, 2006; Hancock, 2017).

Information science expert Helen Nissenbaum suggests that ethical digital research requires a nuanced understanding of the right to privacy. She argues that it "is neither the right to secrecy nor a right to control but a right to appropriate flow of personal information." Users' understandings of appropriate information flow are governed by "context-relative informational norms" that vary according to the digital space involved and the type of data produced (Nissenbaum, 2010, p. 127). Understanding these context-relative information norms will require further SBS research into the assumptions, expectations, and values that users bring to different digital spaces (Hancock, 2017).

USER AUTONOMY AND CONSENT

The Common Rule requires that researchers obtain informed consent from research subjects to protect subjects' autonomy. But many Internet researchers believe that informed consent is unrealistic in the online domain for at least two reasons. First, it is not possible to obtain consent from the millions of web users whose digital traces are being studied, and it is a matter of some dispute whether the individuals whose data is studied deserve the same protections as human subjects (Barocas and Nissenbaum, 2014; Buchanan, 2017; Dittrich and Kenneally, 2012). Second, informed consent requires that researchers anticipate the potential risks posed by any given study. To meet the criteria of informed consent, users would have to know what is being collected, with whom it will be shared, under what constraints, and for what purposes. This is challenging not only because so much of the data used in digital research has already been collected, but also because research methods evolve. The many uses to which digital data may be put are often not clear at the time of collection. Researchers also may use material that people post about other individuals, further complicating the meaning of consent (Barocas and Nissenbaum, 2014).

Another provision of the Common Rule is that consent must not be coerced. But if the cost of opting out of having one's online activities monitored, recorded, preserved, and analyzed is opting out of digital services that have become central parts of everyday financial, medical, work, and social transactions, users of digital systems may not be able to exercise noncoerced choice. Some digital ethics experts also question the freedom of choice implied in terms-of-service agreements for this reason; they argue that including consent to monitoring and research in terms of service fails to meet the requirements of informed consent (Brunton and Nissenbaum, 2013).

A number of researchers have taken advantage of the opportunity that the web offers for experimenting on people without their knowledge (Salganik, 2017). But these practices have caused controversies. For example, defenders of the Facebook study mentioned above in which the emotional content of users' feeds was altered insisted that this study was no different from the product testing commonplace in industry, and that such research is essential to developing sound algorithms. Detractors insisted that such research violated user expectations of informational and emotional autonomy on Facebook (Boyd, 2006; Hancock, 2017).

SOCIAL MEDIA AND ONLINE GAMING DATA

Of particular interest to SBS researchers is social media online gaming data, which raises not only privacy issues but others as well. While ostensibly in the public domain, data associated with gaming (most of which operates under the creative commons license) is nonetheless policed by the companies that produce the technologies used in its production (e.g., Twitter and Facebook). These companies self-police. This means that

- not all members of the research community have equal access to data collected through games;
- data collected through a game may be retroactively changed, and its availability may change as well;
- the rules of engagement leading to the generation of the data may change;
- how these technology companies actually generate data, how they store it, how they prioritize its delivery, and other policies are generally not made public;
- the data themselves may contain malware that can infect the scientists' machines or destroy other data; and
- the conditions under which members of the research community can share the data are overly restrictive and/or rapidly changing.

These realities mean that the system for generating data from gaming sites can be exploited and manipulated, making the creation of false data easy. Much of the research performed with such data is done quickly, with no direct replication; and there is a need for extensive, continuous effort to revamp data collection tools to keep up with the changing technology. Adversaries can identify exploits and take advantage of them more easily than scientists can gain access to the data to learn counterstrategies.

Most social media and online data is created by server logs that were not created for the express purpose of SBS research. Instead, this digital trace data (sometimes referred to dismissively as digital exhaust data)[1] is collected to help programmers debug errors in the system. However, technology companies are discovering the value of this data for business, to support, for instance, game design or customer retention. The result has been a more concerted effort by technology companies to actively collect specific data. Therefore, in its quest for more open access, the research community has the opportunity, and indeed the obligation, to partner with companies in the development of platforms that can advance SBS research.

Secondary Uses of Datasets

Research with large datasets may have the effect of identifying individuals and their affiliations with undesirable groups, or perhaps falsely identifying individuals as members of marginalized or dangerous communities. Researchers stress the importance of using multiple checks to guard against misidentification (Benigni et al., 2017). They also stress the importance of avoiding the imputation of guilt by association. Social network research often categorizes and makes judgments about individuals and groups based on their relationships. These associations, whether false or accurate, can have material effects on the lives and well-being of those individuals categorized, particularly when the categories carry social stigma or imply that categorized individuals pose security threats because of their social networks (Lyon, 2007).

Researchers may also need to consider the multiple contexts in which their research tools can be used. Social network analysis designed to identify ISIS supporters on Twitter or Facebook, for example, can also be applied to identify members of peaceful political dissident groups, from civil rights advocates in the United States to advocates of democratization in China (Buchanan, 2017). Researchers may need to weigh the harms of carrying out such work against the potential harms of leaving research undone and

---

[1] See https://www.amazon.com/Digital-Exhaust-Digitization-Digitally-Innovation/dp/0133837963 [July 2018].

foregoing tools for enhancing human safety and security (Wesolowski et al., 2014).

Algorithmic Bias

Algorithms can "reproduce existing patterns of discrimination, inherit the prejudice of prior decision makers, or simply reflect the widespread biases that persist in society" (Barocas and Selbst, 2016, p. 674). If training data contains racial bias, for instance, that bias will be replicated in its operation. For example, if a computer system for categorizing medical school applicants had been designed on the basis of previous admissions decisions that discriminated against racial minorities and women, the algorithm would replicate that bias (Barocas and Selbst, 2016). Algorithms that respond to users can also replicate users' prejudices (Sweeney, 2013). The negative ethical consequences of discriminatory algorithms are magnified in contexts where the algorithms are used to predict outcomes. For example, researchers have shown that an algorithmic system used to predict the likelihood of criminal recidivism was twice as likely to mislabel black offenders as recidivism risks, compared with white offenders (Angwin et al., 2016).

Such systems may unintentionally violate users', researchers', and government officials' commitments to fairness and justice. They may also reduce the accuracy, value, and efficiency of results. To avoid these negative unintended consequences, some researchers have suggested that data scientists and ethicists work together to build systems, training data, and other tools to mitigate bias (Barocas and Boyd, 2017). Other researchers have outlined techniques for assessing the impact of algorithms. While many of their recommendations concern public disclosure of automated systems not suited to intelligence contexts, other recommendations—such as for self-assessment of existing and proposed automated decision systems—are valuable (Reisman et al., 2018).

GREATER SALIENCE OF THESE CHALLENGES IN THE NATIONAL SECURITY CONTEXT

In the contemporary digital landscape, the means used to gather data often reflect significant power imbalances (Brunton and Nissenbaum, 2013). Internet users typically do not know what traces of their everyday lives are monitored; what happens to their information; or what, if anything, occurs because of it. The potential for security community surveillance afforded by digital data compounds the power imbalances already present in digital spaces. Failure to address ethical concerns can have a chilling effect on research. Research projects that raise serious ethical questions may lose their funding or be terminated by sponsoring agencies, as discussed in Chapter 10.

The public may lose its trust in the SBS research community, as well as in government agencies that sponsor such research, including the security community. And widespread concern that the Internet is a space where actions are monitored, stored, and analyzed rather than a site of free information exchange may cause people to censor their online behavior, constraining Internet use itself (Brunton and Nissenbaum, 2013; Mayer-Schönberger, 2009; Penney, 2016). Some digital scholars recommend that Internet users learn practices of "data obfuscation" to protect themselves from digital surveillance and analysis (Brunton and Nissenbaum, 2013).

It is especially important for researchers working on security issues to recognize that they are working in the context of public concern about the power imbalance between Internet companies and individual users and between security agencies and citizens. Concerns about overreach by the Intelligence Community (IC) have marred the history of American national security, as discussed in Chapter 9. Recent news stories about such U.S. government actions as the Total Information Awareness Program (later called the Terrorism Information Awareness program), in which data mining was used to monitor potential security threats, have reignited old fears that the American national security community is unjustly monitoring domestic communications. Previously documented abuses, such as domestic surveillance of civil rights groups revealed by the Church Committee in 1975, are the backdrop for such concerns (Electronic Freedom Foundation, 2004; National Academies of Sciences, Engineering, and Medicine, 2016; Walsh and Miller, 2016).

Researchers and the IC will continue to grapple with the need to balance privacy and autonomy on the one hand and security on the other (Walsh and Miller, 2016). These rights both overlap and conflict. Nissenbaum (2005, p. 64) explains that security has a number of definitions: "security as safety, freedom from the unwanted effects of another's actions, the condition of being protected from danger, injury, attack (physical and non-physical), and other harms, and protection against threats of all kinds." The language of security poses a conflict between security as privacy and protection from more powerful coercive powers on the one hand, and security as a moral national/international good, preventing harmful acts of violence, which gives research moral force (Nissenbaum, 2005). Having examined this challenge in the context of counterterrorism research and policy, a National Academies committee argued strongly in 2008 that "even under the pressure of threats as serious as terrorism, the privacy rights and civil liberties that are the cherished core values of our nation must not be destroyed." That committee's report recommends that government agencies establish and apply "technical, operational, legal, policy, and oversight processes to minimize privacy intrusion and the damage it causes" (National Research Council, 2008, p. 4).

REFERENCES

Acquisti, A., and Gross, R. (2009). Predicting social security numbers from public data. *Proceedings of the National Academy of Sciences of the United States of America*, 106(27), 10975–10980.

Angwin, J., Larson, J., Mattu, S., and Kirchner, L. (2016). Machine bias. *ProPublica*, May 23. Available: https://www.propublica.org/article/machine-bias-risk-assessments-in-criminal-sentencing [December 2018].

Association of Internet Researchers Ethics Working Committee. (2012). *Ethical Decision-Making and Internet Research* (Version 2.0). Available: https://aoir.org/reports/ethics2.pdf [December 2018].

Barocas, S., and Boyd, D. (2017). Engaging the ethics of data science in practice. *Communications of the ACM*, 60(11), 23–25.

Barocas, S., and Nissenbaum, H. (2014). Big data's end run around anonymity and consent. In J. Lane, V. Stodden, S. Bender, and H. Nissenbaum (Eds.), *Privacy, Big Data, and the Public Good* (pp. 45–75). New York: Cambridge University Press.

Barocas, S., and Selbst, A.D. (2016). Big data's disparate impact. *104 California Law Review*, 671. doi:10.2139/ssrn.2477899.

Bellaby, R. (2010). What's the harm? The ethics of intelligence collection. *Intelligence and National Security*, 27(1), 93–117.

Benigni, M.C., Joseph, K., and Carley, K.M. (2017). Online extremism and the communities that sustain it: Detecting the ISIS supporting community on Twitter. *PLoS One*, 12(12), e0181405. doi:10.1371/journal.pone.0181405.

Boyd, D. (2006). Untangling research and practice: What Facebook's "emotional contagion" study teaches us. *Research Ethics*, 12(1), 4–13. doi:10.1177/1747016115583379.

Boyd, D., and Crawford, K. (2012). Critical questions for big data. *Information, Communication, and Society*, 15(5), 662–679. doi:10.1080/1369118X.2012.678878.

Brunton, F., and Nissenbaum, H. (2013). Political and ethical perspectives on data obfuscation. In M. Hildebrandt and K. de Vries Privacy (Eds.), *Privacy, Due Process, and the Computational Turn* (pp. 164–188). New York: Routledge.

Buchanan, E. (2017). Considering the ethics of big data research: A case of Twitter and ISIS/ISIL. *PLoS One*, 12(12), e0187155. doi:10.1371/journal.pone.0187155.

Dittrich, D., and Kenneally, E. (2012). *The Menlo Report: Ethical Principles Guiding Information and Communication Technology Research*. Washington, DC: U.S. Department of Homeland Security. Available: http://www.caida.org/publications/papers/2012/menlo_report_ethical_principles [November 2018].

Electronic Freedom Foundation. (2004). *Total/Terrorism Information Awareness (TIA): Is It Truly Dead?* Available: http://libertyparkusafd.org/Hale/Special%20Reports/ADVISE/Total-Terrorism%20Information%20Awareness%20--%20%20Is%20It%20Truly%20Dead.htm [December 2018].

Forgó, N., Hänold, S., and Schütze, B. (2017). The principle of purpose limitation and big data. In M. Corrales, M. Fenwick, and N. Forgó (Eds.), *New Technology, Big Data and the Law. Perspectives in Law, Business and Innovation* (pp. 17–42). Singapore: Springer.

Hancock, J.T. (2017). Introduction to ethics of digital research. In *Handbook on Networked Communication* (p. 5). Oxford, UK: Oxford University Press.

Harman, J. (2015). Disrupting the Intelligence Community. *Foreign Affairs*, March/April. Available: https://www.foreignaffairs.com/articles/united-states/2015-03-01/disrupting-intelligence-community [December 2018].

Keller, S.A., Shipp, S., and Schroeder, A. (2016). Does big data change the privacy landscape? A review of the issues. *Annual Review of Statistics and Its Application*, 3, 161–180. doi:10.1146/annurev-statistics-041715-033453.

Lee, N. (2014). Trouble on the radar. *Lancet*, 384(9958), 1917.

Lewis, K., Kaufman, J., Gonzalez, M., Wimmer, A., and Christakis, N. (2008). Tastes, ties, and time: A new social network dataset using Facebook.com. *Social Networks, 30*(4), 330–342. doi:10.1016/j.socnet.2008.07.002.

Lyon, D. (2001). Facing the future: Seeking ethics for everyday surveillance. *Ethics and Information Technology, 3*(3), 171–181.

Lyon, D. (2007). *Surveillance Studies: An Overview.* Cambridge, UK: Polity Press.

Mayer-Schönberger, V. (2009). *Delete: The Virtue of Forgetting in the Digital Age.* Princeton, NJ: Princeton University Press.

National Academies of Sciences, Engineering, and Medicine. (2016). *Privacy Research and Best Practices: Summary of a Workshop for the Intelligence Community.* Washington, DC: The National Academies Press. doi:10.17226/21879.

National Research Council. (2008). *Protecting Individual Privacy in the Struggle Against Terrorists: A Framework for Program Assessment.* Committee on Technical and Privacy Dimensions of Information for Terrorism Prevention and Other National Goals, Committee on Law and Justice and Committee on National Statistics, Computer Science and Telecommunications Board, Division of Behavioral and Social Sciences and Education, Division on Engineering and Physical Sciences. Washington, DC: The National Academies Press. doi:10.17226/12452.

Nissenbaum, H. (2005). Where computer security meets national security. *Ethics and Information Technology, 7*(2), 61–73. doi:10.1007/s10676-005-4582-3.

Nissenbaum, H. (2010). *Privacy in Context: Technology, Policy, and the Integrity of Social Life.* Palo Alto, CA: Stanford University Press. Available: https://crypto.stanford.edu/portia/papers/privacy_in_context.pdf [December 2018].

Penney, J.W. (2016). Chilling effects: Online surveillance and Wikipedia use. *Berkeley Technology Law Journal, 31*(1), 117. doi:10.15779/Z38SS13.

Reisman, D., Schultz, J., Crawford, K., and Whittaker, M. (2018). *Algorithmic Impact Assessments: A Practical Framework for Public Agency Accountability.* Available: https://ainowinstitute.org/aiareport2018.pdf [December 2018].

Salganik, M.J. (2017). *Bit by Bit: Social Research in the Digital Age.* Princeton, NJ: Princeton University Press. Available: http://www.bitbybitbook.com/en/preface [December 2018].

Sweeney, L. (2013). Discrimination in online ad delivery. *Queue, 11*(3), 10. doi:10.1145/2460276.2460278.

Walsh, P., and Miller, S. (2016). Rethinking "five eyes" security: Intelligence collection policies and practice post Snowden. *Intelligence and National Security, 31*(3), 345–368.

Wesolowski, A., Buckee, C.O., Bengtsson, L., Wetter, E., Lu, X. and Tatem, A.J. (2014). Commentary: Containing the Ebola Outbreak—the Potential and Challenge of Mobile Network Data. *PLoS Currents*, September 29. Available: http://currents.plos.org/outbreaks/index.html%3Fp=42561.html [December 2018].

Zook, M., Barocas, S., Boyd, D., Crawford, K., Keller, E., Gangadharan, S.P., Goodman, A., Hollander, R., Koenig, B.A., Metcalf, J., Narayanan, A., Nelson, A., and Pasquale, F. (2017). Ten simple rules for responsible big data research. *PLoS Computational Biology, 13*(3), e1005399. doi:10.1371/journal.pcbi.1005399.

Appendix E

Biographical Sketches of Committee Members and Staff

Paul R. Sackett (*Chair*) is Beverly and Richard Fink distinguished professor of psychology and liberal arts at the University of Minnesota. His research interests involve many aspects of testing and assessment in workplace, educational, and military settings. He was cochair of the joint committee of the American Educational Research Association, the American Psychological Association (APA), and the National Council on Measurement in Education that developed *Standards for Educational and Psychological Testing*. He has served as president of the Society for Industrial and Organizational Psychology, chair of APA's Committee on Psychological Tests and Assessments, and chair of APA's Board of Scientific Affairs. He has a Ph.D. in industrial/organizational psychology from Ohio State University.

Alexandra Beatty (*Senior Program Officer*) is a staff officer in the Division of Behavioral and Social Sciences and Education (DBASSE). Previously in DBASSE, she served as the study director for an evaluation of the public schools of the District of Columbia, and she has worked on studies and workshops on topics in educational assessment and equity, child and adolescent education and development, public health, and climate change. Prior to joining the National Academies staff, she worked on the National Assessment of Educational Progress and College Board programs at the Educational Testing Service. She has a B.A. in philosophy from Williams College and an M.A. in history from Bryn Mawr College.

Gary G. Berntson is an emeritus academy professor of psychology at Ohio State University. His research is in the areas of neuroscience, social neuroscience, and psychophysiology. He has served on numerous federal advisory committees, including for the National Institutes of Health, the National Science Foundation, and the Portuguese Science Foundation. He also served on the Task Force on Predicting Violent Behavior of the Department of Defense, and as scientific consultant to the Future Attribute Screening Technology program of the Department of Homeland Security. He is a past president of the Society for Psychophysiological Research. He was the recipient of distinguished teaching and distinguished scholar awards from Ohio State University and received the Paul D. MacLean Award for Outstanding Neuroscience Research from the American Psychosomatic Society. He has a Ph.D. in psychobiology and life sciences from the University of Minnesota.

Sujeeta Bhatt (*Study Director*) is a senior program officer in the Division of Behavioral and Social Sciences and Education. Most recently, she led the study that resulted in the publication *How People Learn II: Learners, Contexts, and Cultures*. Previously, she was a research scientist at the Defense Intelligence Agency (DIA) and an assistant professor in radiology at the Georgetown University Medical Center. Her work at DIA focused on the management of research on the psychological and neuroscience bases for credibility assessment, biometrics, insider threat, and intelligence interviewing and interrogation methods and on developing research-to-practice modules to promote the use of evidence-based practice in interviews and interrogations. For her work in deception detection and interrogation, she has trained law enforcement agents in local, state, and federal agencies. She has a certificate in security studies from Georgetown University and a Ph.D. in behavioral neuroscience from American University.

Kathleen M. Carley is a professor of societal computing in the Institute for Software Research and director of the Center for Computational Analysis of Social and Organizational Systems at Carnegie Mellon University, and she is also CEO of Carley Technologies Inc. Her research combines cognitive science, sociology, and computer science to address complex social and organizational issues. Her work includes the establishment of dynamic network analysis and the associated theory and methodology for examining large high-dimensional time-variant networks, as well as development of a high-dimensional network analysis and visualization system that supports network analytics in general, for social media, and for dynamic and geospatial networks. She is a recipient of the life-time achievement award for mathematical sociology from the American Sociological Association, the Simmel Award from the International Network for Social Network Analysis, and the academic award from the U.S. Geospatial Intelligence Foundation. She has a Ph.D. in sociology from Harvard University.

Noshir S. Contractor is the Jane S. and William J. White professor of behavioral sciences in the McCormick School of Engineering and Applied Science, the School of Communications, and the Kellogg School of Management at Northwestern University, as well as director of the university's Science of Networks in Communities research center. He is also the cofounder and chairman of Syndio, which offers products and services based on network analytics. His work focuses on factors that lead to the formation, maintenance, and dissolution of dynamically linked social and knowledge networks in a wide variety of contexts. He received the National Communication Association Distinguished Scholar Award, and he is an elected fellow of the International Communication Association. He has a B.S. in electrical engineering from the Indian Institute of Technology, Madras, and a Ph.D. in communications from the Annenberg School of Communication at the University of Southern California.

Nancy J. Cooke is a professor of human systems engineering at Arizona State University and directs the university's Center for Human, Artificial Intelligence, and Robot Teaming and the Advanced Distributed Learning Partnership Lab. She is also science director of the Cognitive Engineering Research Institute in Mesa, Arizona. Her research interests include individual and team cognition and its application to cyber and intelligence analysis, remotely piloted aircraft systems, human–robot teaming, health care systems, emergency response systems, and methodologies to elicit and assess individual and team cognition. She is a past president of the Human Factors and Ergonomics Society and served on the U.S. Air Force Scientific Advisory Board. She is a recipient of the Human Factors and Ergonomics Society's Arnold M. Small President's Distinguished Service Award. She is a fellow of the Human Factors and Ergonomics Society, the American Psychological Association, the Association for Psychological Science, and the International Ergonomics Association. She has a Ph.D. in cognitive psychology from New Mexico State University.

Barbara Anne Dosher is a distinguished professor of cognitive sciences at the University of California at Irvine and recently served as the university's dean of the School of Social Sciences. Her research addresses memory, attention, and perceptual learning in humans using a combination of behavioral testing and mathematical modeling. She is a member of the National Academy of Sciences and an elected fellow of the American Psychological Society and the Society for Experimental Psychologists. She is a recipient of the Howard Crosby Warren Medal of the Society for Experimental Psychologists and the Atkinson Prize in Psychological and Cognitive Sciences of the National Academy of Sciences. She has served on the board and as president of the Society for Mathematical Psychology and on the executive board of the Vision Sciences Society. She has a B.A. in psychology from the University of California at San Diego and an M.S. and Ph.D. in experimental psychology from the University of Oregon.

Jeffrey Johnson is university term professor of anthropology at the University of Florida and an adjunct professor in the Institute for Software Research at Carnegie Mellon University. Until recently, he served as director of the Summer Institute for Research Design in Cultural Anthropology of the National Science Foundation. Previously, he was a program manager with the Army Research Office, where he started the basic science research program in the social sciences. He has conducted extensive long-term research comparing group dynamics and the evolution of social networks of overwintering crews at the American South Pole Station and at the Polish, Russian, Chinese, and Indian Antarctic Stations. Using these isolated human group settings as space analogs, he is currently studying the role of informal role properties in fostering team viability in simulated space missions. He has a Ph.D. in social science from the University of California at Irvine.

Sallie Keller is the director of the Social and Decision Analytics Division at the Biocomplexity Institute and Initiate and a professor of public health sciences at the University of Virginia. Her previous positions include academic vice president and provost at the University of Waterloo; director of the Institute for Defense Analysis' Science and Technology Policy Institute in Washington, D.C.; William and Stephanie Sick dean of engineering at Rice University; and head of the Statistical Sciences Group at Los Alamos National Laboratory. Her work focuses on social and decision informatics, statistical underpinnings of data science, and data access and confidentiality. She is a fellow of the American Association for the Advancement of Science, an elected member of the International Statistics Institute, a fellow and past president of the American Statistical Association, and a member of the JASON advisory group to the U.S. government. She has a Ph.D. in statistics from the Iowa State University of Science and Technology.

David Matsumoto is a professor of social psychology at San Francisco State University and director of the university's Culture and Emotion Research Lab. His work involves studies of culture, emotion, social interaction, and communication. In particular, he focuses in the field of microexpressions, facial expression, gesture, and nonverbal behavior. He has a Ph.D. in psychology from the University of California, Berkeley.

Carmen Medina is the founder of MedinAnalytics, LLC, which provides analytic services on national security issues, cognitive diversity, global trends, and intrapreneurship. Previously, she was part of the executive team that led the Analysis Directorate of the Central Intelligence Agency's (CIA), where she oversaw the CIA's lessons learned program and led the agency's first effort to address the challenges posed by social networks, digital ubiquity, and the emerging culture of collaboration. She also led diversity issues at the CIA, serving on equity boards at all organizational levels and across directorates. She conceptualized many information technology applications now used by analysts, including online production, collaborative tools, and Intellipedia. She is a recipient of the CIA's Distinguished Career Intelligence Medal. She also was a member of Deloitte Federal Consulting, where she served as senior advisor and mentor to Deloitte's flagship innovation program, GovLab. She has a B.A. in comparative government from the Catholic University of America.

Fran P. Moore is the chief of intelligence for the Financial Systemic Analysis and Resilience Center (FSARC), whose mission is to identify, assess, and coordinate activities to mitigate risk to U.S. financial systems. Previously, she was a senior executive with the Central Intelligence Agency (CIA), where she also served as the CIA's chair for Harvard's Learning Innovations Lab and a senior ally for the CIA's LGBT affinity group. She serves on the Security Policy Review Committee of the Intelligence and National Security Alliance and on the Intelligence Committee of the Armed Forces Communications and Electronics Association, both of which are independent nonprofit membership groups. She is the recipient of many awards, including the Presidential Rank Award, Distinguished Executive. She has B.A. degrees in international relations and political science from Elmira College.

Jonathan D. Moreno is the David and Lyn Silfen university professor at the University of Pennsylvania, where he is also a Penn Integrates Knowledge (PIK) professor and a professor of medical ethics and health policy, of the history and sociology of science, and of philosophy. He is an elected member of the National Academy of Medicine, and he chairs its Interest Group on Human Rights, Professionalism and the Values of Medicine. He is the U.S. member of the UNESCO International Bioethics Committee, and he has served as an adviser to many governmental and nongovernmental organizations. He is the recipient of an honorary doctorate from Hofstra University, the Benjamin Rush Medal from the College of William and Mary Law School, the Dr. Jean Mayer Award for Global Citizenship from Tufts University, and the Penn Alumni Faculty Award of Merit. He is also the recipient of a lifetime achievement award of the American Society for Bioethics and Humanities. He has a Ph.D. in philosophy from Washington University in St. Louis.

Joy Rohde is associate professor of public policy and history and a faculty member in the Science, Technology, and Public Policy Program and the Science, Technology, and Society Program at the University of Michigan. Her work examines the relationship between the social and behavioral sciences and the American state from the late 19th century to the present. Previously, she was an assistant professor of history at Trinity University and held fellowships at the Miller Center of Public Affairs and the American Academy of Arts and Sciences. She has a Ph.D. in history and sociology of science from the University of Pennsylvania.

Julie Anne Schuck (*Program Officer*) is a program officer in the Division of Behavioral and Social Sciences and Education. She has provided analytical and administrative support, as well as technical writing and editing, for a wide range of studies and workshops. Her projects have addressed law and justice issues; science, technology, engineering, and mathematics education; the science of human-systems integration; and the evaluations of various federal research programs. She has a B.S. in engineering physics from the University of California at San Diego and an M.S. in education from Cornell University.

Jeffrey W. Taliaferro is an associate professor of political science at Tufts University. His research and teaching focus on security studies, international relations theory, international history and politics, U.S. foreign policy, intelligence, and national security. He recently was a fellow at the Woodrow Wilson International Center for Scholars, where he completed a book on the politics of alliance coercion and nuclear nonproliferation in U.S. foreign policy during the second half of the Cold War. He is a member of the Historical Review Panel of the Central Intelligence Agency. He has a bachelor's degree in history and political science from Duke University and a Ph.D. in government from Harvard University.

Elizabeth Townsend (*Associate Program Officer*) is staff officer in the Division of Behavioral and Social Sciences and Education and the Health and Medical Division. She has worked primarily on studies for the the Board on Children, Youth, and Family, including those on the neurobiological and sociobehavioral science of adolescent development, building an agenda to reduce the number of children in poverty by half in 10 years, ethical considerations for research on housing-related health hazards involving children, and working families and growing kids. She has a B.S. from Radford University and an M.P.H. from the University of Alabama at Birmingham.

Gregory F. Treverton is professor of the practice of international relations at the University of Southern California. He directed the Center for Global

Risk and Security, the Intelligence Policy Center, and the International Security and Defense Policy Center at the RAND Corporation. He was also associate dean of the Pardee/RAND Graduate School. His government work has included serving on the first Senate Select Committee on Intelligence; work on Europe for the National Security Council; and as vice chair and chair of the National Intelligence Council. Previously, he also taught at Harvard and Columbia universities and as deputy director of the International Institute for Strategic Studies in London. He has a B.A. summa cum laude from Princeton University and an M.P.P. and a Ph.D. in economics and politics from Harvard.

Jeremy Wolfe is professor of ophthalmology and radiology at Harvard Medical School and head of the Visual Attention Lab at Brigham and Women's Hospital. He has worked extensively in vision, binocular perception, visual attention, and cognitive science. His research focuses on visual search and visual attention, with particular emphasis on socially important search tasks in such areas as medical image perception (e.g., cancer screening), security (e.g., baggage screening), and intelligence. In recent years, he has become increasingly interested in the role of vision and attention in medical and security errors. He is a past president of the Federation of Associations in Behavioral and Brain Science and past chair of the Board of the Psychonomic Society. He has an A.B. in psychology from Princeton University and a Ph.D. in psychology from the Massachusetts Institute of Technology.